MOUNTAIN TRAVEL ®

THE ADVENTUROUS TRAVELER'S GUIDE

TREKS
OUTINGS & EXPEDITIONS

Kunming, China/Leo Le Bon

You may order single copies prepaid direct
from the publisher, $14.95 + $1.00 for postage and handling.
(California residents add 6% sales tax:
Bay Area residents add 6½%.)

TEN SPEED PRESS

P.O. Box 7123   Berkeley, California 94707   Phone (415) 845-8414

Library of Congress Catalog Number: 84-051101
ISBN: 0-89815-130-9

*e Carhuachocha reflecting the peak of
paja (21,765') highest peak of the Cordillera Huayhuash.
hern Peru/Leo Le Bon*

a few words...

Kirghiz nomads with Leo Le Bon
below the Aghil Pass in Sinkiang, China/Nadia Billia

With the appearance of this issue (Volume II) of the Book of Treks, Outings & Expeditions, the idea that "adventure travel" is one of the best kept secrets in the travel world may no longer hold true.

In the pages that follow are 131 unusual and detailed travel itineraries to more than 48 countries around the world, the combined treasures collected over a lifetime of traveling by the founders and staff of Mountain Travel.

Established in 1967 by mountaineer-explorers Allen Steck, Barry Bishop and myself for the purpose of creating back-country wilderness trips with foot travel as the principal means of access, Mountain Travel's emphasis has always been on genuine exploration of some unique feature of our global geography.

These are not just "armchair travel adventures" to read and dream about; these trips really exist. They are designed for active people who love to walk, trek, explore or climb in places where a few decades ago only seasoned adventurers dared to go.

We invite you to join us on a quest to help preserve and protect our planet's special places, by traveling to some of its faraway untouched corners to seek and learn for yourself.

Leo Le Bon
President, Mountain Travel

1398 Solano Avenue
Albany, California 94706
Phone (415) 527-8100
Telex: 335-429
Cable: Mountain Albany California

HOW TO USE THIS BOOK

Our treks, outings and expeditions are presented by geographical region, beginning with Asia and ending with North America.

The Calendar Index on pages 4 & 5 tells you what trips are leaving each month. They are listed by geographical region within the Calendar Index.

The Quick-Reference Activity Index on page 4 will help you locate a trip which includes a particular outdoor activity (such as rafting, skiing or hut-to-hut trekking).

HOW TO JOIN A TRIP

To reserve space on one of the trips, fill out the Trip Application Form which you'll find in the back of the book.

For Information/Reservations, call toll-free (outside California only) 800 227-2384.

Most of our 1985 trips will be repeated in 1986 on approximately the same dates.

Please Note:

We publish dates, prices and itineraries up to a year and a half in advance so you can formulate your travel plans with us well ahead of time. Since we do work so far in advance, there may be some changes in dates, prices and itineraries after the printing of this publication (August, 1984). All changes will be listed in the Trip Itineraries made up specifically for each trip.

Call or write our office for the most current information.

Linda Liscom, author, trekker and trip leader

Roger and other trekkers on the Thorong La just before the storm

A THANKSGIVING AT ANNAPURNA
by Linda Liscom

Linda Liscom began her outdoor career as a Sierra Club cook on the glaciers in the coast range of British Columbia and on the volcanoes of Mexico. A certified scuba diver, she toured as chef for underwater explorations with the Sierra Club in Hawaii, Baja and the Caribbean. Linda came to Mountain Travel in 1974 with her Guatemalan hiking trip, a personalized adventure of volcano-climbing, archaeological travels and living close to the highland Indians: she calls Guatemala her "second home." On a scouting trip in the jungles of Surinam, she met Ed Power and they were later married (Mountain Travel style) on the slopes of a volcano in the Guatemalan highlands. When not leading Mountain Travel trips, Linda pilots her own plane, works as a professional photographer and freelance writer, and is a regular contributor to the San Francisco Examiner and Los Angeles Times.

I like to walk. I've left 10,000 miles of footprints pursuing the pleasures, the perils, the excitement and the peace of elevated places from Mount Tamalpais (our neighborhood Walden in Marin County), and the Sierra Nevada to the alps of Japan and Peru and the volcanic slopes of Mexico, Guatemala and Hawaii. My longest walk, 500 miles, was in the Himalaya from Kathmandu, Nepal, to Darjeeling, India, via Mount Everest Base Camp.

My recent journey with Mountain Travel around the Annapurna massif in Nepal isolates itself as the most special walk of all.

Trailside entertainer with Annapurna and Machupuchare in background

For 25 days, I trekked around the 10th highest mountain in the world, Annapurna-I (26,540') on an east/west route from Dumre to Pokhara. For 25 days I walked beneath a skyline dominated by the great white giants of the deepest gorges of the earth and over an 17,700-foot pass.

On our approach, hanging above us were mountains named Machapuchare (22,033'), Annapurna IV (24,682'), Annapurna III (24,780') and Gangapurna (24,452'), Peak 29 (25,699') and Bauda Himal (21,884').

These awesome monuments became my friends. They draped the lowland horizon of the broad rice and millet terraces of the Marsyandi River. They poised behind frames of flourishing pointsettias and forests of stately conifers. Early one night, Annapurna-II appeared wearing the evening star in an imaginary crown and Manaslu faced her, cloaked in a gown of peach-tinted light. I sat between them taking a soak in a natural hot spring 18,000 feet below.

West of the pass, the Kali Gandaki River cuts the world's deepest gorge. Between Dhaulaguri and the Annapurna massif, only 21 miles apart, the gorge reaches a depth of 18,000 feet. Some locations in this valley get five inches of rain annually. Here the wind howls from the south on a punctual daily schedule from 11 a.m. to sunset and the alluvial sand plains become airborne. In the same drainage, there are mountain views edited through the haze and moss of rainforest and sometimes by rhododendron trees with trunks too large for my widest embrace. Overwhelming country, yes.

Walking around Annapurna is more than an exhilarating wilderness experience. It's a cultural experience with incredible mountain scenery. The trail follows ancient Tibetan-Nepalese trade routes. Only in 1977 was the Marsyandi Valley opened to foreigners. Villages punctuate the walk and trekkers see the rigor, pleasure and routines of daily life as they plod from the tropics to the roof of the world.

Autumn brings scenes of harvest in the lowlands. Haystacks with legs are created by men and women bent under loads of straw three times their width and double their height.

Crafts people—spinners, weavers and basket makers—create their wares by their trailside homes. A sawmill operates with two men on opposite sides pulling and pushing a long serrated blade through a log, making two-by-fours, and the tailor pumps the treadle of his trusty Singer.

Late fall inspires pony parades moving high-country families of Tibetan origin to lower places for a more hospitable winter. In Manang (at 12,000 feet), a large village with 200 houses, I witnessed a dramatic departure ritual. A family, freshly mounted, stood at the edge of town framed on all sides by ice-clad mountains and moraine lakes. The grandfather raised to his shoulder a weapon that resembled a muzzle-loader, then fired it toward the heavens. Echoes rebounded from an icefall, acknowledged by an avalanche, and the procession began.

The ponies, in all their Tibetan trappings, wear wide leather collars with grapefruit-size bells and plush handmade Tibetan rugs as saddle blankets. Ethnic patterns are created in indigos, crimsons, rusts and yellows. My favorite design displayed two animated snow leopards clawing at a snow-covered mountain woven between them. Mounted passengers dress in thick hand-sewn garments; several appeared in regal plum and jade brocades trimmed in fur. Women wear their wealth in chunks of turquoise or lumps of coral. Men lead their riches—yaks and mules, laden with potatoes and animal skins for winter food and barter. Infants are tethered closely to their mothers' backs in a sort of envelope fashioned from blankets.

The "Around Annapurna Trek" begins with a walk along the steeply-ridged foothills flanking the Marsyandi River

A brief walk from Manang, the village of Braga huddles against steep eroding sandstone cliffs both for defense and wind protection. Tight clusters of flat-roofed stone buildings form a hanging city, the only place I've visited where a fixed rope would be useful moving through town. Arriving the last day of the Tibetan month, we were promised a special ceremony at the *gompa* (monastery). A dark tunnel chiseled into the mountainside led into the sanctuary. Musicians sounded trumpets, horns, cymbals and drums; they were answered in rhythmical chants from attending monks. Butter lamps illuminated intent human faces and a thousand Buddha statues covered one entire wall. Offerings of rice and incense were placed on a small altar.

We Americans had our own rituals. It was Thanksgiving and we celebrated that same evening in a tent below. Fifteen fellow countrymen gathered around a shaky table constructed from three lengths of plywood, each fastened to a wicker stool. Someone read Longfellow's last chapter from "The Song of Hiawatha" beginning "On the shores of Gitche Gumee" while I divided equally a bottle of Camus Napoleon cognac which everyone savored by the dropful.

We feasted on braised yak kebabs, fried banana and apple fritters, Tibetan dumplings stuffed with fresh greens, fresh cabbage and a just-baked cake. I relished the warmth of our group fellowship and the *gompa* scene as the mercury fell throughout the night. My canteen froze even though it was inside my pack, within my tent. Frost from my breath gathered around the top of my sleeping bag. I was sublimely content.

To enrich our cultural experience further, 13 Sherpas accompanied our trek—high country people of Tibetan descent who guide, cook and perform most of the tasks that backpackers

and campers usually do for themselves. I know of no other people in the world who radiate such a happy spirit and kindness not only toward each other but to all living creatures, reflecting their deep inner peace.

At least part of each of our 25 trekking days, I walked with our head Sherpa, Tenzing Gyaltso, a man of few English words but with a smile that nearly overlaps into his ears. Walking quietly in his presence, I felt the world's highest mountains as his home, his roots and his family. As a skilled professional, Tenzing managed 49 porters and epitomized the essence of fine management: we were told about problems only after they were solved. At the end of one day he reported "30 porters going; find 30 more; OK everything." Such was his solution to 30 porters who quit one morning after our group began our daily march.

Pemba Sherpa, wired by the dawn with enthusiasm for any day, delivered morning greetings at each tent door with a mug of steaming milk-and-sugar tea to be savored while still in our sleeping bags. Basins of hot water for bathing followed tea-rounds and the final visit brought a jug of "cold boiling water" to fill our canteens.

Our distinguished Sherpa cook, Chung Cheering, had been to restaurant school, and with his four assistants he prepared a combination of Chinese, Indian, Tibetan and American dishes. His variety, endurance and imagination were undaunted by temperature or weather extremes. Soup stocks were fresh—no packets. Vegetables were fresh—turnips, carrots, beans, cauliflower, cabbage and greens. He braised water buffalo, roasted goat leg, fried chicken and kebabed yak. He fried, boiled, baked and mashed home-grown potatoes. The ones he liked best to mash were marble-sized and, yes, peeled first. Clearly his most showy accomplishments were his apple and pumpkin pies with their glistening crusts of golden brown baked in a thin aluminum pot covered with glowing coals.

Camp is set in rice terraces, the best flat ground for setting up tents

Scenes from this trip will be passengers in my memory forever. There was the day I walked at 12,000 feet on land which was once the floor of an ancient ocean. I left Muktinath, the highest village on the western side of the pass, and began my descent on a traverse of steep, high desert that resembled folded suede. I could see toward Tibet and the valley of Mustang and in another direction, toward the peak of Dhaulagiri. Once upon a time, about 200 million years ago, this very location on which I walked, two and a half miles high in the sky, formed the bottom of the Himalayan (or Tethys) Sea. Tightly clenched in my fist was an ammonite I'd found the day before—a snail-like fossil. The downward pitch to the slopes moved my legs automatically and I imagined the energy of being propelled by great ocean swells in a nearly effortless descent to the valley floor.

I'll always remember an elderly Nepalese woman I met on the trail bearing a heavy load of tree branches intended as fodder for her cows. She rolled her aged eyes up under her weighty burden, pointed to them, and said something to me. Pemba translated her diagnosis first person. "Eyes not good seeing; 19 children having; die 18 and crying so much I cannot see anymore."

Then there was the day we crossed the pass. Our entourage of 78 (16 Americans, 13 Sherpas and 49 Nepalese porters) hit the trail at 6 a.m. at 15,000 feet. We were heading over the Thorong la Pass (17,700 feet), then descending to Muktinath at 12,000 feet.

Thirteen hours later I dragged into camp well after dark, the last three hours navigated by flashlight over ice paths with precipitous drop-offs. A snow-packed trail easy to find early in the day was obliterated by a whiteout and snowstorm in the afternoon.

I fell into my favorite walking place—at the tail-end with Tenzing, Ang Sherpa and an energized marathon runner. Several encounters slowed our morning pace.

Roger, our most senior member at 70 years, was charged with undying, stubborn determination but weakened by the altitude. He moved only a few feet at a time with 1,500 feet left to climb. Hours later he stumbled to the summit marker greeted by a temperature of 4 degrees, a wind-chill factor and a view beyond that looked very bleak. A great cloud filled the valley below, shrouded our steep descent and mystified the location of our 73 fellow travelers.

Remaining upright the next few hundred yards on nearly vertical ice steps was difficult for me and nearly impossible for Roger who was fast losing his ability to coordinate. Tenzing and Ang supported him between them, a posture they continued for 10 hours, while I provided morale. The cloud we

Chung Cheering, master chef, buys a chicken for dinner

entered was heavy with snow and I could see little more than my own feet ahead. The going was slow and the unknowns disarming.

Two miracles occurred an hour before dark. We were reunited with our fellow travelers and their Sherpa guides and shortly after the snow cloud made an exodus.

I was the last to camp. The tents were up and supper was ready. I went through the motions of eating but was more nourished by a feeling of quiet peace and gratitude for my presence on earth. I'd experienced new extensions of my endurance, tenacity and faith.

Photos by Linda Liscom

Trekkers learning numbers in Nepalese language

ASIA
& THE PACIFIC

Mt. Dhaulagiri, 6th highest peak in the world, and Tukche Peak, on the trail from Ghorepani to Ghandrung, Nepal/Brian Weirum

NEPAL • MONGOLIA • CHINA • TIBET • PAKISTAN • SIKKIM
SRI LANKA • THE MALDIVE ISLANDS • NEW ZEALAND
BALI • KOREA • JAPAN

Mountain Travel Asia & The Pacific

The pioneer in Himalayan adventure travel, Mountain Travel is still the acknowledged leader in adventure travel and trekking.

What is trekking? Simply walking, following age-old trails through valleys and villages. Anyone who leads an active life and is in good health will enjoy Himalayan trekking. We hire porters and/or pack animals to carry all the gear. We employ a staff to do all cooking and camp chores.

The concept of "trekking" as a means of touring originated in Kashmir, favorite retreat of the British Raj, and in Nepal, a Himalayan kingdom with the largest variety of trekking routes in all Asia.

China continues to open more and more of its fascinating and remote provinces for trekking tourism, and we offer a wide selection of one-of-a-kind treks in China and Tibet.

In India, we focus much of our attention on the Himalayan highlands of Ladakh, where Tibetan Buddhist monasteries preserve a treasury of ancient Buddhist art.

Trekking in northern Pakistan, where there are 17 mountains higher than 25,000 feet, is a specialty of Mountain Travel. We travel to K2, world's second highest peak and explore legendary Hunza.

There are many reasons why trekking is becoming such a popular form of travel —come to Asia with us in 1985 and you'll see why.

Rice terraces of the Siwalik Hills, Nepal/Gordon Wiltsie

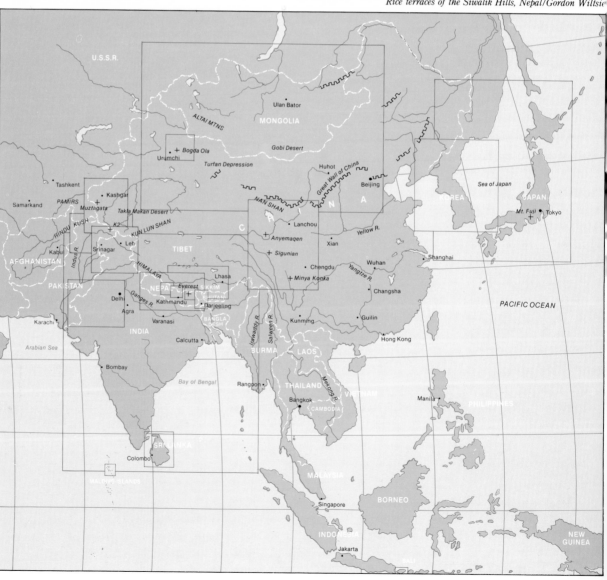

Daku Tenzing Norgay

Ray Jewell

SMOKE BLANCHARD, 65, is a mountaineer with over 40 years of guiding and climbing experience. He has completed extensive mountain walks throughout Nepal, India and Alaska and once spent five months walking in one of his favorite places, the Japanese Alps.

JIM BRIDWELL, 39, is one of America's foremost mountaineers. After establishing many new routes on the big walls of Yosemite, he has more recently turned his attention to alpine-style expeditions, making such notable ascents as Cerro Torre in Chile and a winter ascent of Pumori in Nepal.

JERRY COE, 33, is a mountaineer, woodworker and blacksmith. He is conversant in Japanese and Chinese and leads mountain treks in China and Tibet. When not on trek, he designs metal sculptures and ornamental architectural ironwork.

DAKU TENZING NORGAY, 44, is a Sherpani, born in the Everest region of Nepal. Wife of Everest summiteer Tenzing Norgay, she is an experienced mountain guide and manages a trekking agency in Darjeeling.

CHARLES GAY, 36, lived in Nepal for several years as a Peace Corps volunteer, speaks fluent Nepali, and is an experienced trek leader.

DICK IRVIN, 54, has been leading Mountain Travel treks in Nepal, India and Pakistan since 1979. A former mathematics teacher and recent ecology graduate from the University of California, Davis, he has more than 30 years of mountain exploration and climbing experience and is a veteran of nine major expeditions.

RAY JEWELL, 51, has been with Mountain Travel ever since its inception, and was a member of our very first trip (the first group of Americans ever to trek in Nepal). A former physicist, Ray has over 45 Mountain Travel trips to his credit, specializing in leading treks in Nepal, Pakistan and India.

BRUCE KLEPINGER, 43, has led more than 60 Mountain Travel treks in Asia and South America. His mountaineering background includes over 1,000 climbs, and he has led numerous expeditions on Aconcagua (highest peak in the Western Hemisphere), Huascaran (highest peak in Peru), and peaks in Nepal and India. He has also spent many years as a senior boatman on the Grand Canyon.

LEO LE BON, 50, president and founder of Mountain Travel, has more than 25 years of professional experience in all phases of the travel industry, both in his native Europe and in the U.S. His early interest in wilderness travel led him to the creation of Mountain Travel in 1967. An avid sailor, skier and mountaineer, he has made exploratory expeditions on five continents in search of unusual forms of adventure travel.

SCOT MACBETH, 53, is a field geologist by profession, mountaineer by avocation, and founder of the Alpine Stomach Club. He has spent years in Nepal, calls the Khumbu region his "second home," and was a member of the 1981 American Expedition to Tibet.

LINDA LISCOM, 43, is a professional photographer and free-lance writer, a regular contributor to the San Francisco Examiner and Los Angeles Times. She has 15 years of experience in leading Sierra Club and Mountain Travel trips in Asia and South America.

MIKE PERRY, 28, a New Zealander, is a photographer by profession and has climbed extensively in the Southern Alps of New Zealand for the last ten years.

HUGH SWIFT, 41, author of *The Trekker's Guide To the Himalaya and Karakoram,* has visited just about every nook and cranny of the Himalaya and leads treks in Nepal, India and Pakistan. In 1981 and 1982, he and Arlene Blum walked from Bhutan to Pakistan, a nine-month 3,000-mile foot journey called the "Great Himalayan Traverse."

JOHN THUNE, 67, is a mountain enthusiast, skier and runner. A former Park Ranger in Yellowstone, Survival Training Officer in Naval Aviation and a long-time member of the National Ski Patrol, he is a noted photo-lecturer and has trekked extensively in China and Nepal.

BRIAN WEIRUM, 40, has a graduate degree in South Asian Political Development from U.C. Santa Barbara and has traveled in Asia for the past 20 years. He has lived and hiked extensively in Nepal during the last 14 years and speaks fluent "hill Nepali," which he learned while serving in the Peace Corps in Nepal.

JAN ZABINSKY, 35, is a ski instructor, mountaineer and teacher. He taught for three years at the American School in Lahore, Pakistan, and completed a walk from the southern tip of India to Kashmir in the north. He speaks Urdu and Hindi, and has traveled extensively in Asia.

About Our Asia Trip Leaders

Trip leaders are an important part of what makes a Mountain Travel trip special. Our Asia leaders come to us with a wide variety of backgrounds. Some are chosen for their knowledge of the language or culture, some for their mountaineering experience, but above all, for their ability to assure a safe, enjoyable and successful trip.

Scot Macbeth

Hugh Swift

Leo Le Bon

Charles Gay

Dick Irvin   *Jerry Coe*

Bruce Klepinger   *Mike Perry*

Brian Weirum

John Thune

About Trekking in Nepal

In addition to a professional Mountain Travel leader, each trekking expedition is accompanied by Sherpa guides, kitchen staff and porters, all under the direction of a sirdar, or Sherpa leader.

All camp gear and your own duffle bag of personal gear will be carried by hired porters or yaks; you carry only a small daypack for your water bottle, camera and jacket.

The daily schedule is usually as follows; up at 6 a.m., pack up your duffle and have a light breakfast of oatmeal and tea. The Sherpas break camp and the porters head up the trail with their assigned loads. Trekkers and Sherpas start on the trail around 7 a.m.

Despite the fact that there may be about a dozen trekkers in the group, it is always possible to walk alone if one chooses, since everyone is encouraged to walk at his/her own pace.

Trailside "brunch"/
Brian Weirum

Lunch stop is about 11 a.m. and consists of a hearty "brunch:" eggs, home fries, sausage, beans, etc.

Nepalese legend says that twin goddesses live atop the sacred peak of Machapuchare (23,942'), and therefore its "fishtail" summit has been decreed off limits to mountaineers/
Hugh Swift

Approaching the night's camp in the Annapurna foothills/Linda Goldsmith

IT4TG1MTO1

THE NEPAL ADVENTURE

An introduction to mountains, rivers and jungles

DATES: #1 Feb 7–Feb 23 (17 days)
#2 Feb 21–Mar 9 (17 days)
#3 Nov 28–Dec 14 (17 days)
#4 Dec 12–Dec 28 (17 days)
LEADER: #1 & #2: to be announced:
#2 & #3: Bruce Klepinger
GRADE: B-1
LAND COST: $1595 (6–15 members)

This 17-day adventure samples Nepal's three worlds: its mountains, rivers and jungles.

For a taste of mountain trekking, we will walk a scenic six-day route in the Annapurna foothills near Pokhara and circle up through cool forests and lovely Gurung villages such as Ghandrung (6,400'), with views of Annapurna and Dhaulagiri.

Returning from the mountains, we board rafts and set off on a leisurely float trip down the Seti Khola ("White River"), which flows into the jungles of Chitwan National Park.

Arriving at rustic Gaida Wildlife Camp, we'll spend several days searching for game by elephant-back, by dugout canoe and on foot. The deep *terai* jungle is the haunt of one-horned rhinos, leopards, elusive Bengal tigers and numerous species of exotic tropical birds.

ITINERARY:

DAY 1 to 3: Leave U.S. Arrive Kathmandu. Transfer to hotel.

DAY 4: Sightseeing in Kathmandu. Briefing on trek arrangements.

DAY 5: Fly along the Himalayan skyline to the little town of Pokhara. Meet with Sherpas and porters and begin trekking in the Pokhara Valley to a campsite on the outskirts near the Tibetan Camp at Henja (3,500').

DAY 6: Across rice fields to the small village of Suikhet, climb a steep crest to 6,500 feet then descend to Landrung (5,280').

DAY 7: Down to the Modi Khola river, then up 2,300 feet to a grazing pasture above Ghandrung (6,400'). Spectacular views of Annapurna and Machapuchare (the "Matterhorn" of Nepal).

DAY 8: Back down to the Modi Khola, walking along its right bank to Birethanti (4,300').

DAY 9: Cross the Modi Khola and ascend to the hamlet of Chandrakot, then further up to Lumle (5,000'), over a small pass at Khare (5,600'), and finally down to Naudanda (4,800').

DAY 10: End trek in the afternoon, arrive in Pokhara and check into Fishtail Lodge on Phewa Lake.

DAY 11: Drive to Damauli, the put-in point for our raft trip on the Seti Khola.

DAY 12: On the river.

DAY 13: Arrive by raft near

Gaida Wildlife Camp. Transfer to jeep for a short drive to Gaida. Check into camp and take an afternoon jungle walk.

DAY 14: Game viewing on the river by dugout canoe. Optional nature walk and late afternoon game viewing ride by elephant.

DAY 15: Morning visit to game viewing blind, then depart for five-hour drive to Kathmandu.

DAY 16: Depart Kathmandu on homeward-bound flights.

DAY 17: Arrive home.

Whitewater in the Himalayan foothills/ Linda Goldsmith

Crossing the Rapti River at Gaida Wildlife Camp/Jim Knodell

The afternoon walk begins around 1 p.m. and continues until 4:30, when camp is reached. While camp is being set up, light snacks and tea are served. Dinner is served around 6:30 in a dining tent with a dinner table and small rattan stools.

After dinner one can linger in the dining tent to talk about events of the day, or retire to read or write by flashlight. We provide large, comfortable North Face "Northstar" tents specially designed for us.

Food on the trek will be plentiful. Fresh vegetables, eggs, chickens and other foodstuffs are purchased as available. Meals are supplemented with tinned foods, such as peanut butter, fruit, coffee and fish. The Sherpa cook and his staff are trained professionals.

The Malla Hotel

The Hotel Malla is one of Nepal's finest hotels. Located near the Royal Palace, the Malla boasts neo-traditional Nepalese architecture and private gardens. To top it all off, the hospitality is Nepalese, and that's hard to beat anywhere in the world.

For reservations contact Mountain Travel.

A Word about Costs

The Land Cost listed for Nepal treks is for groups of 6 to 15 members (and some 6–12 members). If group size falls below 6, there will be a surcharge of $200 per person.

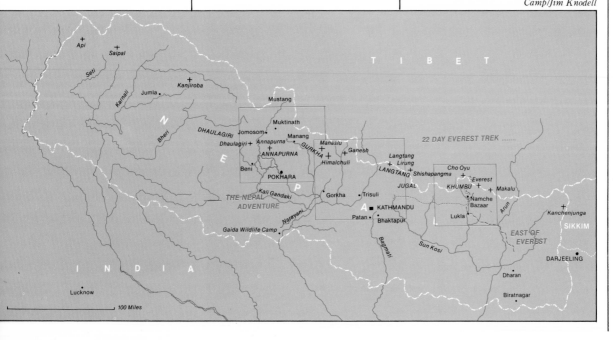

Spinning a prayer wheel/Dick McGowan

On a walk around Annapurna, one crosses through villages populated by Hindu hill tribes along the Marsyandi River, then gradually up into areas of Tibetan culture such as Manang.

Dhaulagiri and Tukche Peak/Stan Armington

Hillside village of Braga, Manang Valley/ Lanny Johnson

Approaching Macha-puchare. Trekkers are encouraged to walk at their own pace/ Gordon Wiltsie

IT4TG1MTO1

AROUND ANNAPURNA

22-day trek via Manang Valley and Tibetan trade route

DATES: *#1 Apr 15–May 14 (30 days)*
#2 Oct 10–Nov 8 (30 days)
#3 Oct 24–Nov 22 (30 days)
LEADER: *#1: Bruce Klepinger*
#2: Jeff Campbell
#3: to be announced
GRADE: *C-3*
LAND COST: *$1990 (6–15 members)*

One of our favorite treks and a classic walk in Nepal is the 22-day circuit around Annapurna, crossing north of the Annapurna massif via the Thorong La (17,771′).

The walk begins in the lush valley of the Marsyandi River, which cuts steeply between the Annapurnas to the west and the Manaslu/Himalchuli peaks to the east.

Turning west into the Manang Valley, a longitudinal gorge which makes a deep furrow behind the Annapurnas, we'll find ourselves in an increasingly Tibetan landscape and culture.

The Manang Valley is inhabited by gypsy traders of Tibetan origin whose villages are striking clusters of medieval stone dwellings often nestled into eroded sandstone cliffs. The main villages are Chame, Pisang, Braga (where there is a magnificent monastery) and Manang (11,450′). Above Pisang, there is a sudden environmental transi-

tion as the dense forests of the lower valley give way to rocky and arid Tibetan scenery and high yak pastures.

The Manang Valley is walled on the south by Annapurnas II and IV, Annapurna III (24,767′), Gangapurna (24,457′) and Glacier Dome (23,191′); to the north, and barring the way to Tibet, is a long ridge of 20,000 to 22,000-foot peaks.

At the head of the valley we cross north of the Annapurnas at the Thorong La and descend by way of the Hindu and Buddhist shrines at Muktinath. Now in the deep gorge of the Kali Gandaki, we descend gradually into green, terraced hillsides and the rhododendron groves of Lete. There are continuous and beautiful views of Dhaulagiri (26,810′), Tukche and the Annapurnas all the way back to Pokhara.

ITINERARY:

DAY 1 to 3: Leave U.S. Arrive Kathmandu. Transfer to hotel.

DAY 4: Sightseeing in Kathmandu. Briefing on trek arrangements.

DAY 5 to 8: Begin trek, hiking gently upward through lush subtropical vegetation and the cultivated fields along the Marsyandi River. Excellent views of Manaslu, Peak 29, Himalchuli, Annapurnas II and IV, Lamjung and Machapuchare. Ascend past canyons coming off rocky ramparts of Peak 29 and Namun Bhanjyang, climbing high above the river to about 7,000 feet among Tibetan settlements.

DAY 9 and 10: Enter the heavily wooded lower Manang Valley and pass the villages of Chame (8,800′) and Pisang (10,450′).

DAY 11 and 12: A beautiful walk on easy terrain through forests to the upper Manang Valley. Rest day at the village of Braga (11,250′). A half-hour's walk above camp leads to a splendid view of the Annapurnas and Manaslu.

Near the Thorong La (17,771′) north of Annapurna/Lanny Johnson

DAY 13: Past Manang village and continue up past yak huts to Chakar Dhunga (13,500′).

DAY 14: Continue through alpine country past Leder (14,200′) to a high camp at Phedi (14,500′), just at the foot of the climb to the Thorong La.

DAY 15: Long day, ascending steeply on a yak and pony trail. Cross Thorong La and descend steeply to Muktinath (12,500′).

DAY 16: Rest day at Muktinath. Visit Hindu and Buddhist shrines and enjoy views of Dhaulagiri.

DAY 17: Descend about 3,000 feet down the Jhong Khola canyon. Camp at the medieval village of Kagbeni (9,000′).

DAY 18: Down along a level but rocky trail through juniper thickets to Jomosom and then Marpha (8,760′), a large Thakali village with an important monastery.

DAY 19 and 20: Continue down the Kali Gandaki flood plain to Larjung (8,400′). Rest day or optional hike to the Dhaulagiri icefall at 12,000 feet.

DAY 21: Through pine woods to Ghasa (6,400′). The Kali Gandaki gorge begins to narrow here and there are marvelous views of Dhaulagiri, Annapurna-I and Tukche Peak.

DAY 22 and 23: Descend lower into the Kali Gandaki canyon, through Tatopani, known for its hot springs, on to Ghorapani (9,300′) and over Deorali Pass (10,000′), with its great views of Dhaulagiri and Annapurna South.

DAY 24 and 25: Traverse through rhododendron forests to Ghandrung (6,400′), a large Gurung village, and down a wide set of stone stairs (the best example of this type of trail in the country) to the Modi Khola. Ascend to Landrung, another Gurung village, and descend to Dhampus (5,900′), a meadow with one of the most spectacular views in Nepal, seen to its best advantage in the morning.

DAY 26: Descend to the Yangri Khola valley, then walk along flat fields to Pokhara (2,800′). Overnight at Fishtail Lodge on Phewa Lake.

DAY 27: Fly or drive to Kathmandu. Transfer to hotel.

DAY 28: Day free in Kathmandu.

DAY 29: Depart Kathmandu on homeward-bound flights.

DAY 30: Arrive home.

Saddhu *(Hindu holy man) at Pashupatinath, Nepal/Brian Weirum*

In the Kali Gandaki gorge, gateway to Tibet for Nepalese traders, goods such as salt and wool are carried between Nepal and Tibet by donkey caravans/ Lanny Johnson

The many faces of Nepal's distinctive ethnic groups, clans and castes are seen on a walk through the Kali Gandaki gorge. There is amazing photographic potential on this easy, colorful trek/Alla Schmitz

Susan Thiele

Susan Thiele

Alla Schmitz

Mustard field below Annapurna South and Hiunchuli Peak/Stan Armington

IT4TG1MTO1

DHAULAGIRI & ANNAPURNA VILLAGES

14 or 19-day "people-watching" trek

DATES: #1 Apr 4–Apr 30 (27 days)
        #2 Nov 21–Dec 12 (22 days)
LEADER: #1: Charles Gay
        #2: to be announced
GRADE: B-2
LAND COST: #1 $1790
           (6–15 members)
           #2 $1590 (6–15)

The Kali Gandaki River has carved a tremendous gorge which splits the Himalaya sharply between the massifs of Dhaulagiri (26,810') and Annapurna (26,545'), creating the deepest canyon in the world. A trek through this great gorge, which for centuries has been a major trade route between Tibet and India, has impressive changes in landscape, population and culture, great views of Dhaulagiri and Annapurna, and doesn't involve crossing any high mountain passes.

Starting at Pokhara and winding through Gurung villages, rhododendron forests and green woodlands, we cross Deorali Pass (10,000'). At Tatopani with its welcome hot springs, we join the Kali Gandaki and walk on ancient pathways as far as the Thakali village of Marpha (8,760').

TRIP #2 (the 14-day trek) turns around here and makes its way back to Pokhara via a slightly different route through the Annapurna foothills.

TRIP #1 (the 19-day trek) continues up to the ancient shrines and temples at Muktinath (12,500'), a pilgrimage site for both Hindus and Buddhists, and also takes time for a side trip to view the spectacular Dhaulagiri Icefall.

This is very much a people-watching trek and we'll see a whole range of fascinating Himalayan groups—the village Brahmins, Chettris and Gurungs (from which the British Army has long recruited its famed "Gurkha" regiments), the Thakalis (renowned traders of central Nepal), and wild-looking Tibetans who frequent this trail with their yak and donkey caravans.

ITINERARY: (19-DAY TREK)

DAY 1 to 3: Leave U.S. Arrive Kathmandu. Transfer to hotel.

DAY 4: Sightseeing in Kathmandu. Briefing on trek arrangements.

DAY 5: Fly or drive to Pokhara, meet with Sherpa crew and begin trek with a short walk to Henja (3,500').

DAY 6 and 7: Cross rice fields to Suikhet, climb up to Dhampus (5,900'), descend to the Modi Khola river before a steep climb to a grazing pasture below Ghandrung (6,400'). Spectacular views of the Annapurna Himal and Machapuchare (the "Matterhorn" of Nepal).

DAY 8: Pass through thick rhododendron forests with a few clearings and climb up through lush growth to a clearing at Deorali Pass (10,000') where there is a spectacular view of Dhaulagiri. Further along, Machapuchare and Annapurna can be seen.

DAY 9: The trail sweeps down the Ghatte Khola canyon during an easy but long descent dominated by the Dhaulagiri ice peaks. Tatopani (3,900') is a town of lemon trees and a hot spring just north of the bridge over the Kali Gandaki.

Three generations of Tibetans/Alla Schmitz

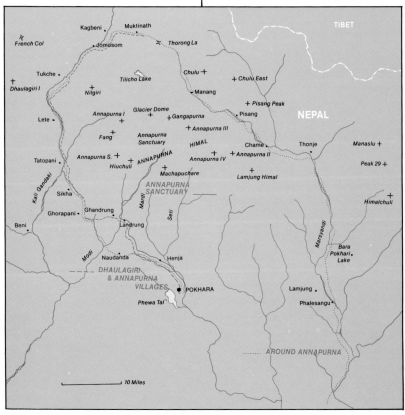

Stan Armington at mani rimdu *festival*/ Bruce Klepinger

DAY 10 and 11: We travel up the gorge of the Kali Gandaki taking a trail literally carved out of the walls high above the gorge. Transition from the tropical zone into the alpine and climb to Lete village. Annapurna-I appears east of the gorge as we trek toward the village of Larjung (8,400′).

DAY 12: The pine woods of Lete give way here to the juniper thickets of Tukche. We reach the government fruit and vegetable farm at the large village of Marpha (8,760′).

DAY 13: Continue through the juniper thickets of Tukche to Jomosom (8,900′), where the scenery is rocky, arid and grand.

DAY 14 and 15: Walk up to the holy shrine of Muktinath, sheltered from the winds of the upper Kali Gandaki, and decorated with small temples and shrines with magnificent Dhaulagiri as a backdrop. Layover day at Muktinath.

DAY 16 and 17: Return down the Kali Gandaki gorge as far as Ghatte Khola.

DAY 18 and 20: Further down to the village of Kalopani, then take a very worthwhile side trip to view the Dhaulagiri Icefall, and continue down through Tatopani to Ghorapani.

DAY 21 and 22: The trail descends the Bhurungdi Khola Valley across the Modi Khola and over a pass at Khare (5,600′).

DAY 23: Trek to Pokhara and check into the Fishtail Lodge on the shores of Phewa Lake.

DAY 24: Fly or drive to Kathmandu. Transfer to hotel.

DAY 25: In Kathmandu.

DAY 26: Depart Kathmandu on homeward-bound flights.

DAY 27: Arrive home.

ITINERARY: (14-DAY TREK)

Same until DAY 12, then as follows:

DAY 13 to 15: Retrace trails back to Tatopani and Ghorapani.

DAY 16 to 17: Descend the valley of the Bhurungdi Khola toward the Modi Khola over a pass at Khare (5,600′). Gradually descend to Naudanda, a ridge above the Pokhara Valley.

DAY 18: Trek into Pokhara and check into Fishtail Lodge on the shores of Phewa Lake.

DAY 19: Fly or drive to Kathmandu. Transfer to hotel.

DAY 20: In Kathmandu.

DAY 21: Depart Kathmandu on homeward-bound flights.

DAY 22: Arrive home.

IT4TG1MTO1

ANNAPURNA SANCTUARY TREK

15-day trek to a spectacular mountain ampitheatre

DATES: #1 Apr-22–May 14 (23 days)
      #2 Nov 4–Nov 26 (23 days)
LEADER: #1: to be announced
       #2: Jeff Campbell
GRADE: B-3
LAND COST: $1650 (6–15 members)

The Annapurna Sanctuary is a glacier-covered amphitheatre at 13,300 feet formed by a circle of the principal peaks of the western Annapurna Himal—including Annapurna South (23,814′), Fang (25,089′), Annapurna I (26,545′), Gangapurna (24,457′), Annapurna III (24,787′) and the spire of Machapuchare (23,942′).

This spectacular mountain-ringed basin can be reached on a relatively short trek (15 days) that goes right to the base of some of the most famous peaks in the Himalaya.

We trek up the Modi Khola through forests of bamboo, rhododendron and oak, and villages of the Gurung and Tamang clans. We'll reach the Sanctuary on about the 7th day and spend two days within its spectacular confines with a possible visit visit to Annapurna South Base Camp.

Return to Pokhara is via the Gurung settlements of Landrung and Ghandrung, with a final grand mountain panorama from our last campsite.

ITINERARY:

DAY 1 to 3: Leave U.S. Arrive Kathmandu. Briefing on trek arrangements.

DAY 4: Sightseeing in Kathmandu. Briefing on trek arrangements.

DAY 5: Drive to Pokhara, about 100 miles west of Kathmandu,

meet with Sherpa crew and begin trek, reaching Henja (3,500′), on the outskirts of the Pokhara Valley.

DAY 6 to 8: Cross the Yangri Khola and wind through rice fields, climb up a steep hill to Naudanda and continue on to Khare (5,600′). Drop down to the Modi Khola and climb very steeply uphill through forests to Ghorapani Pass, from where there are good mountain views. Camp at Ghorapani (9,300′).

DAY 9: Early morning visit to Poon Hill for a spectacular view of Dhaulagiri. Trek eastward along the ridge to forest camp at 9,500 feet.

DAY 10 and 11: Cross the pass leading to Ghandrung and then steeply down to a bridge at about 6,000 feet, then back up high above the Modi Khola, through forests of rhododendron, oak, and hemlock to British sheep breeding project at Kuldi Ghar (7,000′).

DAY 12: Climb steeply high above the river in a bamboo forest to the tiny campsite at Hinko (9,900′).

DAY 13 and 14: A short walk to the Sanctuary (13,300′) and spend these days exploring, photographing and enjoying the mountain scenery.

DAY 15 to 18: Retrace our steps back down through Kuldi Ghar, then continue to the large Gurung village of Ghandrung. Descend on wide stone stairs to the Modi Khola and make a steep climb through Landrung to the pass at Dhampus and camp on the ridge at Tolka.

DAY 19: Down the Yangri Khola valley to Pokhara. Overnight at Fishtail Lodge.

DAY 20: Fly or drive to Kathmandu. Transfer to hotel.

DAY 21: In Kathmandu

DAY 22: Depart Kathmandu on homeward-bound flights.

DAY 23: Arrive home.

Our man in Nepal

Stan Armington was, by coincidence, one of Mountain Travel's very first trip members (number five, we think). He was a member of one of our 1969 Nepal treks and, since then, has spent most of his time in Nepal, developing one of the best trekking operations anywhere. Since his professional background is in computer science, he owns and programs a special computer (one of the few in Nepal) with which he keeps up with such complexities as gear and food inventory, Sherpa assignments, and members' arrival information. He is well acquainted with Sherpa and Nepali culture, speaks fluent Nepali, and is author of the guidebook, **Trekking In The Himalayas.** Stan can frequently be found at the Rum Doodle, his own bar and restaurant in Kathmandu.

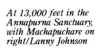

At 13,000 feet in the Annapurna Sanctuary, with Machapuchare on right/Lanny Johnson

IT4TG1MT01

THE DHAULAGIRI TREK

DATES:
*Sep 30–Oct 30
(31 days)*
GRADE: *C-3*
LAND COST: *$1975
(6–15 members)*

23-day trek up the Kali Gandaki gorge, over French Col (17,000′) and into Dhaulagiri Base Camp. Although it was one of the first 8,000-meter peaks attempted, Dhaulagiri (26,810′) was one of the last to be successfully climbed (by the Swiss in 1960). In Tibetan, the name Dhaulagiri means "the Rock That Stands Alone," and it is indeed an impressive mountain.

*Tibetan trader/
Alla Schmitz*

IT4TG1MT01

THE GOSAINKUND LAKES CIRCUIT

15-day trek on Hindu pilgrimage trail

DATES: *#1 Apr 15–May 6 (22 days)
#2 Oct 3–Oct 24 (22 days)*
LEADER: *#1: Siddiq Wahid
#2: Dick Irvin*
GRADE: *B-2*
LAND COST: *$1490 (6–15 members)*

This 15-day route is an excellent first trek in Nepal, offering a good overall impression of the contrasting Hindu-Buddhist hill cultures of Nepal. It circles through a Sherpa enclave on a picturesque trail which is regularly traveled by Hindu pilgrims on their way to worship at the "holy lake" of Gosainkund (14,200′), site of an ancient shrine to Shiva. As we climb up to the lake, we'll have excellent views of high peaks nearby in Tibet and of the plain at Kyirong, a former Tibetan trading town. Above the lakes, as we cross Lauribina Pass (15,100′), we'll have sweeping views of Himalchuli (25,895′), Manaslu (26,750′) and the Ganesh Himal.

We start the trek in the Trisuli Valley, just northeast of Kathmandu, skirting along green ridges with small Tamang villages and some of the most enchanting forests imaginable.

After visiting the holy lakes, we descend to Tharepati, a ridgetop summer settlement which has a wide view along the Himalayan range, then to Tarke Gyang, a compact Sherpa settlement which looks like a Swiss mountain village. Our last few days take us through the Helambu Sherpa district back to Kathmandu.

ITINERARY:

DAY 1 to 3: Leave U.S. Arrive Kathmandu. Transfer to hotel.

DAY 4: Sightseeing in Kathmandu. Briefing on trek arrangements.

DAY 5: Drive from Kathmandu to the roadhead at Trisuli Bazaar. Meet with porters and Sherpa crew and trek along the Trisuli River to Betrawati (2,000′).

DAY 6 and 7: Follow the course of the Trisuli Gorge, climbing high above the bank of the river to about 6,000 feet. This is a beautifully forested canyon with a mixture of subtropical and temperate/

Tibetan women above Trisuli Valley/Jeff Campbell

Above Syabru village with Ganesh Peak in background/Jeff Campbell

deciduous trees. The Trisuli drains the peaks of the Gosainkund Range.

DAY 8: Down steeply and across the Trisuli, then steeply up the other side to Syabru (8,000′).

DAY 9 and 10: Up through fir and rhododendron forests to Sing Gompa, a seldom used Buddhist monastery and a small cheese factory at Chandan Bari (11,200′). Rest day in area.

DAY 11: Climbing steeply in the morning, we will have spectacular views of the peaks of Himalchuli, Manaslu, and the Ganesh Himal. We descend to the shore of the third high lake we pass, which is Gosainkund. A white rock at Gosainkund Lake is reputed to be the remains of an ancient shrine to Shiva and hence the lake has been visited by Hindu pilgrims for centuries.

DAY 12: Wonderful views of the Annapurna, Himalchuli, and Ganesh ranges make a pleasant walk out of our climb past three more lakes to the Lauribina Pass (15,100′). Descend steeply to camp near a cave at Gopte (11,700′).

DAY 13: Continue hiking up and down through forests to a ridge crest named Tharepati with a magnificent view across the central Nepal Himalaya. Camp in a pasture at 9,500 with fine views.

DAY 14: Passing the Sherpa village of Malemchi (8,300′), we descend to the Malemchi Khola, then make a long climb up to Tarke Gyang (8,400′), where there is a recently renovated monastery. We are now amidst the Sherpa people of Helambu, who differ from the Khumbu Sherpas in many ways (including dress and language).

DAY 15: Rest day at Tarke Gyang. Optional day hikes and visits to Sherpa houses.

DAY 16: A day of great cultural change as we descend from the Sherpa mountain villages to the Tamang villages of the valley. Camp at Gheltum (3,200′).

DAY 17 and 18: Cross the river at Taramarang and follow the south bank, then climb steeply to the village of Thakani (6,500′). Good mountain views from the crest of the ridge at Borlang Bhanjang (8,200′).

DAY 19: A long and steep descent brings us to the edge of the Kathmandu Valley. Drive to Kathmandu and transfer to hotel.

DAY 20: In Kathmandu.

DAY 21: Depart Kathmandu on homeward-bound flights.

DAY 22: Arrive home.

Taking time to enjoy the cool air by the river. Days are planned to provide plenty of time for reading, writing or just relaxing/Jeff Campbell

IT4TG1MT01

THE MANASLU TREK

25-day trek in remote central Nepal

DATES: *#1 Apr 11–May 13 (33 days)*
#2 Oct 10–Nov 11 (33 days)
LEADER: *#1: Hugh Swift*
#2: to be announced
GRADE: *C-3*
LAND COST: *$1990 (6–15 members)*

This 25-day trek in central Nepal explores remote, uninhabited valleys and scenic ridges south of the magnificent "Gurkha Himal": Manaslu (26,760′), Himalchuli (25,895′) and Peak 29 (25,705′).

This region is newly opened for trekking and few Westerners have ever traveled here.

Walking from Trisuli to Pokhara, we first pass south of Ganesh (24,298′), the peak most easily visible from Kathmandu. Soon our path heads north of the usual trading routes into rarely traveled gorges beneath Bauda (21,890′), a high peak near Manaslu.

As we leave the terraced fields and villages of the lower hills, our route will take us along narrow paths leading to upper grazing pastures and dense forests. We reach our highest point on the ascent of the Rupina La (15,400′), an unfrequented pass that lies just east of Bauda Peak.

If this pass becomes officially opened to trekkers (it is closed as of May, 1984), we will cross it and return via a slightly different route.

If not, our return to civilization will be via the Chepe and Dordi

valleys, taking us down through thick rhododendron forests with gnarled trunks and moss-covered vines. By the time we descend to chartreuse-hued rice fields, we'll have seen nearly the full range of vegetation that Nepal has to offer. Most areas on this trek are far from the main hiking routes and the welcome accorded us by Gurung, Tamang and Brahmin-Chettri villagers will be delightfully spontaneous.

ITINERARY:

DAY 1 to 3: Leave U.S. Arrive Kathmandu. Transfer to hotel.

DAY 4: Sightseeing in Kathmandu. Briefing on trek arrangements.

DAY 5: Drive from Kathmandu to Trisuli (1,600′). Here we'll meet the Sherpa staff and porters and begin the trek.

DAY 6 to 8: Walk westerly on old paths now nearly deserted, passing ancient *chautaras* (resting places shaded by pipal and banyan trees). At Arughat, we'll see a temple with both Buddhist and Hindu images.

DAY 9 to 11: Walk up the Buri Gandaki Valley which narrows into a gorge as we continue northward on rocky, little-used trails. We are now entering a region rarely visited by foreigners.

DAY 12: Climbing, we turn into a narrow side-valley and arrive at the town of Laprok.

DAY 13 and 14: Leave human habitation and cross a wooded

ridge into the upper Darondi Valley. Reach high camp.

DAY 15: Rest day at high camp with a chance to explore this remote area.

DAY 16: Climb high to the Rupina La, below which lies all of central Nepal. Return to high camp.

DAY 17 to 19: Possible walk to Dudh Pokhari, an isolated lake south of Bauda Peak. Descend southward along a ridge west of the Darondi Valley. Here we'll see Gurung herders in the upper pastures with their flocks of sheep and goats.

DAY 20 to 22: Continue descent to the upper Chepe Valley, cross the river and proceed over a forested spur to the village of Simi.

DAY 23 and 24: Down the Dordi Valley and into lower country, reaching the town of Phalesanga by the Marsyandi River.

DAY 25: Today we follow the busy Marsyandi Valley trade route to the large bazaar of Khudi.

DAY 26: Ascending the Khudi Valley, we reach the ridgetop town of Ghanpokhara with its excellent perspective of Lamjung Himal (22,740′).

DAY 27 and 28: Now we walk across low ridges into Nepal's middle hills where we'll have superb views of Lamjung, Annapurna II and IV and the fishtail peak, Machapuchare (22,942′).

DAY 29: Descending into the broad Pokhara Valley, we will overnight at the Fishtail Lodge on Phewa Lake.

DAY 30: Fly or drive to Kathmandu. Transfer to hotel.

DAY 31: Day free in Kathmandu.

DAY 32: Depart Kathmandu on homeward-bound fights.

DAY 33: Arrive home.

IT4TG1MT01

THE KANCHEN-JUNGA TREK

DATES: *Oct 10–Nov 11 (33 days)*
GRADE: *B-3*
LAND COST: *$2190 (6–15 members)*

The Eastern Himalaya is crowned by Kanchenjunga (28,208′), third highest mountain in the world, whose icy crest forms the frontier between eastern Nepal and Sikkim.

For this 25-day trek, we fly to Biratnagar in east Nepal, drive to Dharan, and walk through the dense forests of east Nepal—rhododendron, bamboo, cedar, hemlock and spruce, visiting settlements of Bhotias, Rais, Limbus, Gurungs. Our approach to the Kanchenjunga massif will be via the Yalung Glacier.

The Trisuli is one of Nepal's major rivers, draining the Langtang and Ganesh peaks along the Tibetan border/Alla Schmitz

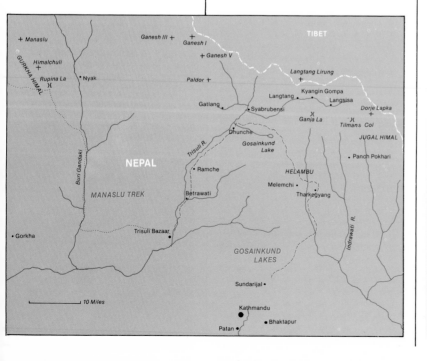

On the moraine of the Ngozumpa Glacier in the Gokyo Valley/Lanny Johnson

On the high trails of Khumbu enroute to Everest Base Camp with Thamserku (22,208') in the background/Lanny Johnson

IT4TG1MTO1

EVEREST BASE CAMP— 22-DAY TREK

One of the world's classic walks

DATES: *#1 Mar 16–Apr 15 (31 days)*
       #2 Oct 7–Nov 6 (31 days)
LEADER: *#1: to be announced*
        #2: Scot Macbeth
GRADE: *C-3*
LAND COST: *#1 $1750*
          (6–15 members)
          #2 $2090 (6–15)

Mt. Everest (29,028'), the world's highest mountain, is known to Tibetans as Chomolungma, "Mother Goddess of the Earth." It is a mountain to describe in superlatives—the most photographed and most written about mountain on earth.

The region below Mt. Everest is now designated as Sagarmatha National Park. It is Nepal's most popular trekking destination. Although the walk from the 4,000-foot lowlands near the Kathmandu Valley to Everest Base Camp at 18,000 feet is long and demanding, the experience of gazing on the majesty of Everest is an indescribable thrill and the realization of a dream for many.

The 22-day Everest Base Camp trek is the classic walk to Everest, following the traditional long base camp march used by most Everest expeditions. The trail from Kiranti-chap to Everest heads generally eastwards at first. Since the deep valleys which drain the Himalaya lie north to south, we'll be cutting "across the grain," for the first week, hiking up and down over many ridges. This is Nepal's banana belt, lush subtropical scenery of bamboo thickets and rhododendron forests. The villages of this region are inhabited by a variety of Hindu hill tribes.

Trekking through verdant rice paddies/ Lanny Johnson

Young Sherpa shepherds at Phortse village in the upper Khumbu region/Brian Weirum

After about nine days of lowland walking (great for altitude acclimatization), we enter the Tibetan Buddhist culture of the Khumbu region, the Sherpa homeland, and spend the rest of our trek in a wonderland of Himalayan grandeur. The trek culminates in a hike to Kala Patar (18,192′) for classic Everest views near the site of Everest Base Camp.

ITINERARY:

DAY 1 to 3: Leave U.S. Arrive Kathmandu. Transfer to hotel.

DAY 4: Sightseeing in Kathmandu. Briefing on trek arrangements.

DAY 5 to 7: Meet with Sherpa crew and begin trek. Drive to Kirantichap (4,200′). Trek through a pine forest to the Bhote Kosi River, then over to Yarsa (6,400′), across Chisopani Pass (8,200′), descend to Sikri Khola, and cross a low pass to Those (5,700′).

DAY 8 to 10: Along the river to Shivalaya, over Chyangma Pass (8,900′) to Bhandar (6,700′). Optional visit to a small dairy and cheese factory at Thodung. Down to the Likhu River and the market town of Kenja. Over Lamjura Pass (11,600′) to Junbesi (8,800′), with beautiful mountain views including Numbur.

DAY 11 to 14: Enter the Sherpa-inhabited Solu Valley for a first glimpse of Mt. Everest in the distance. Over Takshindu Pass to Takshindu Monastery (10,000′), a long, steep descent to the Dudh Kosi canyon then up and down along the Dudh Kosi gorge to Phakding (8,700′).

DAY 15 and 16: Entering the Khumbu region, we ascend to the busy market town of Namche Bazaar (11,300′) and on to Khumjung (12,500′), one of Khumbu's prettiest villages, known for its views of Kangtega (22,340′), Thamserku (22,208′) and Ama Dablam (22,494′).

DAY 17: To Thyangboche Monastery (12,700′), spiritual center of the Khumbu.

DAY 18: To Pheriche (14,000), site of the Himalayan Rescue Association's Trekkers Aid Post.

DAY 19: To the yak grazing pastures at Lobouje (16,200′).

DAY 20: A long day to Gorak Shep (17,000′), walking on boulder fields and glacial debris to the edge of the Khumbu Glacier. Nuptse (25,850′) and Pumori (23,442′) loom above camp.

DAY 21: Hike to the summit of Kala Patar (18,192′) for classic views of Mt. Everest, or hike to base camp itself. Return to Lobouje.

DAY 22 to 25: Back down the Khumbu Valley on a scenic high trail to Dingboche (14,500′), down through Pangboche and around a steep mountainside to Phortse, then through Khumjung, past Namche Bazaar and down to Lukla (9,300′), the mountain airstrip where we will fly out to Kathmandu.

DAY 26 to 29: The next few days will be spent either in Kathmandu or Lukla, depending on flying weather and other factors which often delay the mountain flights. Upon arrival in Kathmandu, transfer to hotel.

DAY 30: Depart Kathmandu on homeward-bound flights.

DAY 31: Arrive home.

Linda Liscom

Sherpani wearing a dablam *(charm box), for which the mountain* Ama Dablam *(22,494′), shown below, is named.*

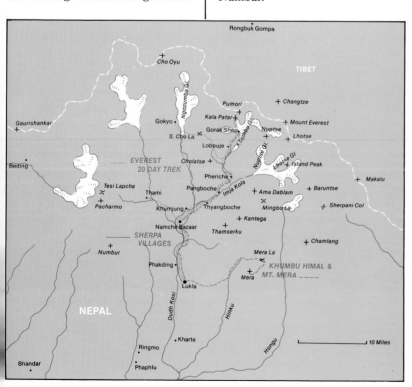

Mina Taylor

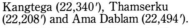
Sherpanis carrying children on our "Family Trek" past a mani *wall/Dick McGowan*

IT4TG1MTO1

EVEREST BASE CAMP— 20-DAY TREK

Khumbu exploration and Sherpa culture

DATES: # Mar 25–Apr 22 (29 days)
#2 Oct 24–Nov 21 (29 days)
#3 Nov 21–Dec 19 (29 days)
LEADER: #1: Dick Irvin
#2: to be announced
#3: Brian Weirum
GRADE: C-3
LAND COST: $1990 (6–15 members)

The 20-day trek to Everest Base Camp begins with a flight to Lukla airstrip at 9,300 feet, bypassing the lowland scenery. Most of the trek is spent well above 11,000 feet in the Khumbu region, at the head of which stands Mt. Everest (and many of the most magnificent peaks in all the Himalayas).

Khumbu is decorated everywhere with prayer flags and carved *mani* stones, and is the homeland of the Sherpa people, Tibetan Buddhist mountain dwellers who have gained fame as high altitude porters on mountaineering expeditions. Besides their traditional occupations as traders and yak herders, many Sherpas also work as trekking guides throughout Nepal's mountain regions.

The 20-day Everest treks include a trip up the Gokyo Valley for a chance to hike up Gokyo Ri (18,000'), a "hill" with stupendous views of the summits of Everest, Makalu and many other peaks. From the Gokyo Valley, a hike across the snow-covered South Cho La Pass (17,800') is an adventurous way to approach the upper Khumbu Valley enroute to Everest Base Camp. (If the South Cho La crossing is not possible due to snow conditions or other factors, we will approach Everest Base Camp and Kala Patar via the usual route up the Khumbu Valley).

ITINERARY:

DAY 1 to 3: Leave U.S. Arrive Kathmandu. Transfer to hotel.

DAY 4: Sightseeing in Kathmandu. Briefing on trek arrangements.

DAY 5 to 7: Fly to Lukla, weather permitting. Meet with Sherpa crew and trek along the Dudh Kosi to Phakding, then steeply up to Namche Bazaar (11,300'), the Sherpa "capital." Spare day at Namche.

DAY 8 and 9: Ascend the Bhote Kosi Valley and trek to Thame (12,500'). Visit Thame Monastery, known for its frescoes, and trek to Khumjung (12,500'), a beautifully situated village with views of

Kangtega (22,340'), Thamserku (22,208') and Ama Dablam (22,494').

DAY 10: Trek to Phortse bridge (11,500').

DAY 11 to 13: Trek gradually up Gokyo Valley, through birchwoods with fine views of Kangtega and on to the yak pasture of Machhermo (14,500'). Continue up a rocky gulch beside the Ngozumba Glacier to beautiful Gokyo Lake. Rest day and optional hike up Gokyo Ri, for magnificent views including Everest (29,028'), Makalu (27,825'), Cho Oyu (26,750'), and a vast expanse of other peaks.

DAY 14: Cross the Ngozumba Glacier and camp at 16,500 feet.

DAY 15: Ascend the 17,800-foot South Cho La pass on boulder fields and a steep, but short, snow slope. Descend the glacier to the beautiful glen of Dzonglha (15,900').

DAY 16: Contour the steep, grassy hillsides above Tshola Lake, enter the upper Khumbu Valley and walk to Lobouje (16,200').

DAY 17: To Gorak Shep (17,000'), up and down by the Khumbu Glacier passing over a tangle of moraine.

DAY 18: Morning hike to the summit of Kala Patar (18,192') for classic views of Mt. Everest. Afternoon walk all the way back down to Lobouje.

DAY 19 to 21: Down past the Trekkers' Aid Post at Pheriche to the Imja Khola, on to Pangboche (12,800'), then continue down the Imja Khola for a short climb to Thyangboche Monastery (12,700'). Spare day at Thyangboche.

DAY 22 and 23: Down to Namche Bazaar and continue along the gorge of the Dudh Kosi to Lukla.

DAY 24 to 27: The next few days will be spent either in Kathmandu or Lukla, depending on flying weather and other factors which often delay the mountain flights. Upon arrival in Kathmandu, transfer to hotel.

DAY 28: Depart Kathmandu on homeward-bound flights.

DAY 29: Arrive home.

The Sherpas, originally from eastern Tibet, migrated to the Khumbu region 400 years ago, where they still retain their Tibetan language, traditions and practice Tantric Buddhism.

Dick McGowan

Charles Gay

Hiking up Gokyo Ri (the brown ridge on the left), known for its exceptional views of Everest and the Khumbu region/Brian Weirum

IT4TGM1TO1

SHERPA VILLAGES & MT. EVEREST

11-day trek in Buddhist highlands of Nepal

DATES: *Dec 9–Dec 27 (19 days)*
LEADER: *Bill Henderson*
GRADE: *B-2*
LAND COST: *$1570 (6–15 members)*

This 11-day Everest trek circles up through the Khumbu region at a leisurely pace, enjoying the unbeatable mountain scenery and Sherpa culture. We'll visit all the major Sherpa villages including Namche Bazaar, Thame, Khumjung, and of course the famed Thyangboche Monastery (12,700'), where there are views of Everest.

Although the trek doesn't walk the extra few days up to Everest Base Camp, it is nevertheless a fantastic trekking experience with close-up views of some of the most beautiful peaks in the Himalaya. There will be a great deal of interaction with the Sherpa people and their Tibetan Buddhist culture.

ITINERARY:

DAY 1 to 3: Leave U.S. Arrive Kathmandu. Transfer to hotel.

DAY 4: Sightseeing in Kathmandu. Briefing on trek arrangements.

DAY 5: Begin trek. Fly to Lukla (9,300'), weather permitting. Meet with Sherpa crew and trek for a few hours along the Dudh Kosi to the village of Phakding (8,700').

DAY 6 and 7: Follow the Dudh Kosi, crossing it at intervals, then hike up the steep Namche hill to Namche Bazaar (11,300'), main trading center for the Khumbu area. Rest day to explore Namche and environs.

DAY 8: Trek to the village of Thame (12,500') and visit Thame Monastery.

DAY 9: Trek to Khumjung (12,500') and visit the Khumjung Monastery, Everest View Hotel and Khunde Hospital.

DAY 10 and 11: Descend into the deep gorge of the Dudh Kosi and up the other side to reach Thyangboche Monastery, the best-known monastery in Nepal.

DAY 12: Up the Khumbu Valley to Pangboche (12,800'). Visit Pangboche Monastery, oldest in the Khumbu.

DAY 13: Return to Thyangboche and continue down to Khunde (12,500') via the steep Dudh Kosi gorge.

DAY 14: Down past Namche Bazaar to Lukla.

DAY 15 to 17: The next few days will be spent either in Kathmandu or Lukla, depending on flying weather and other factors which often delay mountain flights. Upon arrival in Kathmandu, transfer to Malla Hotel.

DAY 18: Transfer to airport. Leave Kathmandu on homeward-bound flights.

DAY 19: Arrive home.

IT4TGM1TO1

FAMILY TREK IN NEPAL

11-day Sherpa culture trek

DATES: *Apr 4–Apr 22 (19 days)*
LEADER: *to be announced*
GRADE: *B-2*
LAND COST: *$1570 (6–15 members)*
Children:
ages 7–14: $785   2–6: $695
under 2: $325

This special trek, visiting the Sherpa villages of the Mt. Everest region, is a wonderful opportunity for parents and children to share the fun of a Nepal trek. On a very relaxed trekking schedule, the 11-day trek begins at Lukla (9,300') and circles up into the Khumbu region at a moderate pace (see itinerary for "Sherpa Villages & Mt. Everest"). Certain extra-amenities will be added to help make things run as smoothly as possible (i.e., extra Sherpa staff and porters to carry the very young children and the older kids when necessary). Much of the emphasis will be on interaction with the Sherpa population. Sherpa families are close-knit and they love being with children. They and their own children are always fascinated to meet "foreign" youngsters, a relative rarity in the Khumbu.

(see "Sherpa Villages & Mt. Everest")

Private Treks In Nepal

In addition to our scheduled Nepal treks, we can arrange treks for private groups and individuals. Ideally, a group of four or more persons is the best number from a cost standpoint, but we can make arrangements for fewer than that.

Since there are so many wonderful trekking routes in Nepal, selecting a trek itinerary can be bewildering! We suggest that you read the descriptions of the treks listed here and pick the one that sounds best for you, according to your time schedule. We can then adapt the itinerary to suit your specific needs.

Dates:
September through May (8 to 36 days)

Leader:
Sherpa sirdars

Landcost:
Depends on number in party and services requested.

Sherpa cooks/ Brian Weirum

Thyangboche Monastery, spiritual center for Khumbu Sherpas, is spectacularly situated on a ridge above the Dudh Khosi gorge. Surrounding views include the peaks of Everest, Ama Dablam, Taweche and Thamserku/ Dick McGowan

Ascending Mt. Mera/Bruce Klepinger

IT4TG1MTO1

KHUMBU HIMAL & MT. MERA

Everest trek plus ascent of 21,000-foot peak

DATES: *Oct 24–Dec 1 (39 days)*
LEADER: *Bruce Klepinger*
GRADE: *C-3/D-2*
LAND COST: *$2690 (6–12 members)*

Always one of our most popular alpine trips, this trek and climb combines a visit to Everest Base Camp and an ascent of Mt. Mera (21,247'), from the summit of which one can see four of the five highest mountains in the world: Everest (29,028'), Kanchenjunga (28,208'), Lhotse (27,923') and Makalu (27,825').

The first half of our trek, which begins with a flight to Lukla, takes us to Everest Base Camp (see "20-Day Everest Treks").

The second half takes us back down to Lukla then east into the high Hinku valley, a wild and uninhabited area. The entire trip from Lukla to Mt. Mera and back is one of high adventure amidst superb mountain wilderness. We'll establish high camp on the Mera La, an 18,000-foot pass from which strong trekkers can attempt Mera's summit. The climb is not technically difficult but the altitude makes it physically demanding.

ITINERARY:

DAY 1 to 3: Leave U.S. Arrive Kathmandu. Transfer to hotel.

DAY 4: Sightseeing in Kathmandu. Briefing on trek arrangements.

DAY 5: Begin trek. Fly to Lukla (9,300') (weather permitting) and trek to Phakding.

DAY 6 and 7: Trek to Namche Bazaar and Khumjung (12,500').

DAY 8 to 10: Trek up the Gokyo Valley to Gokyo Lake at 15,800 feet. Optional hike to Gokyo Ri (18,000').

DAY 11: Cross the Ngozumba Glacier and camp at 16,500 feet.

DAY 12: Weather and other factors permitting, cross the snow-covered South Cho La Pass (17,800'), a flat glacier plateau with magnificent views to the east and west. Descend to Dzonghla.

DAY 13: Trek to the yak pastures of Lobouje (16,200').

DAY 14: To Gorak Shep (17,000') along the edge of the Khumbu Glacier.

DAY 15: Hike to summit of Kala Patar (18,182') or Everest Base Camp itself. Return to Lobouje.

DAY 16. Past the Trekkers' Aid Post and along the Imja Khola to Thyangboche Monastery (12,700').

Each November, Thyangboche Monastery is the setting for mani rimdu, *a colorful Tibetan-Buddhist dance-drama complete with masked and costumed monks. This monk represents Gnossrung, protector-god of the Sherpa valleys/ Bruce Klepinger*

DAY 17: Trek back to Namche Bazaar.

DAY 18: Trek back to Lukla, where we prepare for the second stage of the trek.

DAY 19: Climb through pine and rhododendron forests then yak pastures to Chutenga (11,300').

DAY 20: Climb over a series of three passes at about 14,900 feet. Descend to Chetara (13,700').

DAY 21: Climb up over a rocky spur and descend into the Hinku Valley. Camp near a cave at Kote (11,500').

DAY 22: Through forests and summer pastures to Duhphu, a tiny stone gompa said to be several hundred years old. Camp at Tangnag (13,750').

DAY 23: Climb over moraines and up a ridge to Khare, a yak pasture at 15,800 feet.

DAY 24 to 26: Ascend to the Mera La (18,000') and prepare for the climb. Extra days here to allow for acclimatization and inclement weather.

DAY 27: Establish high camp at approximately 19,500 feet.

DAY 28: Summit attempt today.

DAY 29 to 33: Trek back out to Lukla.

DAY 34 to 37: The next days will be spent either in Kathmandu or Lukla, depending on flying weather and other factors which often delay the mountain flights. Upon arrival in Kathmandu, transfer to hotel.

DAY 38: Depart Kathmandu on homeward-bound flights.

DAY 39: Arrive home.

Innukhu Valley north of Mt. Mera/Bruce Klepinger

IT4TG1MTO1

EAST OF EVEREST

24-day trek on remote route to Everest

DATES: #1 Mar 9–Apr 11 (34 days)
#2 Dec 5, 1985–Jan 7, 1986
(34 days)
LEADER: #1: Bruce Klepinger
#2: to be announced
GRADE: C-3
LAND COST: $2090 (6–15 members)

Nepal is most verdant in its lush eastern reaches, where more rain falls than any other part of the country. On this 24-day trek, we will pass from these green tropics to the high Khumbu area and reach Kala Patar with its world-renowned views of Mt. Everest.

This approach to Everest's base is different from the 22-day trek in its remoteness, its distance from well-trodden paths and in the abundance of vegetation we see along the way.

*Girl of the Rai tribe, lowland Nepal/
Arlene Blum*

*The middle hills of eastern Nepal, with the
peak of Jannu in left background/
Arlene Blum*

The trails we follow are those walked by the lowland porters who supply Namche Bazaar with its food grains. These were also the trails walked by the first Mt. Everest reconnaissance expedition from the south in 1951, led by Eric Shipton.

Our trek begins from a roadhead between the towns of Dharan and Dhankuta and soon heads up the steamy Arun Valley toward Makalu (27,825'). After crossing the Arun (most likely by dugout), we head northwest along the Irkhua River valley, over narrow bamboo bridges and among millet and rice fields.

We cross three passes before reaching Khumbu. The first is the 11,400-foot Salpa Bhanjang, crowned by a twelve-foot-high stupa. Descending into the deep Hongu Valley, we pass the first Sherpa village en route, then trek for several days across two steep gorges before arriving in the Dudh Kosi Valley south of Mt. Everest. Here, perhaps for the first time on our trek, we begin to see other trekkers as we join the well-traveled path north of the Lukla airfield.

The last twelve days of the trek follow the regular hiking route into the Khumbu region and up to Kala Patar (18,192') for superb views of Everest. (See "22-day Everest Trek" for more details on the last half of the trek.)

ITINERARY:

DAY 1 to 3: Leave U.S. Arrive Kathmandu. Transfer to hotel.

DAY 4: Sightseeing in Kathmandu. Briefing on trek arrangements.

DAY 5: Fly to Biratnagar and drive to Dharan (1,200') at the edge of the low Siwalik hills.

DAY 6: Drive to the roadhead near Dhankuta (3,900') and meet Sherpa crew and porters. Begin trek in afternoon.

DAY 7: Ascend to the village of Hille (6,100') on a ridgetop with its Bhotia community and new monastery. Begin walk down ridge, passing a British-run agricultural station.

DAY 8: Magnificent distant views of Makalu as we descend to the hot Arun Valley floor at about 850 feet.

DAY 9: Up the Arun's left bank past Tumlingtar airstrip on a long, low plateau.

DAY 10: Cross the Arun River in a dugout "ferry" and begin walking away from the Arun through low hills.

DAY 11: Passing lush fields, we ascend the Irkhua Valley populated by people of the Brahmin, Chettri and Rai clans. Reach Phedi (6,500').

DAY 12: Now in oak and rhododendron forest, we cross the Salpa Bhanjang (11,400') and descend to Sanam village.

DAY 13: Down into the Hongu gorge with views of snow peaks up-valley, we pass the town of Gudel and reach the village of Bung.

DAY 14: Ascend past a small monastery completely surrounded by evergreens and a wall of prayer stones. Cross the Sipkie Pass (10,120').

DAY 15: We are now in the Inukhu (also called Hinku) Valley. Climb to the Pangum La (10,400') with superb views of peaks both ahead and behind us.

DAY 16: Here in the Dudh Kosi Valley, south of Khumbu, we begin walking north.

DAY 17: Cross a high ridge and join the busy trail beyond Lukla airfield. White peaks appear on both sides of the valley.

DAY 18 to 20: Trek to Namche Bazaar, Khumjung and Thyangboche (12,700').

DAY 21 to 23: Trek to Pheriche (14,000'), Lobouje (16,200') and Gorak Shep (17,000').

DAY 24: Hike to top of Kala Patar (18,192') for classic Everest views.

DAY 25 to 28: Return to Lukla.

DAY 29 to 32: The next few days will be spent either in Kathmandu or Lukla, depending on flying weather and other factors which often delay the mountain flights. Upon arrival in Kathmandu, transfer to hotel.

DAY 33: Depart Kathmandu on homeward-bound flighs.

DAY 34: Arrive home.

Old Codgers' Treks

In response to the great interest expressed in last year's "Old Codgers' Expedition," a climbing trip for mountaineers over 50 in celebration of Leo Le Bon's 50th birthday, we have planned two "Old Codgers' Treks."

These treks are for people who are over the hill, but not out to lunch. If you believe that your body doesn't have to atrophy as you get older, and that at 50 you can still be in better shape than most 18-year-olds, come along and share the trails with others like yourself, including "Old Codger" trip leaders John Thune, 68, a mountain enthusiast, skier and runner, and Lloyd Kahn, 50, surfer, marathoner and publisher of fitness books.

These treks will have the same daily pace and amenities as our other Nepal treks. People under 50 are also welcome (if they think they can keep up!)

For trek description, see Around Annapurna and 20-Day Everest Trek).

IT4TG1MT01

AROUND ANNAPURNA

DATES: *Oct 17–Nov 15 (30 days)*
LEADER: *Lloyd Kahn*
GRADE: *C-3*
LAND COST: *$1990 (6–15 members)*

IT4TG1MT01

22-DAY EVEREST TREK

DATES: *Oct 10–Nov 9*
LEADER: *John Thune*
GRADE: *C-3*
LAND COST: *$2090 (6–15 members)*

Kal Bhairava statue in Kathmandu. During the Durga Festival, hundreds of buffalos and other animals are sacrificed at this place/ Alla Schmitz

IT4TG1MTO1

EXPEDITION 20,000

30-day Khumbu climbing trek

DATES: *Nov 4–Dec 12 (39 days)*
LEADER: *Dick Irvin*
GRADE: *D-2*
LAND COST: *$2690 (6–12 members)*

A 30-day climbing adventure, "Expedition 20,000" will attempt ascents of Island Peak (20,238'), Pokhalde (19,044') and Parcharmo (21,097').

Island Peak is a moderately technical snow climb in an unbelievably magnificent setting. It stands isolated at the foot of the huge Lhotse Wall surrounded by the giants ringing the Lhotse Glacier—Lhotse Shar (27,644'), Nuptse (25,850'), Ama Dablam (22,494'), Baruntse (23,826') and Cho Polu (22,222').

Pokhalde stands to the southwest of the Lhotse Wall, east of the Khumbu Glacier. Views from its summit include Makalu, Pumori and Cholatse.

Private Climbing Expeditions

For mountaineers, we can arrange expeditions on peaks which are authorized by the Nepalese Government for climbing expeditions.

Write for details.

Parcharmo is situated above the Tesi Lapcha Pass on the edge of the Rolwaling Valley. Summit views extend into the heart of the Rolwaling, dominated by the peaks of Menlungtse and Gauri Shankar (23,452') and countless peaks stretching into Tibet.

The peaks are very challenging but not technically demanding. The trekking itinerary includes a visit to Everest Base Camp and the crossing of two rarely-used passes, the Changri La and Kongma La.

ITINERARY:

DAY 1 to 3: Leave U.S. Arrive Kathmandu. Transfer to hotel.

DAY 4: Sightseeing in Kathmandu. Briefing on trek arrangements.

DAY 5: Fly to Lukla (weather permitting). Trek to Phakding (8,700').

DAY 6: Trek to Namche Bazaar (11,300').

DAY 7: Short trek to Khumjung (12,500'). Views stretching from Kwangde (20,293') to Thamserku (21,723') and Kangtega (22,334'), plus Everest (29,028') and Lhotse (27,916').

DAY 8 to 11: Trek up the valley of the Dudh Kosi through Phortse and Machhermo to Gokyo Lake (15,800'). Day free at lake.

DAY 12 to 14: Cross the Ngozumba Glacier and Changri La Pass to Changru Nup Glacier. If conditions are bad on this pass, cross the South Cho La Pass (17,800') into the Khumbu.

DAY 15 and 16: Trek to Gorak Shep (17,000') and hike to Kala Patar (18,192') for views of Everest. Return to Lobouje.

DAY 17: Cross the lower portion of the Khumbu Glacier and camp at 17,200 feet enroute to the Kongma La.

DAY 18: Ascend Pokhalde (19,044'), with its fine views of Makalu, Nuptse, Lhotse, Ama Dablam, Pumori, and Cholatse. Return to camp in the Kongma La.

DAY 19 to 21: Hike to Chukung and farther up the Imja Khola to Pareshaya Gyab, camping by a small lake with fine views up the Lhotse Glacier and Lhotse-Nuptse wall.

DAY 22 and 23: Establish a high camp on Island Peak and, conditions permitting, attempt the summit the following day. The approach is relatively easy but the final pitches are considerably more difficult.

DAY 24 to 27: Trek back down past Pheriche, Thyangboche Monastery and Namche Bazaar to Thame, situated below the Tesi Lapcha Pass.

DAY 28 to 32: Tengbo (14,300') to Glacier Camp at about 17,000 feet, then up to a high camp at 19,000 feet for the ascent of Parcharmo (21,097').

DAY 33 and 34: Trek from Thame to Lukla (9,300').

DAY 35 to 37: The next few days will be spent either in Kathmandu or Lukla, depending on flying weather and other factors which often delay the mountain flights. Upon arrival in Kathmandu, transfer to hotel.

DAY 38: Leave Kathmandu on homeward-bound flights.

DAY 39: Arrive home.

Ascending Parcharmo/Bruce Klepinger

Summit ridge of Island Peak, a challenging but not technically difficult climb/ Bruce Klepinger

IT1AF155RY

TREKKING IN MONGOLIA

7-day walk in the High Altai

DATES: *Jun 25–Jul 15 (21 days)*
LEADER: *Dick Irvin*
GRADE: *B-2*
LAND COST: *$3950 (6–15 members)*

Mongolia is the land of Genghis Khan, whose fierce nomadic warriors once ranged from the Black Sea to the Pacific.

Our Mongolian visit begins with a long flight from Moscow across Siberia, to Ulan Bator, Mongolia's capital, set in grasslands at 5,000 feet. Here we visit Ganden Monastery, where there are several resident lamas and very impressive Buddhist art and artifacts.

From Ulan Bator, we fly to Kobdt, across the sands of the Gobi Desert and up to the lake-strewn northern forests for a seven-day trek in the High Altai, a remote mountain range which rises from the steppes of Central Asia.

With horses to carry our gear, we hike over hills and ridges, occasionally visiting the yurt dwellings of nomadic Kazakh shepherds, seeing beautiful wildflowers in bloom on the hillsides and, with luck, catching a glimpse of some rare Central Asian wildlife such as Argali sheep, ibex and possible even snow leopard.

After the trek, we visit the ruins of Karakorum, Genghis Khan's original capital, abandoned in 1260 A.D. when his son, Kublai Khan, moved the Mongol capital to Beijing.

Our last day in Ulan Bator coincides with festive annual "independence day" celebrations, where we can watch demonstrations of the traditional Mongolian sports of wrestling and archery.

ITINERARY:

DAY 1 and 2: Leave U.S. Arrive Moscow and continue on flight to Ulan Bator.

DAY 3: Arrive Ulan Bator. Transfer to hotel.

DAY 4: Spectacular four-hour flight across Mongolia to Kobdt, then five-hour drive to Sert along the base of the High Altai Mountains.

DAY 5: Begin seven-day trek, hiking up to a beautiful campsite by Khukh Serkh Nuur ("Blue Ibex Lake").

DAY 6: Optional day hike to Urt Sallah Ehk at 13,500 feet. Beautiful wildflowers and a chance to see ibex.

DAY 7: Follow the Khukh Serkh river to a Kazakh village and eventually reach a campsite beneath six pine trees.

DAY 8: Trek steeply uphill with views of Kobdt far in the distance.

DAY 9: Short walk to Burught Belchir. Optional afternoon horseback ride.

DAY 10: Trek downhill along a river seeing many columbines and butterflies.

DAY 11: East down the valley to Tsagaan Tokhoi at the confluence of two rivers. Possible visit with a Kazakh family in their yurt on our way to Tsagaan Tokhoi.

DAY 12: Drive along the Dund Valley and continue to Har Us Nuur ("Black Lake"). The grassy islands in the middle of the lake are the breeding grounds for many water birds, including the herring gull.

DAY 13: Drive to Kobdt and fly to Ulan Bator.

DAY 14: Morning visit to Ganden Monastery, the only functioning Buddhist Monastery in Mongolia today, and Bogda Khan's winter palace.

DAY 15: Fly to Khujert and drive to Karakorum, the ancient Mongolian capital built by Genghis Khan's successors in the 13th century. Destroyed by the Chinese in 1368, Erdene Dzu monastery was built on the same spot and with many of the same stones in 1586. Not a single nail was used in construction. Along the way, we may see several interesting species of birds including sarus cranes. Overnight in yurt camp.

DAY 16: Fly back to Ulan Bator.

DAY 17: Watch the colorful Independence Day celebrations.

DAY 18: Fly to Moscow. Overnight in hotel.

DAY 19: Sightseeing in Moscow (including Red Square and the Kremlin).

DAY 20: Depart Moscow and connect with homeward-bound flights.

DAY 21: Arrive home.

The Kazakh people live in intricately decorated felt yurts on the vast Mongolian steppes.

Mongolian string instrument/ Linda Liscom

Camels are used as beasts of burden and carry all of our gear while on trek/ Linda Liscom

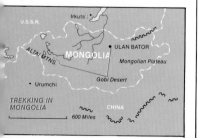

TREKKING IN MONGOLIA

600 Miles

The 13-story-high Potala Palace dominates the entire Lhasa Valley and is said to contain more than 1,000 rooms and chapels. Construction began in 7th century and restoration continues today.

IT5PA1SFMT1

TIBET: THE MT. EVEREST/ SHISHIPANGMA TOUR

Visit Lhasa and northern flanks of the Himalayas

DATES: #1 Mar 31–Apr 27 (28 days)
    #2 Sep 4–Oct 1 (28 days)
LEADER: #1 Jerry Coe
    #2 to be announced
GRADE: A-3/C-2
LAND COST: $5900 (14–16 members)
    $6200 (11–13)

The Tibetan people are a proud and handsome race living on the "roof of the world," where they herd yaks, trade, spin wool and drink salt-and butter tea. Religion is a very important facet of the lives of many Tibetans who practice Mahayana Buddhism.

Tibet photos by Leo Le Bon

Lama from Shigatse.

Spinning wool.

Tibetans on pilgrimage around Tashilumpo Monastery.

"Tibet, forbidden and forbidding, the land of vast sweeping plateaus and giant ranges crowned with eternal snows, the land of a strange and colorful people. From the time of Marco Polo, it has drawn men of the Western Hemisphere to probe its mysteries..."—R. Burdsall, *Men Against The Clouds.*

Of all the places we visit in China, only one can claim the magic and mystery of Tibet. The aim of our Tibetan travels will be visits to the bases of Mt. Everest (29,028′), known to Tibetans as Chomolungma, and to Mt. Shishipangma (26,291′), one of the last 8,000-meter peaks to be climbed. We arrive at both base camps by truck and have several days for optional day hikes, photography and enjoying the spectacular scenery.

First touring Lhasa, Tibet's capital, we visit the legendary Potala Palace, the very symbol of Tibet, a thousand-room hilltop citadel which was the traditional seat of 13 successive Dalai Lamas, God-Kings of Tibet. We also visit Drepung (the world's largest monastery), and the Jokhang "cathedral," the holiest shrine in Tibet and equivalent of Mecca for Tibetan Buddhists.

To reach the mountains, we drive down the valley of the Yarlung Tsangpo to Shigatse and Shegar (14,500′), site of an historic walled village, then further by truck over rough tracks to the base of Shishipangma, where we spend two days taking local walks.

Continuing by truck to the beautiful Tingri Valley, with views of Cho Oyo (26,750′) and Gyanchun Kang (26,140′), we drive over the 17,000-foot Pang La Pass and reach the Rongbuk Valley ("Valley of Precipices"), at the head of which stands Mt. Everest.

At the site of the old Rongbuk Monastery (16,500′), we have four days to explore the area and feast our eyes on the mountain views. Those who are very fit and well acclimatized can hike up the Rongbuk Glacier to advance base camp and Camp I of the historic Everest expeditions of the 1920's.

ITINERARY:

DAY 1 and 2: Leave U.S. Arrive Beijing. Transfer to hotel.

DAY 3: Sightseeing including the Great Wall at Badaling, dating from the Ming Dynasty, with a stop at a beautifully carved stone gate built in the Mongol period; afternoon drive through the 15th century Avenue of Animals, with its huge stone sculptures, to visit the Ming Tombs, built during the emperors' lifetimes to be their underground palaces in the afterworld.

DAY 4: Fly to Chengdu.

DAY 5: Fly to Lhasa on one of the most spectacular mountain flights in the world. Drive 80 miles to Lhasa with a stop to visit a large stone-carved Sakyamuni Buddha.

DAY 6 to 9: Four full days in Lhasa, with visits to the Potala, the Norbulingka, and the three great monasteries of Lhasa (Ganden, Sera, and Drepung), and time to stroll in the bazaar.

DAY 10: All-day bus ride to Shigatse (12,500′), with a ferry ride across the Tsangpo River. In Shigatse, second largest city in Tibet, we will visit Tashilumpo Monastery, the former seat of the Panchen Lama and one of the most important religious centers in central Tibet.

DAY 11: All-day bus ride to the town of Shegar ("White Crystal") at 14,500 feet, crossing the high passes of Tso La (14,800′) and Gyatso La (17,300′), the incongruously named "Ocean Pass" which has yielded many marine fossils to casual collectors. Shegar is the site of a ruined fortress/monastery.

DAY 12: In Shegar.

DAY 13: Drive to Shishipangma Base Camp.

DAY 14 and 15: At Shishipangma Base Camp.

DAY 16: By truck to Tingri.

DAY 17: By truck to Rongbuk (16,500'), winding through numerous remote Tibetan villages. Driving over the Pang La (17,300'), there are spectacular views of the north side of the Himalaya from Makalu to Cho Oyu, including Mt. Everest.

DAY 18 to 21: Four full days at Rongbuk area. Time for local walks and exploration. Those who are very fit can hike to advance base camp and possibly to the site of the early British Camp I (17,800') on the east Rongbuk Glacier.

DAY 22: By truck to Shegar.

DAY 23: By bus to Shigatse.

DAY 24: By bus to Gyantse. Visit site of Younghusband's Fort and Kumbum stupa (largest in Tibet), "the pagoda of 100,000 Buddhas."

DAY 25: By bus to Lhasa.

DAY 26: Fly to Chengdu.

DAY 27: Fly to Beijing.

DAY 28: Depart Beijing and connect with homeward bound flights.

IT5PA1SFMT1

TIBET: THE NAMCHE BARWA TREK

The highest unclimbed peak in the world

DATES: *May 1–May 28 (28 days)*
LEADER: *Leo Le Bon*
GRADE: *B-2*
LAND COST: *$5800 (14–16 members)*
$6100 (11–13)

Namche Barwa (25,445'), highest unclimbed peak in the world, is considered to be the last great rampart of the Eastern Himalaya. It is a lovely icy pyramid standing above the gorge of the mighty Tsangpo River, which curls around its foot and doubles back on itself to become the Brahmaputra. Just seven miles across the river, Gyala Peri (23,458'), another impressive unclimbed peak, rises toward the mountains of China.

The focus of this trip is a 7-day visit to the base of Namche Barwa with a chance to hike and explore extremely remote and unvisited portions of the southeastern Tibetan highlands. We will be the first group of Westerners permitted to visit this region of Tibet.

After a three-day visit to Lhasa, capital of Tibet, we drive for two days by truck to southeastern Tibet, arriving by road at Namche Barwa Base Camp at 9,000 feet. Vegetation around base camp will be lush and subtropical, in great contrast to the peak which rises 15,000 feet above it.

We spend a week at and above base camp for trekking and local exploration. Stronger trekkers can hike up to Camp II on Namche Barwa at 14,800 feet.

Northern ramparts of Mt. Everest from the Rongbuk Glacier.

ITINERARY:

DAY 1 and 2: Leave U.S. Arrive Beijing. Transfer to hotel.

DAY 3: Sightseeing including the Great Wall at Badaling, dating from the Ming Dynasty, and the Ming Tombs, built during the emperors' lifetimes to be their underground palaces in the afterworld.

DAY 4: Fly to Chengdu.

DAY 5: Fly to Lhasa (11,700'), drive 80 miles to Lhasa via the Yarlung Tsangpo River, stopping to visit a large stone-carved Buddha Sakyamuni.

DAY 6 to 8: Visit the major temples and shrines of Lhasa, including the Jokhang, Drepung and Ganden monasteries, the Potala Palace, and Norbulinka (summer palace of the Dalai Lama).

DAY 9 and 10: Drive southeast by truck and arrive at Namche Barwa Base Camp.

DAY 11 to 17: At and around base camp.

DAY 18 and 19: Return drive to Lhasa.

DAY 20: In Lhasa.

DAY 21: Drive to Gyantse via Yamdrok Lake. Visit Kumbum, the largest stupa in Tibet, and the beautiful Palkhor Monastery.

DAY 22: Morning in Gyantse. Afternoon to Shigatse (12,500'), second largest town in Tibet. Visit Tashilumpo Monastery, one of the largest and most important religious centers of central Tibet.

DAY 23: Sightseeing in Shigatse.

DAY 24: Drive to Lhasa. Visit Sakya Monastery enroute (pending permission).

DAY 25: Fly to Chengdu.

DAY 26: In Chengdu.

DAY 27: Fly to Beijing.

DAY 28: Depart Beijing and connect with homeward-bound flights.

The Mahayana Buddhism of Tibet has engendered some of the most beautiful religious art in the world.

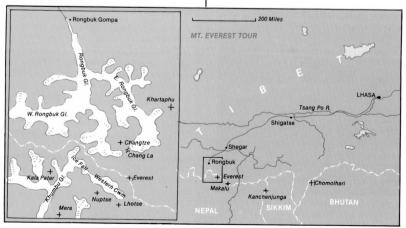

Minya Konka from Rock's Ridge at 15,000 feet/Leo Le Bon

Portrait of Arhat from Temple of 500 Buddhas, Chengdu/Leo Le Bon

Emperor Qin Shi Huang Di (ruled 221–210 B.C.) established the Great Wall as defense against nomadic Mongolian tribes. The wall measures 2,750 miles from near the Bohai Sea to the Gobi Desert/Leo Le Bon

IT5PA1SFMT1

THE MINYA KONKA TREK

12-day trek in the "Alps of Chinese Tibet"

DATES: *Sep 29–Oct 22 (24 days)*
LEADER: *Bruce Klepinger*
GRADE: *C-3*
LAND COST: *$3900 (14–16 members) $4200 (11–13)*

Mt. Minya Konka is the most beautiful mountain in China, a mountain so awesome that "to behold the peak is worth ten years of meditation." This is written on an inscription in the now-ruined Konka Gompa ("Snow Monastery") at the foot of the peak.

Mt. Minya Konka—located in the Alps of Chinese Tibet—was truly unknown and unexplored until about 50 years ago. In the early part of this century, a few travellers reported the distant sight of a great mountain in western Sichuan, on the edge of the Tibetan Plateau. Some thought it might be higher than Mt. Everest. It wasn't until the epic National Geographic Society Expedition of 1927–30, led by Dr. Joseph Rock, that the stupendous range called Minya Konka was definitely located and explored. Its highest peak, Mt. Minya Konka (also called Mt. Minya Gongga) towers 24,950 feet, its base drained by the Tatu River at 3,000 feet, less than 20 miles away.

We'll make our own explorations in this region, completing a 12-day trek through remote "Greater Tibet," an autonomous district in western Sichuan, with a visit to the base camp below Minya Konka, and an optional hike up to "Rock's

Ridge" at 17,000 feet for spectacular views.

Before the trek, we visit Kanding, a small town nestled in the mountain valleys of western Sichuan, and Chengdu, capital of Sichuan Province.

ITINERARY:

DAY 1 and 2: Leave San Francisco. Arrive Beijing. Transfer to hotel.

DAY 3: Sightseeing including the Great Wall at Badaling, dating from the Ming Dynasty, with a stop at a beautifully carved stone gate built in the Mongol period; afternoon drive through the 15th century Avenue of Animals, with its huge stone sculptures, to visit the Ming Tombs.

DAY 4: Fly to Chengdu. Afternoon tour of city.

DAY 5 to 7: Drive to Kanding via Ya'an and Luding, and on to starting point of trek at Yue Ling at 10,000 feet.

DAY 8 and 9: With horses carrying equipment, walk through a landscape dotted with Tibetan houses and tents and striking mountain scenery. Camp at about 13,000 feet.

DAY 10 and 11: Trek over Sam Pan San Pass (also called Djezi La) at 15,685 feet, then walk down Yulongshi Valley through wild country.

DAY 12: Walk through small Tibetan villages where there has been little contact with foreigners.

DAY 13 and 14: Up and over the Tsumei La (15,288') and on to Minya Konka base camp and the site of Konka Gompa at 12,300 feet. Magnificent views of Minya Konka.

DAY 15 and 16: Layover days to photograph, explore, hike to Rock's Ridge and advance base camp for the standard route on Minya Konka.

DAY 17 to 19: Walk back down to Tsumei, once again cross over the Tsumei La to the Yulongshi Valley. Continue past the Sorbu Gompa to Tibetan village of Liuba at the roadhead.

DAY 20: Drive to Kanding.

DAY 21 and 22: Drive to Chengdu via Ya'an.

DAY 23: Fly to Beijing.

DAY 24: Depart Beijing and connect with homeward-bound flights.

Ted Vaill below Mt. Sigunian ("Four Sisters Peak"/Allen Steck

IT5PA1SFMT1

TREKKING IN THE SIGUNIAN VALLEY

6-day natural history trek

DATES: *Oct 6–Oct 25 (20 days)*
LEADER: *to be announced*
GRADE: *B-2*
LAND COST: *$2500 (14–16 members) $2800 (11–13)*

This trip features a six-day natural history trek in the foothills of the Sigunian Alps, a very beautiful region of granite peaks which rise out of heavily forested valleys. The highest peak in the area is Sigunian (21,600'—"Four Sisters Peak"), one of the most impressive granite spires in the world.

Our trek, which takes place at an average altitude of about 11,000 feet, takes us through rhododendron country, up into green meadows and through deep conifer forests draped with Spanish moss.

Birdlife in the region is prolific, including raptors, griffon vultures, lammergeiers, Chinese goshawks and redstarts. We have a good chance of sighting bharal (blue sheep) and musk deer. Higher in this region (although we probably won't be lucky enough to spot them), the forest gives cover to golden-faced monkeys, wild yaks and snow leopards.

We also stop for a visit at Wolon Panda Reserve, a sanctuary established to protect the giant panda and other species. Much research on pandas has been done here by naturalist/author George Schaller.

Our approach to Sigunian is via Chengdu, one of China's most historic cities, called the "Storehouse of Heaven," a center for hand-crafted treasures including embroidery, baskets and pottery. On return from our trek, we also have a chance to visit Zelun, a remote agricultural commune.

There is no difficult hiking on the trek, but those wishing to see wildlife must be prepared for some steep walks. Horses carry the gear on trek.

ITINERARY:

DAY 1 and 2: Leave U.S. Arrive Beijing. Transfer to hotel.

DAY 3 and 4: Sightseeing at the Great Wall, Ming Tombs and Forbidden City.

DAY 5: Fly to Chengdu.

DAY 6: Local sightseeing in old Chengdu—a rich experience for photographers and handicraft enthusiasts.

DAY 7: Drive to Wolon Panda Research Station (6,435'), through agricultural plains and small villages. Overnight at Wolon Guest House.

DAY 8: By special permit, we visit the Wolon Panda Research Station. There are some pandas living in nearby enclosures which we may be able to visit. Also visit the Wolon Natural History Museum, a UNESCO Project housing some fine exhibits of local birds, insects, mammals and a large relief map of the area.

DAY 9: All-day drive over Palung Pass (14,500') down to Zelun (10,500') with fine views of the Sigunian Alps.

DAY 10: Begin six-day trek into the Sigunian Alps. Horses will carry our gear. Leisurely five-hour walk to a fine meadow about half way to base camp (11,500').

DAY 11: Camp at about 12,500 feet in a meadow below the impressive northern face of Mt. Sigunian (21,600'). We've seen up to 22 bharal (blue sheep)in one sighting here.

DAY 12 to 14: Day hikes in the area, or optional backpacking to a spectacular side canyon that leads up around the southwest flanks of Celestial Peak, a shapely granite pyramid of about 18,500 feet.

DAY 15: Return to Zelun.

DAY 16: In Zelun, a commune of about 800 people.

DAY 17: Drive to Wolon.

DAY 18: Drive to Chengdu, with a picnic stop at Two Kings Temple (Erwangsi) built during the Qing Dynasty (221–206 B.C.). The complex contains some of China's most beautiful traditional-style architecture.

DAY 19: Fly to Beijing.

DAY 20: Depart Beijing and connect with homeward-bound flights.

IT5PA1SFMT1

THE VALLEY OF NINE VILLAGES

Exploring remote Sichuan

DATES: *Aug 21–Sep 10 (21 days)*
LEADER: *Linda Liscom*
GRADE: *B-1*
LAND COST: *$2750 (14–16 members)*
$2950 (11–13)

This trip features two short treks in northwestern Sichuan. The first takes us on foot (or by Tibetan pony, if one prefers) for three days into the mountains of the Min Range. This is a remote area which has seldom had foreign visitors (except for a few explorers and botanists during the 1920's). Enroute, we'll pass Tibetan villages of the Awa people, yak herders who cultivate high pastures.

The second three-day trek explores an untouched mountain valley in northern Sichuan called Jiu Zhai Gou ("The Valley of Nine Villages"), replete with Tibetan hamlets and enchanting waterfalls. The valley is prime panda habitat, dense with bamboo. Many Chinese consider the Jiu Zhai Gou Valley to be one of the most scenic in all China.

In between treks, we visit the Huang Long Shi ("Yellow Dragon Monastery") which we reach by hiking along a three-mile ridge of travertine pools.

Visits are also included to Chengdu, Beijing, and the ancient walled village of Son Pan.

Note: At the time of printing (May, 1984), permits for visiting this special region are pending.

ITINERARY:

DAY 1 and 2: Leave U.S. Arrive Beijing. Transfer to hotel.

DAY 3 and 4: Sightseeing including the Great Wall at Badaling, dating from the Ming Dynasty, with a stop at a beautifully carved stone gate built in the Mongol period; afternoon drive through the 15th century Avenue of Animals, with its huge stone sculptures, to visit the Ming Tombs, built during the emperors' lifetimes to be their underground palaces in the afterworld; tour the Forbidden City, once the Imperial Palace, a vast treasure-house begun in the Yuan Dynasty and enlarged over the centuries.

DAY 5: Fly to Chengdu.

DAY 6: Begin three-day bus ride to Jiu Zhai Gou, a journey of about 400 miles. The first day we enter the mountains of northwestern Sichuan and follow the course of the Min River to its source. The Min is one of the four major Sichuan rivers (Sichuan means

"Four Rivers"). Overnight in guest house in Monwen, a town inhabited mostly by Hui Moslems, one of China's national minority people. Our group will be the first party of Westerners into this region since the 1920's.

DAY 7: Continue by bus for about six hours to Son Pan, a village whose ancient city walls can still be seen in places. Overnight in government guest house.

DAY 8 to 10: Three-day excursion on foot or with Tibetan pony into the Min Range, whose highest peak is Mt. Shue Baoding ("Precious Snow Peak"—18,234'), an ice-clad Matterhorn-like spire. Along the trek route, we pass Tibetan villages, with their cultivated pastures and yak herds. Return to Son Pan at the end of the trek.

DAY 11: By bus, crossing Sueshan Pass (14,300'), to visit Huang Long Shi, an ancient Buddhist monastery, which we reach by a three-mile walk along a beautiful ridge of yellow travertine rock filled with deep azure pools. Camp nearby.

DAY 12: Return to the main road via the Sueshan Pass, then over Konkalin Pass (9,500') into the northern watershed of Sichuan Province. Arrive at Jiu Zhai Gou in the late afternoon. Overnight at government guest house.

DAY 13 to 15: Three days exploring the valley, during which we will either camp in a secluded glen and make day hikes, or stay at a lodge and visit the park by bus.

DAY 16: Drive to Son Pan.

DAY 17: Drive to Mon Wen.

DAY 18: Drive to Chengdu.

DAY 19: In Chengdu.

DAY 20: Fly to Beijing.

DAY 21: Depart Beijing and connect with homeward-bound flights.

Drying peas and barley.

Northwestern Sichuan Province has a primarily Tibetan population and some of the most beautiful forests in all China/Jiu Zhai Gou photos by Leo Le Bon

Ruins of Huang Long Shi Monastery.

Boy from Son Pan.

Jiu Zhai Gou, the valley of nine villages.

IT5PA1SFMT1

TRAVELS IN THE TIEN SHAN

Silk Road tour and 4-day trek

DATES: *Jun 30–Jul 23 (24 days)*
LEADER: *John Thune*
GRADE: *B-2*
LAND COST: *$4100 (14–16 members)*
$4500 (11–13)

China's far western provinces are inhabited by a wide variety of "national minorities," such as Kazakhs, Kirghiz and Tibetans.

Photos by trip leader John Thune

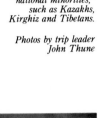

Kazakh girl.

Kazakh horseman.

Tibetan lama.

The Tien Shan ("Celestial Mountains") comprises one of the longest mountain ranges in the world (some 1,000 miles), rising in western Soviet Turkestan, forming the northern ramparts of the huge Takla Makan Desert, and finally ending just east of Urumchi, capital of Sinkiang Province.

The highest mountain in the eastern Tien Shan is Mt. Bogda Ola (17,900′), first attempted in 1946 by British explorers Shipton and Tilman. Bogda's beautifully shaped massif of rock and ice is reflected in Tien Schi (10,000′), the large "heavenly lake" below it.

Driving to Tien Schi Lake, not far from Urumchi, we travel to the end of the lake and make a leisurely four-day trek to the base of Mt. Bogda with Kazakh horsemen and their pack horses carrying our gear. The two-day walk to Bogda's base is relatively easy, with two more layover days at base camp to photograph and take day hikes with great Tien Shan views. Several Kazakh settlements are in this area and we will visit some yurts (portable dwellings made of felt) and probably be invited inside for a cup of tea.

Before the trek we visit some of the most fascinating cultural sites of China's Silk Road. In Lanzhou, with its rich treasure of Buddhist art, we see the "Flying Horse of Gansu," and take a boat cruise to Bingling, a Buddhist temple housing hundreds of stone carvings and a nearly 100-foot-high statue of Buddha carved on a rock face overlooking the Yellow River.

In Xining, we visit Kumbum Monastery, a colorful Tibetan gompa with about 200 monks in residence.

At Dun Huang, we'll explore the "caves of 1000 Buddhas," undoubtedly one of China's finest treasures of Buddhist antiquity. About 450 caves still exist here containing richly decorated carvings and countless wall paintings.

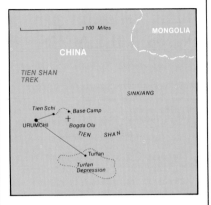

In Turfan, an oasis watered by the melting snows of the Tien Shan, we visit the remains of Gaochan, Bezeklik and other ruined, sand-buried cities from the days when the Silk Road was active.

ITINERARY:

DAY 1 and 2: Leave U.S. Arrive Beijing. Transfer to hotel.

DAY 3: Sightseeing including the Great Wall at Badaling, dating from the Ming Dynasty, the Ming Tombs, built during the emperors' lifetimes to be their undergound palaces in the afterworld.

DAY 4: Fly to Lanzhou (6,500′), capital of Gansu Province. Afternoon visit to the Lanzhou Provincial Museum.

DAY 5: All-day boat cruise along the Huang Ho (Yellow River) to visit temple of Bingling and 100-foot-high statue of Buddha carved out of a rock face over the river.

DAY 6: Six-hour train ride to Xining, provincial capital of Quinghai. Afternoon free.

DAY 7: Visit Kumbum, an active monastery in good condition. Once this was one of the most important monasteries in Northern Tibet (Amdo) and the elder Dalai Lama's brother was its abbot.

DAY 8: Return to Lanzhou by train.

DAY 9: In Lanzhou. Visit White Pagoda Mountain, its white stupa crowning the hills.

DAY 10: Drive to Dun Huang.

DAY 11 and 12: Explore the Dun Huang Caves, the great repository of Chinese cave art spanning the period from the Northern Wei to the Yuan dynasties.

DAY 13: By train to Turfan.

DAY 14: Explore the oasis of Turfan.

DAY 15: Drive to Urumchi, a former oasis town which is now the capital of the desert province of Sinkiang.

DAY 16: In Urumchi.

DAY 17: Drive to Tien Schi Lake.

DAY 18 and 19: Walk to Bogda base camp.

DAY 20 and 21: At base camp.

DAY 22: Return to Tien Schi Lake and drive to Urumchi.

DAY 23: Fly to Beijing.

DAY 24: Depart Beijing and fly to U.S.

Detail of Nine Dragon Screen/Leo Le Bon

Camping at Little Karakol Lake below Mt. Muztagata.

Mary and Sara Groves, Eric Moore and Bob Shanewise taking the camels for a short ride along the flanks of Mt. Kongur.

IT5PA1SFMT

SINKIANG: THE MUZTAGATA & BOGDA TREK

7-day camel trek, 4-day Tien Shan trek, visit Silk Road cities

DATES: *Jun 30–Jul 26 (27 days)*
LEADER: *to be announced*
GRADE: *B-1*
LAND COST: *$4300 (14–16 members)*
$4600 (11–13)

No part of China is more remote and isolated than the western corner of Sinkiang Province. Indeed, this is the very heart of Central Asia, as far away as one can travel from Beijing (3,000 miles) and still be in China!

Sinkiang is immense, encompassing portions of the Karakorum, Tien Shan and Kun Lun mountains as well as parts of the Gobi and Takla Makan deserts.

A major artery of the Silk Road passed through Sinkiang, a province which was known by early travelers as High Tartary, Chinese Turkestan, or Kashgaria. It is now officially the Sinkiang-Uighur Autonomous Region.

Our Sinkiang journey features two relatively easy treks in two very different mountain regions.

From Beijing, we begin with a flight over the Takla Makan Desert to Urumchi, the oasis town which is the capital of Sinkiang Province. Here we have our first taste of the nomadic culture, both Uighur and Kazakh, that predominates the vast grasslands and deserts of Central Asia.

Local dwellings are cozy "yurts" made of felt stretched around a wooden frame. Inside, they are carpeted with hand-made blankets and heated with a wood stove.

The first trek, a four-day walk, takes us to the base of Tien Schi ("heavenly lake") at 10,000 feet in an alpine setting in the foothills of the Tien Shan. We trek from here up into high meadows within view of the snow and glaciers of Mt. Bogda, a shapely ice peak, and return by the same route back to Urumchi. En route we'll see the occasional yurts of nomadic Kazakh families. Horses will carry all our camping gear.

For our second trek, we fly to Kashgar, a dusty desert town much reminiscent of the days of the "Silk Road," when camel caravans passed through here on the trade route between the Yellow River and the Mediterranean. Last outpost on the Silk Road in China, Kashgar has only been open to foreign tourists for three years.

We stroll in Kashgar's medieval bazaars (among the most authentic in Central Asia) then drive out along the rugged Karakorum Highway to the high Central Asian steppes for a seven-day trek near Mt. Muztagata (24,757′) with Bactrian (two-humped) camels carrying our gear.

In a week of easy trekking at and around the dunes, high meadows and rolling hills (mostly at altitudes of 12,000 feet) we will have wide-ranging views of the snowy summits of Muztagata and neighboring Kongur (25,320′), distant views into the brown vastness of the Soviet Pamirs, and a glimpse into the nomadic life of the Kirghiz people.

At the end of the Muztagata trek, we may sponsor a "bushkashi," a traditional polo-like event during which we will admire the horsemanship of the Kirghiz.

On both treks, we'll be able to visit nomadic families (both Kazakh and Kirghiz) in their portable "yurts," dome-shaped dwellings made of felt.

ITINERARY:

DAY 1 and 2: Leave U.S. Arrive Beijing. Transfer to hotel.

DAY 3: Sightseeing including the Great Wall, dating from the Ming Dynasty; drive through the 15th century Avenue of Animals, to visit the Ming Tombs, built during the emperors' lifetimes to be their underground palaces in the afterworld.

DAY 4: Fly to Urumchi. Afternoon sightseeing.

DAY 5: Sightseeing in Urumchi.

DAY 6: Drive to Tien Schi Lake (10,000′).

DAY 7: Walk toward Bogda base camp.

DAY 8: Arrive at base camp.

DAY 9 and 10: Layover days for hikes and exploration.

DAY 11: Walk out to Tien Schi.

DAY 12: Drive back to Urumchi.

DAY 13: Fly to Kashgar.

DAY 14: Local sightseeing in Kashgar.

DAY 15: Drive to Karakol Lake (12,000′). Camp.

DAY 16: At Karakol Lake

DAY 17: Trek with camels up to Muztagata Base Camp at 14,750 feet.

DAY 18: Optional hike up to 17,500 feet (snowline) on the long, gentle slopes of this mountain.

DAY 19: Hike back down and arrive at a camp in a meadow.

DAY 20: Hike through Subashi village and continue to the flats at Konsiver River.

DAY 21: Day hike (or ride camels) up the valley of the Konsiver River, rolling grasslands from which Kongur and Muztagata rise.

DAY 22: Hike back to roadhead at Little Karakol Lake. Possibly sponsor "bushkashi" near Big Karakol.

DAY 23: Drive back to Kashgar.

DAY 24: Fly to Urumchi.

DAY 25: Fly to Beijing.

DAY 26: In Beijing.

DAY 27: Depart Beijing and connect with homeward-bound flights.

Kirghiz are nomadic herders who inhabit the high altitude valleys of far western Sinkiang.

Muztagata photos by Pam Shandrick

Uighur barber shop in the streets of Urumchi/ Leo Le Bon

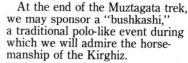

IT5PA1SFMT1

K2 & THE CHINESE KARAKORUM

18-day trek to the world's 2nd highest peak

DATES: *Aug 25–Sep 27 (34 days)*
LEADER: *Leo Le Bon*
GRADE: *C-2/C-3*
LAND COST: *$6900 (13–15 members)*
$7200 (8–12)

The Kirghiz people inhabit a vast area of Central Asia, from the Pamirs of the U.S.S.R. to the Chinese Karakorum.

Kirghiz photos by Nadia Billia

On this hiking expedition in far western China, we will approach the base of K2 (28,741′), 2nd highest peak in the world, set in the majestic grandeur of the Chinese Karakorum.

Explorer Eric Shipton traveled here in 1936 and wrote eloquently about the northern flanks of K2 in his classic book, *Blank On The Map,* "... Nothing interrupted my view of the great amphitheatre about me. The cliffs and ridges of K2 rose out of the glacier in one stupendous sweep to the summit of the mountain, 12,000 feet above. The sight was beyond my comprehension, and I sat gazing at it, with a kind of timid fascination, watching wreathes of mist creep in and out of corries utterly remote."

Shortly after Shipton's visit, the Chinese Karakorum and the province of Sinkiang became inaccessible to outsiders. The trekking route to K2 was just opened in the summer of 1983.

Our approach to K2 begins from the Silk Road cities of Urumchi (3,000′) and Kashgar (4,000′), then takes us by road along the southern edge of the great Takla Makan Desert to Karghalik, an extremely remote Silk Road stopover.

Driving further to the outpost of Khudi (9,678′), we continue up across the western reaches of the Kunlun Mountains to Mahza (12,375′) near the Yarkand River, to meet our Kirghiz camel drivers and the camels which carry our trek gear.

Leo Le Bon enroute to K2 along the Shaksgam River/ Nadia Billia

The trek begins with a hike over the historic Aghil Pass (15,700′), first crossed by Sir Francis Younghusband on his epic journey from Beijing to India in 1887, then a fording of the Shaksgam River by camel, and further to K2 base camp at 12,900 feet on the banks of the Sarpo Laggo River.

The trek length is a total of 18 days: six days to hike in to K2 base camp, six to hike back out, and, once at the base camp, six days to relax and take day hikes or to undertake a strenuous backpacking trip along moraine and glaciers to advance base camp on K2, which has splendid views.

ITINERARY:

DAY 1 and 2: Leave U.S. Arrive Beijing. Transfer to hotel.

DAY 3: Sightseeing in Beijing and environs, including the Great Wall at Badaling, dating from the Ming Dynasty, with a short stop at a stone gate built in the Mongol period, beautifully carved with Buddhist images and inscriptions; drive through the 15th century Avenue of Animals on the way to the Ming Tombs, sepulchres built during the emperors' lifetimes.

DAY 4 and 5: Fly to Urumchi. Day in Urumchi for sightseeing, visiting the museum and tasting some of the melons and grapes which are grown by the local communes.

DAY 6: Fly to Kashgar in far western Sinkiang, the westernmost city in China, little touched by the 20th century.

DAY 7: Sightseeing in Kashgar, including the bazaar.

DAY 8: Drive along the great Takla Makan desert, pass the towns of Yengishar and Soche, and arrive at Karghalik. Overnight at guest house.

DAY 9: Drive south on the Karakorum/Tibet highway, crossing the 10,800-foot Akazu Pass to Khudi. Camp overnight.

DAY 10: Drive over one of the highest road passes in China, the 16,300-foot Chiragsaldi Pass. Descend into the Yarkand Valley to Mahza (12,375′) and continue to Mazha Daria.

DAY 11: Meet with camels and camel drivers and begin 18-day trek. The six-day approach to K2 base camp begins along the bank of the Yarkand then Surukwat River. Camp in a meadow at Ilik.

DAY 12: Trek along the Surukwat River most of the day.

DAY 13: Climb up into the Surukwat Gorge and continue towards Kirghiz settlements, then ascend towards the Aghil Pass. Camp at 14,650 feet.

DAY 14: Walk to the top of the pass at 16,000 feet and descend to the Shaksgam river canyon, 3,000 feet below. Cross the river with camels and camp on a sand bar.

DAY 15: Continue along the Shaksgam River, fording many times. Camp on a sand bar overgrown with willow and tamarisk.

DAY 16: Trek to the confluence with the Sarpo Laggo River. First views of K2. Camp at Suget Jangal base camp at 12,500 feet.

DAY 17 to 22: Six days at or above camp. This camp is quite comfortable, set on the right bank of the Sarpo Laggo River, and offers great views of large mountains all around. Those wanting to go to Advance Base Camp on K2 Glacier must be capable of a six-day backpack trip (carrying 30 lbs.). Camels cannot go up this route and porters are not available. Mountaineering boots and an ice axe (but not crampons) are needed for this excursion.

DAY 23: Spare day to be used as necessary.

DAY 24: Return to Shaksgam Camp.

DAY 25: Cross Aghil Pass.

DAY 26: Return to upper Surukwat Camp.

DAY 27: Return to Ilik.

DAY 28: Return to Mazha.

DAY 29: By bus to Khargalik.

DAY 30: By bus to Kashgar.

DAY 31: Fly to Urumchi.

DAY 32: Fly to Beijing.

DAY 33: Free day in Beijing.

DAY 34: Leave Beijing. Arrive Tokyo and continue to San Francisco.

Nadia Billia preparing for a ride. The Bactrian camel is an ideal beast of burden for high altitude desert trekking/Leo Le Bon

IT5PA1SFMT1

THE MT. SPENDER EXPEDITION

Climbing within sight of K2, Gasherbrum, Broad Peak

DATES: *Aug 25–Oct 15 (52 days)*
LEADER: *Leo Le Bon*
CLIMBING LEADER: *Jim Bridwell*
GRADE: *E-3*
LAND COST: *$8500 (10–12 members)*
             $9000 (8–9)

This is an exploratory expedition to Mt. Spender, an unclimbed 24,000-foot peak near the north side of K2, 2nd highest peak in the world.

We approach Mt. Spender by the same route as our K2 trek (see trek description for *K2 & The Chinese Karakorum*), traveling via Kashgar, Karghalik and Aghil Pass into the Shaksgam river basin, and thence to K2 Base Camp, where our expedition begins.

From K2 Base Camp, route exploration will take place via the K2 Glacier and Sarpo Laggo Glacier (unexplored terrain). The attempt on Spender will be made from the most practical route.

This expedition is for strong, experienced mountaineers and presents the opportunity to explore and climb within sight of the great 8,000-meter giants of the Karakorum, including Gasherbrum I and II, Broad Peak, and K2.

ITINERARY:

DAY 1 and 2: Leave U.S. Arrive Beijing. Transfer to hotel.

DAY 3: Sightseeing in Beijing and environs, including the Great Wall at Badaling and Ming Tombs.

DAY 4 and 5: Fly to Urumchi. Day in Urumchi for sightseeing.

DAY 6: Fly to Kashgar, in far western Sinkiang.

DAY 7: Sightseeing in Kashgar.

DAY 8: Drive along Takla Makan Desert past the towns of Yengishar and Soche, and arrive at Karghalik. Overnight at guest house.

DAY 9: Drive over 10,800-foot Akazu Pass to Khudi. Camp overnight.

DAY 10: Drive over 16,300-foot Chiragsaldi Pass. Descend the Yarkand Valley to Mahza (12,375') and continue to Mazha Daria.

DAY 11: Meet with camels and camel drivers and begin trek to K2 base camp.

DAY 12 and 13: Trek along the Surukwat River then climb up into the Surukwat Gorge and ascend toward the Aghil Pass. Camp at 14,650 feet.

DAY 14 and 15: Cross pass at 16,000 feet and descend to the Shaksgam river canyon, 3,000 feet below. Continue along the river, fording many times. Camp on sand bars.

DAY 16: Trek to the confluence with the Sarpo Laggo River. First views of K2. Camp at Suget Jangal base camp at 12,500 feet.

DAY 17 to 22: Six-day backpacking to Advance Base Camp on K2 Glacier. Porters are not available.

DAY 23 to 42: Climbs and exploration in the area, with attempt on Mt. Spender (approx. 24,000').

DAY 43 to 45: Return to Shaksgam Camp, cross Aghil Pass, return to upper Surukwat Camp.

DAY 46 to 48: Return to Ilik, Mazha and drive to Khargalik.

DAY 49: By bus to Kashgar.

DAY 50: Fly to Urumchi.

DAY 51: Fly to Beijing.

DAY 52: Leave Beijing. Arrive Tokyo and continue to San Francisco.

Kirghiz crafts include fine backstrap-loom weavings.

K2 (28,741') rises impressively at the head of the K2 Glacier/ Leo Le Bon

Balti porters crossing below Masherbrum (25,660').

Scores of Balti men accompany our trekking expedition as porters and camp helpers.

Baltoro photos by Dick McGowan

Lunch stop amid the ice seracs near Goro Camp on the Baltoro Glacier.

Baltis are a mountain people of Tibetan origin whose language is archaic Tibetan but whose culture is strongly Islamic.

IT4BA1YO41

THE BALTORO/ K2 TREK

"The world's greatest museum of shape and form"

DATES: *Aug 31–Oct 5 (36 days)*
LEADER: *Jan Zabinski*
GRADE: *C-3*
LAND COST: *$3890 (11–15 members)*
$4090 (7–10)

"The whole itinerary along the Baltoro seems to have been devised by some prince-poet who had used his genius to hand down to posterity a work whose like was never seen...In the mighty mass of the whole, each single part seems so finely wrought, each one a telling note in a mighty cord; and in the patterning of ridge, couloir, rock face and icefall, thrusting inexorably upwards to the peak, there is the logic of a Bach fugue." Fosco Maraini, *Karakorum*

The Baltoro Glacier has long been the expedition route to the great 8,000-meter peaks of the Karakorum, including K2 (Chogori), the second highest mountain on earth.

The goal of our 28-day trek is that spectacular conjunction of the Godwin-Austen and Baltoro glaciers called Concordia. Here, within a radius of about twelve miles, rise six peaks over 26,000-feet. Author and mountaineer Fosco Maraini was not exaggerating when he referred to it as "the world's greatest museum of shape and form."

Setting out with our 100 expedition porters, we begin successive one-day marches to the villages of

Chakpo, Changpo and then Askole, the last village we will see for three weeks. After Askole, human habitation ends and one enters an incredible wilderness of ice, rock and sky.

Reaching Paiju Camp at the foot of the Baltoro, one begins to feel the pulse of creation: the ice melts, the rocks roll, the glacier creaks and groans, rearranging its icy rivers.

At Concordia, we will be surrounded by K2 (28,741'), Broad Peak (26,400'), Gasherbrum IV (26,180'), Sia Kangri (24,350'), the Golden Throne (23,989'), and razor-edged Mitre Peak (19,718')—undoubtedly one of the most majestic mountain sites in the world.

While in the uninhabited wilderness of the Baltoro, we will have with us a colorful part of Karakorum culture: our 100 expedition porters, the lively Baltis and Hunzakuts who carry all our group trekking gear. We will spend many memorable evenings listening to their songs and watching (and perhaps joining in) their dances.

The trek is graded "C-3," but it is really a true expedition, with all the difficulties and rewards one might expect. The rewards are too numerous to mention; the difficulties will include rough glacier travel, wild river crossings, and possible delays in the mountain flights in and out of Skardu.

ITINERARY:

DAY 1 to 3: Leave U.S. Arrive Rawalpindi. Transfer to hotel.

DAY 4: Free day in Rawalpindi. Trek preparation and briefing.

DAY 5: Fly to Skardu (weather permitting). Overnight in guest house.

DAY 6: Day to explore Skardu, a small village located on the banks of the Indus River.

DAY 7: Jeep to Basha in the Shigar Valley. Short hike to Dasso.

DAY 8: Dasso to Chakpo, a long, hot day.

DAY 9: Chakpo to Chu-mik. Rugged trekking and a thousand-foot ridge. Hot springs en route.

DAY 10: Chu-mik to Askole, passing the last cultivation we see for about three weeks.

DAY 11: Askole to Biafo Glacier camp, farther up the Braldu Valley and across the Biafo Glacier's mouth.

DAY 12: Biafo Camp to Bardumal, past the 19,600-foot Bakhor Das monolith and across the Dumordo River.

DAY 13: Bardumal to Paiju, a moderate day's walk with first views of the Baltoro Glacier.

DAY 14: Layover day at Paiju, a rest day for the porters and ourselves.

DAY 15: Paiju to Liliwah, onto the Baltoro Glacier itself. Views of Paiju Peak and the Trango Towers.

DAY 16: Liliwah to Urdukas, a day of glacier walking with several river crossings.

DAY 17: Urdukas to Biango. Ascend the north bank of the glacier with superb views of Masherbrum and Mustagh Tower.

DAY 18: Biango to Goro, a shorter day as we approach Concordia.

DAY 19: Goro to Concordia, one of the world's most spectacular mountain locations.

DAY 20 to 22: Side trips from Concordia.

DAY 23 to 26: Return down the Baltoro Glacier.

DAY 27: Posssible rest day at Paiju Camp.

DAY 28 to 33: Paiju to Dasso, retracing our route down the Braldu Valley.

DAY 34: Meet jeeps and drive to Skardu. Overnight at guest house.

DAY 35: Fly to Rawalpindi, weather permitting.

DAY 36: Leave Rawalpindi and connect with homeward-bound flights.

IT4BA1Y014

HUNZA & THE BATURA GLACIER

Legendary "kingdom" of the Karakorum

DATES: #1 Jul 9–Jul 29 (21 days)
#2 Sep 10–Sep 30 (21 days)
LEADER: *to be announced*
GRADE: *B-3*
LAND COST: $1990 (13–15 members)
$2150 (10–12)

"An old villager comes by, carrying a stone, sits down beside the Major, and confides to him in Urdu, 'Carrying stones is easy; it's reading books that is difficult.' He pauses briefly, then adds. 'One's hair becomes gray from reading books.' At this, he picks up his stone and moves on. What more impressive comment can there be on longevity in Hunza?" Allen Steck, *Karakorum Journal.*

Legendary Hunza, which explorer Eric Shipton called "the ultimate manifestation of mountain grandeur," is known for its glacier-covered peaks (including 25,550-foot Rakaposhi), fragrant apricot orchards and the longevity of its people.

Hunza's extreme isolation, imposed by the unbelievably steep gorges of the Karakorum, gave rise to a longstanding local diet consisting almost entirely of apricots, wheat, and glacier water, and hence the long-living inhabitants. (Nowadays, Hunzakuts report only an average life expectancy, what with the introduction by the British in this century of such "vices" as sugar, tobacco and tea.)

Until just 1974, Hunza was a semi-autonomous "princely state" presided over by a benevolent Mir, who personally held a daily court and whose subjects paid their taxes in goods rather than money.

The hardy people of Hunza are thought to be descendants of a lost column of the army of Alexander the Greek. It's not unusual to see green-eyed, fair-skinned children (and blue-eyed boys are often named Sikander, for Alexander).

Our approach to Hunza is by jeep on the Karakorum Highway, a thin ribbon of pavement carved into the walls of the stupendous Hunza Gorge (the only gorge which actually cuts through the Karakorum Range). This historic road, completed in 1978, now links by pavement the ancient trails of the Gilgit-to-Kashgar caravan route, part of the Silk Route from western China.

We'll meet the friendly Hunzakuts, taste some of their 22 varieties of apricots, and drive high above the dizzying gorge of the Hunza River to the picturesque village of Gulmit, then further to the roadhead at Pasu, about 70 miles from the 16,000-foot Khunjuerab Pass into China (and as far north as foreigners are permitted to drive on the Karakorum Highway).

Here we begin a nine-day trek which takes us to shepherds' settlements alongside the 25-mile-long Batura Glacier. There are spectacular views of the 25,000-foot Batura-area peaks and from our highest camp at 12,000 feet, we can hike to the uppermost pastures just below snowline for views extending into China and over the vast glacier-wilds of the Karakorum.

ITINERARY:

DAY 1 to 3: Leave U.S. Arrive Rawalpindi. Transfer to hotel.

DAY 4: In Rawalpindi.

DAY 5: Fly to Gilgit, weather permitting. Overnight at Chinar Inn.

DAY 6: Scenic drive to upper Hunza along the Karakorum Highway. First views of Rakaposhi (25,550'). Overnight in Gulmit.

DAY 7: Drive to Pasu. First views of the Batura Glacier. Three-hour walk to Yonz (9,570'). Camp beside the glacier.

DAY 8: Traverse across the moraine-covered glacier for about four hours to Yashpirt (10,659'), a summer shepherds' settlement located in a beautiful wooded glen.

DAY 9: Trek along shepherd's paths to Fatimahel (11,432'). Great views of the Batura Peaks.

DAY 10: Trek through pastures to a green meadow called Guchashim (12,276'), watching yaks grazing in the meadows and viewing the fantastic Batura Peaks and Disteghil Sar (all well above 7,000-meters). The Batura Glacier is the 5th longest in the Karakorum.

DAY 11: Rest day. At the upper pastures, we might observe the centuries-old process by which Hunzakuts make *kurut,* a hard cheese added to soup in the winter months.

DAY 12 to 15: Outbound trek via Fatimahel, Yashpirt and Pasu.

DAY 16: Drive to Baltit. Visit ruby mines and the Mir's 500-year-old palace. Overnight in Karimabad.

DAY 17: Visit the forts of Altit and Baltit.

DAY 18: Afternoon drive to Gilgit, stopping for garnet hunting by the roadside and photographing the spectacular Hunza Gorge. If we are lucky, we might be able to attend a polo match in Gilgit.

DAY 19: Drive to Rawalpindi on the Karakorum Highway.

DAY 20: In Rawalpindi.

DAY 21: Depart Rawalpindi and connect with homeward-bound flights.

About Trekking In The Karakorum

To make your Pakistan trek as comfortable as possible, all camping gear is carried by porters we hire from local villages. Pack animals are not normally available in these regions. You will only need to carry a light day-pack for your jacket, camera, and water bottle.

In addition to a Mountain Travel leader, there will be a camp staff including a cook. It isn't always possible to purchase local food supplies, so our meals will be a combination of local food and high-quality freeze-dried camping food (Mountain House brand) brought from the U.S. Breakfast and dinner are hot meals served in camp. A cold lunch (with hot tea) is served picnic-style each day. All water used for cooking or drinking is boiled and filtered. The staff does all camp chores.

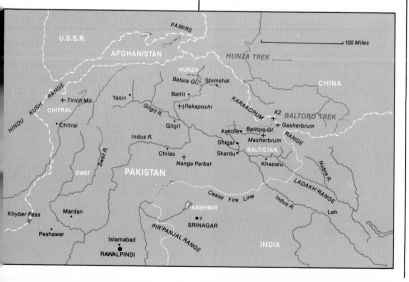

The former palace of the Mir of Hunza/Hugh Swift

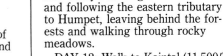

Thiksey Gompa, one of Ladakh's many ancient and well preserved Buddhist monasteries/ John Thune

The Ladakhis are politically a part of India but are culturally pure Tibetan/ Siddiq Wahid

IT5PA1SFMT2

THE TRANS-HIMALAYAN TREK

19-day trek from Kashmir to Ladakh

DATES: #1 Jul 27–Aug 25 (30 days)
#2 Aug 31–Sep 29 (30 days)
LEADER: #1: Ray Jewell
#2: to be announced
GRADE: C-3
LAND COST: $1890 (12–15 members)
$2050 (9–11)

There are few places on earth where it is possible to experience the diversity of landscape seen on this 19-day foot journey, which travels from the densely forested Kashmir Valley to the desert of Ladakh. Moreover, this trek provides an ethnic odyssey, from the Moslem herders' hamlets of Kashmir to the medieval Buddhist villages of Ladakh, known as "Little Tibet."

Trekking through the deep forests for which Kashmir is famous, we hike over the Pir Panjal Range at Shilshar Pass (11,760′), passing shepherds' meadows of the Warwan Valley, a place of Moslem culture and Gujar nomad camps.

Reaching the head of the Warwan Valley, we cross the Great Himalayan Range at Lonvilad Gali Pass (14,530′) into the watershed of the Indus River and enter the Suru Valley, a semi-arid canyon populated by Baltis (who are ethnically Tibetan but long ago converted to Islam). The Suru Valley is cradled between the snowy flanks of the Himalaya and the parched rock of the Zanskar Range to the north.

Continuing up the Suru Valley

Tantric priest dancing at one of the many Buddhist festivals which take place annually in Ladakh/ Siddiq Wahid

Ladakhi villagers/ Ray Jewell

with views of massive Nun Kun (23,410′), we enter a landscape of dry and windswept mountains and reach our first lamaistic temple, Rangdum Gompa, on the outskirts of Zanskar. We are now in the land of the Ladakhi Buddhists.

Crossing the Zanskar Range by the Kanji La Pass (17,240′), we descend past the medieval village of Kanji, a cliff-side settlement whose inhabitants dress in thick red robes, goatskin shawls and winged stovepipe hats. Our last days take us past the multi-colored cliffs of Kang Nalla and to the ancient Lamayuru Monastery, from where we drive to Leh, capital of Ladakh. We spend three days visiting monasteries of the Indus Valley before flying to Srinagar and homeward.

ITINERARY:

DAY 1 to 3: Leave U.S. Arrive Delhi. Transfer to hotel.

DAY 4: Fly to Srinagar. Transfer to houseboats on Dal Lake.

DAY 5: Sightseeing in Srinagar (5,200′), capital of Kashmir.

DAY 6: Drive to Lihenwan and camp.

DAY 7: Hike across Shilshar Pass (11,760′), through forests and meadows.

DAY 8: Steep descent to Inshan (8,000′) on the Warwan River, hiking through stretches of forest. Camp on the banks of the Warwan.

DAY 9: Trek past a number of villages, to Sokhniz (9,100′), the highest village in the Warwan Valley.

DAY 10: Walk alongside the river and camp at about 9,900 feet.

DAY 11: Through lovely countryside today reaching a confluence and following the eastern tributary to Humpet, leaving behind the forests and walking through rocky meadows.

DAY 12: Walk to Kaintal (11,500′) at the snout of a glacier.

DAY 13: A long day over the Lonvilad Gali Pass (14,530′) along the terminal moraine and glacier.

DAY 14: Rest day.

DAY 15: Descent to the Suru River. The countryside, now in the Himalayan rain shadow, is noticeably drier and more barren. First views of Nun Kun and the Zanskar Range. We are now out of Kashmir and entering Zanskar.

DAY 16: Continue over the Pukartse La (12,500′), with its spectacular view of Nun Kun as well as the crevassed Ganri Glacier, and descend to Parkachick, a fascinating adobe village at the foot of the Zanskar Range.

DAY 17: An easy walk along a road to camp at Golmatung Meadow (12,650′).

DAY 18: Rest day.

DAY 19: Trek to beautifully situated Rangdum Gompa, a Tibetan Buddhist monastery.

DAY 20: Visit Rangdum Gompa then walk to the Kanji La South Base Camp (13,900′).

DAY 21: A long but not steep hike up to the Kanji La where there are breathtaking views of the peaks of the Karakorum. A sharp descent brings us into Ladakh proper.

DAY 22: An easy walk down a dramatic maze of canyons to camp near the medieval village of Kanji, a classic Ladakhi town at about 12,000 feet.

DAY 23: Rest day.

DAY 24: Emerge at Hiniskut from between high, steep ridges and pass into a wide valley with an old caravan trail and modern-day road high above.

DAY 25: End trek and proceed to Leh by jeep. Enroute, visit Lamayuru Monastery (11,300′), perched dramatically on an erosion-sculpted cliff above the river.

DAY 26 and 27: Visit Hemis, Tiksey and other major sites around Leh.

DAY 28: Fly to Srinagar (weather permitting). Transfer to houseboats on Dal Lake.

DAY 29: Fly to Delhi. Transfer to hotel.

DAY 30: Depart Delhi and connect with homeward-bound flights.

Crossing the Kanji La into Ladakh/ Gordon Wiltsie

IT5PA1SFMT2

HIMALAYAN PASSAGES

20-day trek through Ladakh, Zanskar and Kishtwar

DATES: *Aug 10–Sep 11 (33 days)*
LEADER: *Nigel Dabby*
GRADE: *C-3*
LAND COST: *$2090 (13–15 members)*
$2290 (9–11)

This rugged 22-day trek in the Great Himalayan Range traverses the parched canyons of the ancient "kingdom" of Zanskar, once part of western Tibet, then crosses over the Kishtwar Himalaya, one of the mountain ranges that forms the backdrop to the green and fertile plains of Punjab.

After visiting Srinagar, capital of Kashmir, we'll drive to Leh (11,000′) and begin the trek near Lamayuru, an ancient monastery perched atop a high, eroded shelf. Entering Zanskar, we'll walk through a dramatic high landscape of narrow river gorges with spectacular views of Zanskar's rugged peaks.

Zanskar is a fascinating Tibetan Buddhist enclave which has had little contact with the outside world —indeed, even the famous Himalayan caravan routes didn't pass this way, since snows keep Zanskar's high passes inaccessible most of the year. Two ceremonial monarchs still reside here, one in Padum and one in the tiny hamlet of Zangla. There are several ancient monasteries in Zanskar, including the large and spectacularly-situated complex at Karsha.

Descending momentarily from the high country, we'll follow the Zanskar River to Padum (11,800′) the area's largest town. Turning westerly, our route takes us over the 17,300-foot Umasi La and down into flower-filled meadows containing the rare blue poppy.

As we continue downward into the Kishtwar Himalaya through the deep Chenab Valley, we enter an area of Hindu culture with small villages and intriguing temples, both Hindu and animistic. Finally, we trek to the roadhead east of Kishtwar in the steep Chenab gorge. After returning to Srinagar, we fly back to Delhi.

ITINERARY:

DAY 1 to 3: Leave U.S. Arrive Delhi. Transfer to hotel.

DAY 4: Morning flight to Srinagar (5,200′). Transfer to houseboat on Dal Lake. Afternoon sightseeing.

DAY 5: Drive from the green Kashmir Valley over the Zoji La (11,580′) into a different world: the western periphery of Ladakh. Arrive at Kargil (9,000′).

DAY 6: Continue to Leh. Overnight in hotel.

DAY 7: Visit the monasteries of Hemis and Tiksey.

DAY 8: Drive to Lamayuru Monastery (11,300′) and begin trek, crossing the Prinkiti La.

DAY 9: Proceed past Shila with its small monastery, old castle and apricot orchards.

DAY 10: Ascend the Snigoutse La (16,120′) amongst the brown folds of the Zanskar Range.

DAY 11: Cross the Sirsir La (15,200′) and wind down into a valley across from Photaskar village, set among fields of wheat and potatoes.

DAY 12: Continue through brilliantly colored, twisted layers of rock and cross the 14,000-foot Kuba La; then, after a short descent, cross the Netushi La.

DAY 13 and 14: Over the Hanuma La (16,000′) and Parfi La, then plunge down into the Zanskar River Valley, walking up and down along steep trails in the river gorge.

DAY 15 and 16: Trek to Karsha, Zanskar's largest and most important monastery.

DAY 17: Rest day at Karsha.

DAY 18: Trek across the wide, flat river plain to Padum, Zanskar's "capital," a village of some 400 inhabitants.

DAY 19 and 20: Hike west past the village of Ating (12,000′) into the Bardar Chu Valley. Ascend to a high camp next to the Zanskar Glacier.

DAY 21: Climb the steep north side of the Zanskar Glacier onto the Umasi La (17,300′). Spectacular last views into Zanskar.

DAY 22: Steeply down alongside the Umasi Glacier. We'll camp in a small meadow at about 12,500 feet.

DAY 23: Rest day. Bid goodbye to our porters and meet the horsemen from Kishtwar.

DAY 24 and 25: Descend the Zanskar Nalla into a valley with idyllic meadows.

DAY 26 and 27: Reach Gulab Garh in the Chenab River gorge.

DAY 28 and 29: Trek up and down through dense forests in the Chenab canyon, passing caravans of Gujar and Gaddi, sheep-herding nomads.

DAY 30: Drive to Kishtwar (5,200′) after reaching the roadhead.

DAY 31: Drive to Srinagar.

DAY 32: Fly to Delhi.

DAY 33: Depart Delhi and connect with homeward-bound flights.

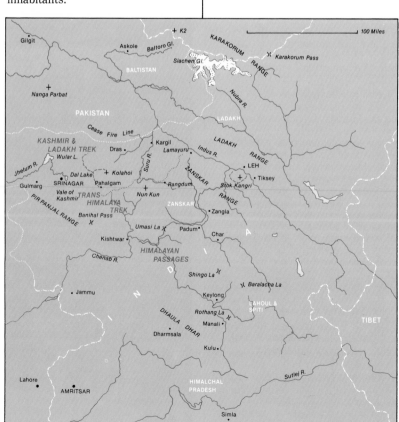

Head lama at Kardung Monastery, Lahoul. A Tibetan lama (master) is distinct from an ordinary trapa (monk) in that he has studied the scriptures such as the Kanjur (Tibetan canon) and passed certain examinations/ Leo Le Bon

IT5PA1SFMT2

TREKKING IN KASHMIR & LADAKH

Visit Moslem Kashmir and Buddhist Ladakh

DATES: #1 Jul 6–Jul 26 (21 days)
   #2 Aug 10–Aug 30 (21 days)
LEADER: #1: Ray Jewell
    #2: Hugh Swift
GRADE: B-2
LAND COST: $1550 (12–15 members)
     $1740 (9–11)

The Kashmir Valley is cool, green and lush in summer, its gentle mountains and hillsides dense with evergreen forests, birch groves and wildflowers. It was long the favorite mountain retreat of the Moghul Emperors and the British Raj, who came here to escape the searing summer heat of the Indian plains. Culturally, the Kashmir Valley is almost entirely Moslem, although thousands of Hindu pilgrims make annual visits to its sacred lakes and holy caves.

After a pleasant stay on houseboats in Srinagar, Kashmir's capital, we'll begin a seven-day hike. An ideal first trek in the Himalaya because of its relatively moderate elevation and terrain, we begin at Pahalgam and meander through remote forested valleys inhabited by a few colorful Gujar nomads. Views include a close look at precipitous Kolahoi Peak (17,800'). Highest altitude reached on this trek is 13,500 feet, the crossing of the Yemnher Pass into the Sind Valley.

Leaving Kashmir, we drive across the Himalayan crest, passing the Himalayan rain shadow, and find ourselves in the arid but extremely spectacular mountain landscape of Ladakh. At Leh and in the Indus Valley, we'll visit some of the most beautiful Tibetan Buddhist monasteries in existence, then make a four-day trek on the flanks of the Indus Valley towards the peak of Stok Kangri (21,000') for grand panoramas of the Indus Valley and mountains of Ladakh from a pass at 16,000 feet.

ITINERARY:

DAY 1 to 3: Leave U.S. Arrive Delhi. Transfer to hotel.

DAY 4: Fly to Srinagar (5,200') and transfer to houseboat on Dal Lake. Afternoon sightseeing.

DAY 5: Drive to Pahalgam (7,800') and begin trek. Hike through a forest over a deserted road to Aru (7,850'); continue uphill to a large open valley above the Lidder River, passing Gujar

Moslem Gujari shepherd in Kashmir/ John Thune

Women of Ladakh and Zanskar still wear traditional costumes and massive turquoise jewelry/Leo Le Bon

shepherd huts. Camp at Lidderwat (8,870').

DAY 6: Trek along the north bank of the Lidder River, heading towards Kolahoi Peak, a beautiful spire of rock, snow and ice. Pass through forests of Kashmiri maple, pine and fir to Satlanjan (10,050'), a summer settlement for Gujar shepherds.

DAY 7: Rest day or optional hike up the valley to the snout of the Kolahoi Glacier.

DAY 8: Back through Lidderwat and begin a climb toward Sekiwas (11,150').

DAY 9: Across the Yemnher Pass (13,500') and descend into the Sind Valley. Spectacular mountain views. Continue to a lovely high camp.

DAY 10: Continue descending the whole day, sometimes steeply, ending at a meadow near Zaivan (9,300').

DAY 11: Walk to Kulan, near Sonamarg and meet with bus. Drive to Kargil (9,000'). Overnight at hotel.

Vegetable vendor at the floating "morning market" on Dal Lake, Srinagar/Ken Scott

DAY 12: Continue the dusty but spectacular drive over the mountains to Leh (11,000'). Transfer to hotel.

DAY: 13: Visit the Tiksey and Hemis monasteries in the Indus Valley.

DAY 14: Begin four-day trek with a hike up through the village of Stok (11,500') and into a long, winding canyon that passes below a spectacularly situated cliffside fort.

DAY 15: Trek towards the peak of Stok Kangri, climbing steadily all day to a camp at about 14,000 feet just below the Matho La Pass. A long day through dramatic terrain of multicolored rock formation.

DAY 16: A short but steep climb up to the Matho La Pass (16,000'), from which there are fine views of snowy 20,000-foot Ladakh ranges. Descend below a yak herders' settlement to a camp at about 14,000 feet with good views of surrounding glaciers.

DAY 17: Descend through a beautiful canyon and end the trek near the village of Matho near the Matho Gompa (monastery). Drive to Leh. Overnight at hotel.

DAY 18: Fly to Srinagar (weather permitting) and transfer to houseboats on Dal Lake

DAY 19: Free day in Srinagar.

DAY 20: Fly to Delhi and transfer to hotel.

DAY 21: Transfer to airport and connect with homeward-bound flights.

Shepherd family in the Warwan Valley/Gordon Wiltsie

Looking into Nepal from the Rothang Glacier

IT5PA1SFMT2

TREKKING IN SIKKIM

14-day trek to Mt. Kanchenjunga

DATES: *Oct 12–Nov 3 (23 days)*
LEADER: *Daku Tenzing Norgay*
GRADE: *B-2*
LAND COST: *$1695 (12–15 members)*
$1795 (9–11)

The summit crest of Mt. Kanchenjunga (28,208′), third highest mountain in the world, forms the border between Sikkim and Nepal. Its satellite peaks—Jannu (25,294′), Tent Peak (24,089′), Siniolchu (22,610′) and Kangbachan (25,925′) —are called "The Five Treasures of the Great Snows." At the present time, the only access to this peak is on a picturesque trail through the foothills on the Sikkimese side, a route we'll travel on our 14-day trek towards Kanchenjunga.

We start our trip in highland India at Darjeeling (8,000′), queen of the British colonial hill stations. We'll walk its steep, narrow streets, sip tea at one of Darjeeling's lovely tea estates, and, from Tiger Hill, view the magnificent sunrise reflected on Kanchenjunga.

Driving into the Sikkimese hills on winding roads through terraced fields of rice, we visit Gangtok, the capital, Rumtek Monastery and Sikkim's Institute of Tibetology, then begin the trek near the great monastery at Pemayangtse.

The walk begins at 6,000 feet in moss-laden forests of pine, magnolia and rhododendron, venturing gradually up into high alpine country. At about mid-point in the trek, we'll have a layover day at a 13,000-foot campsite for an optional side trip up to the Goecha La (16,400′) for classic views of Kanchenjunga.

ITINERARY:

DAY 1 to 3: Leave U.S. Arrive Delhi. Continue by air to Bagdogra. Drive to Darjeeling along the route of the "Toy Train," the old steam engine line. Overnight at hotel.

DAY 4: Morning sightseeing in Darjeeling, afternoon drive to Gangtok (5,000′).

DAY 5: Visit Rumtek Monastery, the largest in Sikkim, and Institute of Tibetology.

DAY 6: All day drive to Yoksum (6,000′). Overnight at Dak Bungalow.

DAY 7: Begin trek, leaving a cultivated area for a wilderness region. Trek through rich wooded hills to Bakhim forest bungalow at 9,000 feet.

DAY 8: A moderately demanding climb through yak and sheep grazing areas to Choka, a resettlement camp for Tibetans and the last village encountered on the trek. Camp at Pittang (12,000′).

DAY 9: Continue through rhododendron forest to Dzongri (13,221′), with its awe-inspiring views of the Sikkimese Himalaya.

DAY 10: Leisurely walk through meadows and gorges to Thangsing (12,467′), magnificent campsite in a giant valley surrounded by high peaks.

DAY 11: Walk toward Kanchenjunga through the great Onglathang Valley, past splendid glacial lakes and numerous glaciers. Camp at Chemathang (15,748′) below Pamdim (21,952′), a beautiful peak only recently climbed by the Indian Army.

DAY 12: Optional four-hour hike up through lichen-covered moraine and steep boulder fields to the top of the Goecha La, with its classic views of Kanchenjunga and the Talung Glacier.

DAY: 13: Descend the valley to Dzongri (13,221′) via the same route.

Trip leader Daku cooking puris for lunch.

DAY 14: North toward the base camp of the Himalayan Mountaineering School beneath a peak called Kabur (15,781′). Cross a 14,000-foot pass enroute.

DAY 15: Rest day or exploratory hikes up to the Himalayan Mountaineering School or Ratong Glacier (16,000′). There are unexplored 6000-meter peaks all around and the views are spectacular (Forked Peak, 20,039′, Kabru Dome, 21,653′, and Kabru 23,228′).

DAY 16: Trek along Ratong Chu to Zamlin Gang Camp, perched on a hillside in dense forest.

DAY 17: Continue trekking to Bakhim Dak Bungalow (9,000′).

DAY 18: Trek to Yoksum ("the meeting place of the three saints"). It was here in 1641 that the first Chogyal was consecrated as the ruler and religious leader of the Sikkimese people. Optional hike to a very old monastery atop a nearby hill. Continue trekking to a campsite perched on the rim of a valley with magnificent terraced rice fields as far as the eye can see.

DAY 19: Trek to Tashiding Monastery atop a hill overlooking the town of Tashiding, the "holiest" of the 60 or so monasteries in Sikkim. Very few groups of tourists are allowed to stay at Tashiding.

DAY 20: Hike down to Legship, meet with vehicles and drive to Pemayangtse. Overnight at lodge.

DAY 21: Morning sightseeing at Pemayangtse Monastery, Sikkim's most important monastery, then drive to Darjeeling.

DAY 22: Sightseeing, including a visit to Tiger Hill (if weather didn't permit on DAY 4). Afternoon drive to Bagdogra and fly to Delhi. Transfer to hotel.

DAY 23: Depart Delhi and connect with homeward-bound flights.

Rice decoration on forehead is part of a celebration of Buddha's birthday.

Pandim Peak from camp at Dzongri.

Sikkim photos by Ken Scott

Looking at the Talung Glacier from the Goeche La.

The "necessary" tent.

Rajasthan photos by Marsha Parker.

During the Pushkar Camel Fair, thousands of traditional desert people ride in from the far reaches of the Thar and convene at the Pushkar marketplace to buy, sell and race their camels.

Marsha Parker leading the group through the desert.

IT5PA1SFMT2

RAJASTHAN CAMEL SAFARI

7-day trek in the "Land of Kings"

DATES: #1 Feb 16–Mar 8 (21 days)
       #2 Nov 9–Nov 29 (21 days)
LEADER: *to be announced*
GRADE: *B-2*
LAND COST: *$1590 (12–15 members)*
          $1690 (9–11)

Rajasthan—land of the maharajas—is one of India's most historic and picturesque regions, a semi-desert graced with the legacy of princely India.

We visit Jodhpur, Jaisalmer and Jaipur, with their massive forts and exquisite marble palaces (one of which we ascend to on elephants).

Between Jaisalmer and Bikaner is an extensive stretch of land called the Thar Desert, through which we'll travel by camel. Unlike the Sahara, the Thar is a younger desert and supports a flora and fauna which is fascinating and diverse. This desert is habitat for nilgai, black buck antelope, Indian gazelle and desert fox. It is also home to some of the rarest birds in the world, including the great Indian bustard and a wide range of birds of prey, such as griffin vultures, eagles and falcons.

An ancient civilization once flourished in the Thar Desert, as is apparent from desert archaeological finds such as Kalibangan. The Thar is currently inhabited by Rajputs and Vishnois who retain unique customs and the traditional desert way of life, tending livestock and riding camels with colorful tasseled saddles.

Our seven-day camel safari is designed to explore a small section of this historic desert, traveling from one settlement (or *dhani*) to another by camel (or on foot if one chooses), camping enroute. In Jodphur, Jaipur, Gajner and Bikaner, our accommodations will be in maharajas' palaces.

Note: The dates of Trip #2 allow for a visit to the famous annual Puskhar Camel Fair. Contact us for details.

ITINERARY:

DAY 1 to 3: Leave U.S. Arrive Delhi. Transfer to hotel.

DAY 4: Sightseeing in Old and New Delhi.

DAY 5: Fly to Jaipur. Sightsee-

Vishnoi villagers in the Thar Desert.

ing at Amber, a complex of forts and palaces (including the carved white marble "Diwan-i-Am" or Hall of Public Audience) and other temples and museums.

DAY 6: Drive to Dunlod Castle. Overnight at the castle and enjoy a traditional village banquet, which may include music and local dancers from the local village.

DAY 7: Drive to Bikaner Palace. Stroll around palace grounds and museum. Overnight in palace guestrooms.

DAY 8: Visit Bikaner Fort and the city. After lunch, short drive to Gajner Palace. Overnight at Gajner Wildlife Sanctuary, where the forests shelter black buck, nilgai, wild boar and a variety of birds.

DAY 9: Morning visit to wildlife sanctuary. After lunch, visit camel breeding farm. Drive to Bithnok and camp.

DAY 10 to 15: On camel safari through the remote villages of Granthi, Pabuser, Burana, Chinnu, Nachna and Ghantiali. We can either ride the camels or walk, according to individual preference.

DAY 16: End camel safari and drive to Jaisalmer. Afternoon sightseeing of fort and city. Overnight at Narayan Niwas Palace.

DAY 17: Morning sightseeing in this 12th century desert stronghold, "a mirage of golden yellow stone" rising from the Thar Desert. Overnight train to Jodphur.

DAY 18: Arrive in Jodphur in the morning. Sightseeing in Jodphur, gateway to the desert and home of the Rathore rulers of Marwar who settled here after the Moslems conquered Delhi and Kanauj. The city has seven gates and colorful bazaars. Overnight at Umaidbhavan Palace.

DAY 19: Fly to Delhi. Transfer to hotel. Rest of day free.

DAY 20: In Delhi for shopping and sightseeing.

DAY 21: Transfer to airport and connect with homeward-bound flights.

IT5PA1SFMT2

INDIA WILDLIFE SAFARI

Exploring Asian game parks

DATES: #1 Feb 23–Mar 11 (17 days)
#2 Dec 7–Dec 23 (17 days)
LEADER: *to be announced*
GRADE: A-1
LAND COST: $1950 (12–15 members)
$2050 (9–11)

The Indian Subcontinent houses an impressive array of wildlife, including Royal Bengal tiger, leopard, one-horned rhino, Indian bison, wild elephant, many varieties of deer and 2,000 species of birds.

Our first stop is Kanha National Park, situated in the heart of the sal forests of central India. This rolling parkland is probably the finest place in all India to see tiger, and on our pre-dawn elephant rides, we may also see blackbuck, chital, Indian bison, hyena and jungle fowl.

At the well-known Bharatpur Bird Sanctuary, once a private princely shooting reserve, we will see vast numbers of waterfowl, including the rare Siberian crane.

In the forests of Dudhwa National Park near the Nepal border, we'll visit Tiger Haven and meet conservation pioneer and "big cat" expert, Arjan Singh, to learn about his efforts to reintroduce zoo-reared tigers and leopards into the wilds.

Accommodations in the wildlife parks will be in bungalows and lodges. We will also tour the cities of Bombay and Delhi and the Taj Mahal in Agra.

ITINERARY:

DAY 1 and 2: Leave U.S. Arrive Bombay and transfer to hotel.

DAY 3: Half-day city tour of Bombay. Afternoon free.

DAY 4: Fly to Nagpur, drive to Kanha National Park. Overnight at forest lodge.

DAY 5 and 6: Game viewing by elephant and landrover in Kanha National Park, where large open meadows give us an excellent chance of seeing beautiful blackbuck, five species of deer, wild pigs, and chausingha (four-horned antelope). In the forests, we're likely to find langur monkeys, the magnificent gaur (Indian bison) and perhaps a tiger. There is also an abundance of birdlife, including pied hornbill, black ibis and racket-tailed drongos.

DAY 7: Drive to Nagpur and fly to Delhi.

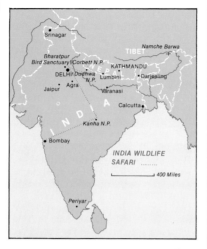

Indian conservationist "Billy" Arjan Singh at Tiger Haven/Alla Schmitz

DAY 8: All day sightseeing tour of Old and New Delhi.

DAY 9: Four hour drive to Bharatpur. Transfer to forest lodge

DAY 10: Bird watching by boat in the marshes of Keoladeo Ghana Bird Sanctuary and nature walks on foot. This sanctuary, a large shallow lake, is a breeding ground for waterbirds, including painted storks, spoon-bills, ibis and jacanas. Migratory birds include the Siberian crane.

DAY 11: Morning of birding, then drive to Delhi via Agra to visit the Taj Mahal.

DAY: 12 to 14: Fly to Lucknow, and drive to "Tiger Haven," the ranch of Indian conservationist, Billy Arjan Singh. Singh has been instrumental in establishing sanctuaries for Indian wildlife. His book, *Tiger Haven,* recounts his experiences in raising two leopards named Harriet and Juliet, who were the subject of a Survival Anglia wildlife film on leopards called "Prince of Cats." Morning and evening game drives through 20-foot tall "elephant grass" in Dudhwa National Park.

DAY 15: Drive to Lucknow and fly to Delhi.

DAY 16: Free day in Delhi. Late evening transfer to airport and depart on homeward-bound flights.

DAY 17: Arrive home.

The endangered one-horned Indian rhinoceros/ Toby Sinclair

By elephant through bamboo forest in search of Asian wildlife/ Nigel Dabby

IT4TG1MTO1

Sri Lanka & The Maldives

5-day highland trek, 3-day wildlife safari, 6-day sailboat excursion

DATES: *Nov 1–Nov 21 (21 days)*
LEADER: *to be announced*
GRADE: *B-1*
LAND COST: *$1550 (12–15 members)*
$1690 (8–11)
+ $130 Maldives flight

Although Sri Lanka is an island off the southeast tip of India, it is *not* an extension of India. It is a beautiful, diverse country with a unique culture all its own.

Its Buddhist history goes back 2,500 years, as we will see in the ancient ruined city of Polonnaruwa. Early Arab travelers came upon Sri Lanka and called it "Serendib" (from which was coined "serendipity," the aptitude for making happy discoveries accidently). The British called this island Ceylon and started world famous tea plantations here.

One of the highlights of our visit will be a leisurely five-day trek across Sri Lanka's green terraced hillsides. Our walk takes place in the interior: delightfully cool and lush terrain at 6,000 to 7,000 feet. This is tea country; we'll walk among many beautiful plantations where close-cropped tea bushes are harvested by Tamil women carrying wicker baskets. We also walk up and into untouched mountainous jungle (with great birdwatching possibilities). Local porters will carry our goods; a cook and assistant round out the camp staff. After the trek, we visit Nuwara Eliya, a colorful town set amid tea plantations and reminiscent of the British era in Sri Lanka.

Driving to the southeast coast, we spend three days in one of Sri Lanka's finest wildlife reserves, 420-square-mile Yala National Park. By night we stay in rustic bungalows and by day we travel by landrover with a local tracker-guide, exploring a protected wilderness park which is teeming with elephant, sambhar, buffalo, wild boar and a huge variety of birdlife, all in a unique seaside setting (we might even see herds of wild elephants roaming the deserted beach!).

The last portion of our trip takes us to the remote Maldive Islands, a snorkeler's paradise where the coral reef wildlife is on a par with the Great Barrier Reef. There are 1800 islands in the Maldives, only 200 of which are inhabited. We'll spend five days exploring by *dhonie,* a local sailing craft which accommodates six people and a crew of three plus cook. We will camp at night in secluded lagoons and travel by day among remote islands, taking time to swim, fish, visit fishing villages, enjoy fresh seafood and snorkel amidst a kaleidoscope of tropical fish in the crystal clear waters of the Indian Ocean. Scuba gear can be rented for those who are qualified and a diving guide can be hired.

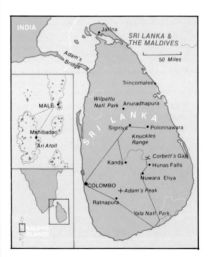

Elephant training in Sri Lanka

ITINERARY:

DAY 1 to 3: Leave U.S. Arrive Colombo, Sri Lanka. Transfer to hotel.

DAY 4: Drive to Habarana. Afternoon visit to ruins of Polonnaruwa, 11th century capital of Sri Lanka.

DAY 5: Drive to Kandy, visiting Sigiriya, 5th century fortress of the reclusive kings of Sri Lanka. Evening visit to Temple of the Tooth to observe a *puja* (religious ceremony).

DAY 6: Drive to Bambarella and begin five-day trek, walking through forest and cardamom plantations. Overnight at camp.

DAY 7: Day hike to Kalupahana Peak through virgin jungle rich in birdlife. Return to camp.

DAY 8: Hike to Meemure, a village with an impressive backdrop of peaks. Overnight at camp.

DAY 9: Day hike to Nitre Caves. Return to camp.

DAY 10: Our final day's walk: trek along rice terraces and ascend to a tea plantation. Drive to Nuwara Eliya, a vestage of British days. An evening to sip brandy and play billiards in the game room of the private Hill Club.

DAY 11: Drive to Yala National Park and check into Pathanangala Park Bungalow. Sumptuous curry dinners will be prepared each night by the resident housekeeper.

DAY 12 and 13: Game drives in open landrovers with a tracker-guide.

DAY 14: Drive to Colombo via Ratnapura, visiting a gem mine en route. Overnight at hotel.

DAY 15: Fly to Male in the Maldive Islands. Check into Ihuru Island Resort. Special seafood dinner and briefing on the four-day sailing itinerary.

DAY 16 to 18: Board *dhonies* and sail to Ari Atoll, stopping at various islands, camping, swimming, snorkeling.

DAY 19: Sail back to Male and check into Ihuru Island Resort.

DAY 20: Fly to Colombo. Late evening transfer to airport and depart Colombo on homeward-bound flights.

DAY 21: Arrive home.

A dhoni, the local sailing vessel we use in the Maldives.

Tea must be carefully harvested by hand to insure getting the proper selection of leaves and bud.

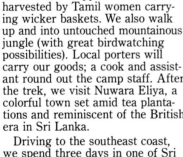

Our landrover in Yala.

Sri Lanka photos by Ken Scott

Starting point of the five-day trek in the Knuckles Range

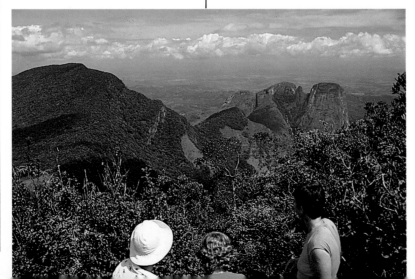

IT5PA1SFMT6

TREKKING IN NEW ZEALAND

Routeburn Walk, Milford Track, Mt. Cook National Park

DATES: #1 Mar 6–Mar 26 (21 days)
#2 Nov 23–Dec 13 (21 days)
LEADER: *Mike Perry*
GRADE: *B-2*
LAND COST: *$1990 (9–12 members)*
$2290 (5–8)
**Cost of domestic flights not included.*

New Zealand's Southern Alps offer a variety of opportunities for the trekking enthusiast. This trip has magnificent hiking in lush rainforest terrain, the challenge of glacier travel, and optional guided snow climbs at moderate altitudes.

We begin on the world-famous Milford Track in Fjordland National Park, trekking for three days through rainforest vegetation in steep valleys with 5,000-foot walls and wonderful birdlife. Our accommodations here (as on the rest of the trip) are in well-stocked and convenient wilderness huts.

After a visit to the serene mountain-ringed fjord at Milford Sound, we move to Mt. Aspiring National Park for a three days on the Routeburn Walk, little known outside New Zealand and Australia, but an extremely beautiful hike along 25 miles of high trails with views down into luxuriant beech forests and out over four or five different mountain ranges.

Our Milford and Routeburn walks will be appropriate warm-up for our activities in Mt. Cook National Park. We fly by ski-plane to the head of the Tasman Glacier, where there is a small and spectacularly situated lodge for climbers and trekkers.

Based in the lodge, we will spend two days making non-technical guided climbs on the surrounding snow and ice peaks (choosing peaks according to the degree of difficulty desired). Those who don't want to climb can sunbathe and enjoy the alpine setting.

The culmination of our mountain experience is a spectacular trek of about 15 miles (taking two days) along the snow-and-ice-covered Tasman Glacier with views all along the way of the icefalls and summits of New Zealand's highest peaks.

ITINERARY:

DAY 1 to 3: Leave U.S. Arrive Auckland and continue by air to Christchurch. Overnight at hotel.

DAY 4: *Fly to Te Anau via Mt. Cook and Queenstown. Transfer to hotel.

DAY 5: Morning free. Afternoon ride by motor launch to the head of Lake Te Anau. Begin hike on the Milford Track with a short walk to the Glade House.

DAY 6: Today's walk gives us time to get acquainted with Fjordland's birdlife and enjoy views of MacKinnon Pass way in the distance. Overnight at Pompolona Hut.

DAY 7: Steadily uphill today to bushline and cross MacKinnon Pass, descending to Quintin, with a side trip to Sutherland Falls. Overnight at Quintin Hut.

DAY 8: Long day of downhill hiking, our last day on the Milford Track. Stop at Boatshed, Mackay Falls, Lake Ada, Giant's Gate Falls, enroute to the Milford Sound hotel.

DAY 9: Launch cruise on Milford Sound, following the walls of this beautiful fjord where we might see seals perched on ledges along the

Hiking the Milford Track.

Distant view of Mt. Cook.

cliffs. Short afternoon flight around the coast to Martins Bay. Afternoon for strolling on the beach.

DAY 10: A choice of jet-boating on the Hollyford River and Lake McKerrow, local bush walks, or a day of beachcombing.

DAY 11: Short flight up the valley and continue by mini-coach ride to start the Routeburn Walk. Walk to Lake MacKenzie Lodge for overnight.

DAY 12: Hike across the Harris Saddle, highest point on the trail, to the Routeburn Falls Hut.

DAY 13: Free day at Routeburn Falls for day hikes or relaxation.

DAY 14: Morning hike out to the trailhead and drive to Queenstown. Arrive late afternoon and transfer to inn.

DAY 15: Drive to Mt. Cook National Park. Overnight in chalets.

DAY 16 to 19: By ski plane to the head of the Tasman Glacier. Two days of optional non-technical snow climbs (according to members' abilities), or two days to relax and photograh, then two-day 15-mile trek down the Tasman Glacier back to the chalets in Mt. Cook National Park.

DAY 20: Morning tour of a high country sheep station, then *fly to Christchurch. Overnight at hotel.

DAY 21: Depart Christchurch and connect with homeward-bound flights.

New Zealand photos by trip leader Mike Perry

Descending to the Tasman Glacier in Mt. Cook National Park.

Terraced rice paddies of Bali with the volcano Mt. Agung in background.

Bali photos by Ken Scott

Balinese make music and dance (especially their renowned trance dances) a part of everyday life.

IT5PA1SFMT3

VOLCANOES OF BALI

Artisans, exotic temples, crater lakes

DATES: *Jun 5–Jun 21 (17 days)*
LEADER: *Steve Penny*
GRADE: *A-2*
LAND COST: *$1050 (12–15 members)*
$1190 (8–11)

Bali is not only one of the most picturesque tropical islands in the world, it also has an extraordinary culture: a life centered around a happy blend of art and religion.

Balinese temples are open, cheerful places and there are thousands of them. Every rice paddy has a small *subah* temple, every lake, every mountain and every residence has its own special temple. Festivals are almost an everyday occasion. Music and dance are a way of life.

A curious mixture of historical events contributed to the uniqueness of Bali's culture. Java and Bali were colonized some 2,000 years ago by Indian traders, blending indigenous cultures with Hinduism and later Buddhism. During the spread of Islam throughout Indonesia in the 14th century, the island of Bali became a refuge for Majapahit princes from Java, who brought with them their entire entourages of Hindu scholars, artists and craftsmen, whose arts were well supported by the princes.

Bali is geologically an extension of the volcanoes that form the backbone of Java. The lush, green volcanic cones that dominate Bali's skyline gives the island much of its legendary beauty. The trails which traverse Bali's volcanic highlands offer spectacular views of steep, terraced rice paddies descending thousands of feet down deep ravines to the sea.

On our trip, we base ourselves in Ubud, a village in the Balinese foothills known for its painters and *gamelon* orchestra (the traditional Balinese band of gongs, chimes and other percussion instruments).

On our optional day hikes, we'll explore many mist-shrouded temples high atop the rim of the island's steep-walled calderas and we'll visit water temples that seem to float on the surface of serene crater lakes.

ITINERARY:

DAY 1: Leave U.S.

DAY 2: Enroute.

DAY 3: Arrive Bali and transfer to hotel on Legian Beach.

DAY 4: After a stop in the market at Den Pasar, travel to Ubud and get established in the hotel which will be our base for much of the trip.

DAY 5: Day hike along the spectacular terraces on the rugged northeast slope of Mt. Agung.

DAY 6 and 7: Optional overnight hike up Mt. Agung from Besakih Temple, the focus of much of the island's spiritual life. Those who wish can complete the 1300-foot hike to the top of the mountain and camp overnight. Others may wish to return to the hotel at Ubud and spend the following day enjoying cultural activities.

DAY 8: Visit Batur Crater, a nine-mile-wide caldera with a beautiful temple perched a thousand sheer feet above Batur Lake, which fills the eastern third of the crater. Hike along the crater rim through bamboo and rhododendron forests. Return to hotel.

DAY 9: Drive around the western volcanic region along a road which may have more temples than any other place in the world. Visit Bedugal Temple, which seems to float on the surface of a serene crater lake nestled bneath the towering cone of Mt. Catur.

DAY 10: Hike past scenic crater lakes and past five volcanic spires, ending the walk at the road at Apuan.

DAY 11: Visit the Elephant Cave, a hermitage for ancient monks. Visit villages of mask carvers.

DAY 12: Explore the area around Tampaksiring with its beautiful gorges and terracing.

DAY 13: Travel to the coast and visit Tanalot, an exquisite temple built on a rugged headland off the west coast. Overnight in hotel on Legian Beach for three nights.

DAY 14: Explore Ulu Watu, a temple high on a cliff on the southwest tip of Bali with a view of Java and the Indian Ocean.

DAY 15: Day at leisure.

DAY 16: Depart Bali and connect with homeward-bound flights.

DAY 17: Arrive home.

IT5PA1SFMT4

TREKKING IN SOUTH KOREA

Explore Buddhist culture, ancient villages

DATES: *Apr 18–May 6 (19 days)*
LEADER: *Adrian Buzo*
GRADE: *B-2*
LAND COST: *$2150 (10–15 members)*

The land surface of Korea has been poetically likened to "waves upon an angry sea." Range upon range of rugged, worn-down peaks stretch into the distance, separated only by narrow valleys in which the clan-based villages of ancestral Korea have evolved a highly distinctive culture.

On this trip, we travel into the countryside and see two widely differing areas of the Korean Peninsula. First, we travel to Mt. Chiri National Park in the southwest for a five-day trek in peninsular South Korea. The trails are undulating but rarely steep, once we reach the ridgeline. They are suitable for the "tenderfoot" while the more energetic can take side hikes off the main ridge into remote valleys.

The endless vistas of "ridge-valley-ridge" in the Chiris contrast sharply with the spectacular granite spires of Mt. Sorak in the northeast. This is the site for our three-day hike from inner to outer Sorak, finishing in style at the fine facilities of the Sorak village resort area.

The two hikes are linked by a four-day tour by bus to explore Korea's unique culture, including visits to Buddhist temples, wayside villages and a full day among the many relics of Kyongju, the ancient capital of the Shamano-Buddhist kingdom of Silla (4th century to 936 A.D.), including Hwangyong Temple, the stone-brick pagoda of Punwang, and a fantastic chain of monuments from Pulguk Temple to the underwater tomb of King Munmu.

Few, if any, foreigners have

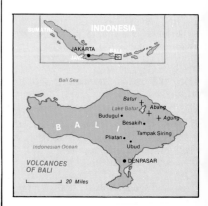

Peaks and valleys of the inner Sorak Mountains of Korea/Adrian Buzo

taken our Chiri and Sorak walking routes, and, for the most part, we'll be traveling and eating Korean-style, using local country inns (*yowans*) where practical.

ITINERARY:

DAY 1 and 2: Leave U.S. Arrive Seoul. Transfer to hotel.

DAY 3 and 4: Sightseeing and walking tours around Seoul. Visit Royal Palaces, Secret Garden, Ch'Ogye Temple, plus optional day trip to Suwon, a city of walls, gates and pavilions.

DAY 5: By bus to the 8th century Hwaom Temple for overnight. Located at the foot of the Chiri Range, this is the greatest of the ancient Korean temples, a fine example of Korea's Buddhist tradition. Optional side trip to Choneun Temple.

DAY 6: Begin five-day trek in the Chiri Range with a hike of 4,000 feet up to the ridge of Nogo-Dan. Overnight at hut.

DAY 7: Along the ridgeline to Paemsa-Gol for overnight. Optional side trek to Panya Peak.

DAY 8: Paemsa-Gol to Chot-Tae Peak, approaching the highest parts of the range.

DAY 9: Chot-Tae Peak to the top of Chonwang Peak and return.

DAY 10: Descend from Chot-Tae Peak down through Paekmu Village and the ancient Zen Temple of Sili-sang to the valley floor. Meet our bus and travel to Unbong Valley for overnight.

DAY 11: Begin three-day bus trip by traveling from Unbong to Kyongju via Haein Temple.

DAY 12: Sightseeing in Kyongju, with its 4th to 10th century temples and tombs.

DAY 13: Travel to the Sorak Mountains via the east coast highway. Overnight at Paekdam in inner Sorak.

DAY 14: Begin three-day hike to outer Sorak by walking to Yangpok.

DAY 15: In the Yangpok area—spectacular sheer granite pinnacles and waterfalls.

DAY 16: Yangpok to Sorak Village resort area.

DAY 17: Morning free. Afternoon bus to Seoul. Overnight in hotel.

DAY 18: Day free in Seoul.

DAY 19: Depart Seoul on homeward-bound flights.

IT5PA1SFMT5

NORTH ALPS OF JAPAN

9-day mountain walk

DATES: *Sep 14–Oct 4 (21 days)*
LEADER: *Smoke Blanchard*
GRADE: *B-3*
LAND COST: *$2175 (12–15 members)*
$2350 (8–11)

Japan is one of the most mountainous countries on earth, with more than 80% of its total terrain too steep for habitation. This trip features a nine-day walk across Japan's most beautiful and precipitous mountain range, the North Alps.

This trip is for people who want to experience Japan exactly as the Japanese do. In the places we go, there is almost no English spoken or written. There are no Western-style accommodations, no Western-style food (and virtually no Westerners!)

Although less than 10,500 feet high, the North Alps rise over a vertical mile above their immediate bases. Their cliff-hung sides are draped with dense forests which at the time of our visit will be covered with wild splashes of red and yellow autumn coloring.

In general, the trails are steep, rocky, narrow and exposed. Japanese literature lists these walks as "climbing" but all of it can be done on what we call a trail in the U.S. Hiking time will be about 6 or 7 hours a day. We prefer to have strong, experienced hikers but we have taken brave novices.

In addition to our time in the mountains, we will have two days in the famous mountain town of Takayama and three days to enjoy the gardens, palaces and gourmet dining of Kyoto.

We can arrange an optional climb of Mt. Fuji before or after the trip.

[Map: NORTH ALPS OF JAPAN / TREKKING IN SOUTH KOREA — showing Toyama, Nagano, NORTH ALPS, Yari, Matsumoto, Takayama, Norikura, Sea of Japan, SEOUL, Sorak, S. KOREA, Chiri, Kyoto, Nara, Mt. Fuji, TOKYO, Narita, 200 Miles]

ITINERARY:

DAY 1 and 2: Leave U.S. Arrive Tokyo. Transfer to hotel.

DAY 3 and 4: Days free for sightseeing or optional two-day climb of Mt. Fuji.

DAY 5: By express train, then regular train through the mountains to Ariake. By taxi to trailhead at Nakabusa Onsen (Nakabusa Hot Springs).

DAY 6: Begin 9-day mountain walk, hiking up a steep forest path to a high ridge at timberline. Overnight at Enzanso Hut. Views of Mt. Tsubakuro and Mt. Yari.

DAY 7: Walk to Nishidake Hut, with good views across nearby valleys, including Mt. Yari to the west.

DAY 8: Walk and climb on steep, narrow rock ridges to Yarigatake (Mt. Yari). Overnight at Yariga-take Hut.

DAY 9: Optional climb up Mt. Yari and continue through a forested canyon to Yokoo Sanso. Hot baths available.

DAY 10: Walk up a forested canyon under Byobu Rocks, a major rock climbing area. Continue up a canyon to Karasawa Hut, situated in a large bowl surrounded by peaks.

DAY 11: Optional hikes to nearby peaks with good views of Mt. Yari and the surrounding area.

DAY 12: Walk out and down forested ridges into the Kamikochi Valley. Overnight at inn with hot baths available.

DAY 13: Optional walk to Dake-sawa, with views of the Kamikochi Valley spread out below, and the Hodaka peaks above. Overnight at inn.

DAY 14: Walk up through forest to Nakao Pass, then descend to Nakao Onsen (Nakao Hot Springs). Overnight at an inn in the village of Nakao.

DAY 15: Bus to Takayama, a spectacular ride through the mountains. Overnight at Hida Gashoen, an inn. Afternoon free to explore town on foot.

DAY 16: Another day to enjoy Takayama. The area around Kami-Sannomachi consists of many shops which have been preserved in the traditional Japanese style. Evening train to Kyoto.

DAY 17 to 19: In Kyoto. Time at leisure for sightseeing and shopping.

DAY 20: By "bullet" train to Tokyo. Overnight at hotel.

DAY 21: Depart Tokyo and connect with homeward-bound flights.

The "road" to Yari is just a notch on a rock ledge.

Forest trail above Yokoo Sanso.

Japan photos by Smoke Blanchard

Don and Virginia Dawson hiking in the Japanese Alps.

*Allen Bechky,
author and safari guide*

A young Masai wife holds a baby beneath her robe, Serengeti, Tanzania

IN THE SERENGETI

by Allen Bechky

Raised in the "concrete jungles" of New York, Allen Bechky's early wild-life horizons did not extend much beyond the Bronx Zoo. After graduation from college, he became interested in the field of natural history and his burgeoning studies led to travels abroad, including meeting tigers face-to-face in India's "forests of the night," and scouring the cloud forests of Central America for a glimpse of the Resplendent Quetzal. Of all the continents, Allen loves Africa the most, and yearly migrates back to the Serengeti Plains to lead safaris for Mountain Travel.

I'm sitting on the veranda at Ndutu Camp listening to the morning bird chorus, an undirected symphony of excited bird song. My friend and frequent safari driver, Rashid, has just left my table.

"How do you sleep, very well?" he inquired.

"Salama tu," I replied. *"Na wewe pia?"*

"Not very well," said he. "I wake up in the night, maybe three o'clock. I hear lions way down in marsh, maybe kill something. I think it six o'clock so I get up to dress. My friend say to me,

The cheetah mounts a termite mound for a better look around the Serengeti woodlands

'what you do now?' I say it time to start safari, find those lions we hear. My friend say, 'you cannot go now. It four o'clock in the morning. Go back to sleep.' My room has no light to see watch. That was the problem." He laughed as he walked off to take his breakfast.

It's a fine day here in the Serengeti. The repetitious cooing of the ring-necked doves is piping down as the heat of the day comes up. It won't be too hot today. The cloud cover is a cooling silvery grey. I'm looking out over a soda lake ringed by graceful flat-topped acacias. Its glassy waters reflect bands of trees and sky and a thin pink line of flamingos feeds near the far shore. Beyond, on the treeless flats stretching off toward Naabi Hill, a mass of black dots mutes the green of the plain. When I raise my binoculars, the black mass sharpens into the individual shapes of wildebeest—thousands of them.

Yesterday I stood on Naabi Hill looking down on "the migration." From the Simba Kopjes to the Gol, flowing out past the woodlands and swamps of Ndutu to Three Trees, the black columns are on the move. It is a sight that never fails to excite me. The ungainly wildebeest, or gnu, with its big bearded head, humped shoulder and too-short hindquarters, could be a beast "designed by a committee." But although the individual is comic, the mass aggregations of tens and even hundreds of thousands covering the plains are simply beautiful. There is nothing more dramatic in nature than this migration of Serengeti wildebeest.

It's not the animals alone which are so profoundly affecting. It is the landscape itself. Its elemental simplicity imparts a powerful sense of freedom to the imagination. The Serengeti is a great undulating sea of grass, punctuated by *kopjes,* islands of sensuously rounded rock outcrops, bordered only by horizons where the prairie just rolls over the edge of the earth into a boundless sky. To cross the plain, surrounded by impossible throngs of free-living animals, is the quintessential African experience.

More than one and a half million wildebeest live here, as do almost half million zebra and a million gazelles. The very size of the herds goes beyond the quantitative: wild animals as far as the eye can see. Where else can that be found? Such a sight is gone now from the plains of Asia and North America, gone now even from most of Africa. It is only here that such herds still roam completely free, a timeless remnant of the abundance of unfettered Nature, of a world unbound by omnipresent Man.

There are lions out there. I could hear them all through the night. A large pride has taken up residence in the salt bush at the end of the lake, roaring repeated warnings to potential challengers. In the Simba *kopjes,* lions watch from atop the wind-sculpted rocks. There are lions guarding the rain puddles near Three Trees. The wildebeests will be at risk to drink there today. There are lions in the Ndutu marshes—fat, happy lions who have been getting easy pickings of the wildebeests filing through from the Macau side of the plain.

Out by the Semiyou River, a rain-fed ribbon of a stream that flows into thin woodlands at the western end of the plain, the wet grass stands two feet high. There are the zebra, not in little groups of a dozen here and there, but herds tens of thousands strong. They are coming to the river pools just now with the first heat. Family groups, ever wary, wade in to drink but are quick to run up the banks in a flurry of thundering hooves if disturbed. In those wild stretches of park, any car is a new and terrible sight to the nervous striped horses.

It is a wonderful feeling to drive among those zebra herds. While wildebeests run in a line, single file, zebras run in a wild mass which flows all around a moving vehicle. A camera might catch the fluid movement of bold black and white through the lush green of the high grass, but not the sound of thousands of hooves pounding, the swoosh of the high grass bending before striped bodies, the piercing dog-like barks from the stallions' throats.

Three male giraffes have emerged from the woods to stand near the pond just in front of where I sit. They are thirsty but will stand and stare a long time before they decide to drink. Above the pond, a flock of terns wheels endlessly. No elephant has come to the pond today, but the black-necked heron hunts as usual and the daily parade of thirsty waxbills (tiny sun-bright finches of a dozen colors and species) is in full swing. One of the giraffes has apparently decided that we human figures do not mean him any harm. His two companions are continuing their silent vigil from their 18-foot-high vantage points, but he has decided that it is safe. He steps to the rim of the pond for a final five-minute scan before spreading his front legs and lowering his knobbed head to the water.

I can't deny that this is my favorite part of Africa. It's not just the abundance of animals, either. It's the wildness of the place, a feeling of having it all to myself. I can drive for hours through remote country and never see another vehicle. It's gotten so that I feel crowded when I meet one other car on the main road. And the animals here are truly wild. I tell my safari members to wait until Ngorongoro Crater to get their "portrait" shots. There, we can drive right up to the game, for they are used to vehicles. Here, the animals are not so tame. Photography is more difficult, but there is more focus on observation.

We always carefully search the "kopjes" for predators before getting out for a picnic

Mountain Travel camp under the shade of a giant fig tree, Ngorongoro Crater, Tanzania

Serengeti Park is over 5,000 square miles, but the great herds accept no boundaries, wandering over surrounding lands which double the migratory ecosystem, creating a "greater Serengeti." In such a vast country, even the colossal migration can be hard to find. During the rains, the wildebeest may be found on the short-grass in a big mass as they are now. But let the rainshowers not come for two weeks and the black dots will gather themselves into long lines and start marching westward into the woodlands where they seek permanent rivers and untrampled grass. Then it gets a lot harder to find "migration." Thousands of wildebeest can vanish overnight, abandoning the plain to the bone-crushing hyenas.

Migration is not predictable like the arrival of birds in our northern spring; rather it is a constant—a never ending movement of animals in search of grazing and water. The weather is variable, and that makes every safari here exciting. We never know where we will find the mass of migration. We have to look for it. And once found, we have to look long and hard for certain animals and special events. It takes time and patience to observe the behavior of free living animals.

On a recent safari, my group came upon a lean and hungry cheetah, on the move and obviously interested in the hunt. We followed her, keeping at a discreet distance so as not to interfere. She approached a group of distant Thompson's gazelles. As the cat moved closer, the "Tommies" could see her perfectly. She made no attempt to hide. There was no point, for the short grass gave no cover. She just kept walking slowly, straight toward the little antelopes, occasionally stopping to look behind with a nervous flick of her tail, or to sit on her haunches, like a big house cat, dispassionately watching her intended prey. The gazelles, heads high and tails wagging, then actually started to walk toward the cheetah. My group expressed surprise, I explained to them that grazing animals frequently approach a predator like this. These animals know their own flight distance, and they feel quite safe as long as the predator is in view. So they move up for a better look.

As we watched, the cheetah again began to walk toward the herd, this time determinedly. She broke into a trot: the gazelles exploded with high stiff-legged bounds. The cheetah ran toward the escaping herd, but we could see that she was not turning out any great effort. She stopped, watching the animals as they ran across her path. Then she began to run again, this time at full speed, faster and faster, until she was a blur of liquid movement steadily closing the gap. She selected a victim. A small Tommie leapt to one side, then the other, in a erratic series of zigzags. The cat followed each twist right along, and in a quick movement, caught up. The gazelle went down.

While zebras live in family groups, wildebeests have no permanent associations

Flamingos on a feed at Lake Natron, a soda lake

Our landrover moved up to within a few feet of the spot where the cheetah held the struggling Tommie in a throat-hold death grip. It was a young animal, at three months old not fast enough to escape a prime cheetah. The cat held the neck until the animal's movements ceased. She then rested a bit, panting hard and looking around nervously. She began to eat just as soon as she caught her breath, for a cheetah must yield its kill to any serious challenger. She is built for speed, not fighting. Even a single hyena may appropriate her kill.

One may have the impression that a Serengeti safari is totally devoted to game watching. The park is, of course, reserved totally for wildlife. But the whole eastern side of the "Greater Serengeti" is the country of the Masai. At this time of year, the Masai out that way are flushed with a prosperity born of rain. The new grass is a nutritious green, fattening their big herds of cattle and goats, brought up from the always-parched Rift Valley and dry weather ranges in the Crater highlands.

We camped last week near Kerian Gorge within earshot of a Masai *manyatta*. Leaving our cameras behind, we followed the call of ringing cow bells through a darkening strip of woods, crossing the sandy bed of a dry river to watch the cattle being herded into the thornbush ring of the temporary village. Three dignified elders, clad in toga-like *shukas* and leaning on tall staffs, directed young boys in driving the lowing cattle into the already tightly-packed paddock. The men exchanged greetings with us. One was the *mzee,* an elder who had brought his sick child to our camp when we first arrived. The boy had chronic malaria, for which we gave him drugs. "Tell him that he must give this boy very good food or he will die," I told Rashid. Rashid replied, "We tell him that the other day. I say must kill cow and give good food. Meat, not just porridge. But him she not do. Masai not want to kill cow or sell cow for money to buy food." We could not make the man change his ways. So we returned to camp.

Rashid learned all his English without benefit of any formal education. Aside from his incurable use of "she" for both he and them, he speaks fluently in a charming style all his own. He also speaks his tribe's Chagga language, as well as Swahili and Masai. He loves to talk in any language, and because of his intelligence and experience, he possesses an inexhaustable supply of fascinating stories of bush life.

The next morning, I led a walk into the gorge to examine the cliffs where hundreds of Griffon vultures nest on rocky crags. When we emerged from the gorge, Rashid was waiting under the shade of an acacia, talking with a lean Masai *moran,* a warrior. My safari members admired the warrior's finery, the ochre corn rows of his hair, the fine beaded jewelry he sported on his neck, wrist and belt, and especially his uninhibited toothy smile. They asked questions for Rashid to translate, but mostly they just enjoyed the contact with a person so different from themselves, for we had already met many Masai on this trip. At Lake Natron, our camp had been constantly filled with beaded laughing girls, nursing mothers, happy children and spear-toting warriors.

While driving off toward the pass in the Gol Mountains which takes us into the Serengeti proper, Rashid explained about the *moran.* "Him she come to ask why I have car here. I tell him that I wait for the *wageni* in gorge. 'Why they go there,' he ask. I tell him for birds. Him she want to know why I not go with people. I say no, I never going, I must not leave

car. I leave car here one time, go in gorge with no one watching. When I come back, my clothes are stolen out of the back. Him she tell me very happy now, just come back from trip for stealing cattle. She go with two friends on the way up to Sonjo country where she stealing very many cattle, maybe 2,000 cows. I say, how can you do like this? Stealing cows no good. Him she say, 'what can I do? I want to get married but I have no cows to pay for wife. Must get cows to pay her father.' Now very happy, have something like 700 cows."

I asked if it wasn't hard to steal so many cattle and bring them so far. "Him she go in dark of the moon, hide cows in the bush or in gorge like this in the daytime."

What about the people they stole the cattle from, I asked. Wasn't that dangerous?

"On yes. This *moran* says that the Sonjo man they stole from came to fight. Him she have gun but Masai also have gun and kill him."

We drove through the pass, observing how much the wide country resembled parts of Wyoming and trying to reconcile the wide smile and easy laugh of the *moran* murderer with our image of our own Wild West.

It's nice to have a few days to myself to relax out here in the bush. I'm always asked if I get tired of guiding safaris so often. I don't. Well, I sometimes get physically tired: it can be rough bounding around in a landrover or stalking game for hours through thick thornbush. But I have been a safari guide for more than ten years and I still see things I have not seen before, and I feel that I still have so much to learn about the web of life out here. This is not the sort of job one gets tired of.

The other giraffes have now finished drinking and all three are disappearing into the woods. Rashid has just come back to tell me that a pack of Cape hunting dogs were spotted this morning. I asked if he thought he could find them this afternoon.

"Oh yes. Them she at pools where we find very shy lion the other day."

Do you think they will still be there later, I asked.

"Dogs never leaving pools this time of day. Him she stay near water till she go hunting maybe 5 o'clock. If she hunting no can find, she run very fast, but not hunting this time of the day."

I asked Rashid to pack our thermos with hot tea. We will be staying out late tonight with the wild dogs.

Rashid, safari driver without peer,
discusses the mornings' sightings with a friend

Photos by Allen Bechky

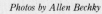

AFRICA
& THE SAHARA

Giraffes at sunset in the Serengeti, one of Africa's premier game viewing areas/Allen Bechky

KENYA • TANZANIA • RWANDA • SOUTH AFRICA • BOTSWANA • NAMIBIA
ZAMBIA • ZIMBABWE • ZAIRE • EGYPT • ALGERIA

se encounter of another kind;
mountain gorilla, Rwanda/Allen Bechky

Mountain Travel Africa & The Sahara

For centuries, Africa has lured the world's greatest adventurers, all determined to solve its geographical mysteries and encounter its lost tribes.

Today's Africa remains a continent of mystery, encompassing enormous tracts of still untamed country which beckons the modern-day adventurer.

Mountain Travel fields deluxe camping safaris in every major wildlife reserve south of the Sahara. From the well-known Serengeti to the remote Etosha Pan, we are there with our naturalist guides and expedition expertise.

In east Africa, we climb to the snows of Kilimanjaro, explore Kenya's Tsavo National Park on foot and experience the incomparable Serengeti migration.

In the south of Africa, we boat the flooded forests of Zimbabwe's Matusadona National Park, tour Kruger National Park (Africa's oldest park), and go birding in Botswana's Makgadikgadi Pans.

In north Africa, we travel the Sahara by camel with Touareg nomad guides. In Egypt, we wander among the archaeological relics of the Nile Valley.

Our group size is kept very small and each trip is led by a top professional guide who will enrich your discoveries with a storehouse of knowledge.

Cheetah on the lookout for game, Kenya/Peter Ourusof

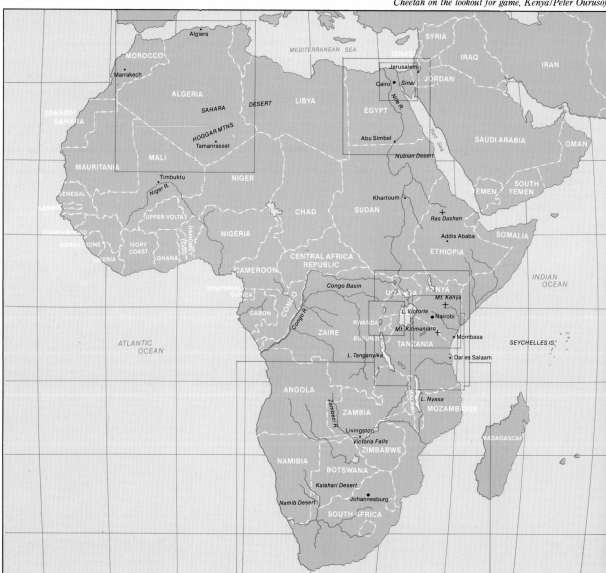

IAIN ALLAN, 35, has lived in East Africa most of his life. A journalist by profession and one of Kenya's leading mountaineers, he is author of the definitive *Guide Book to Mt. Kenya and Kilimanjaro.* He has pioneered new climbing routes on both mountains and is also an experienced safari leader.

ALLEN BECHKY, 37, is an expert naturalist an avid ornithologist who knows Africa from Capetown to Cairo. Manager of our African operations, he spends most of his year guiding in East Africa and scouting new trips. Allen speaks Swahili and has a decade of experience as a professional safari guide.

COLIN BELL, 30, was raised in the Southern Kalahari and Western Cape. A keen wildlife photographer, hiker and ornithologist, he has travelled extensively throughout southern and central Africa. He led his first Botswana safari in 1977.

JEAN-LOUIS & ODETTE BERNEZAT, ages 45 and 39, are professional Sahara adventurers who have spent more than a dozen years exploring the expanses of this great desert, which they love with a passion. Odette is author of a book on Touareg nomads.

DAVID BUITRON, 35, has traveled extensively all over the continent and has managed road-building camps in remote parts of Kenya and Sudan. He speaks Swahili and leads many of our trekking programs in East Africa.

JIM GARDINER, 34, was born in Zimbabwe and has spent his life in Africa as a farmer, soldier and professional safari guide. Now a Swahili-speaking resident of Kenya, he is at home in the bush and specializes in conducting our Kenya foot safaris.

NED ST. JOHN, 30, is an American who has lived in Africa for more than ten years. A professional safari guide, he speaks Swahili and other African dialects and has traveled throughout the continent.

CHRIS MACINTYRE, 26, is a New Zealander by birth but was raised and educated in southern Africa. He was a game ranger for two years in the Zambesi Valley as well as a mineral prospector in Kalahari and Namib deserts. He is an excellent all-around naturalist and has been a professional safari leader in southern Africa for the last four years.

*About Our
Africa
Trip Leaders*

Whether the journey's emphasis is wildlife, natural history or cultural exploration, our African trip leaders bring a special dimension to African travel with their extensive experience.

Iain Allan

Jim Gardiner

Chris MacIntyre

Jean Louis and Odette Bernezat

Please Note:

Allen Bechky

IT3BA1YO19

GREAT PARKS OF EAST AFRICA

Classic game viewing in Masai Mara, Samburu, Aberdares, Serengeti, Ngorongoro

DATES: #1 Mar 11–Apr 1 (22 days)
#2 Jul 1–Jul 22 (22 days)
#3 Aug 12–Sep 2 (22 days)
#4 Sep 9–Sep 30 (22 days)
LEADER: #1, #3 & #4:
to be announced
#2: David Buitron
GRADE: A-1
LAND COST: $3150 (10–15 members)

This is the "grand safari," visiting the prime wildlife parks of both Kenya and Tanzania. We stay in our own deluxe private camps or permanent bush camps. We do our game viewing by landrover, enjoying the flavor and excitement of the African wilderness.

In Samburu Game Reserve we watch elephants come to bathe near our river camp, and we search the surrounding scrub for Grevy's zebra, reticulated giraffe, oryx and gerenuk, all special to Kenya's desert.

In the lush mountain forests of Aberdares National Park, with Mt. Kenya distinctly visible, we see concentrations of rhino, buffalo and elephant, plus unusual species such as giant forest hog, duiker and bongo.

On the celebrated plains of the Masai Mara, we find many wonders including hippo-filled rivers, vast herds of topi, buffalo and zebra and numerous predators.

In Tanzania, we adjust our itinerary to the seasonal rhythms of animal migration. Our March trip features Serengeti when vast herds of wildebeest cover the plain. The July, August and September safaris take advantage of the dry season concentrations of game in Tarangire National Park.

All trips feature the unforgettable experience of camping on the floor of the Ngorongoro Crater, where the variety of wildlife, from prowling lions to throngs of flamingos, never ceases to amaze.

Roof-hatched "go anywhere" four-wheel-drive vehicles ensure classic game viewing on Mountain Travel safaris.

DAY 1 to 3: Leave U.S. Arrive Nairobi. Transfer to Norfolk Hotel.

DAY 4 to 6: In Kenya's northern desert, we camp in Samburu Game Reserve, observing dry-country species (Grevy's zebra, reticulated giraffe, beisa oryx) and seeing crocs, waterbuck and impala along the river. Also visit remote Shaba Reserve and *manyattas* (nomadic villages) of the Samburu people.

DAY 7: Drive into cool highlands to the forests of Aberdares National Park. Enjoy nighttime gameviewing at the flood-lit salt lick of the Ark Lodge.

DAY 8: Explore the Aberdares, a beautiful forest environment of tall cedars, African olive, podocarpus, lush bamboo and alpine moorlands. Rhino and leopard are frequently seen here. Continue to the Great Rift Valley and stop for birdwatching at Lake Naivasha, a large freshwater lake at 6,000 feet.

DAY 9: Drive to the Masai Mara Reserve and camp on the Mara River, where we have Masai herdsmen for neighbors. Wildlife abounds here, and we hear the roar of lions and the whooping call of hyena while we sit around our campfire.

Gesture indicates scenting a female in heat.

The great migration: more than 1.5 million wildebeest still roam freely over the East African plains. The instinct to move and follow overcomes all obstacles. Here they cross the Mara River, Kenya.

Photos by Allen Bechky

No longer warriors, Masai still carry spears as defense against lions, Kenya.

DAY 10 and 11: Two days to explore the Mara, Kenya's premier park in its abundance and variety of wildlife.

DAY 12: Drive to Nairobi. Overnight at Norfolk Hotel.

DAY 13: Drive to Lake Manyara.

DAY 14: Visit Lake Manyara National Park, set at the foot of a spectacular Rift escarpment. The birdlife here makes this an ornithologist's paradise.

DAY 15 and 16: Enter the world of the Serengeti Plains, the last place on earth where vast herds are free to follow their traditional patterns of migration. Sometimes it seems that we are passing through a sea of wildebeest, zebra and gazelle, dotted with little islands where a predator (perhaps a lion or cheetah) rests on the plain. We will spend our nights at Nduto Camp and follow the herds.

DAY 17: Drive to Seronara in the heart of the Serengeti and explore the park's famous rock *kopjes* and woodlands.

DAY 18: Morning at Seronara, then visit historic Olduvai Gorge where the Leakeys made some of the most important discoveries in the search for early man. Continue to Ngorongoro Crater, one of the great natural wonders of the world. Its 100-square-mile floor is framed by steep green crater walls and presents a spectacular setting for wildlife. There is a large year-round population of grazing animals, including wildebeest, zebra, eland, buffalo and elephant, as well as many predators—lion, hyena and jackel. Our camp will be on the crater floor.

DAY 19: Watch the sun rising over Lake Magadi, see the rhinos coming out of the Lerai forest, then spend the whole day observing wildlife on a circuit of the crater.

DAY 20: Another superb day of game viewing in the crater, then drive to Arusha. Overnight in hotel.

DAY 21 and 22: Drive to Nairobi, fly to London and continue on homeward-bound flights.

For safaris in July, August and September, we alter the Tanzania section of the itinerary in accordance with seasonal migrations of game. The itinerary is the same to DAY 14, then continues as follows:

DAY 15: Visit historic Olduvai Gorge, where the Leakey's made important discoveries in the search for early man. Continue to Seronara in the heart of the Serengeti.

DAY 16: Morning game run at Seronera, then drive to Ngorongoro crater, camping on the crater floor.

DAY 17: Early start to watch sunrise on Lake Magadi, then spend the whole day in a fantastic game viewing circuit of the Ngorongoro Crater.

DAY 18: Morning game drive in Ngorongoro Crater, then continue to Tarangire National Park. Overnight at lodge.

DAY 19: Explore Tarangire, where the river attracts game from all over the Masai steppe in the dry season. In the park-like baobab woodlands, we find zebra, gnu and lion, then search the drier parts of the park for fringe-eared oryx and lesser kudu.

DAY 20: A last game drive before moving to Arusha for overnight.

DAY 21 and 22: Return to Nairobi, fly to London and continue on homeward-bound flights.

About Camping Safaris in Africa

Mountain Travel's Africa trips are deluxe camping experiences with such amenities as walk-in safari tents, bathroom tent and shower tent. We travel by "go anywhere" landrover (not mini-bus or truck), with four or five persons plus driver. A landrover is the classic safari vehicle, allowing maximum game viewing and photographic opportunities.

Our camp staff does all camp chores and prepares good meals from fresh local supplies. We maintain a very high standard of camp hygiene.

We are the leading operator of "special interest" tours such as camel treks, mountain hikes and wildlife safaris on foot. Our leaders have extensive experience in Africa and are there to instruct you in the "rules of the bush."

Our campsites are chosen for their scenic appeal and wilderness isolation. When safari lodges are required, we use deluxe facilities which combine charm and wilderness atmosphere.

Near Mt. Kenya.

Grevy's zebra, Kenya.

Enjoying a scratch after a mudbath.

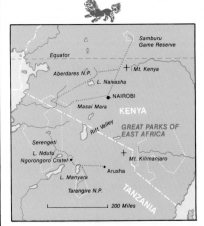

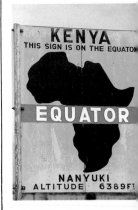

Snow on the equator! Mount Kenya is the second highest peak in Africa. Our trips visiting Kenya and Kilimanjaro both offer hiking traverses. The 5–6 day treks offer a unique opportunity to experience the diverse vegetation and climatic changes surrounding these mountains.

IT3BA1YO15

MT. KENYA & KILIMANJARO TREK

Hiking to the top of Africa

DATES: *#1 Feb 5–Feb 24 (20 days)*
#2 Jun 24–Jul 13 (20 days)
#3 Sep 9–Sep 28 (20 days)
LEADER: *Iain Allan*
GRADE: *C-3*
LAND COST: *$2590 (10–15 members)*

The two highest peaks in Africa are Mt. Kenya (17,058') in Kenya, and Mt. Kilimanjaro (19,340'), in Tanzania. Both mountains rise in regal isolation from surrounding plateaus and plains. Hiking these equatorial giants takes one through three worlds of fascinating beauty: tropical forest, mist-shrouded moorlands, and high altitude alpine zone.

Our Mt. Kenya hike is a five-day traverse beginning in the forests of the little-known Sirimon Route. We ascend to the heights of Point Lenana and descend the other side through the splendid "tropical alpine" flora of the Teliki Valley. Point Lenana (16,355') is the highest point that can be reached without technical cimbing, and has an astounding view of Mt. Kenya's two jagged summits, Batian and Nelion, surrounded by lesser needles and some fifteen glaciers.

Before leaving Kenya, we'll enjoy excellent game viewing in Amboseli National Park in the shadow of Mt. Kilimanjaro.

In Tanzania, our six-day Kilimanjaro trek takes us along the Machame Route, a remote trail skirting the southern glaciers of the mountain. Beginning in rain forest at 6,400 feet, we hike in isolation, enjoying fabulous alpine scenery as we make an altitude gain of nearly 13,000 feet on the way to the "snows of Kilimanjaro" —Uhuru Peak at 19,340 feet.

After the trip, we can arrange an optional seven-day safari in Tanzania's fantastic national parks.

Luxuriant low altitude forest on Mt. Kenya.

Crater Glacier on the summit of Kilimanjaro with Mountain Travel trekkers ascending Uhuru Peak, highest point on the mountain.

ITINERARY:

DAY 1 to 3: Leave U.S. Arrive Nairobi. Transfer to Norfolk Hotel.

DAY 4: Drive 120 miles to the western slopes of Mt. Kenya and camp in the forest at Sirimon Camp (8,000').

DAY 5: Drive to roadhead at 11,000 feet and hike for five miles across open moorland, descending to camp in Liki North Valley (13,000').

DAY 6: Trek up the deep Mackinder's Valley and camp at 14,500 feet.

DAY 7: Making a pre-dawn start, we hike steeply up to Point Lenana from the north, reaching it at about 9 a.m. Descend to the south side of the mountain and camp at 13,600 feet beneath the south face.

DAY 8: Descend the Teliki Valley and its infamous "vertical bog" to the forest clearing at 10,000 feet. Drive to the Ark Lodge in the highlands of Aberdares National Park. This famous lodge features nighttime viewing and the possibility of seeing such rare forest creatures as giant forest hog, bongo and rhino.

DAY 9 and 10: Drive southward to our camp in the Amboseli Game Reserve, which has the slopes of Mt. Kilimanjaro as a magnificent backdrop. We enjoy fantastic wildlife observations—herds of zebra and gnus, giraffe, rhino and family groups of elephants, as well as lion and cheetah.

DAY 11: Enter Tanzania and proceed to the Kibo Hotel to prepare for our Kilimanjaro trek.

DAY 12: Drive to Machame Route and begin hiking at about 6,400 feet. Follow trails up through rain forest and heather to Uniport Hut (10,000').

DAY 13: Climb up to and cross the Shira Plateau to Shira Hut (12,600'). The plateau is often roamed by herds of eland and offers spectacular views of the glaciers of Kilimanjaro.

DAY 14: Trek to Barranco Hut (13,500').

DAY 15: Trek beneath the wild south face of Kilimanjaro to the Barafu Hut (15,000'), situated high on a ridge with views of Mawenzi Peak, Mt. Meru and Moshi on the plains below.

DAY 16: A long, memorable and very strenuous day: up at 1 a.m. and hike about five to nine hours (depending on your speed) to the crater rim, then an hour along the rim to Uhuru Peak (19,340'), and return via crater rim to Gilman's Point (about one hour). Descend to Kibo Hut (15,000') and down to Horambu Hut (12,200'), hopefully reaching it by about 5 to 7 p.m.

DAY 17: Pleasant descent on a good trail through the forest down to the Kibo Hotel.

DAY 18: Return to Nairobi. Overnight in Norfolk Hotel.

DAY 19: Free day in Nairobi. Late evening departure on homeward-bound flights.

DAY 20: Arrive home.

Private Trips

In addition to our regular programs, we can make arrangements for private groups or individuals in Kenya, Tanzania, Rwanda, Zambia, Botswana, Namibia and Egypt.

Ideally, a group of four or more persons is the best number from a cost standpoint, but we will make arrangements for individuals and couples.

Let us know your travel dates, number in party, and lodging preferences about three months (or more) in advance of your proposed trip so we can plan an exact itinerary for you and quote a cost.

Russ Morse at Barranco Hut below Kilimanjaro's summit.

Kili/Kenya photos by Dick McGowan

In the bamboo forest, paths are tunnels made by elephants.

Louise McGowan ascending Point Lenana through Giant Lobelia from Hall Tarns/ Dick McGowan

Iain Allen

Our Man in Kenya

Iain Allan, managing director of Mountain Travel Kenya, was born in Scotland and educated in Kenya, where he has lived since he was nine. He worked for a time in London as a journalist and return to Kenya to become a professional safari guide. Iain is very knowledgeable on African wildlife, speaks fluent Swahili and is deeply involved in Kenya's wildlife conservation problems. A mountaineer of note, he has pioneered new routes on both Mt. Kenya and Kilimanjaro and is author of the definitive trekking and climbing guidebook to both these peaks.

Tsavo National Park is a game reserve the size of Massachusetts!/ Allen Bechky

Masai often come to our camps and invite us to their manyattas (nomadic encampments). Tanzania/Dick McGowan

IT3BA1YO17

DISCOVER KENYA

5-day Mt. Kenya hike, 4-day Tsavo walk, visit Mombasa

DATES: #1 Feb 17–Mar 8 (20 days)
#2 Jul 13–Aug 1 (20 days)
#3 Aug 10–Aug 29 (20 days)
#4 Dec 15, 1985–Jan 3, 1986
LEADER: *to be announced*
GRADE: B-2/C-2
LAND COST: *$1950 (10–15 members)*

Discover the diversity of Kenya the Mountain Travel way. On trek, we experience the grandeur of Mt. Kenya's forests and peaks; on foot and by landrover, we safari to the game-filled savannahs of the national parks, then taste the tropical exuberance of the historic Kenya coast. This is an African safari for the adventurer.

On a five-day hiking traverse of Mt. Kenya, we'll explore its varied environments: the forest (home of the leopard, buffalo and elephant); the moorlands, and the peak-studded alpine zone. The trail scales glaciers and scree to Point Lenana (16,355'), then descends into the beautiful Teliki Valley on the southwest side of the peak.

Our best game viewing adventure is in Amboseli National Park, where permanent water attracts a wide variety of wildlife: elephant, giraffe, antelope, lion and rhino are commonly seen. The park is also well known for its views of Mt. Kilimanjaro.

On the edge of the Taru Desert in Tsavo National Park (a game reserve the size of Massachusetts), we make a three-day "foot safari" along the banks of the Tsavo River and experience intimately the sight, sound and feel of the African bush. Game seen on this non-strenuous trek will include hippo, crocodile and elephant.

On Kenya's coast, we camp and relax on white sand beaches near Mombasa, with time for swimming, snorkeling, shopping and touring this historic Arab town. We return to Nairobi by an overnight train ride on the turn-of-the-century "Lunatic Express."

Hippos are a common sight on the Tsavo River/

Bruce Klepinger

MASAI MARA OPTION:

For those who want more wildlife viewing after the trip, we can arrange an optional three-day "fly-in" safari to a deluxe tented camp (Governor's Camp) in the fabulous Masai Mara Reserve. Cost: approximately $285.

ITINERARY:

DAY 1 to 3: Leave U.S. Arrive Nairobi. Transfer to Norfolk Hotel.

DAY 4: Drive 120 miles to the western slopes of Mt. Kenya, and camp in the forest at Sirimon Camp (8,000').

DAY 5: Drive to roadhead at 11,000 feet, then hike for five miles across open moorland, descending in the afternoon to the Liki North Valley. Camp by a stream at 13,000 feet.

DAY 6: We spend the day trekking up the Mackinder Valley to its head.

DAY 7: Making a pre-dawn start, we ascend Point Lenana from the north, reaching the summit at about 9 a.m. Point Lenana (16,355') is the highest point accessible to walkers. Descend into the Teliki Valley on the south side of the mountain. (We grade this trip a "B-2/C-2" because members who don't want to make the Point Lenana hike can traverse around the mountain by an easier route, catching up with the group at Teliki Camp.

DAY 8: Descend the Teliki Valley to camp in a forest clearing at 10,000 feet. Monkeys, bushbuck and buffalo are often seen here.

DAY 9: Drive to Nairobi.

DAY 10: Drive south into plains country to Amboseli Game Reserve, where the full panoply of African plains animals can be observed and photographed with magnificent Mt. Kilimanjaro as a backdrop.

DAY 11: Full day to explore Amboesli.

DAY 12: Drive through Masailand, gradually entering the dry country of the vast wilderness of Tsavo National Park.

DAY 13 to 15: Three days for trekking along the Tsavo River, a warm-water river running along the edge of the Taru Desert. This is a totally different wildlife experience, tiptoeing quietly through the rugged bush country and meeting wildlife on its own terms. An armed park ranger will be with us at all times for our protection. In our

three nights here, we'll have two or three different campsites, each very scenic and located on the banks of the river.

DAY 16: A complete change of environment from the semi-desert to the inviting tropical coast. Stay at Nomad Tented Camp, a permanent camp on the beach which has walk-in tents with twin beds and private showers.

DAY 17: Day free to relax on the beach, arrange for snorkeling or visit Mombasa.

DAY 18: Free day in Mombasa, then catch the train to Nairobi, a memorable overnight ride on a historic railway line.

DAY 19: Breakfast on the train, as the Lunatic Express chugs through the bush country of Tsavo National Park, and arrive in Nairobi about 8 a.m. Late evening depart Nairobi on homeward-bound flights.

DAY 20: Arrive home.

It takes both patience and luck to be able to locate and observe animals in the wild. Being with expert guides helps in understanding, not just looking.

Lions mating, people watching/Allen Bechky

Kilifi, Kenya coast/Bruce Klepinger

Tradition lives on in the lives of many tribes. Samburu women display their love of color in dress as well as jewelry.

Photos by trip leader Allen Bechky

Mountain Travel Camp in the Ngorongoro Crater, Tanzania. A deluxe camp provides all the comforts of a game lodge while allowing us the privacy of our own camp in the wilds/Allen Bechky

---

IT4BA1YO40

KENYA WILDLIFE SAFARI

Deluxe camping safari in Masai Mara, Samburu, Meru National Park

DATES: #1 Jan 18–Jan 31 (14 days)
      #2 Mar 1–Mar 14 (14 days)
      #3 Jun 28–Jul 11 (14 days)
      #4 Oct 4–Oct 17 (14 days)
LEADER: *Jim Gardiner*
GRADE: *A-1*
LAND COST: *$1490 (5–10 members)*

This safari visits the very best parks in Kenya: Meru National Park, Samburu Game Reserve and the fantastic Masai Mara.

Like our other Kenya safaris, it is a deluxe camping adventure, complete with full camp staff, cook, large walk-in tents (plus shower tent and bathroom tent). All these "creature comforts" afford us the convenience of a game lodge while allowing us the privacy of our own camp in the wilds. We will travel by landrover, with four or five persons plus driver, and, of course, we will always be in the company of an expert safari guide.

Meru National Park was once home to Elsa, the famed lioness of *Born Free*. Elsa is gone, but elephant, buffalo and many antelope species such as oryx and dikdik are found here. Meru's Tana River shelters many hippos and crocodiles.

Samburu Game Reserve is home to the very traditional Samburu people (we may visit one of their villages) and habitat of celebrated desert species such as reticulated giraffe, Grevy's zebra and gerenuk.

The Masai Mara is one of the finest wildlife areas in all Africa, a classic African savannah with roving herds of wildebeest and the best bush country in Kenya for finding big predators such as lion, cheetah, hyena and the always elusive leopard.

ITINERARY:

DAY 1 to 3: Leave U.S. Arrive Nairobi. Transfer to Norfolk Hotel.

DAY 4: Drive north, skirting the western flanks of Mt. Kenya to Meru National Park.

DAY 5: A full day of landrover exploration in the park, a typically beautiful Kenyan setting of golden plains and woodlands.

DAY 6: Drive north to Samburu Game Reserve on the fringe of the great desert of northern Kenya. This thornbush desert features good concentrations of wildlife including waterbuck, elephant and baboon. Possible visit to a Samburu village.

DAY 7: In addition to Samburu's unique desert wildlife, it is particularly beautiful to watch the elephants emerge from the thornbush desert and come to the palm-fringed river for their bath.

DAY 8: Drive to the Great Rift Valley via Thompson's Falls and Lake Naivasha, known for its abundant birdlife.

DAY 9: Drive into the Masai Mara, home of the well-known Masai people, who still retain a traditional pastoral way of life as cattle herders.

DAY 10 and 11: Two days exploring the Mara by landrover and enjoying its renown abundance of wildlife.

DAY 12: Drive to Nairobi. Overnight at Norfolk Hotel.

DAY 13: Day free in Nairobi. Late evening depart Nairobi on homeward-bound flights.

DAY 14: Arrive home.

IT4BA1YO40

KENYA CAMEL TREK & COASTAL SAIL

5-day trek in Tsavo East, 4-day sail in Lamu Archipelago

DATES: #1 Feb 3–Feb 23 (21 days)
      #2 Oct 6–Oct 26 (21 days)
LEADER: *Iain Allan*
GRADE: *B-2*
LAND COST: *$2590 (9–12 members)*

This trip has a very exotic itinerary with unique attractions. As far as we know, no similar itinerary is offered in Kenya today. We trek by camel through the wild bushlands of Tsavo East, sail among the luxuriant tropical islands of the Lamu Archipelago, and make traditional landrover safaris in the little-visited Shimba Hills and magnificent Amboseli National Park.

We begin with game drives in Amboseli, a park dominated by the peak of Mt. Kilimanjaro, then move on to Tsavo East National Park for a four-day camel trek, stalking wildlife on foot and riding camels through a rugged semi-desert landscape.

From the pleasant beach town of Malindi, we fly to Lamu, an island off the northern Kenya coast. The Lamu Archipelago has a blend of Arab and African influences from which the Swahili culture was born. Lamu Island has retained a charming centuries-old flavor, born of its narrow, white-washed streets, Arab architecture and a timeless tranquility enhanced by the absence of motor vehicles on the island. From Lamu, we board small sailboats (traditional Arab dhows) and explore the archipelago for three days.

The trip ends with game drives in Shimba Hills National Reserve, a wildlife park located only 20 miles inland from the Indian Ocean.

ITINERARY:

DAY 1 to 3: Leave U.S. Arrive in Nairobi. Transfer to Norfolk Hotel.

DAY 4: Drive south towards Africa's highest mountain, Kilimanjaro and enter Amboseli Game Reserve. Camp in the shade of flat-topped acacia trees with good views of Kilimanjaro.

DAY 5: Game viewing by landrover in Amboseli, known for its wealth of predators—lion and cheetah. Elephant and rhino can also be seen.

DAY 6: Drive to Tsavo East National Park and reach the Galana Lodge, starting point for our camel trek.

Mt. Kilimanjaro from Amboseli National Park, Kenya/Alla Schmitz

DAY 7 to 11: Days spent wandering through the remote Lali Hills, where we may see herds of elephant and the elusive greater kudu in these hills. All camping equipment and personal baggage will be transported on camels and several passenger-carrying camels will be available.

DAY 12: Drive to the coastal town of Malindi. Overnight in hotel.

DAY 13: Short flight to the delightful Arab island of Lamu, where our accommodations will be in a large Arab house. Lamu is much like an Arab port in the Middle Ages—a scene of dhows full of mangrove headed for Arabia, shipwrights building wooden sailing ships, all with a backdrop of dozens of ancient mosques.

DAY 14 to 16: During these days, we sail an Arab "dhow" around the Lamu Archipelago, visiting Manda Island, Matondoni, Takwa National Monument and a dhow-building village. Plenty of time for swimming and beachcombing. Nights in Arab houses.

DAY 17: Fly to Malindi and drive down the coast to Mombasa, then continue southwards to Shimba Hills National Reserve. Camp.

DAY 18: A day spent driving in these green rolling hills, East African home of the rare roan and sable antelope, and also an environment where elephant and bushbuck can be seen. Camp.

DAY 19: Drive to Nairobi and check into the Norfolk Hotel.

DAY 20: Day free in Nairobi. Evening departure on homeward-bound flights.

DAY 21: Arrive home.

IT3BA1YO16

WILDLIFE TREKKING SAFARI

Trek in Tsavo West and Loita Hills, visit Mombasa

DATES: *Jul 2–Jul 21 (20 days)*
LEADER: *Judith Close*
GRADE: *B-2*
LAND COST: *$1850 (9–16 members)*

Tracking game on foot allows for extraordinary wildlife encounters, an intimate appreciation of the African countryside, and a chance to experience Africa as did the early explorers.

Hiking in the forested Loita Hills, we search for cape buffalo, elephant, and plains game such as impala, wildebeest and giraffe. We also meet the Masai, traditional herders of the plains, visiting a manyatta for a glimpse of life in a typical Masai village.

At the world famous Masai Mara Game Reserve, we do our game viewing by landrover, allowing us to range widely through the verdant plains of this fantastic park to search for lion, cheetah, and leopard and to photograph elephant, rhino and an astounding variety of wildlife.

Entering the vast thornbush wilderness of Tsavo National Park, we'll make a three-day "foot safari" along the Tsavo River through the heart of Kenya's largest reserve, accompanied by an armed "askari" (park ranger).

Arab dhows on the Kenya coast/Dave Parker
Crossing the Tsavo River with an armed askari(park ranger)/Allen Bechky

Our last two days are spent relaxing on the tropical beaches of the Indian Ocean at Mombasa, with a return to Nairobi by overnight train, the historic "Lunatic Express."

ITINERARY:

DAY 1 to 3: Leave U.S. Arrive Nairobi. Transfer to Norfolk Hotel.

DAY 4 to 6: Drive through the Great Rift Valley to the green Loita Hills and camp. Two days of game walks in the hills and forests.

DAY 7 to 9: Drive to the incomparable Masai Mara Game Reserve, Kenya's finest game country, and camp by the Mara River on the boundary of the reserve. In this famous park, we see an abundance of wildlife including elephant, cape buffalo, lion, cheetah, leopard, hippo, zebra and many species of antelope found in great herds.

DAY 10: Return to Nairobi.

DAY 11: Drive to the desert country of Tsavo National Park, one of the largest in Africa. Camp by the Tsavo River.

DAY 12 to 15: The next four days will be spent trekking along the palm-fringed banks of the Tsavo River, a warm-water river running along the edge of the Taru Desert. The river is home to many hippos and Nile crocodiles, and wildlife to be seen along the banks might include elephant, cape buffalo and plains game. Although on this section of the trip we won't see game in the vast numbers one sees in the Mara, we will have the unique experience of tiptoeing quietly through the bush and meeting the wildlife on its own terms—with the excitement of sudden chance encounters. An armed park ranger will be with us at all times for our protection. Tsavo National Park was the setting for some historic confrontations between the British and Germans during World War I, and on our hikes we'll see remnants of some fortifications and bridges.

DAY 16: Drive to Mombasa. Camp by the beach at a permanent tent accommodation with walk-in tents and private showers.

DAY 17: Day for relaxing, arranging snorkeling trips and enjoying the beach.

DAY 18: Day in town or at the beach, and evening departure on the "Lunatic Express," an overnight train ride to Nairobi.

DAY 19: Arrive in Nairobi in the morning. Evening depart Nairobi on homeward-bound flights.

DAY 20: Arrive home.

Africa Options

The following programs are excellent travel options for people visiting Africa on our trips or independently. Contact Mountain Travel for rates and further details.

Kenya's Coast

Kenya's luxuriant tropical coast, with its inviting Indian Ocean beaches, is a perfect place to relax after a safari. You can swim, snorkel and taste gourmet seafood at a beach resort in Mombasa, fly to the romantic Arab island of Lamu, or visit the marine national parks at Malindi and Shimoni. We can arrange a coast experience to suit your taste.

Time: Two days or longer.
Season: All year.

Kilimanjaro Hiking

Mt. Kilimanjaro, the "mountain of springs," is a challenge to strong hikers but those who have trekked to its summit know that the effort is well rewarded—to stand on its glaciers and look down over the hot African plains is an unforgettable thrill. We offer a six-day hike starting from the forests at 7,000 feet and pushing upward to Uhuru Peak (19,340'). Accommodations are in alpine huts and porters carry the gear. This is a great addition to our Tanzania Wildlife Safari and many other East Africa trips.

Time: Seven days.
Season: Most of the year (avoid April/May and October/November).

Somali ostrich

Monitor lizard

Male olive baboon

Bull elephant

Kenyan giraffe

IT3KL1342A22

TANZANIA WILDLIFE SAFARI

East Africa's finest game viewing: Serengeti, Ngorongoro, Mt. Meru, Lake Manyara

DATES: #1 Feb 15–Mar 5 (19 days)
 #2 Mar 8–Mar 26 (19 days)
 #3 Jun 28–Jul 16 (19 days)
 #4 Nov 30–Dec 18 (19 days)
 #5 Dec 20, 1985–Jan 7, 1986
 (19 days)
LEADER: *Allen Bechky*
GRADE: *B-2*
LAND COST: *$2490 (8–15 members)*

This is the Africa buff's "connoisseur" safari. By four-wheel-drive vehicle and on foot, we travel through some of the best landscapes the continent has to offer—and visit the best gamelands on earth at the very best time of year. This area, celebrated in Peter Matthiessen's *The Tree Where Man Was Born,* is truly "Old Africa" as we all have imagined it.

In Arusha National Park, we hike in the company of armed rangers, following game trails through Mt. Meru's lush cloud forest, and peering into Ngordoto Crater, where humans are forbidden to tread.

Leaving the cool highlands, we descend into the Great Rift Valley, land of wild animals and Masai herds, of baobab and whistling thorn.

We then enter the Serengeti ecosystem to witness the greatest wildlife spectacle on earth. Here vast herds of wildebeest, zebra and gazelle stretch to every horizon. It will be calving season and we may well witness the miracle of birth and the drama of predation and death. Our schedule is flexible, allowing us to follow the migration.

We also visit another natural wonder, the 100-square-mile expanse of Ngorongoro Crater, for a mind-boggling wildlife experience within the confines of the earth's largest relic caldera.

At Lake Manyara National Park, we enjoy unbelievably close-up observations of elephant family groups, marvel at massed flocks of waterbirds, and (with luck), find the celebrated tree-climbing lions.

This is a deluxe African camping safari. We travel four or five persons to a landrover, which gives us tremendous flexibility in catering to the personal interests and energies of trip members. We are supported by a full staff of experienced camp assistants. There are Tanzania

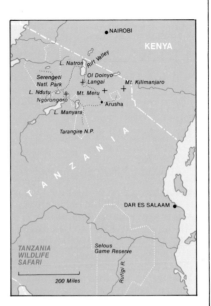

safaris which are lower in cost, but if you compare, you'll find that Mountain Travel's safaris offer more time in the bush and fuller service, leading to a better wildlife experience.

After the safari, we offer a seven-day Kilimarjaro hike or a visit to the Selous.

ITINERARY:

DAY 1 to 3: Leave U.S. Arrive Kilimanjaro Airport, Tanzania. Drive to Momella Lodge in Arusha National Park.

DAY 4: With park rangers as escorts, we hike through the forests of Mt. Meru (14,990') to its beautiful crater.

DAY 5: Drive into Rift Valley wilderness country.

DAY 6: Hike into a gorge that

Masai at our Lake Natron Camp, Tanzania, enjoy the cultural exchanges as much as we: they are amused to hear recordings of themselves singing.

emerges from the steep Rift Valley escarpment. We may see baboon and klipspringer, and can swim near a wild date palm oasis. Camp in the shadow of the active volcano Ol Doinyo Lengai, the Masai "Mountain of God," and hike to the shores of Lake Natron to enjoy the hospitality of nearby Masai manyattas. These traditional people will enliven our camp with memorable cultural exchanges!

DAY 7: Drive up the Rift Escarpment, moving to our camp at the foot of the Gol Mountains. A day for Masai and wildlife. We may spot our first cheetahs.

DAY 8: Hike into a spectacular gorge to view a large colony of griffon vultures, then drive across the short grass plains of the eastern Serengeti, encountering large herds of wildebeest, zebra and gazelle

Female sable antelope with calf.

enroute to Lake Ndutu.

DAY 9 to 12: In the Serengeti, our itinerary is flexible so we can stay in proximity to the migrating animals. Generally, from December to May, the great herds (mostly wildebeest, zebra and gazelle) are on the short grass plain of the southeast. Our June departure will catch migration moving through the western corridor and may even be lucky enough to witness the mass exodus from the plains. In addition to the spectacle of migration, Serengeti is "a kingdom of predators," and we shall see lion, cheetah, hyena, jackal, the elusive leopard and wide-ranging wild hunting dogs.

DAY 13: Visit the famed archaeological site at Olduvai Gorge and drive to the Crater Highland massif. Descend and camp on the floor of Ngorongoro Crater.

DAY 14: We have the Crater entirely to ourselves for our dawn game drive, on which we will see an incredible variety of wildlife in great abundance. Elephant, eland and kongoni live here as well as the larger herds of wildebeest and zebra. Lion and hyena are very numerous.

DAY 15: After a morning game run, drive through fertile farmlands to Gibb's Farm to sample Tanzanian coffee, and continue to Lake Manyara National Park.

DAY 16: Lake Manyara is famed for wonderful concentrations of waterbirds and its numerous elephant herds. Our camp is situated in a lovely groundwater forest, alive with the calls of blue monkeys and silvery-cheeked hornbills.

DAY 17: Stop at an African country market before moving to a lovely permanent camp at Tarangire National Park.

DAY 18: A final game drive in search of Tarangire specialities: leopard, kudu, and python. Afternoon return to Arusha for cleanup, then depart on homeward-bound flight.

DAY 19: Arrive home.

Selous Game Reserve Optional Tour

The Selous of southern Tanzania is Africa's largest and wildest game reserve. Access is by air charter from Dar es Salaam. We stay at the permanent Mbuyu Camp on the banks of the wide Rufigi River, exploring by landrover, on foot and by launch on the river.

Party size: Four or more.
Time: Four or more days.

photos by trip leader Allen Bechky

Lions on a kongoni kill. Tanzania wildlife

Once thought to be among the most dangerous of animals, gorillas are now known to be gentle vegetarians. We'll be able to sit down right in the midst of these gentle apes and observe them in their daily activities.

Gorilla photos by trip leader Allen Bechky

IT3SN1476

RWANDA GORILLA SAFARI

A unique wildlife experience

DATES: #1 *Jan 10–Jan 20 (11 days)*
       #2 *Jan 17–Jan 27 (11 days)*
       #3 *Jun 20–Jun 30 (11 days)*
       #4 *Sep 26–Oct 6 (11 days)*
LEADER: *to be announced*
GRADE: *B-2*
LAND COST: *$1490 (11–15 members)*
              $1690 (6–10)

Straddling the border of Rwanda and Zaire, the Virunga Volcanoes offer a most unusual wildlife experience: observation of one of the rarest animals on earth, the mountain gorilla.

These great anthropoid apes live a very secluded life, avoiding all contact with their one enemy: man. But in Virunga Volcanoes National Park several family groups of wild-living gorillas have become habituated to the presence of observers and can be approached quite closely in their natural habitat. In very small groups, we'll be able to sit down right in the midst of these gentle apes, observing them in their daily activities. It is quite fair to say that no other wild animal has shown as much tolerance for quiet human observance. This is really a one-of-a-kind wildlife experience. We spend three days at Virunga, hiking the lush slopes of these steep, emerald-green mountains.

ITINERARY:

DAY 1 to 3: Leave U.S. Arrive Kigali. Meet with trip leader and drive to Akagera National Park.

DAY 4 and 5: Akagera Park is a unique piece of wild Africa. It is known for its vast papyrus swamps, where the birdlife is always stunning in its diversity. We explore the papyrus by boat. On land, we hope to see lion and leopard as well as waterbuck, warthog, and a variety of other game.

DAY 6: Drive through northern Rwanda, "the land of a thousand hills," and arrive at Ruhengi with its views of the Virunga Volcanoes.

DAY 7: Drive to Virunga Volcanoes Park, and divide into small groups to search for gorillas. We shall attempt to track and observe two different family groups. "Group 11" lives on the slopes of Visoke Volcano where its steep flanks are covered with thick forest. "Group 13" inhabits Sabinyo Volcano and can often be found in the extensive bamboo zone. Sometimes finding the gorillas is easy, as they may have remained close to the area where they had been feeding the previous day. Sometimes, they require constant tracking which can be arduous. The reward is an extraordinary opportunity to observe the gorillas at close range.

DAY 8: Optional hike up Visoke Volcano (12,139′) through the montane forest and an upper forest zone characterized by magnificent moss-strewn hagenia trees and giant St. John's worts (hypercium). Still higher, we reach the zone of Africa's bizarre alpine vegetation: giant groundsels (senecios) and lobelias growing amidst a profusion of everlasting flowers. Nowhere in East Africa is this alpine zone vegetation as lush and mysteriously beautiful as on the misty heads of the Virunga Volcanoes. Descend through a valley filled with un-touched hagenia-hypercium woodland, prime gorilla habitat.

DAY 9: Another morning to search for gorillas. Short afternoon drive, enjoying magnificent views of jagged Mikeno Volcano and the still-active Nyorangonga (in Zaire). Overnight at Gisenye, on the shores of beautiful Lake Kivu, nestled between the rugged hills of Rwanda and Zaire.

DAY 10: Drive to Kigali. Evening transfer to airport and depart Rwanda.

DAY 11: Arrive home.

NOTE: Gorilla safaris can easily be combined with our Kenya Wildlife Safaris.

IT4BA1YO42

RWANDA/ZAIRE GORILLA EXPEDITION

In search of the mountain gorilla

DATES: *Jul 22–Aug 9 (19 days)*
LEADER: *Allen Bechky*
GRADE: *B-1*
LAND COST: *$2900 (11–15 members)*

This is an adventurous safari into the heart of Africa, that mysterious part of Africa first explored 100 years ago by H.M. Stanley, the continent's most celebrated explorer. Here tall tropical forests stand in sight of snow-capped peaks and the jungle floor still shakes from the upheavals of active volcanoes. This is the land of the true Pygmies, who still exist as hunter-gatherers in the deep forests.

Our prime emphasis here will be to seek and observe mountain gorillas, the great apes protected in the lush parks of both Rwanda and Zaire.

In Rwanda, we first view the savannah wildlife of Akagera National Park then move to the Virunga Volcanoes, prime gorilla country, a setting of lush, misty forests and giant vegetation (see *Rwanda Gorilla Safari* for more details).

Crossing the border into Zaire, we visit Parc de Virunga, famous for its thousands of hippos and rich lakeside wildlife habitat. We visit fishing villages and waterfalls before proceeding north along the western edge of the Ruwenzori Range, one of the most scenic regions in all Africa, with its just-cooled lava flows, cloud-making mountains (or snow-capped, if clear) and underground grottos. We'll meet the Pygmies in the forests around Mt. Hoyo. They will demonstrate the traditional hunting techniques they still need for survival.

We shall then visit Zaire's Kahuzi-Biega National Park to track and watch another protected population of gorillas. The gorillas of Kahuzi-Biega are not as "tame" or accustomed to human observors as the Rwanda gorillas. With our Batwa (Pygmy) guides, we walk through forests in search of the apes.

ITINERARY:

DAY 1 and 2: Leave U.S. Arrive Kigali, Rwanda. Transfer to hotel.

DAY 3 and 4: Exploration of Akagera National Park, renowned for the birdlife of its papyrus marshes. We also search for lion and roan antelope among herds of impala and topi.

Pyrethrum plantation at the foot of Virunga Volcanoes/Allen Bechky

The women of Zaire, central Africa/
Allen Bechky

DAY 5: Drive through the beautiful cultivated hills of Rwanda.

DAY 6 to 8: Three days exploring Parc de Volcans and tracking gorillas. Optional hike to the summit of Visoke Volcano (12,139′), where we may encounter forest buffalo or golden monkeys, and possibly wild gorillas (who, unlike the gorillas habituated to human observation, will run from us). This is a fabulous wilderness experience. The upper slopes of the mountain are covered with lush forests of giant lobelia. From the summit, there are splendid views of its crater lake and the other giant volcanoes of the Virunga Range: Karasimbi, the pyramid of Mikeno and jagged Sabinyo.

DAY 9 and 10: Cross over to Zaire and enjoy superb wildlife viewing in Parc de Virunga. Elephant, hippo and buffalo are found here in big herds, as are top and kob. We also visit a fishing village and enjoy African-style barbequed tilapia.

DAY 11: Scenic drive along the Lumbero Escarpment, a spectacular vista of tropical forest, Rift Valley lakes and high mountains. The Virunga volcanoes and Ruwenzori Range may be seen.

DAY 12 and 13: Explore the forests around Mt. Hoyo, and take a dugout canoe ride down a forest river. Hike through the forests with Balese (Pygmy) hunters and observe their unique hunting techniques.

DAY 14 and 15: Visit the "Venus' Staircase" waterfall, underground caverns. Drive through tropical forests enroute to Goma on the shore of Lake Kivu passing over the fresh lava flows of an active volcano.

DAY 16 and 17: Gorilla tracking in Kahuzi Biega Park with Batwa (Pygmy) guides. Here we have better chances to witness such things as the hair-raising mock charges of unhabituated gorillas. We must be on our best behavior!

DAY 18: Return to Kigali, Rwanda. Depart on evening flights.

DAY 19: Connect with homeward-bound flights.

IT3BA1YO73

RUWENZORIS: "MOUNTAINS OF THE MOON"

Trekking in equatorial Africa

DATES: *Jul 1–Jul 19 (19 days)*
LEADER: *to be announced*
GRADE: *B-2/C-3*
LAND COST: *$2390 (8–12 members)*

Since ancient times, legends of the mist-shrouded Ruwenzori Mountains nestled in the heart of the African continent have stimulated the imaginations of armchair geographers and intrepid adventurers alike.

Ptolemy named them the "Mountains of the Moon" and thought that they contained the long-sought source of the Nile. Generations of Greek, Roman and Arab explorers told fantastic stories of snow-covered equatorial mountains inhabited by hairy giants. The geographic questions were finally solved by Stanley, one of Africa's greatest explorers, who applied a native name to the range: Ruwenzori, "The Rainmaker."

Impenetrable jungle (home of chimpanzees) surrounds the range. Hot air rising from tropical forests enshrouds the mountains in perpetual swirling mists. Vegetation which is normally quite small in temperate climates has grown riotously luxuriant on the mist-soaked Ruwenzori ridges. Tree-sized groundsels, lobelia and other bizarre flora, all heavily mossladen, abound in vertical bogs.

There are six Ruwenzori peaks rising to over 15,000 feet and carrying permanent snow and glaciers. The highest is Mt. Stanley (16,673′), first climbed by the Italian Duke of Abruzzi in 1906.

We begin our expedition by exploring the scenic area around Goma in eastern Zaire, enjoying the beauty of Lake Kivu. We hike up Nyiragongo Volcano, still quite active and named for a fiery local god. Camping on the crater rim, we may be treated to a pyrotechnic display in the volcano's bubbling lava lake. We then enjoy superb wildlife viewing by vehicle along the shores of Lake Albert in Virunga National Park.

Commencing our rugged seven-day trekking expedition in the Ruwenzoris, we approach through the wet forests of the western slopes where resident wildlife includes elephant and leopard. Porters will carry our gear and our accommodations will be in mountain huts or tents. We will attempt to trek up onto the glacial

moraine of Mt. Stanley. Conditions permitting, members experienced in glacier travel can attempt to climb to Point Margharita, the highest of Mt. Stanley's nine separate summits.

These peaks are very seldom frequented by climbers or trekkers due to their remoteness and the difficulties of terrain and climate. This is an expedition for the true African explorer.

ITINERARY:

DAY 1 to 3: Leave U.S. Arrive Goma, Zaire. Transfer to hotel.

DAY 4: Hike to summit of Nyiragongo Volcano and camp on the crater rim.

DAY 5: Explore the lava flows of Nyirongongo. Return to Goma for overnight.

DAY 6 to 8: Wildlife viewing in Zaire's Virunga National Park, a lake environment which supports elephant, buffalo, topi, lion and hippos.

DAY 9: Drive to Mutsora, starting point for the Ruwenzori trek.

DAY 10 to 15: Trekking in the "Mountains of the Moon."

DAY 16: Return to Goma for some well-deserved relaxation.

DAY 17: Fly to Kinshasha, modern capital of Zaire.

DAY 18: Depart Kinshasha and connect with homeward-bound flights.

DAY 19: Arrive home.

Gorilla tracking guide, Rwanda/Allen Bechky

Rwanda Tracking Optional Tour

Tracking the Great Apes through the misty forests of Virunga Volcanoes is one of the most unique wildlife experiences imaginable. We can arrange gorilla tracking options in conjunction with many of our regular East Africa trips.

Time: Four days. Season: All year except November, April, May. Cost: Approximately $800.

Crater lake on Visoke Volcano, Rwanda/Allen Bechky

Pony trekking in the highlands of Lesotho/
Dick McGowan

IT5PA1SFMT15

THE SOUTH OF AFRICA

Pony trekking, visit Kruger, Zululand, Swaziland

DATES: #1 Mar 6–Mar 26 (21 days)
#2 Nov 6–Nov 26 (21 days)
LEADER: *Colin Bell*
GRADE: *A-2*
LAND COST: *$2390 (8–15 members)
plus Blue Train fare
$299–$561*

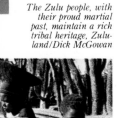

The Zulu people, with their proud martial past, maintain a rich tribal heritage, Zulu-land/Dick McGowan

By pony, by landrover and on foot, this is a journey of discovery in the South of Africa, a region with a spectacular landscape and a justly-famed variety of African wildlife, protected in the oldest game reserves on the continent.

Much of the fascination of this part of Africa, chronicled in James Michener's recent best-seller, *The Covenant,* lies in observing the rich diversity of cultures that have shaped the history of the continent. Zulu, Basutho, Swazi, Cape Dutch, English and Indian have all left their mark on the land.

We begin in Kruger National Park (Africa's oldest, established in 1898), celebrated for its variety of animals. We visit nearby Londolozi, which shares Kruger's magnificent fauna and has the advantage of being privately owned, allowing us the freedom to seek game on foot as well as by landrover.

We visit Swaziland, an independent African kingdom, and browse the Swazi markets for crafts, then continue to Umfolozi Game Reserve, situated in the heart of Zululand.

With a local Zulu-speaking guide, we will move from one Zulu village

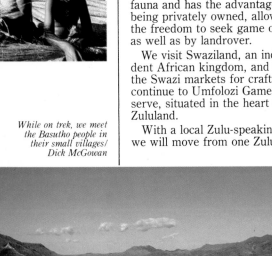

*While on trek, we meet the Basutho people in their small villages/
Dick McGowan*

to another, meeting the people and perhaps observing a "coming of age" ceremony, a wedding or other local festivity.

Moving southwest to the Drakensburg Range, highest mountains of southern Africa, we visit the independent country of Lesotho to make a four-day pony trek through its mountainous highlands. Enroute, we ride across grassy plains, stop to swim in sparkling rivers and enjoy the unique opportunity of meeting local villagers.

With three days in Capetown ("the Fairest Cape of them all"), we can hike to the top of Table Mountain, drive to the Cape of Good Hope, and visit wine country, where we'll stay in a traditional Cape Dutch homestead.

Return travel to Johannesburg is by the famed "Blue Train," one of the most prestigious and luxurious rail journeys in the world.

ITINERARY:

DAY 1 and 2: Leave U.S. Arrive Johannesburg. Overnight in airport hotel.

DAY 3 and 4: Fly to Nelspruit in the Transvaal *lowveld,* meet with trip leader and drive to Londolozi Game Reserve. Game drives and wildlife hikes.

DAY 5: Game viewing by vehicle in Kruger National Park.

DAY 6 and 7: Visit Swaziland, an independent kingdom, and Mlilwane National Park.

DAY 8 and 9: Visit Umfolozi Game reserve and Zululand.

DAY 10: Travel to Nk Walini and drive by bush vehicle into the more remote areas of Zululand, moving from village to village with a Zulu-speaking guide.

DAY 11: Drive to the Drakens-burg Mountains. Overnight at lodge.

DAY 12: Travel to Maseru, capital of Lesotho, a mountainous land inhabited by the Basotho tribe.

DAY 13 to 16: Pony trekking in the mountains of Lesotho.

DAY 17 to 19: In Capetown area, with many optional side trips.

DAY 20: Board the "Blue Train" in the morning for the journey to Johannesburg.

DAY 21: Arrive Johannesburg in the morning. Afternoon visit to a gold mine. Evening depart Johannesburg on homeward-bound flights.

IT5PA1SFMT15

THE BOTSWANA SAFARI

Okavango Delta, Chobe National Park, Makgadikgadi Pans

DATES: *May 10–May 27 (18 days)
Jul 26–Aug 12 (18 days)
Oct 10–Oct 28 (18 days)*
LEADER: *Chris MacIntyre*
GRADE: *B-1*
LAND COST: *$2190 (5–13 members)*

A safari into northern Botswana is a true expedition, a journey into a very wild and remote land. We'll travel by four-wheel drive vehicle, carrying our own mobile camps, and visit all of Botswana's great wildlife areas.

We begin with a camp in the Makgadikgadi Pans, where we meet the wildlife of the open plains: gemsbok, zebra and gnu. Here we sharpen our senses to the pleasures of the "veld"—the rush of zebra through high grass, and pink mirage that materializes into a throng of flamingos, the unfamiliar night sounds around our campfire. Game sometimes congregate here in such great numbers that Makgadikgadi is called a "southern Serengeti."

In the celebrated Okavango Delta, we travel by boat to enjoy the environs of this great swamp, a gentle, timeless wilderness where lechwe stamp through the grassy shallows, sitatunga take shelter in the reeds, and hippo and crocs reside in the clear black waters. The birdlife is spectacular.

We also visit Moremi Wildlife Reserve and the famed Savuti Channel, whose waters attract fantastic concentrations of game.

We end with a safari in the "big game" woodlands of Chobe National Park (elephant country at its finest) and a visit to Mosi-oa-Tunya ("The Smoke That Thunders"), better known as Victoria Falls.

ITINERARY:

DAY 1 and 2: Leave U.S. Arrive Johannesburg, South Africa. Transfer to hotel.

DAY 3 and 4: Fly to Botswana and proceed into the game reserves of Makgadikgadi Pans or Nxai Pans. (Our exact destination will depend on the seasonal migration of game.) In this area, we see animals of the open grass plains like wildebeest and zebra, as well as gemsbok, the beautiful oryx of the deserts of southern Africa. When the pans hold water, they are a paradise for birds, often hosting great masses of flamingos.

DAY 5: Dawn explorations around camp then drive through

*Sometimes you don't even have to leave camp to
see animals, Botswana/Allen Bechky*

through the camp and the roaring
of lions is a common night sound.

DAY 14 and 15: Move to the
Chobe River, elephant country par
excellence. We may see congrega-
tions numbering in the hundreds.
We hope to see the beautifully
marked Chobe bushbuck here, and
perhaps find colonies of Carmine
bee-eaters.

DAY 16: Drive across the Zimbabwe border to Victoria Falls.
Check into the elegant Victoria
Falls Hotel and visit this spectacular waterfall which has a flow
of more than 200 million gallons
per minute in flood!

DAY 17: Optional excursions
around Victoria Falls. Evening
depart Johannesburg on homeward-bound flights.

DAY 18: Arrive home.

*Rock paintings reveal
bushmen's mastery of
the hunting arts/
Allen Bechky*

he plains of north central
Botswana to Maun, for a charter
flight into Xaxaba Camp in the
Okavango Delta. Here in crystal
clear waters, the magnificent fish
eagle is a common sight, as are a
wide variety of storks, herons,
bises and other water birds including pygmy geese and malachite
kingfishers. Larger wildlife includes lechwe and sitatunga. Hippo
and crocodile are common.

DAY 6 to 8: We board makoros,
the traditional dugout canoes of the
Delta natives, and paddle into the
waterways of the Delta, for fishing,
swimming and wildlife viewing. We
explore the larger Delta islands on
foot. Overnights at Xabaxaba Camp
in the Okavango Delta.

DAY 9 to 11: Charter flight to
Maun. Drive to Moremi Game
Reserve, one of the most interest-
ng and beautiful reserves of

southern Africa. Antelope such as
sassaby, kudu, roan and impala can
be found here, as well as buffalo,
elephant and the ever elusive
predators: lion, cheetah, leopard,
and wild dog. We spend three days
in the reserve, for game drives, explorations on foot and swimming.

DAY 12 and 13: Drive northward
into the drier bush country of the
Mababe Depression, a section of
Chobe National Park. We camp
along the Savuti Channel, an im-
permanent waterway which holds
the floodwater spill of the Chobe
River. The numbers of hippo and
elephants in this area can be very
impressive. In the bushier areas,
we have good chances to encounter
the magnificent sable antelope, as
well as kudu and roan. Camping
along the Savuti Channel is always
an experience, as hippo, buffalo
and elephant frequently graze

Zambia: The Luangwa Valley Foot Safari Optional Tour

*Zambia's Luan-
gwa Valley is one
of Africa's premier
national parks.
Massive concentra-
tions of wildlife
inhabit its vast
wooded plains.
More than 60,000
elephants live here,
and the park's 2000
rhinos are the last
truly viable popula-
tion of that endan-
gered species. With
an armed ranger
and naturalist
guide, one can take
a marvelous five-
day "foot safari"
in the game-filled
bushlands. This
option works well
with our Botswana
and Namibia safaris.*

*Party size: Four
or more.
Time: Eight days
or longer.
Season: June
through November.
Cost: Approx. $1400*

*Rhino are on the brink of extinction; the white
rhino can still be found in southern Africa/
Dick McGowan*

The vast salt pan of Etosha/Allen Bechky

Nama women are descendents of the ancient Hottentots; other native tribes of Namibia are Ovambo and Herrero/ Allen Bechky

IT5PA1SFMT15

NAMIBIA/ KALAHARI EXPLORATION

Desert wildlife safari

DATES: *Aug 13–Sep 2 (21 days)*
LEADER: *to be announced*
GRADE: *B-1*
LAND COST: *$2190 (12–13 members)*
$2390 (6–11)

Namibia (South West Africa) is one of the least known parts of the African continent. A former German colony on the southern tip of the Atlantic coast, it contains some amazing environments: the Namib Desert, with its towering dunes in vivid colors, the vast thornland of the Kalahari Desert, the Fish River Canyon ("Grand Canyon" of Africa), and the eerie Skeleton Coast, so called for the treachery of its fog-bound shores, where countless ships have wrecked while rounding the Cape. This southwestern tip of the continent is home to hardy wildlife like the noble gemsbok and mountain zebra, which cling miraculously to sparse desert niches.

A major safari highlight is Etosha National Park, recently celebrated in a *National Geographic* television special. The vast salt pan of Etosha is a wildlife paradise where herds of delicate springbok dot the land and elephants emerge from the shimmering haze of the salt pan like distant ships approaching land. Both prey and predator thrive near each water hole. Giraffe, kudu, cheetah, lion and plenty of small game are found here.

We also explore Namib Desert Park, where ocean-born fog is the only moisture to reach its unique plants and wildlife, and Fish River Canyon, little known outside Africa but as spectacular in its savage rock-hewn grandeur as our own Grand Canyon.

At Kalahari-Gemsbok National Park, named for the graceful oryx of the southern deserts, we should encounter cheetah, bat-eared foxes, secretary birds, kori bustard, large herds of springbok and the Kalahari lion.

ITINERARY:

DAY 1 and 2: Leave U.S. Arrive Johannesburg. Transfer to airport hotel.

DAY 3: Continue by air to Windhoek, capital of Namibia, a small, very modern city with its blend of Namibian peoples: Afrikaners, Germans, English, Namas (Hottentots), Hereros and Ovambos.

DAY 4: Drive northward through bush country to Etosha National Park.

DAY 5 to 7: Three full days at Etosha National Park. We'll wait near the waterholes to watch the parade of animals come to drink. Lion, jackals, hyena and cheetah may be seen as well as black rhino and the very rare black-faced impala. The birdlife at Etosha is always very impressive.

DAY 8: Drive south through dry bush country, explore a forest of petrified wood and look for Bushman rock engravings.

DAY 9: Drive through increasingly desolate country to the Skeleton Coast, whose shores were much feared by sailing men. To be shipwrecked here meant certain death because the land behind the beach holds no fresh water.

DAY 10: A full day exploring the Skeleton Coast. We may be able to find shipwrecks locked in the sands.

3,000-foot-high dunes at Sossosvlei (Sossos Valley) are the highest in the world/ Allen Bechky

DAY 11: Drive southward along the Skeleton Coast, with a possible visit to the great colonies of southern fur seals found at Cape Cross. Arrive at Swakopmund, a town that maintains much of its German colonial character.

DAY 12 and 13: Enter the Namib Desert, one of the driest deserts in the world. We may be lucky enough to encounter gemsbok and the rare Hartman's mountain zebra. Explore the moonscape of the eroded bed of the Swakop River.

DAY 14: Drive to Sossusvlei, scenic bed of a seasonal lake which is surrounded by the highest sand dunes in the world (up to 1000 feet). Hike to the dunes for spectacular views of the desert landscape.

DAY 15: Drive to Fish River Canyon National Park, camping on the rim of the canyon.

DAY 16: Hike down to the floor of the canyon and spend the day exploring and possibly swimming in Fish River.

DAY 17: Drive to Kalahari Gemsbok National Park.

DAY 18: A full day to explore Kalahari Gemsbok National Park, with its bare dunes interspersed with thornbush.

DAY 19: Drive back to Windhoek.

DAY 20: Fly to Johannesburg. Afternoon free. Evening depart Johannesburg on homeward-bound flights.

DAY 21: Arrive home.

Fish River Canyon National Park, Namibia/ Allen Bechky

Visitors examine a welwitchia plant which has adapted itself to exist on the moisture from sea-born fog, since it never rains in the Namib/Allen Bechky

IT3BA1YO14

THE ZAMBIA/ ZIMBABWE EXPEDITION

Zambesi canoe trip, foot safari in Luangwa Valley

DATES: #1 *May 28–Jun 17 (21 days)*
#2 *Aug 6–Aug 26 (21 days)*
LEADER: *Ned St. John*
GRADE: *B-1*
LAND COST: *$2350 (8–12 members)*

This special safari offers unique gameviewing from houseboats, canoes and on foot in a spectacular region of Africa.

A scenic charter flight takes us to Matusadona National Park. Backed by the steep foothills of the Matusadona Range and facing man-made Lake Kariba, the park is known for its uniquely beautiful tree silhouettes in the flooded forests along its shores. This area is a photographer's and birdwatcher's paradise. Staying in houseboats on a river tributary of the lake, we'll take game viewing excursions, boat along the shoreline, and walk into the mopane scrub forest of the national park. Game likely to be seen includes impala, kudu, rhino, lion, eland and sable.

A five-day canoe safari on the Zambesi River gives a thrilling perspective on African bush game as we glide past hippo pools and sunning crocodiles, watching elephant and cape buffalo grazing along the banks. This historic river figured prominently in the epic explorations of Livingston and Stanley. We'll paddle down it in stable, easy-to-maneuver two-person canoes and camp under the stars at night.

In Zambia's Luangwa Valley National Park, we'll undertake an exciting five-day foot safari, hiking to remote bush camps through a national park which is home to 60,000 elephant, 2,000 black rhino, and vast herds of buffalo. Hippos and crocodiles abound in the Luangwa River and there are more than 400 species of birds in the park.

Our last stop is famous Victoria Falls, with the option of a one-day Zambesi whitewater adventure.

ITINERARY:

DAY 1 to 3: Leave U.S. Arrive Harare, Zimbabwe. Transfer to hotel.

DAY 4: Morning flight to Kariba. Connect with charter flight to Matusadona National Park. Transfer to houseboat accommodations on Lake Kariba.

DAY 5 and 6: Game viewing excursions by boat and on foot from Matusadona House Boat Camp.

DAY 7: Morning charter flight back to Kariba. Begin five-day canoe trip on the Zambesi River. Canoe from the Kariba Gorge to Nyamuomba Island.

DAY 8: Full day on the Zambesi, reaching Chirundu in the late afternoon.

DAY 9: A more relaxed day with time to spend on extended "drifts" and refreshing stops under shady trees. Camp at Kakomakamorara Hill.

DAY 10: Continue the canoe safari as the Zambesi flows into a wilder area and more wildlife is encountered. Reach Rukomeche River in the late afternoon and camp.

DAY 11: End river journey in the afternoon at Nyamepi Camp in Mana Pools National Park. Transfer to Chikwenya Camp. Late afternoon game drives by landrover.

DAY 12: Game drives and walks from Chikwenya Camp in Mana Pools National Park.

DAY 13: Drive to Lusaka for charter flight to Zambia's Luangwa Valley. Overnight at Chibembi Camp.

DAY 14 to 17: Foot safari in Luangwa Valley.

DAY 18: Fly by charter to Lusaka, continue by air to Livingston, and transfer to Victoria Falls Hotel.

DAY 19: Optional excursions at the falls. Overnight at Victoria Falls Hotel.

DAY 20 Fly to Harare. Late evening depart for London and connect with homeward-bound flights.

DAY 21: Arrive home.

This Zambian witch doctor shows his power by allowing sand to be poured in his eyes/ Allen Bechky

River crossings are part of the foot safari experience, Luangwa Valley National Park. Looking for crocodiles makes them stimulating!/Allen Bechky

The swift Zambesi current carries canoes past watchful hippos/ Dick McGowan

Victoria Falls, Zimbabwe/Dick McGowan

Each day, pools like this one in the Wasi Tala provide a relaxing place for lunch and a bath.

The supply camels can also provide rides for those trekkers who are interested in the experience.

Sinai photos by Dick McGowan

IT4TW14047

EGYPTIAN SINAI CAMEL TREK

9-day desert trek with Bedouin nomads

DATES: *Nov 28–Dec 16 (19 days)*
LEADER: *to be announced*
GRADE: *B-2*
LAND COST: *$1825 (13–15 members)*
 $1990 (9–12)

This trip combines the delights of desert travel—austere landscapes, Bedouin campfires, oasis pools and star-studded nights—with the mystery of exploring the Mediterranean's last great wilderness, the Sinai.

Flying from Cairo to the coast of the Sinai Peninsula, we'll make a five-day trek with a camel caravan, then stop for a visit to St. Catherine's Monastery (with its Byzantine treasures) and a hike up Mt. Sinai. We then continue our desert trek for four more days, hiking through steep canyons and Bedouin encampments.

Our desert trek takes us through a multicolored sandstone region where flat valleys are strewn with huge, fantastically-shaped sandstone blocks. Traversing narrow canyons, swimming in clear, cool pools, visiting nomadic settlements and sleeping under the starry desert sky, we'll appreciate the mysterious power which the desert has always had over the human soul.

Bedouin mountain guides will accompany us. Camels will carry our gear and be available for riding on some stretches.

After the trek, we tour some of the many wonders of ancient Egypt, including the Pyramids at Giza, Memphis and Sakara.

The Bedouin camel drivers usually bake pittot for lunch.

ITINERARY:

DAY 1 and 2: Leave U.S. Arrive Cairo and transfer to hotel.

DAY 3: Fly to Sharm al-Sheikh. Drive north along the coast, stopping to swim and snorkel at colorful coral reefs. Camp on the beach at the beautiful oasis of Dahab.

DAY 4: Visit the oasis of Bir Ugda and return to beach camp.

DAY 5: Meet with camel caravan and begin Sinai camel trek. Ride and hike through a canyon to the lovely oasis of Moyet Malha. Continue to the geologically interesting valley of Freia and camp.

DAY 6: Hike through the fantastically shaped and colorful sandstone canyons of the Laglug abu Arta ("Canyon of Colors"), ride and hike to the oases of Bir Biriya, Bir Sawra and Moyet Sawana.

DAY 7: Ride and hike over Ras al Galb Pass to the large oasis of Ein umm Ahmad, shared by the Tarabin and M'zeina tribes. Time for swimming in pools and visiting the Nawamis, a necropolis of well-preserved burial structures from the early Bronze Age (c. 3200 B.C.)

DAY 8: Day hike up the huge dome of Jabel Burga (3,800'), the highest peak in the area.

DAY 9: Hike out to the oasis of Ein Khodra, leave our Bedouin guides and camels, and proceed to St. Catherine's Monastery.

DAY 10: Day to visit the monastery and hike up Mt. Sinai.

DAY 11: Begin another trek, this one starting with a hike up Jabal Abbass Basha for breathtaking views of the entire area. Descend the canyon of Wadi Shag and swim in its pools. Hike on through another canyon and camp in the gardens of the Tweita canyon.

DAY 12: Descend into a gorge and spend the day swimming in pools. Hike along a stream to our night's camp near the Bedouin encampment of Farsh Rumana.

DAY 13: Hike up Jabel Bab Peak for a magnificent westward view. Camp near a Bedouin garden in Wadi Jbal.

DAY 14: Walk through cultivated and steep canyons, hike up Jabel Ahmar and descend to the village of Milga.

DAY 15: Transfer to the Mt. Sinai airport and fly to Cairo. Overnight at hotel.

DAY 16 and 17: Two full days of sightseeing in Cairo and environs.

DAY 18: Depart Cairo and connect with homeward-bound flights.

DAY 19: Arrive home.

IT4TW14046

ANCIENT EGYPT

Camping and sailing on the Nile

DATES: *#1 Feb 12–Feb 27 (16 days)*
       #2 Nov 15–Nov 30 (16 days)
LEADER: *to be announced*
GRADE: *A-2*
LAND COST: *$1790 (10–16 members)*
            $1990 (6–9)

Herodutus wrote of Egypt in the 5th century A.D. "there is no other country which possesses such wonders." And that is still true today.

In Cairo, we visit the Great Pyramids, the Sphinx and the Egyptian Museum of Antiquities (filled with King Tut's treasures). From Aswan, we visit Abu Simbel, site of the Nile-side temples of Ramses II. We then begin a special part of our Egypt tour, a leisurely four-day *felucca* sail on the Nile from Aswan to Luxor.

Our vessels for the sail will be feluccas, the traditional native open sailboats. Living on these little boats involves "roughing it" by Western standards. Toilet facilities are primitive, privacy is limited, and since there are no berths on the boat, we will sleep on the beaches at night. What the boats lack in comfort, they make up for in flexibility. We think they provide a far better Nile experience than the sterile cruise ships which are floating hotels. Egyptian sailors handle the boat and do all the cooking. We'll have a relaxed pace on the river, visiting the major temples on route, and meeting white-robed Nubians as they conduct the commerce of the Nile from their felucca boats.

Arriving at Luxor, where the legacy of the pharaohs is at its most astonishing, we'll discover the world of ancient Thebes, visiting the Valley of the Kings, Tutankhamen's tomb and other wonders.

All trips are escorted by a professional Egyptologist. Travel between Cairo and Aswan is by sleeper train.

ITINERARY:

DAY 1 and 2: Leave U.S. Arrive Cairo and transfer to hotel.

DAY 3 and 4: Two full days sightseeing, including Egyptian Museum, Great Pyramids, and an excursion to Memphis, ancient capital of Lower Egypt and its necropolis, Sakarra. Evening of Day 4, board the night train to Aswan.

DAY 5: Arrive in Aswan about noon. Visit Kitchener Island, Elephantine Island and the Mausoleum of the Aga Khan.

The colossus of Memnon, Luxor.

DAY 6: Short morning flight to Abu Simbel. Visit the dramatic temples of Ramses II and his wife, Queen Nefertari. These Nile-side temples were dismantled by an international engineering project and reassembled several hundred feet above their original site to save them from the rising waters of Lake Nassar. Fly back to Aswan and take a short sail to Philae, site of a lovely temple to Isis.

DAY 7 to 10: Board the felucca boats, our floating homes for the next four nights, and enjoy the quiet pleasures of the Nile, a beautiful river whose waters are edged by green palm thickets and flanked by golden desert escarpments. We'll stop each day to visit the major temples enroute, and have close contact with the friendly Nubian people living along the banks of the Nile, getting a glimpse into the lives of Egyptian shepherds and farmers. This experience is totally different than a Nile cruise in a big luxury liner.

DAY 11: Arrive in Luxor, bid our felucca crew goodbye, and transfer to a hotel for showers and cleanup.

DAY 12 and 13: Visit the "Thebes Necropolis," Valley of the Kings, Queens and Nobles, funerary temples of Queen Hatshepsut and Ramses III, the tombs of Ramses IV and Tutankhamen, and the extensive temple sites of Karnak and Luxor.

DAY 14: Morning visit to a small village; afternoon depart on the overnight train to Cairo.

DAY 15: Arrive in Cairo and transfer to hotel. Day free to explore on your own.

DAY 16: Depart Cairo and connect with homeward-bound fights.

Felucca under sail on the Nile.

The Great Pyramids at Giza.

Sinai Trekking Option

We can arrange a one week trekking option in the Sinai or Judean Desert of Israel after the trip.

Feluccas are the picturesque sailboats used by Nubians for their commerce on the Nile. We use them to sail the 200 kilometers from Aswan to Luxor.

Harold Pinsch with our felucca captain, Mamud.

Egypt photos by Ken Scott

The Touaregs, tall and slender, have a natural elegance enhanced by their full-length blue robes and turbans (seche). They are a fair-skinned race of Berber extraction and are the most free of all Saharans, roaming at will in the vastness of the African desert.

IT5PA1SFMT7

THE SAHARA CAMEL EXPEDITION

13-day desert and mountain experience with Touareg nomads

DATES: *#1 Jan 28–Feb 14 (18 days)*
　　　　#2 Oct 30–Nov 16 (18 days)
LEADER: *Jean Louis Bernezat*
GRADE: *B-2*
LAND COST: *$2100 (8–15 members)*

The Sahara, the largest desert in the world, is not an unending sea of sand, as fiction and film would have us believe. It has an infinite variety of landscapes: rock-ribbed plateaus, sandstone canyons, the volcanic Hoggar Mountains, beach-like golden washes filled with oleander, tamarisk acacia-thorn trees, date palms and many wildflowers.

We will travel a mountainous region of the Sahara—the Hoggar Mountains—by camel and on foot, enjoying the mystique of the Sahara and experiencing the way of life of our nomadic Touareg guides, the blue-robed "nobles of the desert."

Our circular trek from Tamanrasset will last two weeks, traveling around the central Atakor pillar, a geological remnant dating back to the Pre-Cambrian era. There are rock carvings, paintings, archaeological remains, unclimbed domes, basalt gorges, awesome volcanic spires, shifting sands and erosion-carved river beds.

We will also hike up to the famous hermitage of Father Charles de Foucauld, 10,000 feet high on the summit of the Assekrem Plateau.

We will sleep under the stars, as there is no need for tents.

Note: no previous camel riding experience is required!

ITINERARY:

DAY 1 and 2: Leave U.S. Arrive Paris. Transfer to flight for Algiers, Algeria. Transfer to hotel.

DAY 3: Fly to the oasis town of Tamanrasset. Overnight at hotel.

DAY 4: Early morning rendezvous with our Touareg guides and camels, and set off into the desert, traversing the plain of Tam. Camp near the Daouda, a magnificent rock spire.

DAY 5: Follow the Oued ("dry river bed") Takecherouat through a setting of enormous and beautiful granite boulders. Cross a series of small passes and plains, and camp at the base of the rocky hills of Aleheg, where there are neolithic engravings of cattle and hunters as well as grafitti in Tifinar (the writ-

...rekkers approach the landmark Tezouaig ...aks near the hermitage of Father Charles de ...ucald.

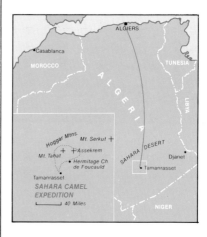

These are not real Touaregs but Mountain Travel trekkers "gone native."

ten language of the Touaregs).

DAY 6: Today we can either go north arou for some beautiful views. Camp in Oued In Dalag ("Place of the Palm Trees").

DAY 7: Cross a plateau to large dry riverbeds bordered by green tamarisks.

DAY 8: Along Oued Isigen toward the beautiful peak of Aguelzam. Afternoon at leisure, or for those who wish, an easy climb up Aguelzam for panoramic views.

DAY 9: Heading east, we'll see a multitude of sharp peaks, each more needle-like than the next. We'll spend the day walking around the base of the peaks and into the gorge of Terara with its fine neolithic drawings of giraffes.

DAY 10: Across a narrow pass where an epic battle among the Touaregs took place around 1880. We'll see many old gravesites. The path ascends to the Assekrem Plateau. Side hike to see some engravings.

DAY 11: Today we arrive at the foot of the Tezouiag (9,000'), among the most beautiful summits of Atakor. We leave the camels to go around the south side and hike up a pass with magnificent views. Descend the west slope and join the route which comes from Tam.

DAY 12: If possible, we will visit a small Touareg encampment en route. Optional hike up Saouinane, a beautiful volcano. Two-hour hike to Assekrem Plateau to visit the rock hermitage of Father Charles de Foucauld. In the afternoon, rejoin our camels at the foot of the Assekrem Pass.

DAY 13: Cross Aril Pass with majestic views of the summit of Ilaman, and descend past the old site of a battle between the Touaregs and the French Foreign Legion.

DAY 14: Up onto a plateau and descend the Oued Terhenanet.

DAY 15: Over a series of

plateaus and plains bordered by smooth-faced mountains. Afternoon visit to the village of Tagmart, where we'll have tea with some local Touaregs.

DAY 16: Arrive in the afternoon at Tamanrasset. Overnight at hotel.

DAY 17: Morning flight to Algiers. Overnight in hotel.

DAY 18: Fly Algiers/Paris and connect with homeward-bound flights.

Sahara photos by Alla Schmitz

North Africa & The Middle East

Mountain Travel is North American representative for EXPLORATOR, the major French adventure firm. Owned and managed by Jean Picon, EXPLORATOR'S odysseys range throughout the world and extensively in North Africa & the Middle East. These trips are not as "trekking" oriented as ours and instead often feature jeep travel and overlanding. Many of their leaders are English-speaking. We think EXPLORATOR's journeys capture the spirit of adventure and will be of interest to Mountain Travel enthusiasts. If you would like to join one of their trips, write to us for a copy of the current EXPLORATOR catalog (text in French) and we'll arrange the rest.

Abdel Kader Chellali, our head guide.

Allen Steck at a wayside cafe in Greece

A "kaiki" in port

VIGNETTES OF GREECE

by Allen Steck

There is a saying among mountaineers that there are many old climbers and there are many bold climbers, but few old, bold climbers; Allen Steck, a dedicated survivor approaching 58, is a member of that small group. His interest in people, the outdoors, good wines, and Austrian songs led him first to guide small groups to Europe and then, later, to become one of the founding partners of Mountain Travel. Known affectionately as the Silver Fox, he is co-author of Fifty Classic Climbs of North America *and co-editor of* Ascent, *a collection of mountain writing and photography published every four years by the Sierra Club. An enthusiastic Greek dancer with a fondness for all things Greek, Allen, together with his friend and partner, Maki Idosidis, leads our vagabond trips to Greece.*

Athens, June, 1983

Maki, my Athenian-born friend, and I are taking our evening walk along a lonely, stony trail on the Ymittos mountain above Athens. The sun is sinking toward a low range of hills opposite us and we languish in the aroma of wild oregano and pine resin. Below us, bathed in dusty, gold-orange light, lies the city of Athens. The Acropolis lies at our feet and we can see the ring of mountains rising above the northern suburbs. A soft, persistant hum emanates from that concrete megalopolis, reminding us that more than two million people carry on their daily lives down there.

A flock of sheep join the roadside picnic

On the slopes below the Acropolis we can see the Plaka, an ancient section of the city where, tomorrow night, we will dance at the *Sissiphos,* our favorite *taverna,* and become acquainted with the members of our newly arrived Mountain Travel group.

My thoughts are drifting among countless recollections of five summers of travel throughout Greece while leading "vagabond" trips for Mountain Travel. My mind comes ultimately to rest on a vital query: why the persistant urge to return?

The reasons seem almost as foolish as they are plentiful: I think of light playing on water beneath a limestone cliff the color of rust, the smell of lamb roasting on a spit, of a Cretan dancer moving wildly to compelling rhythms fashioned by the *lauto* and *lyra;* I think of dining outdoors at a seaside *taverna* in full sunlight, indulging in such delicacies as grilled octopus, squid and succulent eggplant together with the legendary *xoriatiki* (peasant salad), while listening to the waiters arguing in the kitchen.

And then there is the matter of Greek spirit, the drama of their everyday existence. In getting out of the towns into the countryside, away from bottom-line commerce, I find a more direct approach to life: hospitality to strangers, frankness, intellect, cunning. Kazantzakis said it all in *Zorba.*

I am thinking of Maki and all the trip members and Greeks who have come into our lives: we are all of us loose fragments in a Grecian kaleidescope. Each turn of the device produces new, fascinating and unexpected images. I shall try to explain.

Sally, Captain Zisimos and Katrina

The modern *kaiki* is a vessel of tourism, from 18 to 22 meters in length (but can be longer) with bunks, often private, for 6 to 14 passengers, plus galley and captain's quarters. The word *kaiki* is of Turkish origin, used to describe a Levantine vessel of commerce that crossed these seas in ancient times.

The events leading to our boarding the elegant *kaiki, Sally,* in Sifnos instead of Pireaus, were a typical mixture of Greek negotiation and intrigue. Some four weeks previously, Maki and I visited all the marinas in and around Pireaus on a Sunday and found ten or so *kaikis* that we liked. We left business cards indicating our interest in a charter; a few days later, over plates of *mezedes* (small hor d'ouvres) and glasses of *ouzo,* we had fashioned a contract for the *Sally* with our yacht broker, whom we called "the Shark."

However, the day before departure, the Shark called to explain that the *Sally* was in Rhodes with a broken shaft and asked if we could delay our departure for four days while repairs were made. Maki translated quickly: the Shark actually had made another charter that overlapped ours by four days. Our contract, a four-page document of arcane nautical and legalistic jargon, was so easily violated that I wondered how Greeks could carry on their vast commercial enterprises when written agreements were such slippery things.

But, to the shark's credit, he did find us another *kaiki,* the *Iaonnis,* captained by Zorzos Emmanoel, on which we ultimately found our way to the *Sally* in Sifnos. The four-day trip on the *Iaonnis* was uneventful except for Elaine, one of our trip members, and the bachelor captain, who managed in that brief time to fall in love, somewhere between the islands of Kea and Kithnos. But that is another story.

It was in Sifnos that Katrina, another of our Mountain Travel group of eight, saw Stratis, who was painting watercolors in a small *atelier* by the tiny harbor. Stratis, handsome, with dark hair, mustache and crisp manner, is typically Greek. But it was his new BMW motorcycle that first attracted

Katrina to his small shop. Katrina drives a mail truck in rural Oregon and knows a lot about motorcycles, since she owns one herself. Soon the watercolors are forgotten and she is riding into the interior of Sifnos Island with Stratis on the back of his motorcycle. Unfortunately, she must soon bid him farewell since we must depart for the island of Sikinos farther to the south. Katrina becomes known as the "BMW lady" and at each landfall, Maki's first gestures are to flag down the first motorcycle so Katrina may have her ride into the interior. However, it is not the BMW scene that endears me to Katrina, but later her dance of the *tsiftiteli* with Captain Zisimos on the island of Skinoussa.

As we motor into the remote and tiny port of Skinoussa, we sense that here life is slow, reduced to more elemental components. Gone are the tourist shops selling local trinkets, beads, scarves and plastic shoes. The horizon is defined by the meeting of olive trees, parched earth and cloudless sky.

A lobster boat with a fresh catch lies by the dock; fishermen are drying and repairing nets. Nearby is a small *taverna* recently built to accommodate the infrequent visitor to this out-of-the-way place. The only other building, off to the side, is an old hut with thatched roof where two years previously, I had sipped honey-flavored *tsipero* and chewed hardened bread soaked in water with Captain Tacticos and his gnarled old friend, Kostas, the sole occupant of the hut.

We hike over a small hill into the village and take our coffee in a small seaside *kafeneon*. Maki remains dockside to barter for lobster. Flowers adorn every house. The villagers, who seldom see outside visitors, are anxious to know who we are and our feelings about their island. Tonight will be festive; perhaps there will be dancing. Maki and I have been teaching two of the popular dances of Greece, the *syrto* and *hassapiko*.

The *syrto* is a line dance with ancient roots and though the basic rhythm remains the same, the style of the dance varies significantly among the many ethnic regions of Greece. Each island, for example, has its own *syrto*. The leader of the dance is permitted a great freedom of expression and he or she sets the mood, be it stately or lively. In contrast, one variety of the *hassapiko* is a more modern dance which has origins in the anti-establishment *tavernas* of Salamis and Pireaus prior to World War II. It is best danced with three persons who are all obliged to follow the steps set by the leader; these steps can be surprisingly complex. Often, the passion of the *hassapiko* is nourished by inebriation and each of the dancers must assist the other in remaining upright.

Evening arrives, and the family who owns the *taverna* serves our dinner outside on the porch, where we can hear the movement of the sea and watch the stars. Later, after the last plates of lobster shells are removed to the kitchen, someone puts a tape in the deck and there is music, a *tsiftiteli*. This is a sensuous couple dance of Turkish origin, with the character of a belly dance, but less intense. It is a dance for the woman to show her sensuality to her partner, who in turn must encourage his lady.

Katrina had told me that she had learned to belly dance in Oregon, but I had forgotten. Anyway, as the vibrant beat of the music reached out to us, suddenly Katrina is out onto the rough concrete floor, the tables having all been scraped to the side. She knows the rhythm well and is dancing sensuously to the heavy beat when just as suddenly, Captain Zisimos is there in front of her, dancing in homage to her Scandinavian beauty. Soon Zisimos is down on his knees in front of Katrina, his arms waving around like slowly writhing snakes. He is

Dancing in the amphitheatre at Epidavros

looking intently at Katrina, who seems disconcerted, distracted. I realize then that she does not know the significance of the dance. For her, Zisimos is an intrusion, not a partner for whom and to whom she should be dancing. In a moment, she is gone and Zisimos is left kneeling in the middle of the floor, looking at the concrete wall. Unruffled, the rotund captain leans forward, puts his hands on the floor and rocks forward into a mock headstand.

Retsina, Tolon and Epidavros

In the northeastern portion of the Peleponnesos, we had journeyed by bus down from Athens through ancient Corinth, Mycenae, Tiryns, thence to Epidavros, all of which have impressive ruins.

After a brief stop at Tiryns, we spent the better part of an evening in a *taverna* at Nafplion and then sought our sleeping place on a small promontory overlooking the Gulf of Argolikos near the village of Tolon. Later the following day, we took an afternoon walk along the beach and found an *ouzeria* in which to relax while pondering plans for the evening. Our *ouzeria* host and his family made us comfortable and soon the *ouzo* and *retsina* were flowing.

I must comment here on the controversial *retsina* and to do this, I feel compelled to choose the words of Lawrence Durrell from *The Greek Islands,* for it seems that Durrell and I are kindred spirits regarding this beverage (except that we spell it differently).

"*Rezina*," he wrote, "may well taste 'like pure turpentine which has been strained through the socks of a bishop,' as someone wrote to me; but it is to be recommended most warmly. You should make a real effort with it, but be warned that it is never as good bottled as it is fresh from the blue cans of the Athenian Plaka. It is a perfect adjunct for food which is oil-cooked, and sometimes with oil not too fresh. Its pungent aroma clears the mind and the palate at one blow. Yet, it is mild, and you can drink gallons without a hangover; nor does it ever provoke the disgusting, leaden sort of drunkenness that gin does—but rather high spirits and wit. If you drink *rezina*, you will live forever, and never be a trial to your friends or your waiters."

Soon it was time to leave, and, after I paid the bill, we started out along the beach. I was the last to leave and attempted in my halting Greek to thank our host. In a kindly manner, he asked in Greek where I was from and I said San Francisco (since no Greek could be expected to know where

*Maki Idosidis (left) and trip members
at lunch on the "kaiki"*

Photos by Allen Steck

...from the popular tourist areas, most of the Greek islands retain a very traditional culture

Berkeley is). His eyes shone and he quickly shifted to English:

"You know the Minerva Cafe on Eddy Street?

"Yes, of course," I say, doubly surprised at both his good English and his knowledge of this cafe, "we often go there for dancing."

"Well," he replies, "I was chef there for two years, but now I have my own *taverna.* The next time you go there, you tell Vassilis (the owner) not to put so much water in the wine and the lamb!"

The following day we left Tolon and began the drive toward Epidavros through rolling hills flooded with olive groves. The early morning mists were all but gone and the tiny road seemed nearly submerged among the shimmering leaves of olive trees, which contrasted so strongly with the sepia earth below. The sky had a deep, cleansed appearance, as after a rain shower, a kind of sky in which one has the desire to bathe, to paraphrase Henry Miller. The music of Theodorakis from our small cassette deck added to the cumulative effect.

We arrived at the ancient site of Epidavros to visit the 14,000-seat amphitheatre built in 4th century B.C.. We were well ahead of the tour buses and there were less than twenty persons scattered among the seats. Charged by the exuberance of the moment, we placed our tape deck in the center of the earthen floor of the amphitheatre and danced a *hassapiko,* much to the amusement and then pleasure of our tiny audience. Later we were chased away by a formidable Greek lady wearing the official armband of the Greek National Tourist Office, and into the theatre came the first busloads of tourists. We stayed and took our seats in the topmost rows, to hear a match being struck at the center of the orchestra, evidence of the amphitheatre's nearly perfect acoustical properties.

Sikea at Eastertime

It is the day before Easter. The air is redolent of spring and flowers abound as we drive south from Kalambaka in central Greece. The massive rock formations at Meteora fade slowly in the distance as we enter rich agricultural farmland nourished by the Pinios River. We pause briefly to observe a flock of storks that inhabits a marshy area by the side of the road.

We stop to have a picnic near a suitably grassy place near a farmhouse. We break out the picnic baskets, open the wine and prepare an enormous Greek salad of tomatoes, feta cheese, dill, dark Kalamata olives, cucumbers, capers and

olive oil. Dark peasant bread is passed around with the wine glasses. Greek music is soon playing on our ever-present cassette deck and it does not take long for the dancing to begin.

Passing truck drivers sound their horns in acknowledgement of this festive occasion. A shepherd and his flock pass through our picnic area. Suddenly, a farmer, who has an enormous mustache and is wearing a dirty undershirt and baggy pants, steps out of the farmhouse and starts yelling and gesturing in our direction.

"Maki, this fellow looks in an angry mood," I say. "I think we'd best be on our way."

"Just I go and talk with him," says Maki, "you load the bus."

Maki is soon back with the surprising news that we have all been invited in to participate in an Easter celebration with the farmer and his family, a delightful offer that we must unfortunately decline, since we have already made arrangements for our Easter lamb in the mountain village of Sikea with Dimitrios Bekos, a friend of ours from previous trips to this village. We pack up and arrive there at dusk.

The village of Sikea is located on a hillside at an elevation of about 1500 meters at the foot of the immense western escarpment of Mt. Giona. There are perhaps 50 inhabitants left; most of the young people have left to seek a more promising life in Athens. Even the school is closed this year for the first time. The center of the village, 50 meters of paved road, is flanked by a *taverna,* a huge plane tree, a church on one side, and Dimitrios' *taverna* on the other.

Normally, Sikea is a quiet place, but this week the population has trebled, for everyone has returned home for Easter, the most joyous of Greek celebrations. The fragrance of roasting lamb is everywhere; music filters through the trees from half-hidden houses. The two *tavernas* are bursting with activity. An old man is playing a *clarino,* while his family dances on a carpet of grass in front of his house.

We take a long afternoon walk down to the river below the village and by the time we return, our lamb, which has been roasting in Dimitrios' outdoor oven, is done. We take seats around his rustic table and watch as he places the lamb on an ancient chopping block, a tree stump to which three legs have been wired and nailed. While his wife and 14-year-old daughter set the table, Dimitrios grabs the cleaver and attacks the steaming lamb. He chops straight through to the tail; nothing recognizable remains, just bits and pieces of meat and splintered bone. I want to tell him to dismember the lamb in a more delicate way, but I remain silent respecting his village ways. It is a fragrant and tasty meal in spite of the butchery.

Afterward, we move the chairs outside onto the roadway in front of the church, to "check the action" as Maki would say. The musicians have arrived and the dancing begins. The villagers and their relatives insist that every member of our small group participate in the *syrto.* The dance is led by the owner of the village's other *taverna,* a man well past sixty. He is taking enormous leaps like a young goat as the line of dancers, with small children hanging desperately on at the end, swings around the plane tree. The revelry continues well into the night, long after we have retired to our campsite in the abandoned schoolyard.

I reflect on this remarkable Easter celebration and the joy we experienced in being part of it. The language barrier did not matter, for dancing projects its own communication. I will remember this event for a long time. Contented, I drift off to sleep.

EUROPE
& THE U.S.S.R.

The Chamonix Aiguilles and Mont Blanc, Europe's highest summit outside the Caucasus, from Le Brevent/Susan Thiele

GREENLAND • ICELAND • NORWAY • IRELAND • UNITED KINGDOM
FRANCE • SWITZERLAND • ITALY • GERMANY • AUSTRIA • CORSICA • SPAIN
PORTUGAL • GREECE • BULGARIA • ROMANIA • YUGOSLAVIA
CZECHOSLOVAKIA • TURKEY • U.S.S.R.

Sagrada Familia," the unfinished
cathedral of Barcelona/Chipper Roth

Mountain Travel Europe & The U.S.S.R.

We see the continent of Europe as an ideal place for an outdoor adventure because of its easy access from America, and its still-pristine wilderness regions, side by side with the creature comforts for which Europe is known.

Our walking tours in Britain have been hailed for many years as a fine combination of hiking and sightseeing. We have successfully applied this walking/touring concept to many other regions of Europe, including Ireland, France, Spain, Germany and Switzerland.

Most of our European trips don't involve backpacking but for those who want that challenge, we offer several backpacking expeditions and guided climbs in the French and Swiss Alps, the alpine wonderland where the sport of mountaineering was born 100 years ago.

In the U.S.S.R.'s Caucasus and in the Altai of Soviet Central Asia, we offer hiking and climbing camps which are unique and very reasonably priced.

With us, you'll see a Europe that you didn't think still existed, in many places where travelers may be a rarity. Our groups are very small—usually not more than 10, and our European leaders are superb and experienced guides.

On a traditional "kaiki" in the Aegean/Allen Steck

MIKE BANKS, 58, is one of Britain's leading polar explorers and mountaineers. He was awarded the Polar Medal by Queen Elizabeth for his epic 800-mile crossing of the Greenland icecap, and received the M.B.E. (Member of the British Empire) for climbing Rakaposhi (25,550′) without oxygen. He is the author of six books on the polar regions and mountaineering.

HELGI BENEDIKTSSON, 27, is mountaineer, skier and founding member of the Icelandic Alpine Club with many first ascents in the Icelandic Mountains. He is a professional mountain guide, mountain rescue instructor and has also climbed in the Alps and on Mt. McKinley.

ROD BUNTZ, 64, is a retired colonel in the French Marine Corps and a world traveler who with his wife, Maryvonne, leads the "Other France" walking tours.

Mike Banks   *Helgi Benediktsson*

Rod & Maryvonne Buntz

Pierre Jamet with Pemba Chiki

Silvana Camus

SILVANA CAMUS, 36, is a skier and mountaineer who lives in the mountains of Italy. She has led trekking expeditions in Nepal, Ethiopia, Bhutan, Canada (with huskies) and New Guinea.

CESARE CESABIANCHI, 33, is an experienced mountain guide with a thorough knowledge of the Italian Alps. He has climbed and trekked throughout Europe and has led two Himalayan expeditions.

ANGUS ERSKINE regularly takes visitors around the Scottish Highlands (in between his Arctic expeditions). He is an experienced mountain guide well versed in the history, folklore and natural history of North Britain.

MAKI IDOSIDIS, 37, is a Greek mountaineer who divides his time between living in Greece and the U.S. He knows Greece well, is a fine Greek dancer and leads our Greek sailing and hiking journeys.

PIERRE JAMET, 50, of France, leads mountain treks and ski tours in France, Switzerland, Italy and Austria. A mathematics professor turned trekking guide, he has been a member of several climbing expeditions in Nepal and India.

WOLFGANG KOCH, 32, of Stuttgart, is a chemist by profession and has been hiking, skiing and climbing in Europe for many years. He knows the German and Tyrolean Alps and leads our Bavarian hiking tours.

LINDA LISCOM, 43, is a professional photographer and free-lance writer, a regular contributor to the San Francisco Examiner and Los Angeles Times. She has 15 years of experience in leading Sierra Club and Mountain Travel trips in Asia and South America.

SHANAN MILLER, an Australian and now resident of Britain, has traveled extensively in Africa, Asia and South American and leads treks full-time in the Alps and mountains of Asia.

Martin Zabaleta & Chipper Roth

PADDY O'LEARY, 48, director of Ireland's National Association for Adventure Sports, has 25 years of mountaineering experience in Britain and the Alps and has led expeditions in the Karakorum, Himalayas and Andes.

ALLEN STECK, 58, one of the founding partners of Mountain Travel, is a veteran mountaineer and one of America's pioneer rock climbers with first ascents throughout the world. He is co-author of *Fifty Classic Climbs,* a climbing guide for North America. Allen is also a noted Greek dancer and specializes in leading our "vagabond" trips in Greece.

CHARLES WILKINSON, from Britain, is an experienced climber and trekker with experience in Nepal, Kashmir, Peru, Greece, Corsica and Peru.

MARTIN ZABALETA, 34, is a Basque mountaineer who in 1981 became the first Spaniard to climb to the summit of Mt. Everest. He has worked professionally as both a safari leader and climbing guide and has a passion for nature photography and Basque cuisine.

Charles Wilkinson   *Shanan Miller*

Maki Idosidis

Allen Steck

About Our Europe Trip Leaders

Our exceptionally talented staff of European trip leaders have skills, enthusiasm and an understanding of the local culture which adds immeasurably to the success of each trip.

Angus Erskine

Cesare Cesabianchi

Paddy O'Leary

IT4SK1MTDS

DOGSLEDDING IN GREENLAND

A true arctic expedition

DATES: *Mar 27–Apr 10 (15 days)*
LEADER: *Mike Banks*
GRADE: *Grade: B-2*
LAND COST: *$2490 (8 members)*

This is an opportunity to enter the spectacular world of the polar explorer. With Mike Banks, one of Britain's most experienced arctic explorers, we will travel the breathtaking coast of west Greenland by husky dogsled in the company of Eskimo hunters.

We must emphasize that this is not a "tourist" trip where one observes the splendor of the arctic from a cruise ship. This is a real arctic adventure using traditional and proven Eskimo methods of mushing. Dogsleds here have remained a vital form of transport outside the villages, and this is a chance to experience the last of a quickly vanishing way of life. Dogsledding is a stimulating, boisterous affair for which you should be fit and robust. It is not for anyone who is frail or out of condition.

We will travel at an ideal time of year, just before the arctic spring.

From a small village above the Arctic Circle, we undertake a four-day dogsled and camping journey with the Eskimos (one person to a sled with driver), roaming as far along the coast as conditions permit, with snow-covered frozen fjords as our grand highways.

After the trip, we visit Copenhagen, one of Europe's most charming capitals, home of Hans Christian Anderson.

ITINERARY:

DAY 1 and 2: Leave U.S. Arrive Copenhagen. Overnight at hotel.

DAY 3: Fly to Sondre Stromfjord, inside the Arctic Circle. Continue by helicopter to Christianhaab, 125 miles to the north, a Greenlander (Eskimo or Inuit) community of some 3000 people and rather more husky dogs.

DAY 4: In Christianhaab, collecting the special equipment we will need on our journey. Overnight at hotel.

DAY 5: Spend the day dogsledding to familiarize ourselves with the techniques we will need for our journey. Each member will be allocated a sled which will be driven by a Greenlander with his own dog team. Much of the time, we sit on the sled while traveling. However, when going steeply uphill, we walk, easing the strain on the dogs. On steep snowbanks, we pitch in and help push the sleds over any obstacles.

DAY 6 and 7: Another day preparing for the journey, checking food, tents, equipment and personal items.

DAY 8 to 11: On a four-day dog sled journey, Eskimo style. Our exact itinerary will be governed by the weather and particularly by the

condition of the sea ice, which varies each year. We will certainly approach the "ice fjord" into which the famous Jakobshavn Glacier discharges millions of tons of ice a day and moves at the extraordinary speed of three feet an hour —the fastest in the world. From time to time, we will see the dome of the immense inland icecap.

DAY 12: In Christianhaab. Optional walks.

DAY 13: By helicopter back to Sondre Stromfjord and continue by jet to Copenhagen. Overnight at hotel.

DAY 14: At leisure in Copenhagen.

DAY 15: Depart Copenhagen and connect with homeward-bound flights.

Explorer Mike Banks received the coveted Polar Medal for leading an epic 800-mile crossing of the Greenland Icecap. He has an unrivalled knowledge of Greenland extending over 30 years.

Greenlanders (Inuit or Eskimo) from Christianhab, a remote community of the west coast.

We sit on the sled while traveling most of the time. When going steeply uphill, we walk, easing the strain on the dogs. On steep snowbanks, we pitch in and help push the sleds over any obstacles.

Greenland photos by trip leader Mike Banks

IT5FIREKMT

NATURAL HISTORY OF ICELAND

Camping, hiking, exploring by jeep

DATES: *Jul 9–Jul 22 (14 days)*
LEADER: *Helgi Benediktsson*
GRADE: *B-2*
LAND COST: *$1490 (8–12 members)*

Iceland, that peculiar environment of fire and ice, is a living laboratory for geologists. Natural cataclysms are constantly shaping and reshaping the land with major volcanic eruptions on the average of every five years.

We will travel in southern Iceland by four-wheel drive vehicle, camping enroute and visiting some of its most interesting spots, including Great Geyser (a famous thermal spout from which the international word geyser was derived) and Gullfoss, one of Europe's highest waterfalls. We'll hike up Mt. Hekla (4,927′), Iceland's best known volcano, and (for those who are fit) climb Iceland's highest peak, Mt. Oraefajokull (6,952′).

In contrast to the creaking glaciers, spouting geysers and steaming lava fields, we'll find that Iceland's landscape can also be very serene. In mid-summer (the time of our visit), there will be almost continuous daylight illuminating a pleasant and pristine landscape of deep fjords, glittering lakes, green valleys and coastal farm country which has been inhabited by Icelanders for more than 1100 years.

The climate is mild (tempered by the Gulf Stream) and the air is probably the clearest and cleanest in the inhabited world.

Ornithologists take an interest in Iceland, too, since most of Iceland's wildlife (except for arctic fox and reindeer) is winged: more than 240 species of migrant birds visit Iceland, with 76 species nesting here regularly.

GREENLAND OPTION:

After the trip, we can arrange an optional four day tour to Angmagssalik, an Eskimo fishing and seal-hunting settlement on the eastern coast of Greenland. Cost: $500 including round trip air fare from Iceland to Greenland.

ITINERARY:

DAY 1 and 2: Leave U.S. Arrive Rekjavik, Iceland. Meet with trip leader and drive to Pingvellir National Park. Short hike in the area and overnight at hotel.

DAY 3: From Pingvellir, drive to Pjorsardalur at the foot of Mt. Hekla, and camp. Enroute visit the Great Geyser and Gullfoss ("the golden waterfall").

DAY 4: Easy hike to Mt. Hekla, Iceland's most famous volcano, then drive to Thorsmork, a breathtakingly beautiful valley surrounded by glaciers, massive mountains and glacial rivers on all sides. Camp.

DAY 5: Hiking in Thorsmork area.

DAY 6: Hike down to Skogar and drive to Hjorleifshofoi. Good birdwatching opportunities from our campsite.

DAY 7: From Hjorleifshofoi, we drive to Skaftafell National Park and camp.

DAY 8: Optional hike up Mt. Oraefajokull, Iceland's highest mountain and third largest volcano in Europe. This is a strenuous hike, and those not wishing to participate can take other local walks.

DAY 9: Visit Breioamerkurlon, an iceberg-strewn glacial lake. Hike in the afternoon and return to camp.

DAY 10: Drive from Skaftafell to Eldgja.

DAY 11: Drive to Landmannalaugar and soak in a natural hot spring.

DAY 12: Drive to Reykjavik. Overnight in hotel.

DAY 13: Free day in Reykjavik.

DAY 14: Depart Reykjavik and connect with homeward-bound flights.

Landmannalaugar National Park has a tranquil landscape with wonderful natural hot springs.

Geologically speaking, Iceland is a very young country and has the most constantly active volcanoes in the world.

Horned puffin

Blue poppy

In mid-summer, the time of our visit, there will be almost continuous daylight illuminating a pristine landscape of fjords, lakes and green valleys.

Iceland photos by Phillipe Patay.

Ofaerufoss waterfall

Minnie Schambra at Lake Gjende, Norway, where there is a trail-head lodge with marked trails that extend out into the glacial mountains.

Norway's ski huts are well-equipped, conveniently located and offer good amenities to top off a day of exhilarating skiing.

Our optional eight-day hut-to-hut ski tour with husky dogs at Hardangervidda, Norway.

Norway photos by trip leader Dave Parker

IT4SK1MTSN

SKI TOURING IN NORWAY

For beginners and experts alike

DATES: *Mar 10–Mar 25 (16 days)*
LEADER: *Dave Parker*
GRADE: *B-3*
LAND COST: *$1390*
            (12–15 members)
            $1475 (8–11)

Norway's national parks and wilderness mountains are the birthplace of nordic skiing. They offer unparalleled back-country touring and comfortable ski lodges situated in remote areas where skis are the only form of transportation.

There are marked routes throughout the rolling plateaus, frozen lakes and high slopes, as well as unlimited open wilderness for cross-country tours.

We visit three areas which offer differing experiences: Jotunheimen Park is known for deep glacial valleys and jagged peaks; Rondane Park contains rounded mountains and gentle, open foothills with dry snow; the Finse Plateau, located high in the treeless plains, has wide open skiing mixed with flat glaciers.

The comfortable lodges, all in remote areas and built just for nordic skiers, have hearty food and offer perfect access to skiing.

The skiing is suitable for most skiers who enjoy off-track touring. Beginners are welcome if they are in good physical condition and want to learn and experience ski touring in the best possible conditions.

OPTIONAL HUT-TO-HUT TRIP:

At the end of the trip at Finse, we can arrange an optional eight-day hut-to-hut trip through Hardangervidda, accompanied by a dogsled. For strong intermediate skiers. $575.

ITINERARY:
DAY 1 and 2: Depart U.S. Arrive Oslo. Transfer to hotel.

DAY 3: Morning train up the long Gudbrandsdalen Valley, an area of forests, farms and long river gorges. By van from Otta to our trailhead lodge at Lake Gjende.

DAY 4 to 6: Marked routes extend from our lodge out into the glacial mountains and frozen lakes of Norway's highest mountains. The routes vary from flat, to moderate, to steep slopes for telemark turns. There is a variety of terrain, so all levels of skiers can find suitable skiing. The lodge has double rooms with bunks, good food and hot showers.

DAY 7: By van to the trailhead for Rondane National Park, a three-hour ride through some of the oldest farmland in Norway, where log barns and wooded churches are still common. Ski from the trailhead to Rondvassbu Lodge.

DAY 8 to 10: Our rustic lodge is located in the middle of Rondane Park, below rounded peaks that tower several thousand feet above. The entire countryside is higher than treeline and there are unlimited tours down and across the undulating ridges and moraines nearby.

DAY 11: Ski out of the park and catch the train to Oslo, then up to Finse in the mountains of southwest Norway.

DAY 12 to 14: Finse is accessible only by train, and although it is not a national park, the surrounding glaciers and mountains are unspoiled. The skiing is easy but there are also challenging ascents of the Hardanger Glacier and local ridges.

DAY 15: Afternoon train to Oslo and evening free in town.

DAY 16: Depart Oslo and connect with homeward-bound flights.

IT4SK1MTNT

NATURAL HISTORY OF NORWAY

10-day walk in forests and glens

DATES: *Jun 28–Jul 12 (15 days)*
LEADER: *to be announced*
GRADE: *B-2*
LAND COST: *$1290 (8–15 members)*

The rolling forests and fells of eastern Norway are a wonderland for summer hiking. The sun is up almost round the clock, the meadows are filled with wildflowers, reindeer are seen grazing on hillsides, and the birds are nesting in remote lakes and marshes. Things have changed little here since Swedish botanist Linneaus walked these wildlife-rich hills in the 18th century, developing his famous system for the classification of plants and animals.

Our summer ramble begins with a scenic train ride along the Norway/Sweden border, taking us deep into old Norwegian farm country. From here we follow a well-planned trail and hut system through forests and glens which conjure up images of trolls, mythical creatures of Nordic folklore.

The hiking time per day is about five hours and the terrain is moderate and varied. En route, we pass Stone Age settlements, Lapp reindeer herders, and numerous active summer farms.

The Norwegian hut system is the best in Europe: immaculate wooden cabins complete with food, bunks and everything needed for a pleasant stay. The huts are staffed by Norwegian students who enjoy spending the long, light summer evenings sharing their knowledge of the local wildlife and folklore.

Only a small daypack need be carried while walking. This is an excellent tour for families who want to enjoy a European hike together.

ITINERARY:
DAY 1 and 2: Leave U.S. Arrive Oslo. Transfer to hotel.

View from Mt. Galdhopiggen, highest peak in Norway

DAY 3: By train to Tynset and continue by bus to Rausjodalseter. Overnight at an old "seter" (summer farm) that serves as a hikers' lodge.

DAY 4: Hike from Rausjodalseter up to Rausjo Peak (4,281'), then down into the forest to Ellefsplass on the Hola River.

DAY 5: Hike across glens and marshes, past tarns and becks to the old summer farm at Saether.

DAY 6 and 7: A three-hour walk, then a boat journey across Lake Femund into Femund National Park, ending with a one-hour stroll through the pine woods to Svukurset Lodge. Layover day to look for reindeer and perhaps meet some Sami people, the Lapps who herd reindeer in the borderlands.

DAY 8 and 9: Hike along cairned paths to the barren and boulder-strewn country around Roveltjorn Lakes. Much of Femund National Park is strewn with glacial debris from the last ice age; there are numerous small tarns and rivers. Continue to Stromrasen Hill and the River Mugga. There is time here for an easy ascent of Mt. Svuken (4,400') for panoramic views of the Norwegian/Swedish border country.

DAY 10 and 11: Easy hike from Ljosnavollen down through the forest to the village of Langen. Layover day for exploring the countryside.

DAY 12 and 13: Scenic walk to Marenvollen Hut, followed by an easy walk to Roros, a small mining town with a long history. Overnight at hotel in Roros.

DAY 14: By train to Oslo. Afternoon sightseeing. Overnight in hotel.

DAY 15: Depart Oslo and connect with homeward-bound flights.

IT4SK1MTJH

ALPS & FJORDS OF NORWAY

11-day trek in the Jotunheimens

DATES: *Aug 17–Sep 2 (17 days)*
LEADER: *to be announced*
GRADE: *B-3*
LAND COST: *$1475 (8–15 members)*

One of the most dramatic meetings of mountains and sea on earth can be found in Norway, where high glaciated peaks rise abruptly from an incredibly indented coastline of fjords.

Our journey here will explore the Jotunheimens, "home of the giants," a coastal range which contains Scandinavia's highest peaks, looming directly over the deep waters of Sognfjord. More than 250 peaks here are above 6,000 feet, not high by world standards but impressive when you consider that their base-to-summit rise equals that of many peaks in the Alps. We'll spend ten days in the heart of the Jotunheimens, hiking and scrambling to the summits of Galdhoppigen (8,098') and Glittertind (8,045'), Norway's two highest mountains, and down to the coast at Sognfjord itself.

This is one of the world's classic mountain walks. The hiking is challenging, but because of the fine lodge system, we don't have to carry heavy packs. Norway's mountain lodges are known for their comfort, hospitality, and good food, even in the remotest alpine settings.

After the trip, we descend into the fjords for a ferry trip and leisurely train ride to Voss and Bergen, the quaint seaport with buildings dating back hundreds of years to the time of the Hanseatic League.

ITINERARY:

DAY 1 and 2: Leave U.S. Arrive Oslo and transfer to hotel.

DAY 3: Day free for visiting the Viking Museum and Oslo Fjord.

DAY 4: By train and bus to Krossbu in the Jotunheimen Mountains. The train passes through some of Norway's loveliest farm country.

DAY 5 and 6: Cross Smorstabb Glacier to Leirvassbu, then an easy hike down a deep valley to Spiterstulen, at the foot of Galdhoppigen.

DAY 7: Ascent of Galdhoppigen, a strenuous climb with a vertical rise of 4,000 feet—nontechnical but demanding.

DAY 8: Hike from Spiterstulen past Glittertind, second highest peak in Norway. At Glittertind there is an isolated lodge surrounded by glaciers and barren peaks.

DAY 9: Hike over several ridges to Gjendesheim, one of the oldest lodges in the Jotunheimen, situated in the mountains immortalized by Ibsen in *Peer Gynt.*

DAY 10: Ascent the "Peer Gynt" ridges above Lake Gjende and hike down to a lodge at Memurubu.

DAY 11: Scenic hike with good views of the central Jotunheimen to Gjendebu, situated at the far western end of Lake Gjende. Continue to Olavsbu, a self-service hut where everyone helps with fire-making and cooking.

DAY 12: Hike to one of the most idyllic spots in the Norwegian mountains at Skogadalsboen, surrounded by glaciers and high peaks.

DAY 13: Ascent of Fannaraken (6,758'), where clear-weather views extend from the North Sea to Sweden. This is a good day's scramble, a strenuous but non-technical ascent.

DAY 14: Hike down to Vetti, passing Vetti Falls. Overnight at a summer farm.

DAY 15: Hike to Hjelle, bus to Ardalstangen, ferry through picturesque Sognfjord, then by train to Voss. Overnight in hotel.

DAY 16: By train to Bergen. Afternoon stroll around this old Hanseatic North Sea port. Overnight in hotel.

DAY 17: Depart Bergen and connect with homeward-bound flights.

The hut system makes it possible to hike in very remote terrain without carrying heavy packs, Femundsmarka, Norway.

Photos by Helge Sunde

The famous "Peer Gynt" ridge above Lake Gjende, Jotunheimen Mountains, Norway

IT4EI15027

THE IRISH COUNTRYSIDE

Walking tour from Kerry to Connemara to Wicklow

DATES: #1 May 18–Jun 4 (18 days)
#2 Aug 24–Sep 10 (18 days)
LEADER: *Paddy O'Leary*
GRADE: A-1
LAND COST: $1695 (7–12 members)

Trip leader Paddy O'Leary enjoying a picnic on the rock island of Skellig Michael.

Going to market in South West Kerry.

Ireland photos by Bob Bernard

This walking tour is a relaxed and low-key look at little-known areas and aspects of Ireland, conducted by mountaineer Paddy O'Leary. It's an unusual chance to see "an Irishman's Ireland," with its quiet county towns, wild moors, and lonely coastal cliffs.

We begin with a visit to Clare, "Land of Castles," and the peculiar landscape of the Burren country, where mild weather and the proximity of the sea has led to exquisite flora.

We take a ferry to the Aran Islands, then return to Galway and visit the lake-dotted wilds of Connemara, one of Ireland's most beautiful regions.

Driving south, we tackle the rough mountain and coastal country of South West Kerry, staying in a secluded cove on the Ring of Kerry.

Heading through a region steeped in the lore of the Norman Conquest, we tour Kinsale with its sheltered harbor then walk in St. Mullins, an unspoiled river village and burial place of the Kings of Leinster.

Our last lap takes us through the prosperous farms of County Wexford and the Wicklow Hills, where we'll walk in wooded and historic valleys and glens, including Glendalough, with its 6th century monastery founded by St. Kevin.

Travel will be by minibus; accommodations are in small hotels.

ITINERARY:

DAY 1 and 2: Leave U.S. Arrive Shannon, Ireland. Meet with trip leader and drive to a hotel in the Burren. Afternoon stroll on the Cliffs of Moher.

DAY 3: Walk in Burren country and enjoy a session of Irish traditional music in a pub at Doolin.

DAY 4: By ferry to Inisheer and on to the Aran Islands, where islanders proudly foster the Gaelic language and traditions. In the evening, attend a banquet and pageant at Knappogue Castle, 15th century home of the McNamara clan.

DAY 5: Drive around Galway Bay to Galway, called "City of the Tribes," in reference to the four-

teen Anglo-Norman families which once dominated the town. Continue through the lake-dotted wilds of Connemara, and on to Kylemore Abbey and Gaeltacht.

DAY 6: Drive through Limerick to Adare, with its thatched cottages, and ruins dating from the 13th to 15th century, and on to Tralee, county town of Kerry.

DAY 7: Walk in the vicinity of Carrauntoohil (3,414'), Ireland's highest mountain, and drive around the glorious Ring of Kerry. Overnight in the seaside village of Waterville.

DAY 8: By fishing boat to Skellig Michael, a dramatic rock pinnacle with an old church clinging to its 700-foot-high summit.

DAY 9: Walk along flower-hung country lanes and skirt the lovely shoreline of Lamb's Head. Afternoon visit to the home of Daniel O'Connor, the Liberator.

DAY 10: Drive to Kinsale, stopping at Staigue Fort.

DAY 11: Day in Kinsale, with its sheltered harbor and history-filled streets.

DAY 12: Drive through Cork to Waterford, with its famous glass factory. Continue to a secluded guest house on the banks of the peaceful River Barrow.

DAY 13: Stroll through the little hamlet of St. Mullins, with its village green and fine example of early Norman fortification.

DAY 14: Drive to Kilkenny.

DAY 15 and 16: Drive through the farm country of County Wexford to the Wicklow Hills.

DAY 17: Drive to Dublin. Evening at the Abbey Tavern in the nearby fishing village of Howth to enjoy traditional music and dancing.

DAY 18: Depart Dublin and connect with homeward-bound flights.

IT4BA1Y039

IRELAND & BRITAIN WALKING

Walks in County Wicklow, Welsh Coast and Scottish glens

DATES: #1 Jun 30–Jul 20 (21 days)
#2 Jul 21–Aug 10 (21 days)
LEADER: *Paddy O'Leary & Mike & Pat Banks*
GRADE: A-1
LAND COST: $1890 (10–12 members)
$2150 (7–9)

This tour combines walks in Ireland, Wales, England and Scotland all in one trip, with an itinerary that does not overlap any ground covered by our other Ireland and Britain journeys.

A week-long Irish ramble will take us through the lake-dotted territory of "the Ferocious O'Flaherty's", and the Atlantic-washed haunts of the great pirate queen, Grace O'Malley. We'll visit the fabled "Mountains of Mourne" overlooking the Irish Sea, and walk in a lovely green landscape filled with Ireland's storied past, including 4000-year-old dolmens, early Christian settlements and Norman castles.

Crossing the Irish Sea to Wales, land of music and song (with a language older than English) we hike the spectacular Pembroke coast and visit the fishing village said to have inspired Dylan Thomas' "Under Milk Wood."

Journeying to England, we tour the Wye Valley, beloved of composer Elgar and poet Housman. Driving northwards, we visit Chester, a 2000-year-old city with medieval city walls, then north again to hike the Pennine Way along the mountainous backbone of England.

Lastly, we cross into Scotland to hike its glens and explore "Robert Burns" country before ending our tour in ancient Rowallan Castle as guests of its owner.

ITINERARY:

DAY 1 and 2: Leave U.S. Arrive Shannon, Ireland. Meet with trip leader and drive through County Clare to our hotel. Afternoon walk along the 700-foot Cliffs of Moher.

DAY 3: Hike in the Burren, with its many reminders of Ireland's past from megalithic tombs to Norman castles. Drive around Galway Bay, a Gaelic-speaking area. Free time in Galway, the "city of tribes."

DAY 4: Drive north to Westport, County Mayo, and hike on Achill Island, past whitewashed cottages

Shore walk, Cornwall/Mike Banks

and onto a beach with views of Clare Island, once the stronghold of pirate queen, Grace O'Malley.

DAY 5: Travel through County Mayo and Sligo, visiting the hilltop grave of the great Queen Maeve and the haunts of poet W.B. Yeats, then continue through lake country to Enniskillen in Northern Ireland.

DAY 6: Visit the cathedral city of Armagh and hike the famous Mountains of Mourne along the Brandy Pad, an old smugglers' trail.

DAY 7: Drive down the coast to Dublin. Visit the favorite pubs of playwrights Behan and O'Casey, and enjoy traditional Irish music in the Abbey Tavern.

DAY 8: Visit the hills of County Wicklow, walk in the historic valley of Glendalough, and continue to Wexford.

DAY 9 and 10: Depart Ireland on a three-hour ferry ride from Rosslare to Fishguard, Wales, where our British leaders, Mike and Pat Banks, will meet us. Hike the Pembroke hills, legendary land of Merlin the magician and the Druids.

DAY 11: Head east past the varied landscape of South Wales and stop at Laugharne, home of poet Dylan Thomas. At the ancient border town of Monmouth, we spend the night in a 300-year-old inn.

DAY 12 to 14: In Gloucestorshire, one of the most unspoiled counties of England, we explore tranquil villages and hike gentle green uplands.

DAY 15 and 16: Drive north and visit the historic walled city of Chester, founded by the Romans 2000 years ago.

DAY 17 and 18: Continuing north, we visit Martin Mere Wildfowl Reserve in Lancashire and have tea in a great historic mansion, Brownsholme Hall, built in 1507 by the Parker family who still live there. The next day we hike in the Pennine Mountains and venture into the largest limestone cavern in Britain.

DAY 19 and 20: North again to the Scottish border, a region immortalized by poet Robert Burns, whose house we visit. We'll hike the border hills and spend a night at Rowallan Castle.

DAY 21: Depart Glasgow and connect with homeward-bound flights.

IT4BA1YO39

HIGHLAND HIKES OF NORTH BRITAIN

The Lake District and Scottish Highlands

DATES: *Sep 8–Sep 24 (17 days)*
LEADER: *Angus Erskine*
GRADE: *B-2*
LAND COST: *$1390 (10–12 members)*
$1490 (6–9)

The aim of this tour is to venture over the peaks, passes and valleys of north England's "Lake District" and the famous Highlands of Scotland.

In the Lake District, all that is needed, said the poet Wordsworth, is "an eye to perceive and a heart to enjoy." Here in the land of Wordsworth and Coleridge, we hike up Scafell Pikes, Great Gable and Helvellyn, some of the most scenic corners of this 'miniature Switzerland.' There will also be time to visit the Lake District's villages, farms and tarns (some of which were the locations of Beatrix Potter's books for children).

Moving north to the Scottish Highlands, hills of purple heather, rock and rowan tree, we will climb Britain's highest mountain, Ben Nevis (4,406′), and view the wooded slopes around the Trossaches, scene of Sir Walter Scott's poems and novels. We also hike over such craggy summits as Ben Lawers, Cairngorm and Glas Maol, and have plenty of time to see the banks of Loch Lomond, visit ancient castles and watch the local whisky being distilled (perhaps sample some).

ITINERARY:

DAY 1 and 2: Leave U.S. and arrive Prestwick, Ayrshire. Drive to Carlisle, visit Hadrian's Wall, continue to Lake District. Overnight at a hotel which is our base for three nights.

DAY 3: Hike up Great Gable (2,949′) and Scafell Pikes, the highest peak in England (3,206′).

DAY 4: Hike up Helvellyn (3,116′) and visit Dove Cottage, the Wordsworth Museum.

DAY 5: Drive north through Carlisle and Paisley to Aberfoyle to Bailie Nicol Jarvie Hotel, base for the next three nights.

DAY 6: Hike up Ben Venue (2,393′) then take a ride in a small steamer on Loch Katrine, a lake which is associated with Scott's poem, "The Lady of the Lake."

DAY 7: Hike up Ben Ledi (2,873′), which has a superb view from its summit.

DAY 8: Drive to Loch Tay and climb Ben Lawers (3,984′). Botanists in the party may find some rare alpine flowers here. Drive to Glen Shee and the Spittall of Glenshee Hotel, our residence for two nights.

DAY 9: Drive to Cairnwell Pass and walk to the summit of Glas Maol (3,502′), where we are likely to see rare mountain birds such as golden plover and golden eagle.

DAY 10: Sightseeing drive into the Dee Valley for a distant view of Balmoral, the Queen's highland residence. Visit Craigievar Castle, dating from 1626, with its charming gardens and grounds. Stop at a whisky distillery to see the intricacies of whisky-making. Overnight at Red MacGregor Hotel for the next two nights.

DAY 11: The mountain range called "The Cairngorms" is the largest area of wilderness in Britain, a plateau with rounded peaks over 3,500 feet high. On its northern slopes is the Rothiemurchus Forest, a relic of the old Caledonian forest. Weather permitting, hike up Cairngorm and Ben Macdui.

DAY 12: Hike up Braeriach (4,248′) and descend by a circular route to see more of the Rothiemurchus Forest.

DAY 13: Drive to Inverness, "capital" of the Highlands, and then proceed to Loch Ness, keeping a sharp eye for "Nessie," the monster. Visit Castle Urquhart and continue down the Great Glen to Fort William. Two overnights at Croit Anna Hotel.

DAY 14: Weather permitting, make a long climb up a well-marked trail to the summit of Ben Nevis.

DAY 15: Drive south to Glencoe, Scotland's most dramatic glen, and along a road which winds down the west side of Loch Lomond. Stay two nights at Winnock Hotel, Drymen.

DAY 16: Hike up Ben Lomond (3,192′). Also stop at a small nature reserve where many ducks and other birds may be seen.

DAY 17: Drive to Prestwick and connect with homeward-bound flights.

On Britain & Ireland Trips

We stay in small hotels and guest houses of character and travel by mini-van.

Mike and Pat Banks and their six-passenger mini-vans.

Sheila Noble enjoying the view over the northwest highlands of Scotland/John Noble

Adventure travel in the grand "manor," Langton Hall, on "the Other Britain" trip/ Linda Liscom

Hill walk in Wales. Days will be spent exploring the scenic countryside. Nights will be spent in comfortable country inns/ Mike Banks

IT5PA1SFMT8

THE OTHER BRITAIN

Walking tour of Cornwall, Wales, Yorkshire

DATES: #1 *Jun 13–Jun 30 (18 days)*
            #2 *Aug 15–Sep 1 (18 days)*
LEADER: *Mike & Pat Banks*
GRADE: *A-1*
LAND COST: *$1690 (10–12 members)*
                    $1890 (8–9)

This tour reveals Britain from a totally fresh viewpoint, striking a balance between sightseeing and hiking, finding Britain's favorite walks among tranquil hills and along windswept cliff paths from Cornwall to Wales to Yorkshire. With Mike Banks, British author and mountaineer, and his wife Pat, we will discover the lovely, unspoiled rural England that the English themselves enjoy.

Starting in legend-laden Cornwall, we shall hike its spectacular coastline, explore hidden fishing coves, and ramble over lonely Dartmoor in Devon.

We'll enjoy the elegance of Georgian Bath and visit medieval Cotswolds villages before crossing the border to spend three days in Wales, land of song, castles and mountains.

In the Lake District, we will hike its fells and follow its becks to the famous waters that inspired Beatrix Potter to weave her fairytale world, and by which still stands Dove Cottage, where Wordsworth lived and wrote.

In Yorkshire we hike through "James Herriot country" and visit the ancient walled city of York, one of Britain's historical treasures, still entered by its medieval gates.

Best of all, we will constantly be meeting friendly British people, in their own homes and in their equally friendly pubs.

The tour finishes with a night's stay in Langton Hall, a 16th century manor house where we will be the welcome guests of the owner, Robert Spencer, cousin of Princess Diana, future Queen of England.

Travel is by two comfortable minibuses. Accommodations are in small country hotels of character.

ITINERARY:

DAY 1 and 2: Leave U.S. Arrive London, meet with trip leaders and enjoy a relaxed drive to the West-country, calling at mystic Stonehenge. Overnight at 300-year-old coaching inn in Wiltshire.

DAY 3: Continue west to Devon to hike Dartmoor's haunted wilderness and glimpse its wild ponies. Stroll the cobbled streets of historic Plymouth, where the Pilgrim Fathers and Drake embarked on their epic voyages. Sample delicious Devon cream teas in old country cottages.

DAY 4 to 6: To Celtic Cornwall, land of King Arthur, to enjoy its rugged coastline, old smugglers' coves and taverns and to make a private visit to Lord Eliot's castle and estate. Then on to Bath to enjoy, as Jane Austen did, the delights of the elegant Georgian spa built over an ancient Roman city.

DAY 7: Driving to the Cotswolds, the "heart of England," we experience the tranquil charm of villages of honey-colored stone cottages and 14th century wool merchant's houses, with flower-filled gardens set in green countryside, through which we walk before having private tea in a beautiful old house.

DAY 8 to 10: Over the border into Wales, we hike along Offa's Dyke, the great entrenchment built on the frontier in A.D. 785, then explore Snowdonia National Park, visit a woolen mill and a massive medieval castle. Our last evening, we'll be entertained by traditional harp and song at a banquet in ancient Ruthin Castle.

DAY 11 and 12: In the Lake District, our walks will let us enjoy the perfect harmony of hills and water which inspired Wordsworth's finest poetry and the fairytale world of Beatrix Potter.

DAY 13 to 15: Driving east to Yorkshire, we walk the dales and moors and visit James Herriot's own village. Then on to the walled city of York, where we explore narrow cobbled streets, museums and colorful taverns, marvelling at the soaring splendor of the superb Minster, the largest Gothic church in England, whose windows contain nearly half of Britain's medieval stained glass.

DAY 16: Drive south to Leicestershire and stay in Langton Hall, magnificent private home where we enjoy a candlelight dinner with the owner.

DAY 17: Drive to London with afternoon at leisure.

DAY 18: Depart London and connect with homeward-bound flights.

IT5PA1SFMT9

THE OTHER FRANCE

Walks in Basque hills, Loire Valley, Bordeaux

DATES: #1 Jun 2–Jun 19 (18 days)
　　　 #2 Sep 1–Sep 18 (18 days)
LEADER: *Rod & Maryvonne Buntz*
GRADE: *A-1*
LAND COST: *$2350*
　　　　　　 (10–12 members)
　　　　　　 $2575 (7–9)

In the style of our popular "Other Britain" walking tours, we will tour rural western France, immersing ourselves in French country life as we visit the Basque hills, the Pyrenees, the coastal plains of Aquitaine, the vineyards of Bordeaux, and the Loire countryside with its famed chateaux.

We begin with a swift train ride from Paris south to the French Pyrenees. Here we tour Basque villages and hike in the beautiful high altitude mountain pastures of the Ossau and Aspe valleys.

Driving north through the largest conifer forest in Europe, we discover the medieval city of St. Emilion, known for its wines. We hike its vineyards, sample some wine, then stop in Cognac and visit the Martell cellars.

At La Rochelle, we stroll the streets along this 17th century city's fortified harbor and enjoy delicious fresh seafood.

Heading for the Loire Valley and the heart of France, we visit some famous chateaux and take walks in the countryside.

Travel will be by comfortable minibus, with accommodations in hotels and inns.

ITINERARY:

DAY 1 and 2: Leave U.S. Arrive

Formal garden in Loire Valley chateau.

Paris. Continue by train to Dax in the south of France. Overnight in hotel.

DAY 3: Morning visit to a spa known for its healing mudbaths. Afternoon boat ride on the "courant d'Huchet" through an almost tropical underwood. On the return trip, we'll hike in a lofty pine forest, visit immense sand beaches on the Atlantic Coast and drive back to Dax.

DAY 4: Morning drive to Pomarez to visit a typical duck market of this region. Drive to Orthez and hike along the river Adour, ending at the trip leaders' 17th century country house, where we'll have dinner. Overnight at hotel in Dax.

DAY 5: Drive to Bayonne, Biarritz and St. Jean de Luz, with short visits to these typical old towns. Picnic in a private summer house with time to enjoy the wonderful scenery of the bay at St. Jean de Luz. Afternoon drive through the Basque hills and visits to Basque villages. Overnight at St. Jean-Pied-De-Port, a very attractive old fortified town.

DAY 6: An entire day's hike in the beautiful "Foret des Arbailles," then drive to Oloron-Ste. Marie.

DAY 7: Early morning drive to one of the wildest valleys in the Pyrenees, the Ossau Valley. Here we can choose either a full day's hike or a shorter walk before and after lunch.

DAY 8: Full day's hike in the Aspe Valley to meet shepherds.

DAY 9: Drive to St. Emilion, the world-famous wine-making city, through the Landes forest. Afternoon walk in the forest. Overnight at St. Emilion.

DAY 10: Morning walk in the vineyards. Visit the wine cellar at Chateau Lignac, owned by friends of the trip leaders.

DAY 11: Driving north, we visit a monolithic 6th century cathedral then drive to La Rochelle through the Cognac vineyards. Visit the old town of Saintes, where there are important Roman ruins.

DAY 12: Day at leisure in La Rochelle, strolling along the harbor.

DAY 13: Drive to Montreuil Bellay, a little town surrounded by the Anjou vineyards. We shall tour a "fairytale castle," visit a mushroom farm, and sample excellent Saumur wine. Overnight at Chinon, Joan of Arc's town.

DAY 14: Drive to Candes, where St. Martin died in the year 397. Morning walk on the hills above the Loire and Vienne rivers. Back to Chinon in time to enjoy a stroll down its narrow, medieval streets.

DAY 15: Visit the Loire Valley, "valley of the kings," and the chateaux of Usse-Villandry and Chenonceaux.

DAY 16: Drive to the Fontainebleu forest for a walk and picnic, arrive in Paris in the evening and transfer to hotel.

DAY 17: Free day in Paris.

DAY 18: Depart Paris and connect with homeward-bound flights.

Mountain Travel escort.

France photos by trip leader Rod Buntz

The Ossau Valley, Pyrenees.

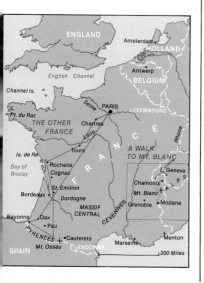

*Trip leader
Pierre Jamet.*

*Castles, lakes and
villages of the
Auvergne region in
central France.*

*Photos by trip leader
Pierre Jamet*

IT5PA1SFMT9

A WALK
IN CENTRAL
FRANCE

*12-day trek across Cevennes and
Chaine des Domes*

DATES: *Jun 7–Jun 22 (16 days)*
LEADER: *Pierre Jamet*
GRADE: *B-2*
LAND COST: *$1190 (9–12 members)*
$1350 (6–8)

This hiking tour travels through
two very beautiful regions in the
heart of central France: Auvergne
and the Cevennes.

Auvergne is a green and pleasant
place with wide upland meadows,
verdant valleys and a mild climate.
Our six-day Auvergne hike takes
us across rolling hills dotted with
fine Romanesque churches, ruins
of medieval castles, and shepherds'
hamlets. In the nearby "Monts
Dore," we venture up to high
crater lakes then along the "Chaine
des Domes," a volcanic range.

Our second six-day hike takes
place in the unspoiled wilderness
of the Cevennes, the lovely region
of long ridges, moors, chestnut
forests and apple orchards traveled
in and written about by Robert
Louis Stevenson in 1878. As we
hike along ridges which form the
watershed between the Atlantic
and the Mediterranean, we'll come
upon ancient hill towns and farming communities which have
changed little in the last 100 years.
Our route eventually leads to the
plateaus and deep gorges of the
Causse Mejean, an environment of
sheer cliffs, natural arches and
rock towers of fantastic shapes.

Most nights will be spent in
hotels, with one night at a farm
and one in a mountain refuge. We
will stop enroute for meals in wayside inns and picnic-style lunches.
We will carry rucksacks weighing
20–25 lbs., depending on personal
gear.

ITINERARY:

DAY 1 and 2: Leave U.S. Arrive
in Paris. Transfer to hotel.

DAY 3: By train to Riom. Overnight at hotel in Tournoel.

DAY 4: Drive to the Col de la
Nugere and begin hike along the
Chaine des Domes, the highest of
which is dome-shaped Puy de
Dome (4,806'). Hike up Puy de
Pariou, visit its crater, then hike
the Puy de Dome for views of the
whole volcanic range. Visit the
ruins of a Roman temple dedicated
to Mercury then hike down the old
Roman road to an old house which
has been converted into a hotel.

DAY 5: Continue southwards
along the Chaine des Domes, hiking
up the twin volcanoes of Lassolas
and La Vache, remarkable for their
large reddish craters. Reach the
village of Saulzetle-Froid where we
will find a hotel.

DAY 6: Hike into the "Monts
Dore," remnants of larger and
much older volcanoes than the
Chaine des Domes. Walk to a little
lake in an ancient crater; climb up
the Puy de Combe Perret and Puy
de l'Ouire. Continue to Le Mont
Dore, a health resort since the time
of the Romans, who appreciated its
hot mineral springs. Nowadays it
is also a winter ski resort.

DAY 7: Up to the Col de la Croix
Saint Robert, passing a waterfall
called "La Grande Cascade," then
along to the spectacular ruins of
the medieval castle of Murol. Overnight in hotel below the castle.

DAY 8: Short walk to Saint-
Nectaire and visit its beautiful
Romanesque church. Drive to
Issoire.

DAY 9: Visit Issoire's Romanesque church and take the train to
Villefort. Overnight in hotel.

DAY 10: Start the Cevennes hike.
From Villefort, hike the long ridge
of Mont Lozere.

DAY 11: Continue along the
ridge and hike over Roc Malpertus,
continuing to the hamlets of Salarial
and l'Hopital. Follow the *draille,* a
shepherds' trail to the hamlet of
L'Aubaret. Overnight in hotel.

DAY 12: Follow the ridge of
Montagne du Bouges to the town
of Florac. Fine views on the various
ridges of the Cevennes.

DAY 13: Climb steeply to the rim
of the Causse Mejean and walk
across this dry chalky plateau to
La Parade where there is a rustic
hotel. The villages in this area are
inhabited by shepherds.

DAY 14: Short walk to Aven
Armand, a beautiful cave. Walk
to the little hamlet of La Viale.
Dinner and overnight in a farm.

DAY 15: Reach the south rim of
the Causse Mejean and hike down
to Le Rozier by a spectacular trail
amidst rocks with fantastic shapes.
At Le Rozier, drive to Millau and
take an overnight train to Paris.

DAY 16: Arrive Paris. Depart
Paris and connect with homeward-
bound flights.

Refuge Bayssellance with Mt. Petite Vignemale on the left.

IT5PA1SFMT9

TREKKING IN THE PYRENEES

Alpine scrambles on the French/Spanish border

DATES: #1 Jun 30–Jul 14 (15 days)
       #2 Sep 1–Sep 15 (15 days)
LEADER: *Pierre Jamet*
GRADE: *B-3*
LAND COST: *$1050 (6–10 members)*

This 11-day trek offers challenging hiking in the beautiful Vallee d'Aspe of the western Pyrenees, part of the French national park system.

One of the great attractions of the Pyrenees, besides the peaks themselves (50 over 10,000 feet), is the large alpine area between tim-

berline and the summits. Timberline is about 6,800 feet and snowline is about 9,000 feet. For those who love to wander through alpine high country at its finest, this is one of the most appealing regions in Europe. The climate favors a wide-ranging and lovely flora, including daffodils and alpine roses.

We'll hike about eight to ten hours a day, carrying rucksacks. Accommodations and meals will be in mountain huts maintained by the French Alpine Club.

The route is almost all on the French side of the frontier, except for two brief crossings into Spain. No technical climbing skills are necessary, but we will cross some snowfields on the passes.

ITINERARY:

DAY 1 and 2: Leave U.S. Arrive Paris. Continue by train to Pau. Transfer to hotel.

DAY 3: Travel to Urdos by train and bus. Overnight at hotel.

DAY 4: Drive down the Valley d'Aspe and begin trek with a long walk over a good trail with gradual elevation gain. Cross Col d'Ayous (7,168′) and descend to the Refuge d'Ayous.

DAY 5: Descend into the Bious Valley (4,900′) and climb steeply to Lac de Peyreget, a delightful spot for lunch. Cross Col de Peyreget

(6,804′) and descend to Refuge de Pombie, with views of the south face of the Pic du Midi d'Ossau, one of the classic climbs of the Pyrenees.

DAY 6: Day for rest or optional hikes.

DAY 7: Descend to the Brousett Valley (4,600′), then climb steeply into the Arrious Valley and eventually to the Col d'Arrious (7,411′) overlooking Lac d'Artouste.

DAY 8: Hike over Col du Palas (8,257′), where we cross into Spain and traverse to the Port du Lavedan (8,597′) and back into France. From here the trail drops past alpine lakes to the Refuge de Larribet (6,758′).

DAY 9: Descend to the Azun Valley (5,100′), then up to Campo Plano (7,043′) and Col de la Fache (8,740′). Overnight at Refuge Wallon. This is a long day's hike (about 10 hours), but there are no refuges in between to stop at.

DAY 10: Rest day at Refuge Wallon.

DAY 11: Climb to the Col d'Arratille, where we enter Spain, then drop into the Ara Valley and traverse to the head of the valley, entering France at the Col des Mulets (8,500′). Continue down to Refuge Oulettes with its inspiring view of the Vignemale (10,820′), a sheer-walled limestone peak with glaciers at its base.

DAY 12: Ascend Hourquette d'Ossoue, a pass at 8,969 feet, and descend to Refuge Bayssellance (8,401′). Optional hikes available in the afternoon.

DAY 13: Take a short trail to the Col de Arraille, and into the Lutour Valley, which we follow down to the town of Cauterets. Overnight in hotel.

DAY 14: Afternoon train to Pau. Overnight at hotel.

DAY 15: Fly to Paris and connect with homeward-bound flights.

Louise and Kili McGowan in the Bious Valley below Lac de Peyreget.

Arthur Battagel in the Gaube Valley below Peak Vignemale, Pyrenees.

Pyrenees photos by Dick McGowan

IT5PA1SFMT9

A WALK TO MONT BLANC

12-day trek in the French Alps

DATES: *Sep 7–Sep 22 (16 days)*
LEADER: *Pierre Jamet*
GRADE: *B-3*
LAND COST: *$1090 (9–12 members)*
$1250 (6–8)

This walk takes place on a stretch of the long *Grand Randonee 5,* a 1300-mile walking route which begins in Holland and ends in Nice on the Mediterranean, but whose most impressive section is in the French Alps.

On our 12-day walk along the *"GR5,"* we'll find beautiful villages, European fellow hikers, clean places to stay and friendly local people to welcome us as we trek toward our destination, the Chamonix Valley at the foot of Mont Blanc in the heart of the French Alps.

We begin in Modane, a town on the French side of a tunnel which connects France and Italy. Enroute, we cross two separate regions: the Beaufortain, a province which has kept its traditional pastoral flavor and is famous for its cheeses (still prepared by shepherds in alpine huts), and the Vanoise, much of which is now a national park where glaciers and high peaks are breathtaking and the wildlife includes herds of rare *bouquetins* and chamois. We'll see views of Mont Blanc, the Matterhorn and Monte Rosa as we approach Chamonix.

Alice Jamet on the Col de la Vanoise (8,257')/ Pierre Jamet

Although the hiking days are not long there are some steep hikes on the route. Our accommodations will be in small wayside inns or mountain refuges. We will carry rucksacks weighing perhaps 20 to 25 lbs. (depending on personal gear).

ITINERARY:

DAY 1 and 2: Leave U.S. Arrive Geneva. Transfer to hotel.

DAY 3: By train to Modane, and hike up to the Refuge de l'Orgere (6,348') on a wooded trail.

DAY 4: Continue above timberline to the Col de Chaviere (9,100') and down to the Refuge de Peclet-Polset.

DAY 5: Climb to the Col du Soufre (9,320'), descend the Gebroulaz Glacier, then up again over Col de Chanrouge (8,303') to Refuge des Lacs Merlet near two little lakes.

DAY 6: Down to about 6,100 feet, then climb steeply up to the Breche de la Porteta (8,694'), a narrow gap between vertical towers and pinnacles of rock. From here,

descend steeply to the ski resort of Pralognan. Beautiful views of the Grande Casse (12,647'), highest summit in the Vanoise, and the Domes de la Vanoise, which are covered by a glacier more than 10 kms. long. Overnight in hotel.

DAY 7: Short hike up to the Col de la Vanoise (8,257'), a beautiful pass. Overnight at mountain refuge.

DAY 8: Over Col de le Leisse (9,048'), steep descent, then up again to Col du Palet (8,700'). Overnight at mountain refuge.

DAY 9: Short detour for a beautiful view of the steep northern face of the Grande Casse, then down the valley of the Ponturin to Landry (2,559'). Overnight in hotel.

DAY 10: Cross the valley of the Isere River and hike to the hamlet of Forand. Overnight at Refuge de la Balme (6,591').

DAY 11: Rest day or hikes in the area. Weather permitting, climb the Pointe de Combe Neuve (9,714'), an easy non-technical climb with a beautiful view of all the summits in the North Alps, including the Matterhorn and Monte Rosa in the distance.

DAY 12: Upwards to the Lac de Presset (8,202') and Col du Grand Fond (8,694'), down the valley of Combe Neuve, straight towards Mont Blanc, then traverse the wide-open pass of the Cormet de Roselend to the Refuge du Plan de la Laie (6,069').

DAY 13: Up green pastures to Col du Bonhomme and traverse down to the village of Les Contamines (3,805'), a ski resort.

DAY 14: Up to the Col de Voza (5,423'), below which lies the Chamonix Valley, on the north side of Mont Blanc. Descend to Les Houches and proceed to Chamonix. Overnight in hotel.

DAY 15: Morning free in Chamonix. Afternoon train to Geneva. Overnight in hotel.

DAY 16: Depart Geneva and connect with homeward-bound flights.

IT4SR1MT01

SCRAMBLES IN THE ALPS

Classic climbs on the Haute Route

DATES: *Aug 3–Aug 24 (22 days)*
LEADER: *to be announced*
GRADE: *D-2*
LAND COST: *$2650 (5–9 members)*

On this mountaineering journey, we will attempt to climb some of the most famous peaks of the Swiss and French Alps, including the Matterhorn and Mont Blanc.

Flying to Geneva, we drive directly to a camp at Arolla (6,560') and have a day for checking out our techniques and gear on some local glaciers and peaks.

We then traverse hut-to-hut for five days across peaks, passes and glaciers of the Pennine Alps—the classic route of the alpine "Golden Age," beneath such striking mountains as the Dent Blanche (14,295'), which we will attempt. We descend into Zermatt, the most well-known mountain resort in the world, nestled at the foot of the Matterhorn.

Based in the mountains above Zermatt for the next five days, we will attempt an ascent of the Matterhorn (14,962'), then drive across the border to Chamonix, France.

Little needs to be added to the wealth of material written about the Chamonix-Mont Blanc area. It is one of the world's great climbing places and the birthplace of mountaineering. Here in the Mont Blanc Range we will attempt the Aiquille Chardonnet (12,546') and Mont Blanc (15,771'), the highest point in Europe west of the Caucasus.

NOTE: As on all mountaineering expeditions, weather and snow conditions will determine our exact itinerary. Given a good climbing party and good luck with the weather, the following program is what we hope to accomplish.

Cabine du Mont Fort, Switzerland/Susan Thiel

Descending from Col Riedmatten/Susan Thiele

ITINERARY:

DAY 1 and 2: Leave U.S. Arrive Geneva. Drive to Arolla. Overnight in hotel.

DAY 3: Climbing practice above Arolla.

DAY 4: Trek to Vignettes Hut. Snow and ice climbing seminar enroute. Overnight at hut.

DAY 5: 4 a.m. start for a climb of L'Eveque, a fine snow and ice peak. Overnight at hut.

DAY 6: 3 a.m. start for ascent of Pigne D'Arolla and traverse to Mt. Blanc D'Cheilon, a fine high level route. Descend to Cabane Dix. Overnight at hut.

DAY 7: Traverse the Pas D'Chevres and descend through beautiful flower-filled alpine pastures to Arolla. Overnight at hotel.

DAY 8: Leave Arolla for Ferpecle and ascend to the Dent Blanche Hut.

DAY 9: 3 a.m. start for ascent of Dent Blanche, one of the finest and most sought-after climbs in the Alps. Return to Dent Blanche Hut.

DAY 10: Ascend Tete Blanche and descend the Tiefmatten Glacier to the Stokje and Schonbuhl Hut.

DAY 11: Descend to Zermatt via Zmutt. Overnight at hotel.

DAY 12: In and around Zermatt. Local sightseeing and walks.

DAY 13: Walk to the Hornli Hut beneath the Matterhorn.

DAY 14: Local hikes around Schwartzsee. Overnight at hut.

DAY 15: Ascend Matterhorn (weather permitting). Descend to hut.

DAY 16: Descend to Zermatt and continue to Chamonix. Overnight at hotel.

DAY 17: Ascend to the Grand Mulettes Hut. Overnight at hut.

DAY 18: 1 a.m. start for the ascent of Mont Blanc (weather permitting). Traverse Aiguille and the Dome D'Gouter. Descend to the Tete Rouse Hut.

DAY 19: Descend to Chamonix. Afternoon free. Overnight at hotel.

DAY 20: Climb the Aiguille L'M and descend to Chamonix. Overnight at hotel.

DAY 21: A day of rock climbing at the Guillands and local sightseeing. Overnight at hotel.

DAY 22: Travel to Geneva. Depart Geneva and connect with homeward-bound flights.

On the Hornli Ridge of the Matterhorn, one of the most popular climbs in the Alps. This was the route used by alpinist Edward Whymper in his historic first ascent of the Matterhorn in 1865. Whymper's book about his climbs Scrambles In The Alps, is a classic of mountaineering literature/John Noble

Trekking toward the Trient Glacier, Switzerland/Susan Thiele

IT4SR1MT05

HIKING IN THE SWISS ALPS

12-day trek in the Bernese Alps

DATES: *Aug 20–Sep 4 (16 days)*
LEADER: *to be announced*
GRADE: *B-3*
LAND COST: *$1190 (6–12 members)*

The Swiss Alps are often perceived as terrain for the intrepid mountain climber yet these Alps are laced with literally thousands of miles of beautiful, well-marked trails which any experienced hiker can enjoy.

Our 12-day walk across the Swiss Alps takes place in the Bernese Oberland, a spectacular group of mountains which presents a well-defined wall overlooking the Swiss lowlands and the plains of northwest Europe and is thus known as the "North Face of the Alps."

Enroute, we see some of Switzerland's most famous peaks, including the Monch (13,401'), Jungfrau (11,401'), and the notorious Eiger (13,025'), whose formidable 5,000-foot north face has challenged and tragically defeated many climbers over the years.

We also hike to the villages of Murren (an unspoiled spot which can only be reached on foot or by train), Kliene Scheidegg, which lies beneath both the Eiger and Jungfrau, and finally to Grindelwald, the "glacier village" which is the popular climbing center of this part of Switzerland.

Enroute we stay in dorm-style alpine mountain huts and carry rucksacks weighing perhaps 20–25 lbs. (depending on personal gear).

ITINERARY:

DAY 1 and 2: Leave U.S. Arrive Geneva. By train and bus to the village of Lenk.

DAY 3: Acclimatization and local walks.

DAY 4: Begin trekking through alpine scenery including Wildstrubel (10,640') and Wildhorn (10,656'). Cross the Ammertengrat Pass, viewing the Ammerten Glacier which flows from Wildstrubel's northwest face, ending at the village of Engstligenalp.

DAY 5: Rest day.

DAY 6: Skirt the northern slopes of Felsenhorn before striking south along the western shore of Daubensee, a large alpine lake. Hike over Gemmipass and descend into the Valais, ending at Leukerbad.

DAY 7: To Torrentalp and Torrenthorn.

DAY 8: Long walk to Selden via the Restipass (7,742') and the Lotschenpass.

DAY 9: Short walk to Kandersteg for lunch and continue to Oeschinsee, an alpine lake with impressive cliffs along its southeastern shore.

DAY 10: Steep hike along a cliff trail with fine views of the lake hundreds of feet below it. Climb rocky paths to the Blumlisalp Alpine Hut.

DAY 11: Cross Hohturli Pass (9,114'), with superb views of the valley below to the north. Descend to Oberer Bundalp, a tiny settlement situated on a gentle mountain slope with magnificent views.

DAY 12: Descend through woodland to Grissalp and hike up Sefinenfurke Pass (8,569'), enjoying fine views of Blumlisalphorn and the Hohturli. Descend to Boganggen, a small farmstead set in grassy meadows and continue to Murren.

DAY 13: Murren (5,413') is virtually unspoiled since motor vehicles are not allowed within its precincts. Situated on a sheltered sunny plateau, this delightful spot nestles beneath Schilthorn (9,744'), while around it lie the majestic peaks of Jungfrau, the Monch and the Eiger. Descend through one of the most photogenic sections of our walk, passing through Lauterbrunnen on the way to Kleine Scheidegg (6,672'), a village lying beneath both the Eiger and Jungfrau. There can be few places more spectacularly situated than this! It is a popular tourist spot by virtue of its location, but is nevertheless a town not to be missed.

DAY 14: Kleine Scheidegg lies on the Jungfrau Railway, highest railway in Europe and third highest in the world. We take a ride on it to Jungfraujoch (11,401'), lying between Jungfrau and the Monch.

DAY 15: Walk through alpine pastures and descend to Grindelvald (3,392'), situated in a broad lush valley surrounded by mighty alpine peaks.

DAY 16: By train to Geneva and connect with homeward-bound flights.

IT4SR1MT03

TREKKING THE HAUTE ROUTE

Backpacking traverse from Chamonix to Zermatt

DATES: *#1 Jul 9–Jul 24 (16 days)*
       #2 Aug 5–Aug 20 (16 days)
LEADER: *#1: Rory Edwards*
       #2: to be announced
GRADE: *B-3*
LAND COST: *$1190 (6–12 members)*

No region is more steeped in mountaineering lore than the "Haute Route," a high-level traverse which crosses the Alps between Chamonix, France and Zermatt, Switzerland. Along this route rise ten of the twelve highest peaks in the Alps, including the Matterhorn and Monte Rosa. It was here that the sport of mountaineering, a phenomenon of 19th century Europe, was born.

In the winter, the "Haute Route" is the finest ski tour in Europe; in summer it presents one of the most spectacular hikes in all the Alps.

Besides traveling much of the famed Haute Route, our trekking route covers some rarely-visited parts of the Swiss Valais, crossing high passes of true alpine character and meandering into charming villages where the style of farming has remained unchanged for centuries. Most of the trails are relatively untrodden, giving excellent opportunity to see a variety of alpine flowers and wildlife.

From the Chamonix Valley, we cross the northern part of the French side of the Mont Blanc Massif via the Col de Balme into Switzerland. The remainder of our trek will be in Switzerland, concluding at the famous alpine resort of Zermatt, where we spend a few days enjoying outstanding day walks.

Wherever possible, accommodations will be in mountain refuges, to maintain the high mountain ambiance. There is one three-day section of self-contained backpacking, and on most other hiking days, we carry rucksacks weighing perhaps 20–25 lbs. (depending on personal gear).

ITINERARY:

DAY 1 and 2: Leave U.S. Arrive Geneva and continue by train to Chamonix. Overnight in hotel.

DAY 3: Day free in Chamonix. Optional excursions such as the cable car ride up to Aiguille du Midi (11,526') for views of Mont Blanc.

DAY 4: Train to Argentiere and begin trek amongst fields of alpine flowers. Cross Col de Balme

Village of Grimentz/Susan Thiele

7,230') with panoramic views of
he Mont Blanc massif. Descend to
rient.

DAY 5: Steep hike to the Fenetre
'Arpett (8,743'), and long descent
o the resort of Realis d'Arpette.

DAY 6: Descend to Champex, a
harming village with its lakeside
etting. Sightsee and prepare for
hree-day backpacking trip. By
us, train and cable car then hike
Cabane Mt. Fort (8,061), an
lpine hut with impressive views of
Mont Fort and the Grand Combin.

DAY 7: Steep, cross-country hike
cross the Col du Gele (9,200'), one
f the most remote areas of the
lps. Descend and hike to Refuge
t. Laurent with views of Rosa-
lanche. We cook our own dinner
the refuge tonight.

DAY 8: Steep ascent over Col de
rafleuri (9,728'), a remote area
ith panoramic views of Mont
lanc de Cheelon and Pigne
'Arolla. Overnight at Cabane Pra-
euri, a rustic mountain hut where
e cook our dinner.

DAY 9: Descend to Lac des Dix
nen ascend the long route to the
ol de Riedmatten (9,577') for the
rst view of the Matterhorn before
ermatt. Magnificent views across
ne Val d'Arolla to the Dent Blanche
nd Mont Collon. Overnight in
rolla.

DAY 10: Free day in Arolla.

DAY 11: Bus to Les Hauderes
nd taxi to Villa, seeing local Valais
omen still wearing traditional
ress as they tend their fields.
like up Col de Torrent (9,574'),
ith spectacular views of Val
'Arens and Val Moiry. Descend to
rimentz, an extremely charming
ld Valais town.

DAY 12: Walk via Ayers to
abane de Weisshorn, superbly
ocated with beautiful panoramic
iews.

DAY 13: Walk over Meidpass
),154'), then enter German-
peaking Switzerland. Long descent
 Gruben.

DAY 14: Climb up to Augstbord-
ass (9,495'), highest in our route.
escend to Jungu and take the
ible car to St. Niklaus and train
 Zermatt.

DAY 15: In Zermatt, with its
onderful panorama of mountain
eaks and many excellent walks.

DAY 16: Morning train to Geneva
nd connect with homeward-bound
ights.

IT4SR1MT05

SKIING THE HAUTE ROUTE

*The most famous ski tour in
the world*

DATES: *Apr 21–May 4 (14 days)*
LEADER: *to be announced*
GRADE: *B-3*
LAND COST: *$1390 (8–10 members)*

This is the most famous ski
tour in the world, the "Haute
Route," a high level traverse of
eleven glacier passes between the
greatest peaks of the Alps.

Among its many attractions are
unbelievably beautiful winter views
of the snowy backbone of Europe,
including the Matterhorn, Monte
Rosa, Mont Blanc and other great
peaks of the Alps.

The classic "Haute Route" tour
starts near Chamonix and ends near
Saas Fee. It can be completed in
about a week, but we have allowed
several extra days to adjust for
weather conditions and make possible ascents along the route, according to members' abilities.

Alpine skiing experience or
strong parallel skiing technique on
downhill skis is required. We will
cover about 75 miles, most of it at
an altitude of 10,000 feet.

ITINERARY:

DAY 1 and 2: Leave U.S. Arrive
Geneva and continue by train to
Chamonix. Overnight in pension.

DAY 3: Check equipment, practice avalanche procedures and generally tone up for ski mountaineering. Overnight in pension at
Chamonix.

DAY 4: By cableway to a point
just below the summit of the
Aiguille des Grand Montets, then
descend via the Rognons Glacier to
the Argentiere Glacier. Ski up to
Argentiere Hut.

DAY 5: A strenuous day, crossing
part of another popular ski route,
the Tour de Trois Cols ("Three Col
Traverse") via the Plateau du
Trient. Overnight at Trient Hut.

DAY 6: Ski down Trient Glacier
to the Fenetre du Chamonix and
the Col des Ecandies, further down
into the Val d'Arpette, then Champex. On certain sections we may
require the use of a rope to cross
bergschrunds.

DAY 7 and 8: Via the Valsorey or
Mont Fort huts, as dictated by the
prevailing weather and snow conditions.

DAY 9: Climb the Pigne d'Arolla
enroute to the Vignettes Hut.
Superb views of the Dent Blanch
and surrounding peaks.

DAY 10: Spectacular Haute
Route scenery as we cross Col de
l'Eveque, Col du Mont Brule, Col
de Valpelline and finally the long
descent beneath the Matterhorn
into Zermatt. Overnight at hotel.

DAY 11: Rest day or ski ascent
of the Breithorn, in part by uphill
ski lifts.

DAY 12: From the Monte Rosa
Hut we are among the highest con-
glomeration of 4,000-meter peaks
in the Alps, all accessible to the ski
mountaineer.

DAY 13: To Saas Fee via the
Adler Pass. Depending on condi-
tions, we stay at Britannia Hut or
Sass Fee.

DAY 14: By train to Geneva.
Depart on homeward-bound flights.

*The "Haute Route,"
the classic alpine ski
tour. We will cover
about 75 miles, most of
it at altitudes of about
10,000 feet/
John Noble*

Chalet Hotel De La Balm on the way to Col Du Bonhomme, Mont Blanc, France.

IT4SR1MT02

THE MONT BLANC CIRCUIT

12-day trek in French, Swiss and Italian Alps

DATES: #1 Jun 22–Jul 6 (15 days)
       #2 Jul 13–Jul 27 (15 days)
       #3 Aug 10–Aug 24 (15 days)
       #4 Aug 30–Sep 13 (15 days)
LEADER: #1: Shanan Miller
       #2, 3, 4: to be announced
GRADE: B-2
LAND COST: $1190 (6–12 members)

This is one of the world's great walks, a complete circuit around Mont Blanc, highest peak in Europe.

The classic *tour du Mont Blanc* takes about twelve days. The trail passes in and out of France, Italy and Switzerland. Views enroute make it a photographer's dream, with a background of tumbling glaciers and famous peaks like the Aiguille du Midi, Les Grandes Jorasses, and Mont Dolanot.

Mont Blanc (15,771′) presents an 11,000-foot flank of Himalayan scale and grandeur on the Italian side; the French flank is less steep but higher still. From this massif, seven valleys extend into France, Italy and Switzerland. Each of these alpine countries has its own unique culture, architecture and landscape. In circling Mont Blanc, we pass from one to the other and take time to enjoy their individual delights amidst alpine scenery which has few equals in the world.

This is a vehicle-supported trek,

so we only need to carry small day packs. We'll camp each night, either in our own camps or at organized camping areas with shower facilities. This makes us independent of local mountain refuges, which can be crowded. Daily hiking time is about five hours.

ITINERARY:

DAY 1 and 2: Leave U.S. Arrive Geneva, take the train to Martigny and camp.

DAY 3: Short bus ride to Champex and begin trek, crossing Col Bovine (6,519′) and Col de Forclaz to camp beneath the Trient Glacier at La Peuty, Switzerland.

DAY 4: We cross into France via the Col de Balme (7,188′), with first views of the entire Mont Blanc massif and the Glacier du Tour. Walk or take cable car to Le Tour. Visit Argentiere in the afternoon and see the Glacier d'Argentiere.

DAY 5: Via Tre le Champ, we make a detour to the scenic Lac Blanc (7,716′) before rejoining the Grand Balcon route, which looks across the Chamonix Valley toward Mont Blanc. Descend via cable car to Les Plaz de Chamonix and camp.

Looking toward Mont Blanc and the "Glacier des Bossons" across the Chamonix Valley.

Bionassay Glacier torrent, Mont Blanc, Chamonix, France

Mont Blanc photos by Susan Thiele

Dent Du Geant, Aiguilles de Chamonix and Mont Blanc from Brevent.

DAY 6: Rest day in Chamonix. Possible excursions include a ride the famed cable car up to the Aiguille du Midi (11,526′) for views Mont Blanc, or the cog railway rectly to the edge of Mer de lace, a glacier of Alaskan proortions. Return to camp.

DAY 7: We rejoin the trail at La legere, using the cable car, and ontinue along the Grand Balcon to e Col de Brevent (8,284′), one of e high points of the tour with ce-to-face views of the Mer de lace and Bossons glaciers. This is longish day, but offers some of e trip's finest views. Descend Les Houches where there are xcellent camping facilities.

DAY 8: Cable car to Hotel Belleue (5,906′), walk right under the out of the Bionassey Glacier to ol Tricot (6,955′), descend to the halets de Miage and then hike ver Truc before descending rough forest to the charming wn of Les Contamines. Camp ear the old chapel of Notre Dame e La Gorge.

DAY 9: Make a long ascent to ol du Bonhomme (7,641′), stop at refuge for tea, then descend to hapieux, one of the most attracve campsites of the trek.

DAY 10: Over Col de la Seigne ,245′) into Italy, where a van will ke us to camp in the Val Veni, ast of Courmayeur. On the way e catch views of the spectacular lacier du Miage.

DAY 11: Rest day in Courmayeur eneath the Grand Jorasses and lanpansier Glacier.

DAY 12: By van to road's end nd walk up a track past the classic lacier de Pre de Bar which spills own from Mont Dolent. Cross ither the Petit or Grand Col Fert to re-enter Switzerland and proeed to the excellent Swiss campte of La Fouly (5,230′) beneath e Glacier de l'A Neuve.

DAY 13: Optional hikes or rest ay.

DAY 14: As a climax to the trek, tter members of the party can limb to the Cab D'Ornay (8,799′) n their return to Martigny. Others an take an easier route through e Swiss Val Ferret, one of the veliest hikes of the trip, through rests and fields alive with wildowers, through the charming illages of Praz de Fost and Les rlaches. Overnight at hotel in Martigny.

DAY 15: Train to Geneva and onnect with homeward-bound ights.

IT4SR1MT06

SKI HOLIDAY IN SWITZERLAND

Cross-country touring for gourmets

DATES: *#1 Jan 25–Feb 3 (10 days)*
#2 Feb 15–Feb 24 (10 days)
LEADER: *to be announced*
GRADE: *B-2*
LAND COST: *$990 (8–15 members)*

Some of the best ski touring in Europe is found in Switzerland's beautiful Jura Mountains, a region of forested hills along the Swiss/French border, stretching from north of Geneva to just south of Basel.

The Juras form a barrier between France and the western cantons of Switzerland and are relatively unknown to all but a few knowledgeable Swiss nordic skiers. Well-marked cross country ski trails run across the Jura hills through quiet forests and rural villages.

Little country inns and restaurants dot the area, making ideal spots to stop for a leisurely meal during the day's ski tour. The ambiance is a pleasant mixture of French and Swiss and the food is delicious. The area is known for country specialties like smoked ham and goat cheese.

Lunch, ("midi") is a relaxing affair in this part of Switzerland, typically consisting of hot soup, wine, perhaps some local trout or special cheese, and a fresh baguette. It makes a nice break after a hard morning of skiing. Our nightly accommodations will be comfortable and clean inns which serve hearty meals.

Each day's ski tour will be about five hours (or longer, if you want to ski side trails after reaching the evening's hotel).

While we are skiing from village to village, our baggage will be transported separately, leaving us free to enjoy skiing unencumbered by a heavy pack.

The skiing is on prepared nordic trails and the terrain is moderate enough for beginners and varied enough for experts (who will find challenging trails equal to any in Scandinavia or North America).

ITINERARY:

DAY 1 and 2: Leave U.S. Arrive Geneva mid-morning. By train to Moutier, a typical Jura mountain town surrounded by forests.

DAY 3: Short train ride to the Franche Montagnes plateau and the main ski route, the "Piste du Haut-Plateau." Ski for several hours on rolling terrain, stop for leisurely lunch and continue to Cerneux-au-Marie.

DAY 4: Ski to the little village of Le Boeche, then continue after lunch to Les Barriers, skiing across many small ridges and down into isolated valleys where the ski trails traverse family farms.

DAY 5: Continue towards the Doubs Valley. Lunch at La Pautelle. Overnight at Saignelegier.

DAY 6: A fairly long day across the plateau to Les Rouge Terres and the original center of the area, Montfaucon, which has buildings dating back to the 14th century.

DAY 7: Ski along at an elevation of about 3,000 feet, alternately crossing deserted forests and small villages. In addition to the main "randonee" route, there is a training track at Genevez. Overnight at Breuleux.

DAY 8: Tour up Mont Soleil (4,235′) for magnificent views across Switzerland to the Alps (including the Eiger, Jungfrau, Matterhorn and Mont Blanc on clear days). Return to Les Breuleux.

DAY 9: Ski south to La Chaux Fonds, a fairly long tour that can be shortened, if you want, by riding a tiny train part of the way into Chaux Fonds, a picturesque small town and one of the watch making centers of Switzerland.

DAY 10: By train to Geneva and connect with homeward-bound flights.

Winter in the Jura Mountains, Switzerland. While we ski from village to village, our baggage will be transported separately, leaving us free to ski unencumbered by a heavy pack.

IT5PA1SFMT10

BAVARIA WALKING TOUR

Easy day hikes in Germany

DATES: *Jun 7–Jun 24 (18 days)*
LEADER: *Wolfgang and Renate Koch*
GRADE: *A-1*
LAND COST: *$1575*
(12–14 members)
$1675 (8–11)

This tour visits the hidden valleys and rural villages of Bavaria, where the mountain lifestyle hasn't changed greatly in centuries.

Based in Garmisch for the first few days, we'll take day hikes into the surrounding mountains and ascend the Zugspitze (10,000'), Germany's highest peak, by cable car.

From Berchtesgaden, with its typical Bavarian architecture, we'll take some leisurely walks to high viewpoints, cross Konigsee (the most beautiful alpine lake in Germany) and visit St. Bartholomew's Monastery. In Austria, we'll visit the city of Salzburg.

Continuing into more rural and little-traveled parts of Bavaria, we'll spend several days on leisurely hikes in Bayerischer Wald National Park and Altmuhltal National Park.

Travel will be by van with accommodations in Bavarian-style pensions or castles.

ITINERARY:

DAY 1 and 2: Leave U.S. Arrive Munich. Continue to Garmisch.

DAY 3: Ascend Zugspitze, Germany's highest peak, by cable car. Return to hotel in Garmisch.

DAY 4: Day hike to Hollental Hut through Hollentalklamm, a narrow gulch with wonderful views of the Wetterstein peaks. Return to Garmisch for overnight.

DAY 5: Travel to Berchtesgaden along lovely Bavarian lakes such as Walchensee, Tegernsee and Chiemsee. Visit Herren-Chiemsee Castle enroute. Overnight in Berchtesgaden.

DAY 6: Day hike from Konigsee to Kuhroint Hut with great views of Watzmann Peak. Steep descent to St. Bartholomew Monastery and return to Berchtesgaden by boat across Konigsee Lake.

DAY 7: Travel to Ramsau and hike to Blaueis Hut and Schartenspitze Peak, with views of the Blaueis Glacier and Hochkalter. Return to Berchtesgaden.

DAY 8: Day trip to Salzburg. Return to Berchtesgaden.

DAY 9: Travel to Passau via Burghausen, stopping to visit the fort at Burghausen and Alotting, a famous pilgrimage site. Overnight in hotel at Passau.

DAY 10: Visit Passau and environs. Overnight at hotel.

DAY 11: Travel to Neuschonau. Afternoon hike in Bayerischer Walk National Park. Overnight in hotel.

DAY 12: Travel to Racheldienst Hut via Rachelsee, a pretty alpine lake. Continue by mini-bus to Spiegelhutte. Overnight at a pension.

DAY 13: Day hike to Falkenstein Peak via Hollbachgespreng. Return to pension at Spiegelhutte.

DAY 14: Travel to Kelheim (Altmuhltal National Park), visiting Walhalla and Regensburg. Overnight at hotel.

DAY 15: Day hike to Befreiungshalle and the monastery at Weltenburg. Return to Kelheim via a boatride on the Danube. Overnight at hotel.

DAY 16: Day hike from Schulerloch, a stalagtite-draped cavern with prehistoric wall paintings. Return to Kelheim. Overnight at hotel.

DAY 17: Drive through the Altmuhltal, with its historic villages, and arrive in Munich. Farewell dinner at the Hofbrauhaus. Overnight at hotel.

DAY 18: Depart Munich on homeward-bound flights.

IT5PA1SFMT10

ALPINE TREKS IN BAVARIA & TYROL

Hiking the mountains of Berchtesgaden and Karwendel

DATES: *#1 Jul 7–Jul 22 (16 days)*
#2 Sep 6–Sep 21 (16 days)
LEADER: *Wolfgang and Renate Koch*
GRADE: *B-2*
LAND COST: *$1190 (12–14 members)*
$1395 (8–11)

This journey combines alpine trekking with visits to some of the prettiest mountain towns in Germany and Austria.

From Innsbruck, Austria's most famous alpine center, we will trek for five days through the Karwendel Mountains, a region with lovely alpine flora and fine peaks, Ending at Achensee, we drive through green alpine valleys to Berchtesgaden, famed for its landscape and romantic Bavarian architecture.

In the high mountains around Berchtesgaden, we make a four-day alpine trek which takes us over Watzmann Peak and to St. Bartholoma, a monastery on Lake Konigsee. We'll boat across the lake back to Berchtesgaden and end the trip with a visit to Salzburg.

ITINERARY:

DAY 1 and 2: Leave U.S. Arrive Munich. Drive to Innsbruck. Overnight at hotel.

DAY 3: Acclimatizing and visiting historic parts of Innsbruck, including the site of the Olympic winter games. Overnight at hotel.

DAY 4: Five-day trek through the Karwendel Mountains, beginning with a ride by cog railway to Hungerburg. Continue via Pfeis Hut to the Halleranger Hut for overnight.

DAY 5: A long hike and climb of the peak of Birkarspitze (9,100'), descending to the Karwendel Hut for overnight.

Weltenburg Abbey on the Danube / Wolfgang Koch

The Karwendel Mountains, a non-glaciated range of rock crags and alpine meadows, are ideally suited for walking / Wolfgang Koch

Trip leader Wolfgang Koch in the Eastern Alps.

DAY 6: Trek through a region with lovely alpine flora to Falken Hut, with views of the rock climbing area of Lalliderer Walls. Overnight at Falken Hut.

DAY 7: Continue trekking over the peak of Lamsenspitze. Overnight at Lamsenjoch Hut.

DAY 8: Descend to Achensee and enjoy a refreshing swim in the lake. Overnight at hotel.

DAY 9: Travel to Berchtesgaden with a short visit to Kitzbuhl, one of the most famous ski resorts in Europe. Overnight in hotel.

DAY 10: Tour Berchtesgaden.

DAY 11: Four-day trek through the Berchtesgaden Mountains. Hike up Watzmann Peak via Wimbachklamm, a narrow valley with impressive water cascades. Overnight at Watzmann Hut.

DAY 12: Day hike up some of the main peaks of Watzmann, with breathtaking views down the steep rock faces of the Eastern Alps. The altitude is about 6,600 feet. Overnight at Wimbachgries Hut.

DAY 13: Short hike to Karlinger Hut with time to relax and enjoy the scenery along the way.

DAY 14: Hike to St. Bartholomew Monastery at Konigsee, the most beautiful alpine lake in Germany. Sample the beer brewed at the monastery, then boat across to Berchtesgaden.

DAY 15: We end our journey with a tour of Salzburg then proceed to Munich. Dinner in the world famous Hofbrauhaus. Overnight in hotel.

DAY 16: Depart Munich on homeward-bound flights.

Dolomites, Italy/
Dick McGowan

IT5PA1SFMT10

EASTERN ALPS CLIMBING CIRCUIT

Non-technical ascents of highest peaks in Germany, Austria, Italy

DATES: *Aug 4–Aug 25 (22 days)*
LEADER: *Wolfgang and Renate Koch*
GRADE: *B-3/D-1*
LAND COST: *$1490 (10–13 members)*
$1755 (8–9)

This trip visits the major mountain areas of the Eastern Alps for hut-to-hut trekking and easy, non-technical ascents of the three highest points within Germany, Austria and Italy.

Traveling to the German mountain town of Garmisch, we trek for five days on a circuit through the Wetterstein Mountains. Our route takes us past Schachenhaus (an old castle at the very top of a peak) and along narrow valleys with impressive waterfalls. During the trek, we'll hike up the Zugspitze (10,000′), Germany's highest peak.

Traveling to Vent, a highland village in Austria, we trek for four days in the Otzaler Alps, with an ascent of Wildspitze (12,850′), the highest peak in Austria.

Crossing the border into Italy, we'll visit the famed Dolomites for some trekking and a climb of Ortler (13,016′), highest peak within Italy.

This circuit is for strong hikers or mountaineers (it is not intended as a technical mountaineering trip). Transport will be by van, with accommodations in pensions and mountain refuges.

ITINERARY:

DAY 1 and 2: Leave U.S. Arrive Munich. Continue to Garmisch.

DAY 3: Tour Garmisch then begin trek through Wettersteingebirge with an easy walk through the Hollentalklamm, a narrow valley. Overnight at Hollental Hut.

DAY 4: Ascend Zugspitze, Germany's highest peak. Overnight at hut.

DAY 5: Descend to Oberreintal and overnight at Schachen Hut.

DAY 6: Climb the Dreitorspitze (8,960′), located in a famous rock climbing area. Overnight at Schachen Hut.

DAY 7: Descend to Garmisch via Partnachklamm. Overnight at hotel.

DAY 8: Drive to Fernsteinsee, a lovely lake, and continue through the Otztal region to Vent, a little highland village and starting point for our four-day trek in the Otzalter Alps. Overnight at hotel.

DAY 9: Easy hike to Martin-Busch Hut. Overnight at hut.

DAY 10: Climb Saukogel (11,900′), descend by crossing the Hochjoch Glacier to Hochjochhospiz. Overnight at hut.

DAY 11: Hike via the Wurzburger Hut to Breslauer Hut for overnight.

DAY 12: Climb Wildspize (12,850′) via Mitterkar Glacier and descend to Vent. Overnight at hotel.

DAY 13: Leaving Austria today, we drive to Grodner Joch in Italy via Timmelsjoch Pass. Overnight at hut.

DAY 14: After climbing the breathtakingly steep Pisciadu Route, which winds up the Exner Tower, we reach Pisciadu Hut. Continue to the bottom of the clefted Sella peaks to Bamberger Hut for overnight.

DAY 15: Trek to Pordoi Joch, after crossing the peaks of Piz Boe (10,400′) and Pordoispitze (9,850′). Overnight at Sella Joch Hut, magnificently situated between the Sella towers and Langkofel.

DAY 16: From Langkofelscharte, which we reach by cable car, we descend to Langkofel Hut and hike up the Oskar Schuster Route to climb Plattkofel (9,880′). Return to Sella Joch Hut.

DAY 17: Travel to Trafoi via Bozen and Meran. Overnight at hotel.

DAY 18 and 19: On our last trek, we return to the world of snow and glaciers. Ascend to Payer Hut for overnight, and cross glaciers to Ortler (13,016′), highest peak in the Eastern Alps. The descent follows the same route. Overnight again at Payer Hut.

DAY 20: Return to Trafoi. Overnight at hotel.

DAY 21: Drive via the spectacular Stilfser Joch Pass to Lake Como and arrive in Milan.

DAY 22: Depart Milan on homeward-bound flights.

The Cima Grande De Lavaredo, the most famous Dolomite wall.

IT4LH131A

THE DOLOMITES TREK

11-day trek in the spectacular South Tyrol

DATES: #1 Jul 20–Aug 3 (15 days)
　　　 #2 Aug 10–Aug 24 (15 days)
LEADER: #3: Enrico Bertolini
　　　　 #2: to be announced
GRADE: B-3
LAND COST: $1450 (8–12 members)
　　　　　　$1560 (5–7)

Although the mountains of the Dolomites are not exceptionally high (the highest peak is 10,965-foot Mt. Marmolada), they are among the most striking mountains in Europe, steep spires of fantastic form colored in weathered hues of rose, yellow and grey.

Below the "fairytale" spires and dramatic walls lie bright green meadows alive with wildflowers all summer. In the lower valleys, there are orchards, vineyards and a checkerboard of cultivated fields.

Continuously sheer cliffs flank most of the Dolomite's peaks. The great mountaineers of the 1920's and 1930's practiced the emerging sport of rock climbing on these cliffs, forging routes which remain classics to this day.

The name Dolomites is generally considered to include all the lime-stone mountains of the Alto Adige, Trentino and Veneto, a region favored with sunny, dry weather.

Up until World War I, this was part of the Austrian South Tyrol. The present-day people of the Dolomites speak their own special patois (Ladin) as well as Italian and German.

Our nights will be in traditional mountain "refuges," often spectacularly situated and offering rustic dorm-style accommodations.

Visits are also included to Verona (city of Romeo and Juliet) and Milan.

Dolomites cow inspecting Dick McGowan.

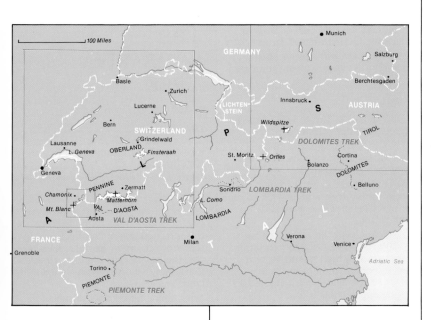

Lunch at a typical Italian mountain inn.

Dolomites photos by Dick and Louise McGowan

View of the Cristallo peaks while crossing Prato Piazza Plateau to 6,500 feet on the way to the luxurious Hotel Hohe Gaisl.

ITINERARY:

DAY 1 and 2: Leave U.S. Arrive Milan. Overnight at hotel.

DAY 3: Drive to Cornuda, cross Duran Pass (5,249′) and arrive at the Hotel San Sebastiano, a little mountain inn.

DAY 4: Begin 11-day trek, starting at Duran Pass and reaching Refuge Vazzoler (5,623′). The walk takes us along the base of the huge rock faces of the 10,500-foot Civetta Range, known by rock climbers all over the world.

DAY 5: Hike to Refuge Sonnino at Coldai (7,979′), along the foot of the northwest face of Civetta.

DAY 6: Hike to Refuge Palmieri (6,692′).

DAY 7: Walk through woods and meadows of the Ampezzo Valley to Refuge San Marco (4,855′), with its exceptional views of the 10,400-foot Pelmo massif.

DAY 8: Early start to hike up Forcella Grande for views of Torre Dei Sabbioni, Sorapis (10,515′), Marmarole (9,714′), and Antelao (10,705′). Descend the Sanvito Valley through the Somadid Nature Reserve, an ancient forest where the Serene Ventian Republic drew timbers for the masts of its vessels. Overnight at Hotel Palus San Marco (3,608′).

DAY 9: Rest day or local hikes in Palus San Marco.

DAY 10: Hike to Refuge Fonda Savio (7,775′), crossing the Cadin Del Nevaio Saddle, an 8,500-foot pass with wide-ranging views of the Dolomites.

DAY 11: Hike to Refuge Locatelli (7,972′), following a trail to Refuge Lavaredo at the base of the three summits called Tre Cime De Lavaredo (9,842′), the most famous rock trinity in the Alps. Tonight's refuge has superb views of the north faces of the Tre Cime peaks.

DAY 12: Rest day on local hikes from Refuge Locatelli.

DAY 13: Descend to Lake Landro and drive to Cortina. Overnight in hotel.

DAY 14: Drive to Milan, stopping for lunch at historic Verona. Overnight at hotel.

DAY 15: Depart Milan and connect with homeward-bound flights.

Italian guide Gary Paoletti and Louise McGowan (carrying her daughter, Kili) on the Dolomites trek between Refuge Savio and Refuge Locatelli.

IT4LH131A

VAL D'AOSTA TREK

11-day trek in highest Italian Alps

DATES: *#1 Jun 22–Jul 8 (17 days)*
#2 Jul 6–Jul 22 (17 days)
LEADER: *Pietro Giglio*
GRADE: *B-3*
LAND COST: *$1690 (10–12 members)*
$1790 (8–9)

Val d'Aosta is a spectacular valley in the heart of the highest Alps of Europe, where the mountainous borders of Italy, Switzerland and France meet.
Surrounding Val d'Aosta are some of the most magnificent and well-known peaks in the Alps: the Mont Blanc massif, whose 15,771-foot summit is the highest point in Europe west of the Caucasus, and the great peaks of the Pennine Alps, including the Matterhorn (14,692′), Monte Rosa (15,203′) and Gran Combin (14,154′).

The first part of our trek will take us along miles and miles of ancient footpaths connecting valleys, villages and alpine meadows, all with views extending from Monte Rosa to the Matterhorn to Mont Blanc. The second portion of the trek will take us through Gran Paradiso National Park, where the delicate mountain environment remains unspoiled and we may see a graceful ibex or chamois posed among the rocks. In the summer, a profusion of wildflowers add brilliant color to every vista. The climate here is generally fair and dry, since the massive flanks of Mont Blanc shelter the valley from wet weather and storms.

Rich in human history since the Neolithic Age, Val d'Aosta's medieval era is represented by many ancient forts, castles and churches.

The region is bilingual and bicultural in French and Italian. There are other ethnic communities such as the Walsers, who migrated here

Nadia Billia by Lac Blue with "Cervino" (the Italian name for the Matterhorn)/ Leo Le Bon

in the 12th century and still speak their own German-based language.
At night we will stay in small inns, alpine villages or in mountain refuges.

ITINERARY:

DAY 1 and 2: Leave U.S. Arrive Milan. Transfer to hotel.

DAY 3: Drive to Aosta, main town of the Aosta Valley. Afternoon free to explore the city.

DAY 4: Drive to St. Jacques. Begin 11-day trek with a walk to Refuge Casole. Good views of Monte Rosa.

DAY 5: Cross the Col de Nana (9,100′) to Cheneil (6,975′) through meadows and high pastures with wildflowers all along the trail. Views of the Matterhorn (14,492′) will be spectacular today.

DAY 6: Descend to the village of Valtournanche (5,000′), with its ancient houses and church, then up the other side of the valley to Cignana Lake (7,086′). Overnight at Refuge Barmasse.

DAY 7: To Torgnon (5,577′), passing by alpine houses and open meadows. Overnight at a village inn.

DAY 8: Cross over Col Fenetre (7,246′) and reach the village of Lignan (5,357′). Overnight at inn.

DAY 9: To Oratoire de Cuney (8,700′). The trail heads uphill to a 17th century church. Overnight in a small refuge next to the church.

DAY 10: Cross over Col Vessona, with its views of Monte Rosa (and our first views of Mont Blanc and Gran Combin), and reach Dzovenno.

DAY 11: Hike from Dzovenno to Aosta. Overnight at hotel.

DAY 12: Visit Aosta and nearby Roman ruins, stop for lunch in a local restaurant in Cogne, then hike up to Refuge Vittorio Sella (8,477′).

DAY 13: To Eaux Rousses (5,446′). Today we are in the heart of Gran Paradiso National Park. Cross Col Lauson (10,813′), with its views of La Grivola (13,021′), Gran Paradiso (13,641′) and surrounding glaciers.

DAY 14: Up again to the Col de Entrebor (10,120′) then descend to the village of Rhemes Notre Dame.

DAY 15: We cross from one valley into another, over Col Fenetre (9,317′) and end our trek at Valgrisenche.

DAY 16: Drive to Milan. Afternoon sightseeing. Overnight at hotel.

DAY 17: Depart Milan and connect with homeward-bound flights.

IT4LH131A

THE LOMBARDIA TREK

11-day trek in Bernina Alps

DATES: *#1 Jul 13–Jul 29 (17 days)*
#2 Aug 3–Aug 19 (17 days)
LEADER: *Cesare Cesabianchi*
GRADE: *B-2*
LAND COST: *$1690 (10–12 members)*
$1790 (8–9)

Lombardia is the region of north central Italy which extends from the fertile plains of the Po River to the snow-crowned Bernina Alps and the peaks of Bregaglia, which mark Italy's border with Switzerland.

Its alpine landscape, crowned with rock spires and snowy peaks, is seen in the background in many of Leonardo da Vinci's most beautiful paintings. In fact, da Vinci spent the most productive years of his career in Lombardia and traveled widely through the region.

We will trek across two of the most interesting and remote valleys of Lombardia: the Val Masino and Val Malenco, both on the Swiss border. Here we find beautiful snow peaks, including Mt. Bernina (13,284′) and Mt. Disgrazia (12,066′), a huge, isolated massif and one of the most picturesque in the Alps. Great glaciers flow from these mountains, among which are the Scerscen and Fellaria, which feed the large lakes of the lowlands. Also situated here is the rock massif of Mt. Badile (10,853′), well known among European climbers. The 3,000-foot high granite slabs of its northern flanks are considered by mountaineers to be one of the "six classic north faces in the Alps."

As we walk from hut to hut, the chestnut woods gradually give way to pine forests. Higher, above the 7,000-foot level, thickets of stunted rhododendrons and wildflowers compliment a typically grand alpine landscape. Marmots and royal eagles are very commonly seen.

At night, we will sleep in traditional mountain "refuges," similar to the refuges in the Dolomites and many other mountain regions of Europe.

Visits are also included to Lake Como and Milan.

ITINERARY:

DAY 1 and 2: Leave U.S. Arrive Milan. Transfer to hotel.

DAY 3: Drive to Bagni Masino. Overnight at inn.

DAY 4: Begin 11-day trek. From Bagni Masino (3,845'), we trek through fields and pastures to the end of the Oro Valley. Overnight at Refuge Omio (6,890').

DAY 5: To Refuge Giannetti (8,310'), a long traverse along the foot of the Oro peaks.

DAY 6: To Refuge Allievi (8,395'), crossing two passes: Camerozzo (8,925') and Qualido (8,760'). This is a typical alpine trail surrounded by snow-covered peaks.

DAY 7: To Cataeggio (2,580'), descend along the Val di Mello, a rock climbing area. Overnight at a small inn in the village of Cataeggio.

DAY 8: To Refuge Ponti (8,395'), with spectacular views along the way of Mt. Disgrazia.

DAY 9: To Refuge Bosio (6,840'), crossing Corna Rossa Pass and entering Valle Airola, with its lovely waterfalls.

DAY 10: To Refuge Porro (6,430'), across the remote Val Torreggio with its huge granite walls, and over Ventina Pass with views of Mt. Disgrazia from the glacier.

DAY 11: To Refuge Tartaglione, through pastures and shepherds' huts, passing the peaks of Alpe de Locca and Alpe Sentieri.

DAY 12: To Refuge Longoni. Wildflowers decorate the trailsides today.

DAY 13: To Chiesa de Val Malenco (2,952'), descending to the main village of the Malenco area. Overnight at inn.

DAY 14: Visit stone quarries and a small historical museum at Chiesa de Valmelenco.

DAY 15: Sightseeing around Lake Como. Overnight at hotel.

DAY 16: Drive to Milan. Afternoon sightseeing. Overnight at hotel.

DAY 17: Depart Milan and connect with homeward-bound flights.

IT4LH131A

THE PIEMONTE TREK

Walking in rural Italy

DATES: *Sep 14–Sep 29 (16 days)*
LEADER: *Silvana Camus*
GRADE: *B-2*
LAND COST: *$1575 (10–12 members)*
$1680 (8–9)

In the western part of the Italian Alps, near the Maritime Alps, lies Piemonte (literally "foothills"), an area of green and gently rolling hills at altitudes of 5,000 to 7,000 feet.

Piemonte traces its human history back to medieval times. The oldest existing historical documents on this area date to 1200 A.D., as do many of its fine old churches.

With a geography which has left it relatively isolated from the mainstream of modern Italy, the pastoral villages of Piemonte have maintained a traditional way of life ruled by the passing seasons. Farming and cattle raising are the summer activities, and the making of handicrafts (particularly wood carving) fills the winter.

To walk these valleys is to wander back in time, strolling on stonepaved paths, exploring ancient churches with historic wall paintings, meeting shepherds and enjoying old-style Italian country life.

The people of Piemonte descend from an ethnic group which still speaks an ancient dialect of French called "provencal." They are proud of their heritage and celebrate it often in their dances and festivals.

The walks will be easy, with our baggage carried by pack mules. Our longest walking day will be about six hours. From the highest point on the trek (8,000'), we have a close view of the isolated pyramid of Monviso (12,600'), highest peak in the area. Nearby springs the source of Italy's longest river, the historic Po.

Our accommodations will be farmhouses or small inns.

Visits are also included to Torino, 19th century capital of Italy, and Milan.

ITINERARY:

DAY 1 and 2: Leave U.S. Arrive Milan. Transfer to hotel.

DAY 3: Drive to Alba. Lunch in typical country restaurant and continue to Rore. Overnight in hotel.

DAY 4: Begin 11-day trek. Hike to Pagliero, a panoramic and varied walk through woods and pastures. Lunch stop at Birrone Pass (5,577').

DAY 5: Walk through fields and pastures to the village of Cella Macra (4,169'), with its typical ancient architecture.

DAY 6: Cross the Maira Valley with its cobbled pathways, small chapels and old houses and reach Stroppo.

DAY 7: Climb up to Col Bettone for views of the Elva Valley. A quick descent brings us to the town of Elva, where we can admire the paintings of the "Maestro d'Elva" dated 1504 in the local church. Overnight at Elva (5,370').

DAY 8: Walk through pastures and pine woods to the Blins Valley, the heart of the "Ousitanes" culture. The Ousitanes settled here in the Middle Ages; their traditions are still alive in the regional language and architecture. Overnight at Blins.

DAY 9: Hike to Pontechianala. Beautiful views of the south face of Mt. Monviso. Lunch stop at Colle Della Battagliola (7,414').

DAY 10: Walk along the Fintursa Valley up to Col Rostel, then follow a hillside path to Chinale (5,895'), the highest point on the trek and one of the best preserved villages in the region.

DAY 11: Follow a path through gentle pastures and farms where local cheeses are made.

DAY 12: Today we cross the largest "cembri" pine forest in Italy. Overnight at Ciampanesio.

DAY 13: From Colle de Luca, we gain our closest view of the southeast face of Monviso. Enroute today we might meet local shepherds and farmers and have a chance to hear about life in this region. Overnight at Oncino.

DAY 14: Hike up to Colle Cervetto (7,385'), walk down to Dragoniere for lunch and end in Rore, where we started our trek. Overnight at hotel.

DAY 15: Drive to Milan, with a sightseeing stop in Torino. Overnight in hotel.

DAY 16: Depart Milan and connect with homeward-bound flights.

Romeo and Juliet's balcony, Verona, Italy/ Dick McGowan

IT4TW14052

ACROSS CORSICA

10-day Mediterranean backpacking traverse

DATES: *Jul 20–Aug 4 (16 days)*
LEADER: *Charles Wilkinson*
GRADE: *B-3*
LAND COST: *$875 (6–12 members)*

Trekking in Corsica, one of the most mountainous islands in Europe.

Corsica is primarily a mountain rising out of the sea. Almost its whole length, coastal cliffs and headlands surge out of the blue sea to heights of 3,000 feet or more. Monte Cinto, highest peak on the island is 8,881 feet high; dozens of needle-like smaller peaks surround it. Terraced gardens, small cultivated fields, olive groves and vineyards spread out below the peaks.

Our ten-day trek across Corsica follows a portion of the *Grand Randonee 20*, a marked trail linking 177 miles of ancient shepherds' trails that wind across the mountainous interior of the island. The route crosses only three roads and one village during its entire length. The hiking is challenging, and the scenery is truly impressive, with the herbal fragrance of the *maquis* scrub softening the mountain harshness.

There are two three-day stages of the trek on which we carry backpacks weighing 25 lbs. Our accommodations will be a mixture of bivouacs, hut nights and camping. Average walking time is about six hours a day.

After the trek, we have two days to relax on the beaches at Calvia.

ITINERARY:

DAY 1 and 2: Leave U.S. Arrive Ajaccio, Corsica via Paris.

DAY 3: Bus to Bastelica, pack up our backpacks and hike through woods of beech and silver birch to our lunch stop at the *bergeries* (shepherds' huts) at Messaniva. Continue up and camp at an extremely pleasant spot above the Bergeries at Possi.

DAY 4: Follow the *Grand Randonee 20* to the Berg de Capanelle, making a detour to climb to the summit of Monte Renoso. Rejoin our support vehicle.

DAY 5: Carrying only a daypack today, we contour around the Punta de Zorpi, descending through forest to Vizavonna, the only village on the *Grand Randonee 20*. Camp by the river.

DAY 6: Day hike up Monte d'Oro (7,837') via the Agnone Valley. Return to Vizavonna by descending the steeper north side.

DAY 7: With backpacks again, we ascend gradually then more steeply to the Refuge Pietra Piana (6,043').

DAY 8: Climb to the ridge above the refuge and follow it to Refuge de Manganu, enjoying spectacular views along the way. Optional traverse out across the ridge to climb Corsica's second highest peak Monte Retondo (8,602').

DAY 9: An easier day with a pleasant walk to Lac de Nino, where one could make an optional climb of Monte Tozzo (6,584') before the gradual descent through forests of rare Laricio pine to the Col de Vergio. Overnight in a dorm-style hotel.

DAY 10: Donning our backpacks again, we hike from Col De Vergio to Berg de Ballone, past the impressive peaks of Paglia Orba and Capu Tafonatu. Optional climb of Paglia Orba.

DAY 11: Steeply up to Col Perdu. Good views into Cirque de la Solitude then on to lunch at a small lake near Bocca Minute. Afternoon descent to Haut Asco.

DAY 12: Climb Monte Cinto (8,881') and return to Haut Asco.

DAY 13: Climb from Haut Asco through woods to rejoin the *Grand Randonee 20*. Steep descent into the Spasimata Valley and the Auberge de la Foret, followed by a short drive to Calvi, where we camp near the beach.

DAY 14: Day on the beach at Calvi.

DAY 15: By train to Ajaccio, a six-hour ride on Corsica's funicular mountain railway.

DAY 16: Depart Ajaccio and connect with homeward-bound flights.

Trip leader Chipper Roth at a picnic at Brecha de Rolando in the Basque Pyrenees/ Martin Zabaleta

IT4TW14048

THE OTHER SPAIN

Walks in Basque Country, Pyrenees, Catalonia

DATES: *#1 Jun 9–Jun 26 (18 days)*
#2 Oct 27–Nov 13 (18 days)
LEADER: *Martin Zabaleta & Chipper Roth*
GRADE: *A-2*
LAND COST: *$1675 (6–12 members)*

Exploring the mountains, villages and coasts of northern Spain, this tour is a combination of hikes in completely untouristed areas and visits to the ancient towns in Aragon, Catalonia, and Euskadi (Pays Basque).

We meet our trip leaders (one of whom is a Basque mountaineer and Everest summiteer), in Madrid. After a stop in Avila, holy city of St. Teresa, we begin our walk along the green meadows, aquamarine lakes and splendid granite cirques of the Sierra de Gredos. Then we'll see the Gothic and Romanesque art treasures in medieval Leon and the golden university town of Salamanca before roaming into the Picos de Europa, a *cordillera* (mountain range) with a mysterious labyrinth of gorges and valleys cut by streams alive with fish.

The next few days are spent exploring along the verdant Basque Coast, with its caves, sheltered bays, and charming fishing villages, including San Sebastian, where we dine on amazing seafood and hike along the fertile Cantabrian coast and Bay of Biscay.

In the Pyrenees at Ordesa, we follow a grandiose canyon with 3,000-foot escarpments towering above an alpine meadowland remarkably like Yosemite.

Driving through Huesca, ancient capital of Aragon, to Catalonia, we hike into the Sierra de Guara, fantastically carved and colored canyons reminiscent of our own southwestern desert.

After a final walk in the Monserrat Massif, we end the trip with a stay in the magnificent city of Barcelona, capital of Catalonia.

ITINERARY:

DAY 1 and 2: Leave U.S. Arrive Madrid. Overnight at hotel and briefing with trip leader.

DAY 3: Drive to the monastic and martial city of Avila. Afternoon hike in the Sierra de Gredos and spend the night in a lakeside refuge.

DAY 4: Easy hike along the trails of the Sierra de Gredos where we see many *capra hispanica* (mountain

The rolling countryside of northern Portugal.

goats), then drive to Salamanca. Overnight at hotel.

DAY 5: Free morning in Salamanca, then drive to Zamora, stopping for lunch in Parador Nacional "Condes de Alba y Aliste" (a *parador* is a historic building or monument which has been converted into a hotel). Onward to Leon for a stay in that medieval city's old quarter.

DAY 6 and 7: Hikes in the Picos de Europa, highest range in the Cantabrian Cordillera. Overnight at local village hotels.

DAY 8: Beautiful drive along the indented Santander coastline. Afternoon in Santillana del Mar, a well-preserved and charming village, famous as a destination for pilgrims in the Middle Ages. Overnight at hotel.

DAY 9: Morning hike in the Sierra de Hornijo and visit the caves of Santimamine with their prehistoric cave paintings. Overnight in the fishing village of Lequeitio.

DAY 10: Drive along the fertile emerald slopes and solitary, steep-cliffed beaches of the Basque Coast. Dinner at Gastronomique Society (a private eating club) and overnight in San Sebastian.

DAY 11: Free day to enjoy the beach, the *tapa* bars and shops in the heart of Basque country.

DAY 12: Roam through pastoral countryside and villages of the Baztan Valley. Lunch in a *caserio* (farm) whose owners are friends of the trip leaders. Short stop in Pamplona, then on to spend the night in a splendidly refurbished *parador* in Sos de Rey Catolico.

DAY 13: Visit a 9th century monastery at the foot of the Pyrenees. Hike in Sierra de San Juan de la Pena.

DAY 14: A whole day to hike in Ordesa National Park, a canyon ringed with practically vertical walls and full of astonishing vivid vegetation and wildlife. Overnight in Ainsa.

DAY 15: Hiking in the Sierra de Guara, a fantastic "badlands" in the foothills of the Aragonese Pyrenees. Overnight in Huesca.

DAY 16: Drive through Huesca to Catalonia and walk in the grand Sierra de Montserrat, an interesting range of sawtooth mountains.

DAY 17: Short drive to Barcelona. Free day to stroll and shop.

DAY 18: Transfer to the airport and connect with homeward-bound flights.

IT7TW15451

WALKS IN PORTUGAL & MADEIRA

Hill rambles and coastal hikes

DATES: *Oct 12–Oct 25 (14 days)*
LEADER: *Martin Zabaleta & Chipper Roth*
GRADE: *A-2*
LAND COST: *$1590 (6–12 members)*

Hill hikes and coastal walks are the focus of this journey to Portugal and the island of Madeira. Our travel is by mini-van and our accommodations are in small hotels and guest houses.

We begin our travels on Madeira, a volcanic island known for its roller-coaster hills rising from the sea, its charming medieval towns of white villas with orange window shutters, and a strikingly handsome populace. Called "Pearl of the Atlantic," Madeira is lush with orchids, hydrangeas, bougainvillea, birds of paradise, calla lillies, willows and sugar cane.

Hiking is taken seriously by the locals, and there's no such thing as a dull walk. 1,300 miles of *levadas,* (water channels which make up Madeira's sophisticated irrigation system) and well-maintained access paths open up the beautiful interior of the island and take us to otherwise inaccessible corners of the island. One of our walks will be a level 10-mile hike at an altitude of 3,000 feet which meanders through mountains ablaze with flowers and forests of eucalyptus and fragrant mimosa.

Flying to Lisbon, the port city built on seven hills, we take a loop tour of the central and northern mountain provinces—Alentejo, Biera Alta, Beira Baixa, and Tras-os-Montes, hiking and stopping to chat with gypsies and local shephards, and to sample the astounding array of wines and renowned Portuguese cuisine. Our walking circuit returns to Lisbon along a coastline of incredible variety, with traditional fishing villages and

beaches of fine sand sheltered by dunes and cliffs.

ITINERARY:

DAY 1 and 2: Leave U.S. Arrive Santa Cruz, Madeira, and meet with trip leaders. Hike to a hidden beach which lies in a cove well-protected by basalt cliffs. Overnight in hotel at Machico.

DAY 3: Day hiking along the coast to the Porto Da Cruz. Overnight in the pretty village of Santana.

DAY 4: Walk from Queimadas to Pico Ruivo.
Overnight in Eira Do Serrado.

DAY 5: Hike to Encumeada, with views extending down over both sides of the island. Drive to the coast and overnight in Porto Moriz.

DAY 6: Drive along the coast, visiting small villages. Overnight in Madeira's capital, which lies at the end of a beautiful bay.

DAY 7: Fly to Lisbon and spend the day sightseeing. Overnight in hotel.

DAY 8: Drive to Alentejo, the Portuguese granary and habitat of the cork oak, the evergreen oak and the olive tree. Overnight in Evora, a walled town dating from Roman times, now Moorish in character, with alleys cut by arches, hanging gardens, terraces and tiled patios.

DAY 9: Drive to Serra Da Sao Mamede, a small island of greenery in an arid and stony region. Overnight in Marvao, a fortified medieval town set below a castle.

DAY 10: Hiking in the Serra Da Estrela, highest massif in Portugal, whose boulder-strewn summits rise above cultivated fields. Overnight in Guarda.

DAY 11: Visit Tras-os-Montes Province, where mountain villages have granite and shale houses which merge into the landscape. Overnight in Montalegre, with its red-roofed houses and 14th century castle.

DAY 12: Visit Peneda-Geres National Park, a hilly region from which the deep valleys of the Lima, Homen and Cavada rivers divide into "serras" (mountain ranges). Overnight in Oporto, and a chance to visit the Vela Nova Da Gai wine storehouses and sample famous port wines.

DAY 13: Drive along the coast of Biera and Extremadura, visiting fishing villages and the monastery of Batalha, a masterpiece of Portuguese Gothic architecture. Return to Lisbon.

DAY 14: Transfer to airport and depart on homeward-bound flights.

Moorish castle in Sentia, Portugal/ Chipper Roth

IT4TW14049

THE GREEK ISLANDS

Exploring by boat in the Western Cyclades

DATES: #1 Jul 6–Jul 19 (14 days)
#2 Jul 23–Aug 5 (14 days)
LEADER: *Maki Idosidis
and/or Allen Steck*
GRADE: *A-1*
LAND COST: $1790 (9–10 members)
$1990 (7–8)

For this free-form journey, we charter a *kaiki* and cruise to several of the most interesting and remote islands in the western Cyclades.

We travel island to island, avoiding the tourist areas, to explore remote fishing villages where the old Greek way of life still exists. This trip will have a very flexible itinerary and a few surprises.

We also plan to do some beach hiking, swimming, snorkeling, and spend many evenings dancing in small *tavernas*.

Our boat will be a motor-sailer, called a *kaiki,* a term which refers to a variety of hull shapes and boat designs. It will be a very comfortable and livable boat. There will be a crew of two.

A typical day on the boat may go like this: up early for a light breakfast on board, then leave port (usually by motor) for the next island. We stop around noon on most days for a swim at a secluded beach followed by a Greek salad-style lunch on board. Continuing to the next port, we might go ashore for coffee, perhaps some ouzo and octopus, then walk to a nearby village. The evening meal will be taken in a *taverna,* where we hope to do some Greek dancing.

Much of the emphasis of the trip is on enjoying the scene in the local tavernas and outdoor cafes, where we spend a lot of our time.

*Almost every island harbor is a photographer's dream /
Ken Scott*

Greece is one of the few places where the national dances are not just relegated to the performing stage, but are part of everyday life. Every joyous occasion calls for music and dancing, and we will dance with the Greeks in their *tavernas* and cafes, or sometimes by ourselves on isolated beaches... wherever the spirit moves us! Nightly accommodations will be four-bunk cabins on the boat.

ITINERARY:

DAY 1and 2: Leave U.S. Arrive Athens. Transfer to hotel.

DAY 3: Day free in Athens. Evening visit to our favorite dancing spot in the Plaka.

DAY 4: Drive to Pireaus or Porto Rafti and board the boat.

DAY 5 to 13: For the next nine days, we will motor (or occasionally sail when winds and currents are favorable) among the following islands: Kithnos, Sifnos, Sikinos, Thera, Skinoussa, Antiparos, Tinos, Delos, Kea and back to Pireaus and Athens. We will keep the sea itinerary flexible according to weather conditions.

DAY 14: Depart Athens and connect with homeward-bound flights.

IT4TW14051

MT. OLYMPUS & NORTHERN GREECE

4-day trek in Vikos Gorge, 4-day traverse of Olympus

DATES: *Jun 2–Jun 17 (16 days)*
LEADER: *Maki Idosidis
and/or Allen Steck*
GRADE: *B-2*
LAND COST: *$1175 (6–12 members)*

The rugged Pindos Mountains on Greece's northern border are among the most spectacular yet least traveled mountains in the whole country. On our four-day trek in these remote reaches, we hike through the dry river bed of the Vikos Gorge, a beautiful canyon flanked by immense, jagged limestone cliffs and filled with wildflowers. We venture high up through forested terrain, then alpine pastureland, descending to the Zagorian village of Tsepelovon.

Traveling to Mt. Olympus (9,750'), the many-ridged home of Zeus, we traverse the mountain for four days, beginning in the hill village of Ellasona on the west, crossing the summit and ending at the beach town of Litochoron in the east. Athough less than 10,000 feet high, Olympus has impressive rock walls and snow which lasts most of the year.

In between treks, we visit the famed medieval monasteries built on the rock towers of Meteora, and after our Olympus hike, we relax on the sunny beach at Stomion.

ITINERARY:

DAY 1 and 2: Leave U.S. Arrive Athens. Drive to the small seaside community of Varasova. Overnight at local inn.

DAY 3: Continue by bus to Ioannina, capital of Epiros, then onto Monodendri, a small hamlet located high above Vikos Gorge. Overnight at local inn.

DAY 4: Begin four-day Pindos Mountains trek with an all-day hike to Papingo. From Monodendri, an indistinct trail leads down through lush forested terrain to the dry riverbed of the Vikos Gorge. Continue to the Viodomatis, a full-size mountain river that gushes out of the dry riverbed from underground channels. Hike up an old trail system to the hill town of Megalo Papingo. Overnight at a local inn.

DAY 5: Continue hiking through forested terrain, then alpine pastures to the Astraka Refuge at 6,000 feet, maintained by the Greek Alpine Club.

*Fishermen discussing the catch of the day/
Ken Scott*

The rugged Vikos Gorge in Northern Greece/Allen Steck

DAY 6: Free day for short hikes or ascents of the nearby peaks.

DAY 7: Mid-morning departure for a hike to the Zagoria village of Tsepelovo, descending through a limestone gorge. Meet our bus and drive to the Mt. Olympus region.

DAY 8: Drive to the lovely mountain village of Metsovon. Overnight at local inn.

DAY 9: Drive to Kalambaka, where we will visit the famed medieval monasteries built on the rock towers of Meteora. Overnight at a local inn.

DAY 10: Drive on to Ellasona, a hillside village near the roadhead on the western approach to Mt. Olympus. Overnight at inn.

DAY 11: Hike up to Vryssopoules Refuge (6,233') on Mt. Olympus.

DAY 12: Ascent of Mt. Olympus' main summit, which is called Mytikas (9,750'), snow conditions permitting. Descend to the Spilios Agapitos Refuge (6,889') on the eastern side of the peak.

DAY 13: Rest day.

DAY 14: Descend along lovely forested path to Litochoron, and meet our bus for the drive to Stomion Beach, an ideal place to relax after the traverse of Mt. Olympus. Overnight at local inn.

DAY 15: A long day's drive back to Athens. Overnight at hotel.

DAY 16: Depart Athens and connect with homeward-bound flights.

IT4TW14050

TREKKING IN GREECE & CRETE

3-day Pelopponesos walk, 3-day Gorge of Samaria trek

DATES: *Sep 7–Sep 22 (16 days)*
LEADER: *Mattanyah Zokhar*
GRADE: *B-2*
LAND COST: *$1660 (11–12 members)*
$1790 (8–10)

This hiking journey ventures into the back-country to come into close contact with the hospitable mountain villagers of Greece and Crete.

These rugged hills and coasts are an exquisite place for hiking, a Mediterranean panorama of wooded mountains, barren rock summits, silvery-green olive groves, golden beaches and a wide blue sea.

Our first trek takes us for three days through the Taiyetos Mountains which rise above Sparta, and our journey follows Spartan warrior paths through forests of chestnut and oak.

On Crete, largest and most mountainous of the Greek islands, a second three-day trek takes us into the Levka Ori ("White Mountains"), a tremendous range from whose peaks we can see almost the entire western half of Crete. Besides meeting local villagers, we visit some of the most famous Mycenean and classic sites of Greece, and the mysterious sites of the Minoan civilization on Santorini, the most beautiful island in the Cyclades.

Our camp gear is transferred by vehicle while we walk, so we only need to carry day packs. Accommodations are in mountain huts, tents and in very simple pensions.

ITINERARY:

DAY 1 and 2: Leave U.S. Arrive Athens. Transfer to Piraeus harbor and continue by ferry to Hydra. Overnight in pension in the fishing village of Kaminia.

DAY 3: By ferry to Hermione and continue to Epidavros, site of the temple of Aesclepius and his holy snakes. Drive to Nafplion, first capital of modern Greece. Camp nearby.

DAY 4: Drive to Mycene, Agamemnon's capital, and continue across the Tayetos Range to Sparta. Camp near the beautiful monastery of Phaneronamy.

DAY 5: Hike to the village of Parury with excellent views of the valley of Sparta, the Parnon Range and the Aegean Sea. Continue hiking up to Mistas, the well-preserved Byzantine "ghost town" that was the capital of the Peleponnesus during the Middle Ages.

Drive to Anoya and continue by bus and tractor to Krionerion. Begin four-day trek in the Tayetos Range. Hike to a mountain hut maintained by the Greek Alpine Club.

DAY 6: Hike over Pilgrim's Pass to the summit of Prophitis Elias, highest peak in the Tayetos Range. A small chapel consecrated to the prophet Elijah is at the summit. Descend and camp by a shepherds' colony in the valley of Ayo Dimitrio.

DAY 7: Descend on an ancient Spartan path along a spectacular canyon to the village of Exochorion. End trek and drive to the seaside village of Kardamili, an ancient site mentioned in Homer's writings. Overnight at pension.

DAY 8: In Khardamili to rest, swim and wander in the village.

DAY 9: Drive southward along the steep coast to Githion and board an overnight ferry to Crete.

DAY 10: Morning arrival in Kastely in northwestern Crete. Drive to Hania, picturesque capital of the island. Overnight in hotel.

DAY 11: Drive southward across the western part of Crete. Visit the ancient site of Lyssos and continue driving to the Omalas plain. Begin Levka Ori trek with a walk to the alpine hut of Kalergy atop a tremendous cliff which dominates the Gorge of Samaria.

DAY 12: Optional rest day or climb of Gingilos, second highest peak in the Volakias Range.

DAY 13: Descend the Gorge of Samaria, one of the largest canyons in Europe. A clear, cool stream flows along its entire length.

DAY 14: Drive along the wild southern coast toward central northern Crete, where most of the Minoan sites are found. Visit Knossos and Fesstos and continue to Heraklion. Overnight in hotel.

DAY 15: Free day in Heraklion. Board overnight ferry to Athens.

DAY 16: Arrive in Athens. Afternoon depart Athens and connect with homeward-bound flights.

Meeting the villagers of Greece/Allen Steck

No visit to Greece is complete without seeing the Acropolis, Athens/Ken Scott

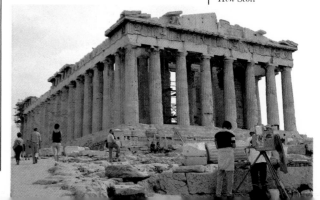

IT4TW14053

Mountains Of The Balkans

Hikes in northern Greece, Bulgaria, Romania, Yugoslavia

DATES: *Sep 9–Sep 30 (22 days)*
LEADER: *Maki Idosidis*
GRADE: *B-2*
LAND COST: *$1790 (8–14 members)*

Visiting Greece, Yugoslavia, Romania and Bulgaria, this unusual journey combines hikes in beautiful mountain regions with visits to historic cities. Needless to say, this is one of the least "touristed" parts of Europe! Our accommodations will be small inns and mountain huts. Travel will be by van or mini-bus.

We start with a hike up Mt. Olympus (9,570'), highest summit in Greece, then drive to Yugoslavia's mountainous southern tip, called Macedonia in ancient times. We visit several Macedonian villages, hike to the summit of Salunska Glava (8,380') and visit Belgrade, the capital.

Continuing by road into Romania, we find ourselves in the Transylvanian Alps, wooded hills with abundant wildlife and feudal-era castles (one we visit is Castle Bran, former haunt of Count Dracula). Our hiking itinerary takes us up Mt. Negoiu (8,359'), second highest peak in Romania, after which we tour Bucharest, the 500-year-old capital.

Our last lap brings us to Bulgaria, in the heart of the Balkan Peninsula. Bordered by the Blue Danube and the Black Sea, Bulgaria traces its historical roots back to the Thracians (1,500 B.C.) and was part of the Turkish Ottoman Empire until 1878. We visit Sofia, the capital, then journey through countryside for a hike up Mt. Musala (9,596').

ITINERARY:

DAY 1 and 2: Depart U.S. Arrive Athens and continue by air to Salonika. Transfer to hotel.

DAY 3: Drive to Litochoron. Swimming, sunbathing, and overnight at beach inn.

DAY 4: Drive to the roadhead on Mt. Olympus and hike for three hours to the Spilios Agapitos Hut at 6,900 feet. Overnight at hut.

DAY 5: Five-hour hike up to the summit and back, descend to roadhead and return to Litochoron. Overnight at beach hut.

DAY 6: Drive across the Yugoslavian border to Tito Veles, a small, traditional Macedonian town. Overnight at local inn.

DAY 7: Drive to the village of Bogomila then continue by four-wheel-drive vehicle through lushly forrested terrain to the Ceples Hut for overnight.

DAY 8: Three-hour hike to the summit of Salunska Glava (8,380'). Return to hut for lunch and drive back to Tito Veles.

DAY 9: Long drive to Belgrade, capital of Yugoslavia. Overnight at hotel.

DAY 10: Sightseeing in Belgrade, including old town, confluence of the rivers Saba and Danube, Kalemegdan Park, Manasijia Monastery.

DAY 11: Long day's drive to Sibiu, Romania. Picnic lunch enroute. Overnight at inn.

DAY 12: Drive to the village of Arpasu de Jos then hike for about three hours to Cabana Negoiu Hut through dense forest with spectacular views. Overnight at Cabana Negoiu Hut.

DAY 13: Four-hour hike to summit of Negiou and return. Overnight at hut.

DAY 14: Hike down to roadhead and drive to Castle Bran for a visit. Lunch in Bran village and continue to Bucharest via the towns of Azuga, Sinia and Pidiesti.

DAY 15: Sightseeing in Bucharest.

DAY 16: Drive to Sofia, capital of Bulgaria. Overnight at hotel.

DAY 17: Sightseeing in Sofia, including mausoleum of Georgi Dimitrof, St. George Church (with two tons of gold on its dome), and the Alexander Nevsky Memorial Church.

DAY 18: Depart Sofia for Mt.

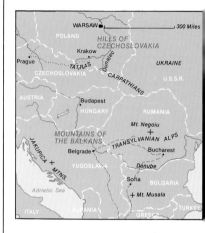

Masula. A two-hour drive brings us to Borovits, a rather fancy ski resort by Balkan standards. From here we take a gondola lift to Yastrebts Peak, and hike from there to the Musala Hut.

DAY 19: Easy three-hour hike to the summit of Musala. Picnic lunch and return to hut.

DAY 20: A long day, beginning with a hike down to the teleferique. Drive on a winding mountain road for two hours to Rila Monastery, situated among high and spectacular mountains. visit monastery and continue across the Greek border to Salonika. Overnight at seaside hotel.

DAY 21: Sightseeing in Salonika, including White Tower, Church of St. Dimitrios, and waterfront. Overnight at hotel.

DAY 22: Fly to Athens and connect with homeward-bound flights.

Alpine country in the Tatras.

Romania, Bulgaria and Czechoslovakia are some of the least traveled parts of Europe yet they are a treasure house of historic, cultural and natural wonders. Our accommodations are in small inns and mountain huts. Travel is by van or mini-bus.

The High Tatras of Czechoslovakia.

IT5PA1SFMT

THE HILLS OF CZECHOSLOVAKIA

Hikes in the High Tatras and northern Bohemia

DATES: #1 Jun 15–Jun 29 (15 days)
       #2 Sep 14–Sep 28 (15 days)
LEADER: *to be announced*
GRADE: *A-2*
LAND COST: *$1050 (7–15 members)*

This walking tour encompasses Czechoslovakian hill country at its finest—both in the alpine High Tatras and the romantic valleys of northern Bohemia.

The peaks of the High Tatras, astride the Polish-Czech border, are the highest portion of the long Carpathian chain. A compact and spectacular mountain range, the Tatras are somewhat like a scaled-down version of the Alps, a scene of fine granite pinnacles, aretes and rock walls rising as much as 4,000 feet above timberline. The highest peak in the Tatras is Gerlach (8,710'). The region's residents are farmers and shepherds who are far removed from the mainstream of modern Czechoslovakian life and still retain their traditional costumes in everyday life.

This is fine hiking country, with its gentle meadows and beech forests, and we'll spend four days based in a mountain lodge with a beautiful Tatras panorama. Time is set aside for a variety of hikes and climbs to suit individual tastes.

Before visiting the Tatras, we journey to northern Bohemia, another area where ancient dress is still worn and folk traditions are cherished. The history of Bohemia dates to medieval times when the Hussites defeated the 70,000-strong armies of the Crusaders. Today it is a land of rich orchards and cultivated fields, a rural landscape dotted with castles and churches of Gothic and Baroque architecture, and beautiful old villages of stone and half-timber folk tradition.

In Bohemia, we will make a leisurely three-day trek in the Krkonose Mountains (rugged hills known as the "Giant Mountains"), hiking from village to village and spending nights in small hotels.

The trip begins and ends in Prague, the graceful capital city built on the shores of the Vltava River, and full of well-preserved buildings and monuments dating from the 13th to 19th century.

ITINERARY:

DAY 1 and 2: Leave U.S. Arrive Prague and transfer to hotel. Afternoon free and dinner at hotel.

DAY 3: Half-day sightseeing in Prague. Overnight at hotel.

DAY 4: Full-day excursion visiting Karlstejn Castle, Koneprusy Caves, and Konopiste Castle. Return to Prague.

DAY 5: By bus to Harrachov in Krkonose, north of Prague. Afternoon hiking in the surrounding forests. Overnight at inn.

DAY 6: A whole day of hiking (about 12 miles) through the western part of Giant Mountains National Park, overnight at the village of Spindleruv Mlyn.

DAY 7: Hike about 11 miles to the village of Pec Pod Snezkou. Overnight at local hotel.

DAY 8: Hike in the area around Pec Pod Snezkou.

DAY 9: Morning free. Afternoon drive to Prague and by train to Poprad in the High Tatras.

DAY 10: Arrive in Poprad then take the electric train to Strbske Pleso (4,455') in the High Tatras. Afternoon hike. Overnight at hotel.

DAY 11: Drive to Sliezky Dom Mountain Hotel (6,560'). Overnight in hotel.

DAY 12 and 13: Hikes and climbs, including Gerlach, highest peak in the Tatras.

DAY 14: In the late morning return to Poprad. Board the overnight train to Prague.

DAY 15: Arrive in Prague. Morning free. Transfer to airport and connect with homeward-bound flights.

Museum of Anton Dvorak in Prague.

Czechoslovakia photos by P. Sirotek

Vranov Castle, Czechoslovakia.

Old Prague.

Assyrian warrior (detail) bas relief. Turkey.

Turkey photos by Leo Le Bon

Springtime in the Taurus Mountains, central Turkey.

IT5PA1SFMT12

TURKEY: MT. ARARAT & THE TAURUS MOUNTAINS

In search of Noah's Ark

DATES: *Jul 28–Aug 18 (22 days)*
LEADER: *Leo Le Bon*
GRADE: *B-2/C-3*
LAND COST: *$1750 (10–15 members)*
$1950 (6–9)
+ $100 domestic flights within Turkey

When Mt. Ararat was opened to foreign travelers last year, Mountain Travelers were there, standing on its summit, looking out over northern Turkey, Soviet Armenia and the plains of northern Iran.

Mt. Ararat is a magnificent sprawling dome whose snow-covered summit is 16,945 feet above sea level. Many Armenians revere this peak as "Mother of the World" and most Christians believe it is the site where Noah's Ark came to rest after the Great Flood.

A climb of Ararat is really just a steep walk (non-technical but requiring a bit of stamina). The upper third of the volcano is covered in snow and the last hundred meters to the summit is icy. (The actual climb to the summit from

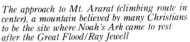

The approach to Mt. Ararat (climbing route in center), a mountain believed by many Christians to be the site where Noah's Ark came to rest after the Great Flood/Ray Jewell

Camp II at 14,760 feet is optional). The approach to Ararat is through the dusty frontier town of Dogu Beyazit, with its cobblestone streets and horse carts.

Before hiking on Ararat, we'll warm up with a six-day trek in the Taurus Range, a limestone group on the southern coast with a complex system of spires, peaks and ridges of almost mystical beauty. On trek, we cross a high plateau beneath the rocky 12,000-foot summits of the Aladag group, highest portion of the Taurus Mountains.

Turkey has many of the world's most famous sites of antiquity, and we will be sure to see Cappadocia, with its rock-hewn chapels and the remarkable underground cities of Derinkuyu and Kaymakli. We also

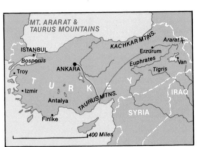

visit Silifke, site of the Byzantine Cennet Cehennen Caves ("Caves of Hell and Heaven") as well as Tarsus, birthplace of St. Paul.

ITINERARY:

DAY 1 and 2: Leave U.S. Arrive Istanbul and fly to Ankara. Transfer to hotel.

DAY 3: Morning tour of Ankara and drive to Cappadocia. Visit rock churches, monasteries, cave dwellings.

DAY 4: Sightseeing in Cappadocia.

DAY 5: Drive to Nigde, visiting the "underground cities" of Derinkuyu and Kaymakli enroute. Begin Taurus Mountains trek with a walk to the foot of Mt. Demirkazik.

DAY 6: Excursion to the remote Cimbar Valley with impressive views of Mt. Demirkazak (12,322').

DAY 7: Trek to Seven Lakes Valley, visiting a nomadic family enroute. Optional hike up Mt. Embler (11,886') or just relax at the lake.

DAY 8 and 9: Trek to Sogukpunar and visit some spectacular waterfalls.

DAY 10: Trek to the Aciman highlands at 7,000 feet and jeep to Karsanti over a rough road with panoramic views of the Taurus Mountains.

DAY 11: Drive to the seaside town of Mersin and visit Tarsus, birthplace of St. Paul.

DAY 12: Free day for ocean swimming and resting. Excursion to Cennet Cehennen Caves (Caves of Heaven and Hell) and Kizkalesi (Maiden Castle).

DAY 13: Fly to Erzurum, tour the city and drive to Dogu Beyazit.

DAY 14: Drive to Eli, where Kurdish shepherds graze their sheep and cattle, and trek to a main camp at 10,500 feet.

DAY 15 and 16: Trek to Camp I (13,780') and Camp II (14,760').

DAY 17: Cimb up to the summit at 16,945 feet, for those who feel up to it, and descend to Camp II.

DAY 18: Descend and drive back to the town of Dogu Beyazit.

DAY 19: Drive to Lake Van, once the center of an Armenian kingdom founded in the first century B.C. Sunset visit to the great citadel of Van.

DAY 20: Afternoon flight to Istanbul.

DAY 21: Tour Istanbul.

DAY 22: Depart Istanbul and connect with homeward-bound flights.

IT1AF155SC

THE CAUCASUS & MT. ELBRUS

7-day mountain trek, optional climbing

DATES: *Sep 1–Sep 24 (24 days)*
LEADER: *to be announced*
GRADE: *B-3/D-2*
LAND COST: *$1890 (8–15 members)*

This is a special trekking and climbing journey to the Caucasus Mountains of the U.S.S.R. Mountain Travel's first trip here was in 1974, when we sent the first-ever American trekking/climbing party to visit the region.

Our itinerary focuses around the Central Caucasus in the Baksan Valley. The mountain scenery here is as beautiful as any in the heart of the Swiss and French Alps. There are deep forests of poplar and beech, high thickets of stunted birch and rhododendron and alpine meadows carpeted with wildflowers. The highest peak in Europe is located here—Mt. Elbrus (18,841'). Around it are other major peaks such as Shikhra (16,529'), Katyntau (16,355'), Jangitau, (16,571'), and Ushba (15,453'), the "Matterhorn of the Caucasus."

Our base will be a hotel in the Baksan Valley below Mt. Elbrus. From this central location, we'll make a variety of excursions, including a seven-day backpacking trip across the major passes of the Caucasus into Svanetia, a Georgian mountain region with 1000 years of history dating back to the Crusades.

Returning to the Baksan Valley, climbers in the group will have a chance to ascend Mt. Elbrus, a challenging (but not technically difficult) high altitude climb. During the two-day climb, trekkers in the group can hike up to the Priutt Refuge on Mt. Elbrus for great mountain views.

Mt. Elbrus, highest mountain in Europe outside the Alps, seen from the seldom-visited Irik Tchat Valley.

ITINERARY:

DAY 1 and 2: Leave U.S. Arrive Moscow. Transfer to hotel.

DAY 3: Fly to Mineralnye Vody. Continue by bus to the Baksan Valley. Overnight at hotel.

DAY 4: By chair lift up to Cheget (11,480'), for a leisurely hike with panoramic views of the Baksan Valley and the two white peaks of Mt. Elbrus. Return to hotel.

DAY 5: Day excursion to "Refuge of Eleven" on Mt. Elbrus, up by tram to 11,480 feet, then a hike over snow to the refuge, which is located at 13,800 feet. Descend by tram and return to hotel.

DAY 6: Begin seven-day trek across the passes of the Caucasus and into Svanetia, Georgia, with a hike to a campsite below Betcho Pass (10,580'), which leads from the Baksan Valley into Georgia.

DAY 7: Cross the Betcho Pass over a steep trail and easy snow slopes. Descend into the Betcho Valley and camp.

DAY 8: Descend through meadows and forests to about 9,200 feet.

Camp along the Betcho River near the roadhead.

DAY 9: Short hike through the village of Masery. Continue by bus to Mestia, a small Georgian village famous for its ancient watchtowers. This is the main town of Svanetia. Camp or overnight at hotel.

DAY 10: Sightseeing in Mestia, with its little stone streets and ancient town squares, many of which date back to the time of Genghis Khan. Overnight at hotel.

DAY 11: By bus to the Nacra Valley, then hike up through forests and meadows to a camp along the Nacra River (8,800').

DAY 12: Cross Dongus-Orun Pass (12,795') and descend into the valley on the other side. Traverse through meadows to the middle station of a chairlift by which we descend back into the Baksan Valley. Arrive back at our hotel.

DAY 13: Rest day; optional local walks.

DAY 14: to 16: For mountaineers, an optional climb of Mt. Elbrus; for non-climbers, hike to refuge on Elbrus.

DAY 17: Descend to the Baksan Valley. Overnight at hotel.

DAY 18: Rest day at hotel.

DAY 19 to 21: Three-day excursion by road to Georgia, including visits to Kasbegi and Tbilissi.

DAY 22: Fly to Moscow. Transfer to hotel.

DAY 23: Day free in Moscow for sightseeing.

DAY 24: Depart Moscow and connect with homeward-bound flights.

Women of the Baksan Valley in the Caucasus. Hand-made goods can be sold at the "free market" adjacent to the hotel for climbers.

Caucasus photos by Dick McGowan

Backpacking camp in the Irik Valley at 8,000 feet. Soviet climbers are fond of making a traverse of all peaks in one day!

U.S.S.R. International Mountaineering Camps

The U.S.S.R. Sports Committee hosts an important series of International Mountaineering Camps open to climbers, skiers and hikers. The camps are truly international and are attended by people from dozens of nations. This program has been on-going since 1974.

Base camp at Lake Akkem in the Siberian Altai.

Participants must supply their own personal camping, climbing and/or skiing equipment. Cost includes all expenses within the U.S.S.R. The Soviet staff provides assistance in planning your activities at the camps, but there is no pre-planned itinerary; each individual must arrange his/her own activities. No change is allowed from the set program dates. Mountain Travel will provide some written material and maps.

At the time of writing, the exact dates and prices for 1985 are not known. As soon as they are, we will print an Information Sheet on the 1985 U.S.S.R. International Mountaineering Camps. Send for a copy.

IT4AF155SY

TRAVELS IN ARMENIA

An ancient civilization on the Plains of Ararat

DATES: *Sep 14–Oct 4 (21 days)*
LEADER: *Linda Liscom*
GRADE: *A-2/B-2*
LAND COST: *$1690 (8–15 members)*

Armenia is the oldest Christian country in the world (converted by St. Gregory the Illuminator in 301 A.D.); Armenians provided Byzantium with a whole series of emperors; the Crusaders arrived here in 1097 A.D.; Marco Polo visited in 1271 A.D.; Russia annexed eastern Armenia in 1828; the Young Turks massacred the Turkish Armenians in 1915; and in 1920, Soviet Armenia was formed, encompassing about 1/10th of Armenia's historic territory.

During our visit to Soviet Armenia, we hope to travel "Mountain-Travel-style," camping, hiking and exploring out-of-the-way places.

We will see the massive group of extinct volcanoes which dot the Armenian plateau, including Mt. Alagoz (Aragats), rising from the Araxes Valley to a height of 13,410 feet and forming a distant and snowy backdrop for Armenia's capital city, Yerevan.

Yerevan is one of the oldest cities in the world, founded in 782 B.C. One of the legends surrounding it is that when Noah came into sight of land after the Great Flood, he exclaimed, "It is seen" (*yerevoum*), hence giving the city its name.

Among our wanderings outside of Yerevan, we visit the summer resort of Lake Sevan (6,340′), a mountain lake confined by the long ridge of mountains which divides Armenia and Georgia, and sites of antiquity including Echmiadzin, where we find the first Christian churches in the U.S.S.R., a 4th century cathedral and the 7th century Ripsime Temple, classic examples of Armenian architecture.

Traveling down the picturesque Avan Ravine, we visit the fortress Garni, former summer residence of the Armenian kings, and a cave-monastery on the upper reaches of the Azat River.

As we go to press, the daily itinerary is not yet firm, but you may contact us for the latest details.

Pik Bronja is a popular climb in the Ak-Ojuk Basin, a few hours walk from Lake Akkem. The one-day climb is usually done along the lefthand skyline.

IT4AF155SY

SKI HOLIDAY IN RUSSIA

Downhill and nordic skiing in the Caucasus

DATES: *Approx. Feb 18–Mar 6 (17 days)*
LEADER: *to be announced*
GRADE: *B-2*
LAND COST: *$1245 (10–15 members)*

The Caucasus Mountains are one of the major ski areas in the U.S.S.R. On our Caucasus ski holiday, we base ourselves in a comfortable hotel in the Baksan Valley at the foot of Mt. Elbrus (18,841′) highest peak in Europe, and undertake ten days of skiing. The Soviets have several chair lifts operating in the area and there is also a gondola which goes up to 13,780 feet on Elbrus. Some nordic skiing is also available.

Development of ski resorts in the Soviet Union is not on a par with the U.S., of course, but in a way this is a refreshing situation. The skiing is good and there is a unique opportunity to meet and enjoy the Soviet people. Our group will be assisted by Soviet skiers who will help arrange daily activities for all levels of skiing ability. A climb of Elbrus is possible for good strong alpine skiers.

ITINERARY:

DAY 1 and 2: Leave U.S. Arrive Moscow. Transfer to hotel.

DAY 3: Fly to Mineralnye Vody. Continue by bus to the Baksan Valley. Overnight at hotel.

DAY 4 to 14: Skiing activities in the Caucasus, based out of hotel in Baksan Valley.

DAY 15: Drive to Mineralnye Vody and fly to Moscow.

DAY 16: Tour Moscow.

DAY 17: Depart Moscow and connect with homeward-bound flights.

IT1AF155SA

EXPEDITION TO SIBERIA

Mountaineering in the Altai

DATES: *approx. Jul 24–Aug 17 (25 days)*
LEADER: *Dick Irvin*
GRADE: *E-2*
LAND COST: *Approx. $2875 (8–15 members)*

The Altai is one of the truly wild regions of the world, rising from the Siberian steppes in a complex system of high ridges and broad valleys covered by steppe vegetation. Snowline varies from about 7,600 to 10,000 feet. Its 50-degrees-north latitude places it in a similar position to the North Cascades, Coast Range or Selkirks of Washington and British Columbia but since it is in the extreme north of Central Asia, its climatic patterns are unique.

The goal of this expedition is a climb of Mt. Belukha (14,800′), highest peak in the Altai, a twin-summited peak covered by glaciers (about 27 square miles of ice). An ascent requires five to seven days, depending on weather conditions.

From the Altai Base Camp, several other climbs can be attempted. We will also undertake a rugged five-day backpacking trek to Lake Kutscherla in an alpine setting that truly feels like the remotest place on earth.

To get to the Altai, we fly to Moscow and then half way across Siberia, stopping just north of the Chinese border and a bit west of Mongolia at Barnaul, then continuing by jet to the Siberian outpost of Ust Koksa, and finally by helicopter to Altai Base Camp, located by Akkem Lake at 6,900 feet.

One of the attractions of this expedition is the opportunity to meet and climb with the hospitable Russians who staff and guide here during the annual U.S.S.R. Altai International Mountaineering Camp, which is held concurrently with our expedition.

ITINERARY:

DAY 1 and 2: Leave U.S. Arrive Moscow. Overnight at hotel.

DAY 3: All-day sightseeing in Moscow and evening flight to Barnaul, arriving next day.

DAY 4: Breakfast at Barnaul airport and board flight to Ust Koksa. Afternoon helicopter shuttle to Altai Base Camp.

Ascending Riga Turist Pass enroute to Lake Kutscherla, looking back toward the Siberian Altai.

DAY 5: Preparation for climbing Belukha.

DAY 6: Load carrying to Camp I on Belukha (ten to twelve hours of backpacking). Return to Base Camp.

DAY 7: Rest day.

DAY 8: Return to Camp I at 10,000 feet.

DAY 9: Carry loads to Camp II at 12,000 feet.

DAY 10: Camp II to summit via the upper Mensu Glacier and East Ridge. Return to Camp II.

DAY 11: Descend to Camp I and Base Camp.

DAY 12: Rest day at Base Camp.

DAY 13: Optional one-day climb of Pik Bronja.

DAY 14 to 18: Five-day backpack excursion to Lake Kutscherla.

DAY 19 and 20: Rest days or other climbs.

DAY 21: Helicopter shuttle to Ust Koksa.

DAY 22: Fly to Barnaul. Overnight at hotel.

DAY 23: Visit Siberian agricultural station. Evening flight to Moscow.

DAY 24: Sightseeing in Moscow.

DAY 25: Depart Moscow on homeward-bound flights.

Louise McGowan, first Canadian woman on the summit of Belukha, highest peak in the Siberian Altai.

For 1985, the programs will take place in four mountain regions:

The Caucasus:

24-day climbing/ hiking program in the Mt. Elbrus region (two July camps); 17-day alpine skiing program (camps in February, March and May).

The Pamirs:

30-day program of expedition mountaineering with climbs in the Pamir Range. Five July camps. Minimum four in party.

The Western Tien Shan:

15-day program of skiing and climbing in the Chimgan region. One camp is offered in February.

The Altai:

24-day climbing/ hiking program with an ascent of Mt. Belukha (14,800'), highest peak in the Altai. One July camp is planned.

Camp II on the Mensu Glacier at 12,000 feet on Belukha. The summit was reached the next day by a Canadian-American team of nine climbers.

Altai photos by Dick McGowan

Picnic by a glacial lake with Mt. Ausangate in background/Pam Shandrick

THE ANDES VIA THE ROYAL ROAD

by Gail Bryan

© Copyright 1983

Gail Bryan is a professional writer and photographer with a lifelong love of the mountains. She travels to "get to know people, to understand them in spite of a different language and culture." She has traveled extensively, including a trek in Nepal with Mountain Travel in 1977 to visit the mountains she always dreamed of, and to Alaska, a special place for her, since she is a keen whitewater canoeist and kayaker. She is currently working on a book of photographs of the women of India and Nepal.

Llamas and alpacas are constant trailside companions on a hike through the Cordillera Vilcanota/Bruce Klepinger

Just follow the Inca road." and with that, Jaime, my guide, was gone—down a long, dizzingly steep slope of crumbling red scree, down along the edge of the huge glacier to our left, whose surface had been smoothed by severe wind and etched by debris to the look of burnished silver. He was quickly a small black figure lost under the towering white brilliance of Salcantay, the mountain peak that dominates everything within miles. I was left alone on the razor edge that is the summit of the Incachilaska Pass, 16,000 feet up in the Peruvian Andes.

Across high, bare, undulating olive land, the imprint of the road curved below me—a thin thread, still visible after three centuries. Along it, far in the distance, walked tiny specks, strung out over and between the great rounded wrinkles, the other seven members of my Mountin Travel trek.

The builders of the road called it Capac Nan, the beautiful highway. It was the technical means by which they administered an empire that at its height reached 3000 miles along the Pacific coast of South America. It was the royal road of the Inca—supreme ruler—whose title the conquering Spaniards, reaching Peru just at the apogee of imperial expansion, misapplied to the whole civilization.

So magnificent were the roads—over 5000 miles of them with almost 1000 bridges—that Hernando Pizarro himself was awed: "The royal road over the mountains is a thing worthy of being seen, because the ground is so rugged. Such beautiful roads could not, in truth, be found anywhere in Christendom."

The Andes are precipitous ridges of rock, the second highest range in the world. On one side is the arid coastal desert, and on the other the almost impenetrable jungle of the Amazon basin. High fertile valleys among the mountain peaks provided a habitat conducive to the development of civilization. A road system was essential to empire in such terrain, but the obstacles to its construction were so great that it stands as an engineering feat of extraordinary brilliance, far greater than that of Rome—unbelievable in scope and precision, were one not actually walking on the stones.

The feat that it was became indelibly clear to me as I stood under Salcantay. It had been imprinted deep in the fiber of mind and muscle with every step to the top of the long and extremely steep pass. We had begun the trek two days ago in Cuzco, a city of golden Spanish provincial architecture, underlaid with massive walls of original Inca buildings —a city with the austerity of both the Inca and El Escorial. Cuzco—capital of the Inca empire, and for the Inca civilization, literally the "navel of the world."

Out from the city, we were immediately immersed in the intense quality of Peruvian light. The landscape itself is arguably the most spectacular on earth. The Andes are like elegant soaring white wings. They are not massive in aspect like the Himalayas nor weathered like the Alps, but rather are thin and tapered, jagged knife edges. But the dark, brooding light that falls around the mountains imparts a power to the landscape that is much more than simply beautiful. Gray often hangs low and ominous over the peaks while sun streaks the high plains brilliant green. Shadows color great swaths of the brown hills dark lavender-blue.

We climbed initially through steep, arid ridges far above a wild, churning stream, past stands of twisted trees baroque with lichens and bromeliads.

It is a landscape with red butterflies stationary in the trail, and bright blue buntings fluttering about unafraid among voluptuous blossoms. It is a garden of miniature colors: purple berries, bits of tiny red leaves, dandelion and daisy-like flowers hugging close to the earth, patches of small cactus turning glowing platinum in the low sun.

Walking always toward the white of Salcantay, we came to a great highland meadow of light brown grass. And there we camped under the mountain in the thin silent air of a long dusk.

Silence, too, was the hallmark of our ascent. Rushing meltwater from the glaciers, cold and immense above us, was the only constant—along with the brittle crystal sound of ice falling.

The next day we scaled two more high passes, walking on this tiny track through a world unknown below this altitude: empty, desolate, echoing country, bare and chillingly remote. It is without snow and ice, a vast expanse of unrelieved rock falling away into a far distance. A pair of condors swept very close below us, gliding back and forth, black and white, riding the wind in this great serene space.

Names for the land in Peru are descriptive references to what grows in each zone of altitude. There is the *junga,* or jungle, the *quechua,* "where the corn grows," and the *puna,* "where no corn grows." Altitude is so vital in Peru that the name of the level that produces life-sustaining corn is also the name of the Inca language, Quechua.

We camped, poised to descend through the inhabited strata of Peru's vertical agriculture. The next day, we would pass men harvesting potatoes from small fields blocked out from the enormous scale by what seemed doll-like stone walls. And much farther down we would pass through a whole village taking in corn. But on our second night, we stayed in the high *puna.*

To say that we "camped" is accurate in that we stayed in tents on the ground in sleeping bags. But trekking with Mountain Travel is trekking with style. Our dining room table came with us on mule back—and the dining room with it (in the form of a large tent). We sat down to tea at the end of our first day with strawberry preserves and English biscuits. At the second camp we dipped into freshly made popcorn. I will long remember a superb lunch prepared in the middle of one of our longest days—a day of climbing steeply up through wet forest, down over irregular jumbled rocks, and immediately up again, up a mountain side so steep that we crept along a zigzag of switchbacks. Juan, our chef, managed elegant plates of *papas a la Huancaina* in the spectacular setting of a round pre-Inca ruin.

Mountain Travel puts every effort into seeing that all members complete the trip—not a trivial concern with 16,000-foot passes in rapid succession. It is a rigorous trek. There is a wonderful exhilaration in the physical exertion. But the leaders help the exhilaration along by bolstering flagging confidence. "We *all* make it" was the smiling response to a few hesitant verbalized self-doubts at the end of the first long day. And the leaders ensure that we do make it by ruthless paring down of daypack loads and in adjustments to equipment.

Below Salcantay, we turned onto what was originally a minor spur of the Inca road. It was for centuries unknown or ignored as an unimportant dead end. It is now by far the most heavily travelled portion and is known as "the Inca Trail." It leads to the sacred late-Inca city of Machu Picchu.

Because this secondary road did not receive the heavy traffic carried by the rest of the system well into the 19th century, it is well-preserved. Precise curbing remains; stairways with great stone slabs as risers lead up to lookout posts; steps are cut into bedrock through natural tunnels. There is also increasing evidence of what Inca civilization was like before the Spanish conquest: the garrisons of Sayacmarca, Phuyupatamarca, and Huinay Huayna.

Each is different in character and orientation to its site, but the salient characteristics of Inca workmanship stand out: long concentric terraces down the steep mountainsides, trapezoidal windows looking out to triangles of sharp peaks; and, above all, the huge stones superbly and precisely joined without mortar.

At the turn onto "the Inca Trail," we passed to the wet side of the mountains and entered a lush cloud forest, dripping orchids and tendrils of vines—a cool, still-silent world of tree ferns over and beside the rock. The last bit of trail edges along a precipice. Several times I put my walking stick down beside my foot into what looked like foliage but was, in fact, empty space. The precarious way the road hugs the mountain is disguised by the luxuriance. For a long stretch, the ground is coated with large, thick, white blossoms fallen from giant trees that tower in the canopy.

I came to a high fortress-gateway in late afternoon. Machu Picchu lay below just as I had seen it in innumerable photographs—a collection of almost intact stone ruins on a small saddle of ground in the midst of sheer green mountains. But Machu Picchu can never be captured in postcard images. Nothing but space and height surround it. It is part of the mountains.

There are many guidebooks to Machu Picchu, and living guides throng the ruins at midday. But there are no facts about the city beyond what the perceptive eye can see. There are only many theories—and enigmas. Machu Picchu is a place in which to give imagination free reign. What was its purpose: Agriculture? Religion? Defense? What is the reason for its many intricate parts? Why and when its demise?

The site can, of course, be enjoyed on many levels. You can give yourself over totally to the visual and walk through Machu Picchu as through the Museum of Modern Art. Superlatives hang limp and ineffectual beside the magnificence of Inca art and masonry.

An enormous stone in the "Ceremonial Room" has 32 angles worked on all six sides. The Intihuantana, the most sacred of Inca shrines, at the highest point in the city, is bedrock carved into abstraction, every side of which is differ-

Camp below Mt. Salcantay/Bruce Klepinger

ent and bold and subtle. Examples of the daring and accuracy of Inca stonework are everywhere: the exquisite cascade of fountains, the great carved stone by the "Watchman's Hut."

Machu Picchu is a great, terribly intricate and beautiful Rubik's Cube.

Rock and water are clearly paramount. The Incas seem to have venerated both, and often bedrock was left untouched next to detailed carving. The planning of the trek allowed us to experience in an immediate way the parallel of art and nature.

After a brief rest at an inn in the sacred valley of the Urubamba river, we set out to circle the highest peak in southern Peru, Ausangate. We walked above the *puna* into the area the Incas reserved to the spirits of the mountains. We walked by huge glaciers, with Andean geese, among Chinese watercolors of rock and cloud. The power of the ice and the rugged rock, the arid austerity, was a constant presence. We saw below the sheer white of one glacier face a small pool of silent green water. On it floated gracefully one glistening clear iceberg. There was an encompassing tranquillity next to and part of the power, with only the delicate "clink...clink" of ice slowly touching ice.

There were other lyrical moments. We sat in an unexpectedly lush green meadow laced with thin curving streams—the water reflecting black silhouettes of llamas. And we mingled with the llamas themselves: curious and gentle, walking demurely on small feet with ladylike steps, dowagers appropriately ample but with a very correctly erect carriage and mein.

But just when you settle in to love the land and reach out to embrace its beauty, adversity stands stark in your path and reminds you that this is an extraordinarily unforgiving mother earth. The rock sacred to the Inca is magnificent but brutally harsh.

The Incas built the Royal Road in harmony with the harsh land, in harmony with the sacred rock. And great irony it is that the very excellence of their achievement was the avenue to their destruction. It was by following the beautiful road, that the small band of 183 Spanish *conquistadores* was able to penetrate the Andes with the horse and thus eventually to obliterate the Inca.

SOUTH AMERICA

& MEXICO

High country of the Cordillera Raura, Peru/Bruce Klepinger

PERU • ECUADOR • BOLIVIA • CHILE • ARGENTINA • BRAZIL
COSTA RICA • MEXICO

na, high altitude beast of burden,
/Bruce Klepinger

John Cleare below Nevado Rondoy (19,347'), Cordillera Huayhuash, Peru/Leo Le Bon

Mountain Travel South America & Mexico

In Peru, a lofty Andean wilderness where more than 100 peaks top 18,000 feet, the legacy of the Inca Empire is every-where. It is at its most astounding in the massive stone monuments of Cuzco and Machu Picchu, and still impressive in little-known mountain valleys where today's paths follow Inca-built trails.

For 1985, we offer twelve different Peruvian journeys, some for touring and cultural exploration, some for mountain trekking.

We trek to Machu Picchu via a spectacular 15,000-foot pass below Mt. Salcantay (20,564'). We follow a llama traders' trail to Paucartambo to attend the once-a-year Indian "Fiesta del Carmen." We climb the snowy ridges of the Cordillera Blanca, highest tropical mountain range on earth.

Our South American journeys are not only in Peru: we also sail the world-famous wildlife habitat of the Galapagos (Darwin's Islands), explore the fjords and pampas of Patagonia, and ascend Ecuador's tropical yet ice-covered volcanoes.

In Central America, we search wildlife-rich Costa Rica, and climb up three of Mexico's highest mountains.

Mountain Travel offers the most comprehensive adventure travel program on the continent, with imaginative itineraries designed for very small groups and led by expert guides.

TERRY BRIAN, 33, is an experienced wilderness guide with expertise in the ethnology and natural history of South America. An avid river-runner, he is a senior guide on the Colorado River and has made many first descents of South American rivers. Fluent in Spanish, with a knowledge of various Indian dialects, he has explored most of South America and has led Mountain Travel treks for eight years.

JAMES DIRKS, 37, a Canadian, was born in Peru and raised in the Peruvian jungle among the Campa Indians. He has traveled throughout South America and once walked from Bolivia to Chile for three months, crossing much of the Atacama Desert). He lives on a farm in Curahuasi, Peru, and guides our "Peru Festival Trek."

Sara Steck

LINDA FARLEY, 34, was raised in the Canadian Rockies, which she explored on foot and by cross-country skis for years. She spent a year traveling in South America, including an expedition by balsa raft on Peru's Tambo River. She is interested in Peru's native crafts and is studying knitting designs in the Cuzco area, where she lives on an anise farm with her husband, Mountain Travel leader James Dirks, and their two children.

SERGIO FITCH WATKINS, 33, of Mexico, is a professional climbing guide with experience in the U.S., the Alps, Spain and the Himalayas. He leads our climbing expeditions on the volcanoes of Mexico and Ecuador as well as on Aconcagua, highest peak in the Western Hemisphere.

BRUCE KLEPINGER, 43, has led more than 50 Mountain Travel treks in Asia and South America. His mountaineering background includes over 1,000 climbs, and he has led numerous expeditions on Aconcagua (highest peak in the Western Hemisphere), Huascaran (highest peak in Peru), and peaks in Nepal and India. Bruce also has ten years experience as a boatman on the Grand Canyon of the Colorado River and on several South American rivers. He speaks fluent Spanish.

Bruce Klepinger

JOSE "PEPE" NORIEGA, 30, of Cuzco, Peru, spent most of his younger years living in Europe and the U.S. with his father, a member of Peru's diplomatic corps, and it was in Europe that he developed his love of the mountains. Settling in Cuzco after his schooling, he has spent the last three years leading hiking and rafting expeditions.

SARA STECK, 30, is Mountain Travel's South American operations manager. She has lived in Central America, speaks fluent Spanish, and spends six months of each year leading treks in Peru, Ecuador and the Galapagos.

CARLOS VELOACHAGA, 44, has a degree in cultural anthropology. A native of Peru, he has lived in Cuzco for the last seven years, where he leads trekking expeditions and continues his studies of both Quechua and Inca cultures.

Lindy Farley

Terry Brian

About Our South America Trip Leaders

Our South American trip leaders have unique backgrounds, an individual blend of cultural expertise and wilderness knowledge. They are capable guides whose experience will enhance the special delights of South American travel.

Narcisso Cahuana, playing the quena. *With his fluency in both Quechua and English and his insights on highland culture, Narcisso is a great asset to our Peru trekking staff/Bruce Klepinger*

Please Note:

Sergio Fitch Watkins

James Dirks

Jose "Pepe" Noreiga

*The Inca Trail...
which way?/
Barbara Kaplan*

IT3EA1MT02

DISCOVER PERU

Inca culture and natural history

DATES: #1 Jan 11–Jan 25 (15 days)
#2 Mar 8–Mar 22 (15 days)
#3 Nov 1–Nov 15 (15 days)
#4 Dec 20, 1985–Jan 3, 1986 (15 days)
LEADER: *Carlos Velaochaga*
GRADE: *A-2*
LAND COST: *$1650 (10–16 members)
$1790 (4–9)*

This is both a cultural and natural history journey, exploring archaeological sites such as the famous Nazca Lines and the magnificent mountain sites of Machu Picchu and the Urubamba Valley. We'll delve into many rich natural environments from Paracas Wildlife Park on the Pacific Coast, with its colonies of marine mammals, to the snow-capped Arequipa Volcanoes and Lake Titicaca, the great "inland sea" shared by Peru and Bolivia.

There is no trekking or camping on this trip and all the walks are non-strenuous.

*Indian girl near Tambomachay, Peru. A major part of the enjoyment of trekking in Peru is meeting the people who have inhabited these highlands for centuries and through whose villages and lives we will pass/
Pam Shandrick*

*Bill Le Bon admiring the ruins of Machu Picchu, the greatest mystery of the Inca Empire, discovered in 1911 by American archaeologist Hiram Bingham, who followed up rumors told him by his Indian guide of a lost city hidden in the ridges of the Cordillera Urubamba, Peru/
Leo Le Bon*

Moisture-laden air has provided the Inca Trail with a rich flora including a wide variety of bromeliads, Spanish mosses and Andean hardwoods. The section between Runkuraqay and Phuyupatamarca is particularly remarkable, with its overhead canopy of trees festooned with vines and creepers and the trail itself a stony path often consisting of white stone slabs weighing hundreds of pounds and forming a path three feet wide.

ITINERARY:

DAY 1: Leave U.S. Arrive Lima and transfer to hotel. Afternoon city tour of Lima and visit to the city's well-known archaeological museums.

DAY 2: Drive south along the Pacific Coast to Paracas, visiting the Pachacamac ruins (circa 500 B.C.) enroute.

DAY 3: Boat trip to Islas Ballestas, islands off the shores of Paracas Wildlife Park with large colonies of flamingos and sea lions. Return to mainland and drive south to Nazca.

DAY 4: Morning tour and scenic overflight above the famous archaeological site of the Nazca Lines, enormous mysterious markings cut into the coastal desert during Nazca Civilization (800 B.C.). Maria Reiche, the German expert who has studied the Nazca lines for over 25 years, maintains that the lines represent a vast astronomical pre-Inca calendar.

DAY 5: Drive south along the coast, turning inland to the town of Arequipa (8000').

DAY 6: Half-day tour of Arequipa, a lovely white stone city built in the colonial era and set in an arid highland environment. The big peaks of the Cordillera Volcanica can be seen from town—snow-capped El Misti (19,200') and Chachani (20,000').

DAY 7: Drive to Nacional Aguada Blanca Vicuna Reserve, a sanctuary for vicunas, which have become an endangered species. The road goes through high desert terrain and over a pass between the volcanoes of Misti and Chachani. Continue driving higher up on the altiplano ("high plains") to Puno, a town on the shores of Lake Titicaca (12,500'). Lake Titicaca is the highest navigable body of water on earth.

DAY 8: All-day excursion out onto the lake to visit Takili Island, with its population of Aymara Indians. We'll also pass by the floating reed islands of the Uros Indians, with their hand-made reed boats that are still the main form of transport on the lake.

DAY 9: By train from Puno to Cuzco (11,204'), the Inca capital, arriving in the afternoon.

DAY 10: Early morning train to Machu Picchu, a scenic four-hour ride through the beautiful Urubamba Valley. Arrive at Machu Picchu station and proceed up to the ruins by bus. Afternoon to explore the vine-covered stone buildings of this "lost city" of the Incas. Overnight at the Machu Picchu Hotel.

DAY 11: More exploration at Machu Picchu and a chance to climb Huayna Picchu (9,000'), a small peak above the ruins. Catch the afternoon train to Urubamba and check into a small country inn.

DAY 12: Morning walks in the very beautiful Inca ruins at Pisac and Ollantaytambo, then continue by bus through the Urubamba Valley to Cuzco.

DAY 13: In Cuzco. Day free for sightseeing and shopping.

DAY 14: Fly to Lima. Day free in Lima. Depart on evening flight.

DAY 15: Arrive Miami and connect with homeward-bound flights.

IT3EA1MT02

THE PERU ADVENTURE

Sample the mountains, rivers and jungles

DATES: #1 Mar 16–Mar 30 (15 days)
　#2 Apr 13–Apr 27 (15 days)
　#3 May 11–May 25 (15 days)
　*#4 Jun 8–Jun 22 (15 days)
　#5 Jun 15–Jun 29 (15 days)
　#6 Jul 6–Jul 20 (15 days)
　#7 Aug 3–Aug 17 (15 days)
　#8 Aug 31–Sep 14 (15 days)
LEADER: *to be announced*
GRADE: *B-2*
LAND COST: $1690 (4–6 members)
　　　　　$1490 (7–16)

*Note: The June 8 departure is set aside as a "family trek" for parents and children (special rates apply for children).

Sampling the best of wilderness Peru, our "Peru Adventure" includes a five-day trek on the Inca Trail to Machu Picchu, a leisurely two-day rafting trip on the Urubamba River, visits to Cuzco and the Inca ruins of the Urubamba Valley and an Amazon visit with a chance to explore jungle rivers by canoe.

The mists of the Urubamba Valley below a high section of the Inca Trail with Pumasillo Massif in distance/Bruce Kelpinger

ITINERARY:

DAY 1: Leave U.S. Arrive Lima. Continue by air to Cuzco. Transfer to hotel.

DAY 2: Drive to Urubamba Valley, "Sacred Valley of the Incas," and begin float trip on the Urubamba River by paddle raft. Float through a rich green mountain valley walled by the ridges of the Cordillera Urubamba. Visit the Inca ruins at Pisac en route. Overnight at inn.

DAY 3: Continue float trip, visiting Ollantaytambo ruins, known for their exceptional stonework. Overnight at inn.

DAY 4: Leaving our rafts and donning hiking boots, we begin a five-day trek on the Inca Trail to Machu Picchu, walking on Inca-built steep stone stairs and over green ridges. Today's walk takes us from Chilca (8,000′) near the banks of the Urubamba River up to the village of Huayllabamba (9,700′). Walk along the upper banks of the river with a view of the ruins at Llactapata.

DAY 5: Hike over the Warmiwan-usqa Pass ("Pass of the Dead Woman"—13,776′), longest and steepest part of the trek, and highest point on the Inca Trail. Descend and camp below the ruins of Runkuraqay (11,800′).

DAY 6: Over Runkuraqay Pass (12,494′) to Sayacmarca. Stop to visit the ruin, and continue on to camp near Phuyupatamarca ("Town in the Clouds") at 11,906 feet.

Porters Celso Monarco, Gregorio Giuspe, Mariano Yapu and Venancio Monarco preparing their lunch/Leo Le Bon

DAY 7: A three hour walk, passing the ruins of Winaywayna ("forever young") to Intipunku at 8,900 feet, the original entrance to Machu Picchu, through which we will enter the ruins.

DAY 8: All morning to explore the ruins and hike up Huayna Picchu (9,000′). Catch the late afternoon train and arrive in Cuzco in early evening.

DAY 9: Morning free in Cuzco. Afternoon city tour, including the major ruins at Sacsayhuaman and Kenko.

DAY 10: Day free in Cuzco.

DAY 11: Fly to Puerto Maldonado, and proceed by motorized dugout canoe to a lodge on the tributary of the Amazon River.

DAY 12: Time for walks in the jungle, visits to a nearby Indian village or exploring the river environment by dugout canoe.

DAY 13: Transfer to airport for morning flight to Lima. Afternoon free. Overnight in hotel.

DAY 14: Morning tour of Lima. Afternoon free. Late evening transfer to airport and depart Lima.

DAY 15: Arrive Miami and continue on homeward-bound flights.

Alfredo Ferreyros

Our Man in Peru

Alfredo Ferreyros, director of trekking operations in Peru, was raised in Peru's northern mountains and educated in Europe and the U.S. (at Cornell University). He knows the Andes intimately and makes trekking logistics run smoothly, even in the most remote places. He has traveled to Nepal to compare the fine points of Andean versus Himalayan trekking, and he organizes, without a doubt, the very best treks in Peru. During off-season, he is an environmental activist, consultant to Peru's newly developing national park system (his special interest is the new Machu Picchu National Park), and is spearheading an effort to maintain the environmental integrity of Manu National Park, one of his favorite places and one of the Amazon's most pristine wilderness regions.

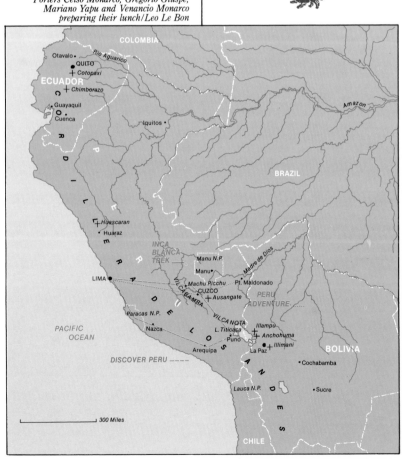

Mountain Travel catalog editor Pam Shandrick and the glaciers of Mt. Ausangate, Cordillera Vilcanota, Peru/Alberto Miori

IT3EA1MT03

THE PERUVIAN HIGHLANDS

6-day Inca Trail trek, 7-day Vilcanota trek

DATES: #1 May 4–May 25 (22 days)
#2 Jun 15–Jul 6 (22 days)
#3 Aug 10–Aug 31 (22 days)
LEADER: #1 & #2: Terry Brian
#3: Sara Steck
GRADE: C-2
LAND COST: $1850 (13–16 members)
$2150 (10–12)

This is a Peru "classic," starting with a walk on the fabled Inca Trail to Machu Picchu (but with a unique approach via the remote valleys of the Cordillera Vilcabamba) and ending with a trek across the vast, golden *altiplano* of the Cordillera Vilcanota, where we hike among herds of llamas and alpacas, meet the occasional Indian herdsman and enjoy panoramic views of 18,000 to 20,000-foot ice peaks.

Our six-day foot journey to Machu Picchu begins in the Cordillera Vilcabamba, a range which juts out of the lowlands and has glaciers feeding the Amazon, and whose valleys are replete with remnants of Inca terraces and irrigation canals. We begin in a remote section of the Vilcabamba and cross a spectacular 15,000-foot pass in the shadows of magnificent Mt. Salcantay (20,574') and Mt. Palcay (18,654'), linking up with the Inca Trail for the last three days of the trek.

The trek culminates with the incomparable experience of walking into Machu Pichu, the citadel abandoned by the Incas, reclaimed by the jungle and only rediscovered in 1911.

Spinning and weaving are ancient folk arts among highland Indians, who produce some of the finest hand-woven fabrics in South America/ Barbara Kaplan

The second section of the trip is a seven-day trek in the Cordillera Vilcanota, a mountain range of stunning, isolated ice peaks which rise from the rolling grasslands of the *altiplano*. Our route completely circles glacier-covered Mt. Ausangate (20,945') and our camps are in splendid meadows at 14,000 feet.

We also plan to spend time enjoying the Inca ruins and Indian markets of Cuzco. In between treks, we relax at a comfortable country inn in Urubamba, visiting the superb ruins at Ollantaytambo.

ITINERARY:

DAY 1: Leave U.S. Arrive Lima and continue by air to Cuzco. Transfer to hotel. Afternoon free.

DAY 2: Morning excursion by bus to Indian market at Chincheros.

DAY 3: By bus to the hilltop ruins of Pisac in the Urubamba Valley. Return to Cuzco.

DAY 4: All-morning drive to a rustic hacienda at Mollepata (8,500').

DAY 5: Begin six-day trek to Machu Picchu, with a long, gradual uphill hike to a high meadow at Soray (10,000'), just beneath the spectacular southwest face of Salcantay.

DAY 6: Steep push up over the Incachilaska Pass (about 15,000'), then descend a long, flat valley to a camp at about 12,000 feet.

DAY 7: Following the remnants

of Inca terraces, hike over another 15,000-foot pass. Camp at 11,000 feet.

DAY 8: Hike past remnants of Inca irrigation canals to a camp at about 10,000 feet, where we join the "regular" Inca Trail.

DAY 9: Continue along the Inca Trail, crossing over the Warmi-wanusqa Pass (13,776'), highest point on the Inca Trail. Camp at a meadow at about 11,000 feet.

DAY 10: Hike to Phuyupatamarca, descend about 2,000 feet to Inti-punku ("Door of the Sun"), and arrive at Machu Picchu.

DAY 11: All day at Machu Picchu. Optional hike up Huayna Picchu (9,000'). Afternoon train to the town of Urubamba. Overnight at inn.

DAY 12: Visit the town of Ollantaytambo and its beautiful Inca ruins.

DAY 13: Six-hour drive to the highland village of Tinki (13,000'), crossing over a rugged 14,000-foot pass.

DAY 14: Begin five-day Vilcanota trek, walking across an expanse of golden pampas from which the peak of Mt. Ausangate, highest mountain in the Cordillera Vilcanota, rises. Camp at Upis (13,500') near some hot springs.

DAY 15: Hike over the sand-colored slopes of the Incapampa Pass (15,400') and then alongside a deep glacial lake called Pucacocha, above which towers Mt. Ausangate. Camp by the lake at about 14,000 feet and hear Ausangate's glaciers drop huge blocks of ice into the lake.

DAY 16: Over a 15,750-foot pass and down to Lake Ausangatecocha, then over Palomani Pass (16,900') with views of Ausangate and neighboring Mariposa. Camp at 15,000 feet.

DAY 17: Trek along the Rio Jampamaya and above Lake Ticlla-cocha, with views of the 19,000-foot ice peaks of Jatunjampa and Collque Cruz. Cross Pacchanta Pass (16,725') and camp.

DAY 18: Meander down the Pacchanta Valley and camp near Pacchanta hot springs at about 14,000 feet.

DAY 19: Hike to Tinki where we started our trek and board a bus for a five-hour drive to Cuzco.

DAY 20: In Cuzco for last-minute shopping and sightseeing.

DAY 21: Fly to Lima. Day free. Evening transfer to airport.

DAY 22: Depart Lima, arrive Miami and connect with home-ward-bound flights.

Our guide Wilbur Aparicio and Bill Le Bon overlooking the Pacamayo Valley, Inca Trail/Leo Le Bon

IT3EA1MT08

TREKKING IN THE CARABAYA

14-day trek from Lake Titicaca to the Vilcanota

DATES: #1 May 18–Jun 8 (22 days)
　　　 #2 Jun 29–Jul 20 (22 days)
LEADER: #1: Bruce Klepinger
　　　　 #2: Sara Steck
GRADE: C-3
LAND COST: $1990 (13–16 members)
　　　　　 $2275 (10–12)

The Carabaya, a mountain range in the easternmost reaches of Peru's *altiplano*, just north of Lake Titicaca, is little traveled by outsiders and has fantastic mountain scenery, colonial-era Inca ruins and some of the most beautiful pampas in the Andes. It also has a fine share of Andean wildlife, including condor, vicuna and flamingos. At its western end, it links with the impressive Cordillera Vilcanota,

Maxi, our chief cook, Porfirio and arrieros *(animal handlers) at Oconcate/Bruce Klepinger*

and both ranges together stretch nearly 100 miles across the highlands from Lake Titicaca to Cuzco.

Our 14-day Cordillera Carabaya trek begins near Lake Titicaca's northern shore. Our route follows trails through moderately high altitudes with surprising subtropical vegetation, hot springs and waterfalls. Views extend upwards to the Carabaya's carved and fluted 18,000-foot ice peaks and down thousands of feet to the mists of the Amazon Basin.

At mid-point in the trek, we cross a 16,500-foot pass with views of the Andean ice cap and a 360-degree panorama of ice peaks. This pass is the line where the Carabaya changes names and becomes the Cordillera Vilcanota (see *Peruvian Highlands* trek). From here we descend to Lake Sibinacocha (15,000'), where we might see flocks of pink flamingos. Finally, we pass along the ramparts of Mt. Ausangate (20,945') and end the trek at the highland village of Tinki (13,000').

Before the trek, we'll visit Lake Titicaca and at the end of the trip we enjoy the markets of Cuzco and museums of Lima.

ITINERARY:

DAY 1: Leave U.S.

DAY 2: Arrive Lima. Continue by air to Juliaca. Drive to Puno on the shores of Lake Titicaca (12,500'), visiting pre-Inca tomb towers at Sillustani enroute. Overnight at hotel.

DAY 3: By boat across the lake, passing the floating island-villages of the Uros Indians and visit the island of Takili. Continue to the northern shore and camp at Taraco.

DAY 4 and 5: Drive to Macusani, crossing a high pass, and camp. From camp, take a day hike around Lake Chungara and descend by bus to the remote village of Ayapata to visit a native market.

DAY 6: Begin trek, hiking into a valley with many lakes and Inca ruins. Camp at one of the lakes.

DAY 7: Cross a 13,500-foot pass with extensive views north toward the Yungas (the deep valleys which lead to the Amazon) and southward toward the Carabaya. Descend to Olleachea and relax in public hot springs.

DAY 8: Ascend from Olleachea, past the town of Asiento, to the crest above Rio Corani. Cross a pass and camp near a small mountain lake surrounded by grassy meadows.

DAY 9: Over two passes with splendid views of open pampas, flanks of steep carved mountains and the deep gorge of the Rio Corani.

DAY 10: Trek west through immense pampas, approaching snow-capped peaks. Camp at about 14,000 feet.

DAY 11 and 12: Rest day and optional hike to the head of the Rio Corani valley, where the peaks of the western Carabaya are at their most magnificent. The Peruvian icecap is seen to the south and many jagged ice peaks to the northwest.

DAY 13 and 14: Cross a 17,000-foot pass, entering the "Departmento de Cuzco" and the mountain range called the Cordillera Vilcanota. Descend past a large cirque of 20,000-foot peaks and camp at the pueblo of Finaya. Rest day or optional hikes to the base of the ice cap or to Lake Sibinacocha (15,000').

DAY 15 and 16: Trek along the banks of Lake Sibinacocha with incredible views of lakes and towering ice peaks and cross a 17,500-foot pass to Jampa.

DAY 17 and 18: Cross two more passes and descend toward Lake Ticllacocha, then cross Pacchanta Pass (16,900') and camp near the hot springs at Pacchanta.

DAY 19: Walk to the highland village of Tinki (13,000') and drive to Cuzco.

DAY 20: Free day in Cuzco.

DAY 21: Fly to Lima. Day free.

DAY 22: Depart Lima, arrive Miami and connect with homeward-bound flights.

About Trekking in the Andes

To make your Peru trek as comfortable as possible, all camping gear is carried by pack animals and/or porters. You will only need to carry a light day-pack for your jacket, camera and water bottle.

In addition to the Mountain Travel leader, there will be a camp manager, camp staff and cook. Breakfast and dinner are hot meals served in a dining tent; a plentiful lunch is served picnic-style each day at a scenic spot on the trail.

All water used for drinking and cooking is filtered and boiled; we maintain a high standard of camp hygiene. The staff does all camp chores.

Most of our Peru treks take place in sparsely populated highland regions, often at 10,000 feet or higher. Campsites are chosen for their scenic beauty and proximity to sources of water and fodder for the pack animals.

Settling into camp at Huallabamba on the Inca Trail/ Bruce Klepinger

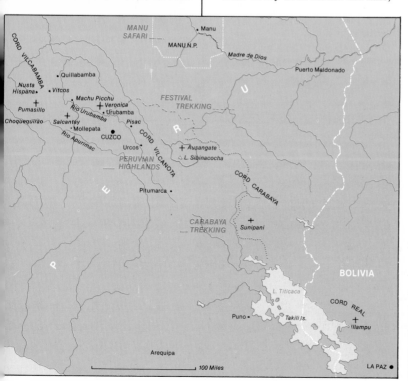

IT3EA1MT13

PERU: THE FESTIVAL TREK

15-day trek through remote Cordillera Urubamba

DATES: *Jun 30–Jul 19 (20 days)*
LEADER: *James Dirks*
GRADE: *C-3*
LAND COST: *$1575 (13–16 members)*
$1780 (10–12)

This 15-day trek through the Cordillera Urubamba is timed to coincide with the lively Indian "Fiesta del Carmen" at the town of Paucartambo.

Villagers come from all around to attend this once-a-year celebration and festival. It is a joyous "dance parody" of life, complete with hundreds of dancers in brilliant costumes and masks. The dances parody certain occupations—from herders and traders to doctors and lawyers—and many aspects of daily life from Inca and colonial times.

The trekking route to Paucartambo is strenuous, following a major trade route used by alpaca and llama herders. On the way we'll pass many villages and remnants of Inca terracing and Inca irrigation canals. There will be long days and much up and down walking on steep ridges, but this trek is a special opportunity to glimpse into a mysterious, ancient culture before "progress" changes it forever.

ITINERARY:

DAY 1: Leave U.S. Arrive Lima and continue by air to Cuzco. Transfer to hotel.

DAY 2: Afternoon tour of the city and Inca ruins.

DAY 3: All-day excursion to the "Sacred Valley of the Incas," for visits to Pisac and Ollantaytambo. Overnight at an inn in Urubamba.

DAY 4: Begin trek, hiking along the Patacancha River, a major trade route from Urubamba to Lares. Camp at Huilloc.

DAY 5: Walk to Queunaococha on high and rocky terrain through rare *quenual* tree groves. On clear days there is a view of Salcantay (20,574′).

DAY 6: Cross a high pass beneath Mt. Colque Cruz, hiking past the beautiful village of Huacahuasi to the Inca-built Lares Hot Baths.

DAY 7: Hike past the town of Lares and camp by the Lares River.

During festivals, the community puts aside the chores of farming and herding and gives itself over to dancing, celebrating and drinking home-brewed chicha *with friends.*

Photos by Bruce Klepinger and Leo Le Bon

DAY 8: Hike over a rolling pampa ridge to the Inca village of Choquecancha. Two sides of the main plaza of this town are Inca walls, a third is now a colonial church.

DAY 9 and 10: Continue to Ampares, crossing the main pass on the trip and descending on a long downhill stretch to Chimor and the Chimor Hot Baths.

DAY 11: A short hike today to the Mapacho River; in the evening enjoy a *pachamanca,* or Peruvian barbeque.

DAY 12: Hike up 4,000 feet today on a llama trail and camp by a lake in high grasslands with views down into the jungle.

DAY 13: Hike along rolling country, past numerous lakes, with jungle views and views of Mt. Pitusiray. Mt. Ausangate (20,945′) comes into view on a clear day.

DAY 14: Hike along a ridge and arrive at Tres Cruces, once the site of two large Inca roads that descend to the tropics and an area called *patiti,* where in 1980 the remains of an Inca road built of turquoise mosaic was found.

DAY 15: Long day down the Mapacho River.

DAY 16: Hike to Paucartambo for the beginning of the Fiesta del Carmen. Camp outside of town.

DAY 17: At the Fiesta del Carmen. Watch hundreds of dancers in brilliant costumes performing traditional, ancient ritual dances. Return to camp for overnight.

DAY 18: Morning drive to Cuzco, arriving in the afternoon.

DAY 19: Fly to Lima. Day free. Overnight at hotel.

DAY 20: Depart Lima and connect with homeward-bound flights.

IT3EA1MT14

MANU JUNGLE WILDLIFE SAFARI

Amazon's most pristine forest reserve

DATES: *Aug 17–Aug 31 (15 days)*
LEADER: *Terry Brian*
GRADE: *A-2*
LAND COST: *$1890 (10–16 members)*

Join a wildlife expedition in Manu National Park, the largest national park in the Amazon.

This special four-million-acre park is one of the most beautiful and most untouched natural areas on the entire continent. Its isolation on the eastern slope of Peru's southern Andes has helped keep its ecological integrity. In 1977, Manu was declared a Biosphere Reserve by UNESCO, joining a select group of reserves whose scientific value is internationally recognized.

The impenetrable forest of Manu National Park gives shelter to jaguars, pumas, 13 species of monkeys, Andean deer, and rare spectacled bear. A dazzling abundance of birds (more than 500 species) flutter in the high canopy of orchid and vine-laden trees. The rivers and lakes are home to caimans, turtles, piranhas, anacondas and very rare giant otters.

The "highways" which allow us to penetrate the green walls of the Amazon are the reddish waters of the Manu River and the clear-flowing Madre de Dios River. Each day, we'll glide on the rivers by motorized dugout canoes. Each evening, we'll set up a tent camp on sandbars along the shores and listen to the haunting night sounds of the jungle.

First day of Vilcanota trek, Mt. Ausangate (20,945′) in background/Bruce Klepinger

Laguna Paron and Nevado Piramide in the Cordillera Blanca, highest tropical mountain range in the world, Peru/Bruce Klepinger

Pirana in Manu National Park, largest protected region in the Amazon, Peru/Bruce Klepinger

The trip also visits the beautiful highland town of Cuzco (11,200′), ancient capital of the Incas, with its many Inca ruins.

ITINERARY:

DAY 1: Leave U.S. Arrive Lima and continue to Cuzco. Transfer to hotel.

DAY 2: Morning free. Afternoon tour of Inca ruins at Sacsayhuaman and Kenko.

DAY 3: Drive to the Paucartambo Valley, an important trading center in colonial and republican times, and continue to Tres Cruces de Oro. Reach Manu National Park and camp.

DAY 4: Continue driving to Shintaya, arriving mid-day. Proceed by canoe to upper Madre de Dios, leaving the jungled hill country and entering the flood plains. At confluence with Manu River, head upstream to Playa Romero and camp.

DAY 5: By boat to Salvador or Orotongo.

DAY 6 to 8: Daily excursions deep into the jungle to see birdlife and perhaps red deer, tapirs and monkeys.

DAY 9 to 11: By boat to Cocha Cashu. Camp at Cocha Totora.

DAY 12: Float downstream to Boca Manu and camp.

DAY 13: Fly to Cuzco via Puerto Maldonado.

DAY 14: Fly to Lima. Day free. Evening transfer to airport and depart Lima.

DAY 15: Arrive Miami and connect with homeward-bound flights.

IT3EA1MT04

THE INCA-BLANCA TREK

7-day Inca Trail trek, 6-day Cordillera Blanca trek

DATES: #1 Jul 13–Aug 3 (22 days)
      #2 Sep 7–Sep 28 (22 days)
LEADER: #1: Linda Farley
       #2: Pepe Noriega
GRADE: C-2
LAND COST: $1990 (10–16 members)
          $2190 (10–12)

This is our only Peru itinerary which features treks in both northern and southern Peru.

In southern Peru, a seven-day trek takes us to Machu Picchu via a seldom-traveled route in the Cordillera Vilcabamba, following long, high altitude valleys below Mt. Palcay (18,645′). Joining the Inca Trail at mid-trek, we descend to the misty ruins of Machu Picchu.

In northern Peru, we will trek for six days in the Cordillera Blanca, highest tropical mountain range in the world. We'll walk through a variety of environments from subtropical to alpine, enjoying great panoramas of the Cordillera Blanca's well-known "skyline" of 20,000-footers, including Huascaran (22,204′), highest peak in Peru.

ITINERARY:

DAY 1: Leave U.S. Arrive Lima and continue by air to Cuzco. Transfer to hotel.

DAY 2: Excursion by bus to Sacsayhuaman and other Inca ruins nearby.

DAY 3: Early morning bus ride to the Urubamba Valley, the sacred valley of the Incas, for an all-day float trip on the Urubamba River and a visit to the Inca ruins at Pisac on route.

DAY 4: Visit the Inca site at Ollantaytambo, then continue on to Chilca (8,000′) to begin our seven-day trek to Machu Picchu.

DAY 5 and 6: Hike up into the Silque Valley to a meadow below the Ancascocha Pass (13,950′); cross the pass with views of the peaks of Huayanay and Palcay (18,645′) in the distance.

DAY 7 and 8: Hike down toward the valley of Sisaypampa below Mt. Salcantay (20,574′); continue downhill past the ruins of Incaraqay to the village of Huayllabamba (9,700′).

DAY 9: Hike through Llulluchapampa, cross a pass at 13,300 feet and descend to the Pacamayo River.

DAY 10: Up to the second pass past the ruins of Rukuraqay to Say-acmarca ("the waiting town") and Phuyupatamarca (11,900′). Enter Machu Picchu via Intipunku at 8,000 feet.

DAY 11: Explore Machu Picchu, hike up Huayna Picchu (9,000′), and return to Cuzco on the afternoon train, arriving early evening.

DAY 12: Day free in Cuzco.

DAY 13: Fly to Lima and continue by bus on a seven-hour drive to northern Peru and the highland town of Huaraz (10,200′). On route, visit the pre-Inca ruins of Paramonga.

DAY 14: By truck to the roadhead at Vaqueria, stopping enroute to visit Llanganuco Lakes, and drive over Portachuelo de Llanganuco, a pass at 15,740 feet with a great panorama of the major peaks of the Cordillera Blanca, including Huascaran (22,234′), Huandoy (20,980′), Pisco (18,898′), Chopicalqui (20,816′), and Chakraraju (20,052′). Descend to the east side of the range and camp at Vaqueria.

DAY 15: Begin trek with a hike up the canyon of the Quebrada Huaripampa and camp at Quebrada Paria.

DAY 16: Trek to Tuctubamba and camp. Optional hike up the Alto de Pucaraju (15,150′) for exceptional views of the Cordillera Blanca, including Alpamayo (10,511′), a peak known for its almost perfectly symmetrical pyramid shape.

DAY 17: Hike over Punta Union, a 15,580-foot pass, and camp on the western side. Optional hike for views of Quitaraju (19,816′).

DAY 18: Hike down the Santa Cruz Valley and camp at Llama Corral, passing beautiful meadows and a lake.

DAY 19: Hike out to Cashapampa and return to Huaraz by truck.

DAY 20: Seven-hour drive to Lima.

DAY 21: Visit anthropological museum in the morning, afternoon free to shop or visit Lima's other famous museums. Late night transfer to the airport.

DAY 22: Depart Lima, arrive Miami and connect with homeward-bound flights.

Peru Options

Whether you plan to visit Peru on one of our trips or on your own, we can arrange a variety of outdoor adventures for you, on foot, on horseback, by raft or dugout canoe.

For private treks, we can provide a full range of services such as bilingual guides, pack animals, camp staff and cooks, camp equipment and transport. Contact Mountain Travel for rates and further details.

Among our most popular "after the trek" excursions are:

Iquitos Amazon Exploration

From a remote lodge on the banks of the Amazon River, hike the trails of the jungle, swim in secluded lagoons, and explore the Amazon's tributaries by boat. Time: Three days.

Urubamba River Rafting

Whitewater rafting on the lively Urubamba River as it tumbles through the "sacred valley of the Incas." Also visit the fine Inca sites at Pisac or Ollantaytambo. Time: One or two days.

Puno/Lake Titicaca Excursion

From the red-roofed village of Puno on the shores of Lake Titicaca, journey by boat to visit Indian weavers on Takili Island and watch sunset over the highest navigable body of water on earth. Time: Three days.

The puya riamondi, *world's largest bromeliad (often to 12 meters), found only in the Queshque and Pachacoto valleys of the Cordillera Blanca/ Bruce Klepinger*

IT3EA1MT10

TREKKING IN THE CORDILLERA BLANCA

9 or 15-day treks in highest tropical mountain range in the world

DATES: #1 May 25–Jun 8 (15 days)
 #2 Jul 13–Aug 3 (22 days)
 #3 Jul 20–Aug 3 (15 days)
LEADER: #1: James Dirks
 #2: Terry Brian
 #3: Sara Steck
GRADE: #1 & #3: C-2 #2: C-3
LAND COST: #1 & #3: $1550
 (10–16 members)
 #2: $1875
 (13–16 members)
 $1980 (10–12)

Delicate corniced snow ridges and fluted ice faces make the mountains of the Cordillera Blanca ("White Mountains") among the most beautiful in the world.

In this great ice range, most of which is now protected within "Parque Nacional Huascaran," eleven major summits top 20,000 feet and more than 70 peaks top 18,000 feet.

Because these peaks are so close to the equator, snow conditions here are quite different from those of mountains in higher latitudes.

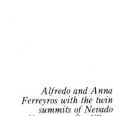

Indian girl of the Cordillera Blanca, Peru/Leo Le Bon

Alfredo and Anna Ferreyros with the twin summits of Nevado Huascaran, Cordillera Blanca/Leo Le Bon

Above snowline, even the steepest slopes are draped with ice, while the summits often consist of incredible overhanging cornices. The glaciers (the longest in the tropics) can almost be reached by road in some places.

Our treks here are fantastically scenic high altitude adventures, with campsites at about 13,000 to 14,000 feet.

TRIP #2 is a 16-day trek with views including most of the Blanca's spectacular northern peaks: Santa Cruz (20,534′), Huascaran (22,204′), Huandoy (20,980′), Chacraraju (20,052′), the "perfect" pyramid of Alpamayo (19,510′), and the glacial slopes of Copa (20,252′) and Toqllaraju (19,790′). As we walk, often along neatly cultivated fields and past lakes and waterfalls, we also see peaks much farther south, as we encircle the massifs of Contrahierbas, Hualcan and Copa.

ITINERARY:
Sixteen-day Trek (Trip #2)

DAY 1: Leave U.S. Arrive Lima. Transfer to hotel.

DAY 2: Seven-hour drive to the highland town of Huaraz (10,200′), with a visit to the pre-Inca Paramonga ruins and views of the southern peaks of the Cordillera Blanca enroute. Overnight at hotel.

DAY 3: Visit market and town of Huaraz and day hike in the Rio Santa Valley.

DAY 4: By truck from Huaraz to the roadhead at Caranca in Quebrada Ragranco, with good views of Huascaran, Santa Cruz and Copa enroute. Camp at 13,000 feet.

DAY 5 and 6: Trek through a gentle valley cultivated with potatoes. Pass Inca ruins enroute. Splendid views of the Cordillera Negra to the west. Enter the Quebrada Los Cedros with views of the classic pyramid of Alpamayo.

DAY 7 and 8: Cross Huilca Pass (15,800′) with sweeping views of the northern reaches of the Cordillera Blanca and up to the base of a pass leading to Quebrada Yanajanka. Camp at 13,500 feet.

DAY 9 to 11: Trek through wooded groves, grassy meadows and the steep glaciated cliffs of the eastern foothills of the Cordillera Blanca. Views include the formidable glaciers of the eastern face of Pukajirca. One day to be used as a rest day if necessary.

DAY 12 to 14: Cross Pucaraju Pass (15,345′) with views of Piramide and Chakraraju. Hike down the canyon of Quebrada Huaripampa. Side trip to the summit of Portachuelo de Llanganuco (15,740′), with its famous panorama including Huascaran, Huandoy, Pisco (17,900′), Chopikalqui (20,100′) and Chakraraju.

DAY 15 to 17: Hike into lower farmlands above Yanama then ascend the canyon of Quebrada Yanayacu and cross Yanayacu Pass. (16,170′). Views include the southern flanks of Huascaran and Contrahierbas (19,550′). Cross Ulta Pass with extensive views to the north including Artesonraju and the peaks of Quebrada Paron, as well as Huascaran and peaks far to the south.

DAY 18 and 19: Hike down Quebrada Putaca, pass the village of Pompeii and on into Quebrada Juitish. Cross Portachuelo Honda and camp at Rinconada.

DAY 20: Long descent down Quebrada Honda through cultivated fields to Ruripaccha. Meet truck for late return to Huaraz.

DAY 21: Drive to Lima.

DAY 22: Depart Lima, arrive Miami and connect with homeward-bound flights.

TRIPS #1 and #3 feature nine-day treks, which cover slightly more than half of the same route covered on the longer trek, only starting in the opposite direction. We'll be circling three major massifs, including Alpamayo, Santa Cruz and Pukajirca. The views are of the northern Cordillera Blanca with beautiful glacial-blue lakes of Azulcocha, Kullicocha and Jankarurish, the immense glaciers of Pukajirca and Santa Cruz, the cultivated fields of the eastern valleys and finally, views of the giant peaks of the Llanganuco Valley (Huascaran, Huandoy and Chakraraju).

ITINERARY

Nine-day Trek (Trips #1 & #3)

DAY 1: Leave U.S. Arrive Lima. Transfer to hotel.

DAY 2: Seven-hour drive to the mountain town of Huaraz, visiting the Paramonga ruins on route.

DAY 3: Visit Wilcahuain ruins and take a short acclimatization hike.

DAY 4: Drive over the Portachuelo Llanganuco, with its impressive panorama of the Cordillera Blanca, to a roadhead and camp.

DAY 5 to 8: Trek to Huaripampa, cross Pucaraju Pass, and visit Lake Huecrococha enroute to Jancapampa.

DAY 9 to 11: Cross Huilca Pass (15,800') to Quebrada Tayapampa and cross a 15,842-foot pass to Quebrada Alpamayo.

DAY 12 and 13: Cross Cuillicocha Pass (16,240'), end trek at Caranca and drive to Huaraz.

DAY 14: All-day bus ride to Lima.

DAY 15: Depart Lima, arrive Miami and connect with homeward-bound flights.

IT3EA1MT07

CORDILLERA HUAYHUASH TREK

10-day trek to the source of the Amazon

DATES: *May 4–May 21 (18 days)*
LEADER: *Sara Steck*
GRADE: *C-2*
LAND COST: *$1775 (13–16 members)*
$1990 (10–12)

This unusual ten-day trek has as its goal a small, azure lake at 15,700 feet in the heart of the Peruvian Andes. This glacier-ringed pool, called Ninacocha ("Lake of the Child"), was determined in 1951 to be the actual source of the Amazon, one of the world's longest rivers.

We begin our trek traveling up and over several passes in the spectacular Cordillera Huayhuash, second highest of Peru's great iceranges. Views here will include the imposing fang of Jirishanca (20,099') and Yerupaja (21,759'), the 2nd highest mountain in Peru and locally known as El Carnicero ("The Butcher").

Continuing across a 15,000-foot pass, we enter the virtually unknown Cordillera Raura, hiking along rocky ridges and grassy slopes at 14,000 feet with turquoise lakes and astounding views of Yurupac and Matador, the two big peaks of the Cordillera Raura. Our goal, the glacier-fed tarn of Ninacocha at 15,700 feet, is reached on the last day of the trek.

Transport will meet us below the lake for a drive back to Lima.

ITINERARY:

DAY 1: Leave U.S. Arrive Lima and transfer to hotel.

DAY 2: Seven-hour drive to Huaraz. Overnight in hotel.

DAY 3: Morning visit to Huaraz (10,000') and afternoon hike.

DAY 4: Day trip by bus to Portachuelo de Llanganuco (14,470') for breathtaking views of the Cordillera Blanca.

DAY 5: Drive to Chiquian (10,560'), main village of the Cordillera Huayhuash.

DAY 6: Begin trek, ascending for about four hours along the Llamac River to a pass at Pitec (10,900') then on to the village of Llamac (10,560').

DAY 7: Hike over Punta Llamac Pass (13,860'), then to a beautiful lake called Jahuacocha (13,200'), our first major viewpoint of the Cordillera Huayhuash, including Nevado Yerupaja (21,759'), the sec-

ond highest peak in Peru, towering 8,000 feet above the Punta Llamac Pass.

DAY 8: Rest day.

DAY 9: Over 15,345-foot Rondoy Pass, with views of Lake Solterococha, the Yerupaja icefall, and the limestone face of Nevado Rondoy. Descend a beautiful valley to the main trail to Pocpa.

DAY 10: Hike over Cacanampunta Pass (14,890') on the Continental Divide. Descend to Queropalca Valley and camp at Mitucocha Lake below the peaks of Rondoy and Ninashanca.

DAY 11: Hike up a valley to the pass of Punta Carhuac (14,950'), with views of Yerupaja and Jirishanca (20,099'). Arrive at the large lake called Carhuacocha.

DAY 12: Rest day.

DAY 13: Cross the river on horseback, hike over Punta Camicero Pass with fine views of the peaks of Siula, Sarapa and Siria. Camp at 13,200 feet.

DAY 14: Leaving behind the Cordillera Huayhuash, we cross a 14,850-foot pass with great views of Yurapac and Matador, two big peaks in the Cordillera Raura. Camp amid a string of glacial lakes.

DAY 15: Slow ascent past Lake Patarcocha, and two more lakes with views of the whole of the Cordillera Raura in the background. Camp below Lake Tinquicocha.

DAY 16: Walk to Ninacocha, the source of the Amazon at 15,700 feet, fed by glaciers in the Cordillera Raura. At a nearby silver mine, we board transport back to Lima.

DAY 17: Free day in Lima for sightseeing. Late night transfer to airport.

DAY 18: Depart Lima, arrive Miami and connect with homeward-bound flights.

Smaller but more spectacular than the Cordillera Blanca is the Cordillera Huayhuash, a crest of knife-edge peaks with seven summits over 6,000 meters.

Huayhuash photos by Leo Le Bon

Nevado Yerupaja and Jirishanca, highest peaks of the Huayhuash.

A climbing seminar in the Peruvian Andes combines learning with an unforgettable scenic and cultural experience.

Climbing photos by Bruce Klepinger

IT3EA1MT07

ANDEAN CLIMBING SEMINAR

Learn mountaineering techniques in the Andes

DATES: *Jun 8–Jun 21 (14 days)*
LEADER: *Sergio Fitch-Watkins*
GRADE: *C-3/D-1*
LAND COST: *$1450 (7–12 members)*

The 20,000-foot peaks of the Peruvian Andes attract expert mountaineers from all over the world.

Our climbing seminar takes place in the high altitude valleys of the Cordillera Raura, a beautiful range with a multitude of gentle peaks as well as precipitous ice faces—all in all, a great variety of high altitude terrain on which to learn and practice snow and ice climbing techniques.

To get to our Cordillera Raura base camp, we hike up and over the eastern flanks of the stunningly beautiful Cordillera Huayhuash, a compact range with six summits topping 20,000 feet. Two of its better known peaks are Yerupaja (at 21,759 feet, Peru's second highest peak) and impressive Jirishanca (20,099′), the "Matterhorn of Peru."

Crossing the Continental Divide into the Cordillera Raura, we'll establish a camp at about 15,000 feet and spend three days in an intensive climbing course. We will review rope handling, snow and glacier travel, ice climbing and crevasse rescue, and spend four days on ascents of two or more 18,000 to 19,000-foot peaks in the region. The course will be geared to the varying abilities of the participants.

ITINERARY:

DAY 1: Leave U.S. Arrive Lima. Transfer to hotel.

DAY 2: Drive to Cajatambo (11,100′) and camp.

DAY 3: Trek up a gentle valley to Laguna Viconga (14,200′). Great views of the peaks of the Cordillera Huayhuash.

DAY 4: Walk around the northern end of the Cordillera Raura to camp at Aguascocha (14,200′). Establish base camp.

DAY 5 to 7: Instruction, practice and review of mountaineering techniques.

DAY 8 to 11: Cross a 16,500-foot pass and descend to Laguna Checchi or Yuracocha (about 14,850′). Proposed ascents of Nevado Leon Yuaccanan (about 16,500′) and Quesillojanca (17,500′), a slightly more difficult peak.

DAY 12: Hike out to roadhead and drive to Lima. Overnight in hotel.

DAY 13: Day free in Lima, evening transfer to the airport and depart Lima.

DAY 14: Arrive Miami and connect with homeward-bound flights.

IT3EA1MT09

CORDILLERA BLANCA EXPEDITION: HUASCARAN

Climb Peru's highest peak

DATES: *Jun 22–Jul 18 (27 days)*
LEADER: *Sergio Fitch-Watkins*
GRADE: *E-1*
LAND COST: *$2390 (7–12 members)*

The goal of this expedition is an ascent of Huascaran (22,204′), highest peak in the Peruvian Andes and one of the highest in the Americas.

A huge massif, Huascaran was first climbed in 1932 (Huascaran Sur, the highest of its twin summits) by the landmark Austrian-German expedition of Kinzl and Schneider, who also made the first survey of the Cordillera Blanca.

Snow conditions have changed on Huascaran in the last few years, increasing the technical difficulties of an ascent. Participants should be experienced in snow and ice climbing.

Before the ascent, we will freshen up our climbing and glacier travel

High altitude traverse from the Huayhuash to Raura.

Nevado Huascaran from Pasaje de Ulta (16,000'), highest pass in the Cordillera Blanca/William Boehm

techniques with climbs in the vicinity of Nevado Kayesh (18,800') and Nevado Chinchey (20,532'). Visits are included to Huaraz and Lima.

ITINERARY:

DAY 1: Leave U.S. Arrive Lima. Transfer to hotel.

DAY 2: All day drive to Huaraz (10,200'), the main town in northern Peru. Expedition briefing. Overnight at hotel.

DAY 3: Day hike along the crest of the Cordillera Negra and walk back to Huaraz through small colorful villages.

DAY 4: Afternoon hike to a viewpoint above the Rio Santa at Monterrey.

DAY 5: Drive to Pitec and hike up the canyon called Quebrada Quelquehaunca. Views of Pukaranra (20,281'), Tullparaju (18,836') and Chinchey (20,532'). Establish base camp at about 13,500 feet.

DAY 6: Practice and review climbing techniques.

DAY 7 to 10: Ascents in the area of Nevado Kayesh.

DAY 11 to 14: Climb Nevado Chinchey (20,532'). (Note: depending on the skills and acclimatization of the party, another peak may be substituted). We'll have views of the entire Cordillera Blanca from Copa (20,420') in the north as far south as Nevado Huantsan (20,980').

DAY 15: Hike out and truck back to Huaraz.

DAY 16: By truck down the Rio Santa Valley. Hike to lower base camp of Huascaran.

DAY 17 to 19: Shuttle loads to our higher camps on the granite slabs of the western side of Huascaran and past Camp I to high camp below Gargantua, the saddle between Huascaran's two summits.

DAY 20 to 22: Summit attempts on Huascaran Sur (22,204'), and extra days to allow for bad weather.

DAY 23 and 24: Return to lower camps and return to Huaraz.

DAY 25: Drive to Lima.

DAY 26: Day free in Lima.

DAY 27: Depart Lima, arrive Miami and connect with homeward-bound flights.

IT3EA1MT24

THE ALPAMAYO EXPEDITION

A challenging climb for experienced mountaineers

DATES: *Jul 18–Aug 11 (25 days)*
LEADER: *Sergio Fitch-Watkins*
GRADE: *E-3*
LAND COST: *$2390 (7–10 members)*

Perhaps the most famous mountain in Peru is Alpamayo, a remarkably alluring snow and ice pyramid perched upon a wall of glaciers and often referred to as "the most beautiful mountain in the world."

Viewed from the northwest, it appears as an extremely steep, completely white and faultlessly symmetrical mountain. At 19,510 feet, it presents a serious challenge to experienced mountaineers. Its north ridge was first climbed in 1951 by a Franco-Belgian expedition. The south peak was reached in 1957 by Gunter Hauser and his party. Alpamayo has been climbed several times since, both by its ridges and the steep east face.

This expedition is for seasoned mountaineers with very solid experience in snow and ice climbing. Applicants must submit a detailed climbing resume with references.

ITINERARY:

DAY 1 and 2: Leave U.S. Arrive Lima. Overnight at hotel.

DAY 3: Drive to Huaraz (10,200'), main town of the Cordillera Blanca.

DAY 4: Acclimatization hike in the Cordillera Negra

DAY 5: Drive to roadhead of Quebrada Llaca and hike to base camp.

DAY 6 to 9: Acclimatization hikes, review of techniques and climb of an 18,000-foot peak.

DAY 10: Return to Huaraz.

DAY 11: Drive to Huaripampa and camp.

DAY 12 and 13: Hike up the Quebrada Cedros to Alpamayo Base Camp (14,700').

DAY 14 to 22: Eight days to attempt the peak and descend to base camp.

DAY 23: Drive back to Huaraz.

DAY 24: Drive back to Lima.

DAY 25: Depart Lima and connect with homeward-bound flights.

The "perfect" pyramid of Alpamayo/ Bruce Klepinger

Students reach the summit of Nevado Leon Huaccanan in the Cordillera Raura.

The gaff-rigged ketch, Sulidae, *our comfortable floating home during the cruise/Sara Steck*

IT3EA1MT18

THE GALAPAGOS ISLANDS

Wildlife journey to "Darwin's Islands"

DATES: #1 *Feb 4–Feb 13 (10 days)*
         #2 *Apr 1–Apr 10 (10 days)*
         #3 *Jun 24–Jul 2 (10 days)*
         #4 *Dec 23, 1985–Jan 1, 1986*
            (10 days)
LEADER: *On-board naturalist*
GRADE: *A-1*
LAND COST: *$1390 + chtr. $325*
            (8–10 members)
            $1590 + chtr. $325
            (6–7)

"Considering the small size of these islands, we feel the more astonished at the number of their aboriginal beings, and at their confined range. . . Hence, both in space and time, we seem to be brought somewhat nearer to that great fact—that mystery of mysteries—the first appearance of new beings on earth." Charles Darwin. 1860, *Voyage of the Beagle.*

Day hike on James Island/Alla Schmitz

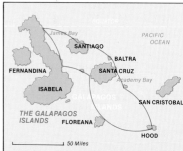

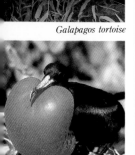

Galapagos tortoise

Displaying frigate bird

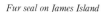

Land iguana on Plazas Island/Sara Steck

The processes of natural selection that inspired Charles Darwin are still at work in the Galapagos today; the islands are a living laboratory and the subject of constant scientific study.

Fur seal on James Island

The Galapagos Islands, situated in quiet isolation some 600 miles off Ecuador's coast, were the focal point for one of the most dramatic chapters in science history. It was here, in 1835, that Charles Darwin observed and catalogued the evidence that led him to formulate his theory of evolution through natural selection.

Galapagos plants and animals vary from island to island; climatological influences, soil textures and different altitudes gave rise to specific plants on specific islands, which in turn influenced differential evolution of wildlife.

The processes of natural selection that inspired Darwin are still at work in the islands today; the islands are a living laboratory and the subject of constant scientific study.

In the 400 years since their discovery, the Galapagos have been sorely affected by the influence of man. Pirates, whalers and sporadic settlers killed many of the tame indigenous animals and introduced domestic animals and plants. In 1934, these practices were stopped when Ecuador set aside the islands as a sanctuary for native flora and fauna. In 1959, the Galapagos became a fully protected national park and tourism on the islands is strictly regulated.

Galapagos wildlife has no fear of human presence and can be approached closely, making this place a photographer's dream!

Our explorations here are eight-day yacht cruises, sailing or motoring island to island with an experienced Galapagos-trained naturalist guide and skilled crew. Our boat is the *Sulidae*, a gaff-rigged ketch which holds up to ten passengers.

ITINERARY:

DAY 1: Leave U.S. Arrive Quito. Transfer to hotel.

DAY 2: Fly to Guayaquil. Continue by charter flight to Baltra in the Galapagos Islands. Board yacht.

DAY 3 to 8: The cruise itinerary varies according to weather, but most trips will visit Plazas Island, Academy Bay and highlands of Santa Cruz Island, Caleta Tortuga, James Island, Bartolome Island, Hood Island and either Tower Island or Floreana Island.

DAY 9: Motor to Baltra. Fly to Guayaquil and continue by air to Quito. Overnight in hotel.

DAY 10: Depart Quito and connect with homeward-bound flights.

IT3EA1MT18

MOUNTAINS OF ECUADOR

Climb snow-capped tropical volcanoes

DATES: *Nov 25–Dec 12 (18 days)*
LEADER: *Sergio Fitch-Watkins*
GRADE: *D-2*
LAND COST: *$1590 (10–12 members)*
$1750 (7–9)

The Andes of Ecuador are actually two separate ranges, the Eastern and Western Cordillera. Running between these ranges for over 200 miles is a central valley lined with more than 30 volcanoes. On this mountaineering journey, we will attempt two of these volcanoes: Cotopaxi (19,347′) and Chimborazo (20,561′), the highest peak in the region.

While not technically difficult, these climbs are physically demanding due to the altitude and snow conditions. Ample time is allowed for inclement weather and acclimatization. Basic mountaineering experience is required.

The trip begins in Quito (9,350′), with time for enjoying the local culture, including the annual Fiesta de Quito, and ends with a relaxing visit to the Banos hot springs.

ITINERARY:

DAY 1: Leave U.S. Arrive Quito, drive to the village of Otavalo. Overnight at hotel.

DAY 2: Visit the Otavalo market, one of South America's oldest Indian markets.

DAY 3: Drive to Imbabura; afternoon fitness and acclimatization hike. Camp nearby.

DAY 4 to 6: Hiking, climbing and glacier practice in the area of Nevado Cayambe, an 18,996-foot mountain situated on the equator.

DAY 7: Return to Quito.

DAY 8: Enjoy Quito Week festivities, including bullfights and dancing in the streets!

DAY 9 to 11: Climb and descend Cotopaxi.

DAY 12: Drive to Ambato, "the city of flowers."

DAY 13 to 15: Climb and descend Chimborazo.

DAY 16: In Banos, a town on the edge of the jungle.

DAY 17: Drive to Quito, arriving in the afternoon.

DAY 18: Depart Quito and connect with homeward-bound flights.

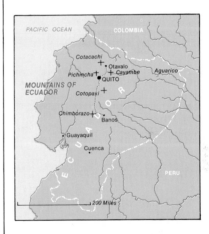

Climbing Cotopaxi (19,347′), second in height to Chimborazo, and considered by many to be the most majestic mountain in Ecuador because of its Fuji-like symmetry/ Sergio Fitch-Watkins

The peak of Chacocomanis in the Cordillera Real/Bruce Klepinger

IT3EA1MT18

HIGHLANDS OF BOLIVIA

12-day trek in remote Andes

DATES: *May 27–Jun 18 (23 days)*
LEADER: *Sara Steck*
GRADE: *C-2*
LAND COST: *$1590 (11–15 members)*
$1690 (6–10)

The main range of the Bolivian Andes is the Cordillera Real ("Royal Mountains"), a superb wilderness where massive blue-white glaciers tumble from 20,000-foot peaks. The high valleys of the Cordillera Real descend thousands of feet into the cloudy forests of the upper Amazon.

Our 16-day trek begins at Sorata, in the shadows of some of the highest peaks of the Cordillera Real, including Ancohuma (21,082') and Illampu (20,873'). Enroute, we'll hike 100 miles through remote Indian villages and llama pastures. We cross several 14,000-foot mountain passes and meet Indian descendants of the Incas and Aymaras who seldom see "outsiders."

Visits are also included to the high city of La Paz (12,000') and enormous Lake Titicaca (12,500'), legend-filled birthplace of the first Inca king.

ITINERARY:

DAY 1: Leave U.S. Arrive La Paz and transfer to hotel.

DAY 2: Morning city tour of La Paz.

DAY 3: Drive to Lake Titicaca (12,500'), visiting the colonial village of Laja, ruins at Tiahuanaco and Puma Kunku enroute. Camp at Taraco Beach on the shores of Lake Titicaca.

DAY 4: By motor launch, visit Inca tombs and monuments on the island of Kalahuta. Continue to eastern side of the lake and drive to Sorata over San Francisco Pass (14,200') where the snow peak of Illampu comes into view.

Bolivian women wearing the traditional "bowler"/ Bruce Klepinger

Reflection of Jhanko Khota, Ancolacaya Valley/Bruce Klepinger

DAY 5: Drive by truck to the picturesque village of Oncoma.

DAY 6: Begin trek with pack mules and/or llamas to carry equipment. Trek to Cocoo (12,250') over Kalamutuni Pass (14,600'), passing silver mines enroute.

DAY 7: Rest day and optional hikes.

DAY 8: Hike past numerous waterfalls and the hanging glaciers on Chearoco. Cross Sarani Pass (15,050') and descend to the valley of Chacolpaya.

DAY 9 and 10: Trek past the flanks of the Chacocomanis massif. Splendid views of glaciers and ice-covered peaks.

DAY 11 and 12: Cross Taipipata Pass (16,100'), with stunning views including Vinohuara and Chacocomanis, and another pass with views eastward toward more tropical regions.

DAY 13 and 14: Ascend the Ancolacaya Valley to a 15,650-foot pass between Cerro Wila Llojeta and Cerro Jankho Hoya. Great views across the entire width of the altiplano as far as Sajama, 150 miles away. Rest day in area.

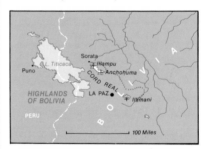

DAY 15: Walk to roadhead and drive to Lago Tuni (14,050').

DAY 16: Walk from Lago Tuni to a lake at the base of Cerro Condiriri.

DAY 17 and 18: Explore around Cerro Condiriri, then cross two passes and descend into the upper Livinosa Drainage (15,800'), continuing down to camp at Chacapampa (12,800').

DAY 19 to 21: Walk across a deserted section of the southern Cordillera Real on an old, well-preserved Inca highway. Arrive at the roadhead and drive to Chiquilini.

DAY 22: Drive to La Paz by bus, crossing valleys with impressive tropical canyons covered with abundant vegetation. Transfer to airport; depart La Paz.

DAY 23: Arrive Miami and connect with homeward-bound flights.

IT4EA1MT23

ANDEAN OVERLAND: PERU, BOLIVIA & CHILE

Exploring the altiplano

DATES: *Feb 1–Feb 23 (23 days)*
LEADER: *to be announced*
GRADE: *A-2*
LAND COST: *$1790 (10–15 members)*
$1890 (7–9)

This is a cultural, geographical and wildlife odyssey which roams from Cuzco to vast Lake Titicaca, out across the remotest *altiplano* (high plains) of Bolivia and south into Chile's wildlife-rich Lauca National Park. We'll travel by vehicle, enjoy occasional day hikes and stay in small hotels or our own camps at night.

After exploring Cuzco (11,204'), the Inca capital, we drive across southern Peru, with views of the Cordillera Vilcanota on our way to Lake Titicaca (12,500'), the great lake shared by Peru and Bolivia, on which the major form of transportation is still hand-made reed boats. We'll camp on its eastern shores and visit Indian settlements.

Entering Bolivia, we drive over a 14,200-foot pass to reach the mountain town of Sorata, with its views north to the Apolobamba Range and east into the Yungas, deep subtropical valleys which stretch into the Amazon. Illampu (20,873') and Ancohuma (21,082'), high peaks of the Cordillera Real, will dominate the mountain scenery.

Continuing across the brown vastness of Bolivia's *altiplano,* geographically reminiscent of the high plains of Tibet, we'll visit small Indian settlements and pre-Inca ruins such as Tiahuanaco, arriving in La Paz (13,000'), one of the world's highest capital cities.

We also explore the Bolivian towns of Cochabamba, colonial-era Sucre (where we might venture to the famed weaving center of Tarabuco) and Potosi, the town in which the Spanish discovered "a mountain of silver."

Heading out into the vast Salar de Uyuni, a brilliant white salt plain extending into the amber Western Cordillera, we camp and look for birdlife such as the pink Andean flamingo.

Our last Bolivian town is Oruru, where the unusually dressed Quechua Indians wear felt hats designed to resemble Conquistador's helmets.

From here, we drive into Chile, crossing a rugged section of *altiplano* and passing by Parinacota (20,767') and Pomarapa (20,472'), the world's highest active volcanoes.

Arriving at Lauca National Park, we establish a base camp near Lake Catacotani and explore for three days, looking for the New World's cameloids: llama, alpaca, guanaco and vicuna (Lauca is the only spot where all four exist together). There are also several species of flamingos here, which we'll see feeding at multi-colored lakes or on salt plains such as at Salar de Surire. This part of the Chilean *altiplano* is small, but it is vastly higher than the famed Bolivian altiplano. We'll also take

time to visit remarkable native Indian villages with thatched roofs and exterior wall paintings, such as those at the village of Gaullatiri.

From Arica, a pleasant coastal town, we drive back into Peru via the Peruvian wine-making region for a final stop at Arequipa, a town set at the foot of two 19,000-foot volcanoes. The trip ends in the capital city of Lima.

ITINERARY:

DAY 1 and 2: Leave U.S. Arrive Lima and fly to Cuzco. Transfer to hotel.

DAY 3: Tour Cuzco and local ruins. Afternoon drive to Sicuani, visiting Racchi ruins enroute. Camp near Sicuani.

DAY 4: Drive south over Abra La Raya, passing llama and alpaca herds and viewing the 18,000-foot ice peaks of the Cordillera Vilcanota enroute to Lake Titicaca. Stop near Taraco and Huancane to view the unusual cone-shaped houses along an inlet near the lake. Camp on the eastern shore of the lake. Excellent views of the Cordillera Real of Bolivia.

DAY 5: Drive across the border into Bolivia and continue along the lake with views of Isla de Sol and Isla de la Luna. Cross San Francisco Pass under the northern

snow-covered flanks of Mt. Ancohuma and spend the night at Sorata.

DAY 6: Morning drive to the pass above Cocoo and Ancoma. Splendid views to the Amazon Basin and the eastern flanks of the Cordillera Real.

DAY 7: Drive to La Paz across the *altiplano* with its patchwork of potato fields and small villages. Stop at Laja, once the capital of Bolivia, and visit the pre-Inca ruins of Tihuanacu.

DAY 8: Tour La Paz.

DAY 9: Drive to Cochabamba, a colorful town with fine Spanish architecture.

DAY 10: Drive to Sucre, the second capital of Bolivia, with its white colonial buildings. Possible visit to San Miguel, the oldest church in continuous use in South America.

DAY 11: Explore Sucre and visit Tarabuco to see fine weaving.

DAY 12: Continue on to the silver mining district of Potosi, largest active mining center in the Andes.

DAY 13 and 14: Camp on the vast white salt plain of Salar de Uyuni. During times of wet weather in the mountains, 2 to 3 inches of water may cover the plain, transforming it into a giant blue mirror. On these occasions, pink Andean flamingos may be seen.

DAY 15: Drive on to Oruro, scene of the famed devil dances of the Quechua Indians.

DAY 16: Drive west from Oruro, crossing rugged portions of the *altiplano* near Sajama, (21,423'), Bolivia's highest peak. Cross into Chile and get fantastic views of the Payachata ("twins"), the two glaciated peaks called Parinacota and Pomarapa, the world's highest active volcanoes. Cross into Chile and establish camp in Lauca National Park.

DAY 17 to 19: Three days to explore the Park. Possible day hike to Lake Chungara for extraordinary views of the Payachata volcanoes and fine birdwatching. Look for llama, alpaca, guanaco, vicuna, flamingo and other Andean wildlife.

DAY 20: Drive to the coastal town of Arica. Late afternoon free to visit beaches.

DAY 21: Drive north back in to Peru and arrive at Arequipa.

DAY 22: Fly to Lima. Day free. Evening transfer to the airport and depart Lima.

DAY 23: Arrive Miami and transfer to homeward-bound flights.

Vegetable seller in a marketplace in La Paz/ Bruce Klepinger

The Uros Indians of Lake Titicaca live on "floating islands" of reeds and construct their houses and boats from the same material/ Bruce Klepinger

Patagonia photos by trip leader Bruce Klepinger

Nature walk in Parque Nacional Torres Del Paine.

Terminus of the Moreno Glacier, one of the most active in Patagonia.

IT5PA1SFMT13

PATAGONIA OVERLAND

"All the attending marvels of a thousand Patagonian sights and sounds...." Herman Melville, Moby Dick

DATES: *Jan 11–Jan 31 (21 days)*
LEADERS: *Bruce Klepinger & Sara Steck*
GRADE: *A-2*
LAND COST: *$1990 (8–15 members)*

Shared by Argentina and Chile on the southernmost tip of south America is a wild land called Patagonia, the "uttermost end of the earth."

Patagonia is a land of Alaskan-size fjords, of glaciers which fall into the sea, of red and yellow Magellan beech trees with parrots nestling in the branches and penguins pacing the ice beneath.

On the Argentine side of Patagonia, there are great lakes and forests, and to the east lie the great rolling *pampas,* where millions of sheep roam, tended by *gaucho* shepherds, wild characters who live on meat and *mate* tea and ride down ostriches with whirling boas.

In Patagonia, the spine of the Andes tapers into the sea, and although the Patagonian Andes are not extremely high, they are among the most spectacular in the world. The fantastic spires of Fitzroy (11,073'), Cerro Torre (10,280') and the great granite "towers" of Paine are sought-after prizes by mountaineers the world over.

Our journey through this wild place will be over rough roads, traveling in our own "expedition" bus, camping and occasionally staying in simple inns.

We begin with a visit to cosmopolitan Buenos Aires, from which we fly to the tiny port of Comorodo Rivadavia and drive across the plains to Glacier National Park, establishing a camp right at the base of the jagged spires of Fitzroy and Cerro Torre. We have three full days to explore the park, walking through beech forests and hiking up Cerro Pliegue Tumbado for fantastic views extending out onto the Patagonian icecap.

Driving out of the park and around the eastern end of ice-blue Lago Argentino, we establish our next central camp in a meadow on

The black slate cuernos (horns) of Paine in Parque Nacional Torres Del Paine, Chile.

Gaucho *on the Argentine* pampas.

the shores of Laguna Roca and take a day excursion to the Moreno Glacier, whose 100-foot headwall constantly calves massive blocks of ice into Lago Argentino.

Continuing over rolling *pampas* into Chile, we approach Paine National Park and have our first sight of the spectacular granite towers and black slate *cuernos* (horns) of the Cordillera del Paine, whose compelling grandeur is an unmistakable landmark of Patagonia.

In three days at Paine, we will hike around the northern flanks of Paine Grande (10,600') for one of the most sensational views in all Patagonia and perhaps take an optional overnight backpack trip to the Grey Glacier. Large herds of guanacos, cousins of alpacas and llamas, roam Paine National Park and the birdwatching is incredible.

Leaving Paine for Puerto Natales, we drive along the Strait of Magellan and take a motor launch ride on the Last Hope Sound to view the glaciers of Cerro Balmaceda

and the rugged peaks at the southern end of the Great Patagonian icecap.

The trip ends in Chile's capital city, Santiago.

ITINERARY:

DAY 1: Leave U.S. Arrive Buenos Aires and transfer to hotel.

DAY 2: Half-day tour of Buenos Aires.

DAY 3: Fly to the little town of Comodoro Rivadavia, driving first along the coast and then across wide open plains. Camp enroute to Glacier National Park.

DAY 4: Arrive at Glacier National

Moreno Glacier and Lago Argentino.

Guanacos, members of the cameloid family, at Parque Nacional Torres Del Paine, Chile.

Park ("Parque Nacional de los Glaciares") after driving across scenic pastoral *pampas.* Set up base camp below the amazingly jagged spires of Fitzroy and Cerro Torre.

DAY 5 to 7: From our central camp on the banks of the Rio de Las Vueltas, we set out on day hikes through Magellan beech forests. Among the possibilities are a day hike with views of Fitzroy, the Patagonia icecap and Viedma Glacier.

DAY 8: Today we drive around the eastern end of Lago Viedma and Lago Argentino, passing the town of Calafate enroute. We establish our next camp at Laguna Roca, near the base of the Cordon Cristales mountains. Good fishing here.

DAY 9: Day excursion by bus to Moreno Glacier, a very active glacier on the south arm of Lago Argentino. Return to camp.

DAY 10: Hike up Cerro Cristal today for views extending from the Paine Towers in the south to the main body of Lago Argentino in the north. Return to camp.

DAY 11: Early morning start today for drive to Rio Turbio where we cross the border into Chile. Continue to a camp in a pleasant beech grove at the Milodon Cave in sight of the Last Hope Sound and Darwin Cordillera. Enroute we will see flamingos and rheas (an ostrich-like bird).

DAY 12: Drive to Parque Nacional de Paine. Set up base camp with fantastic views of Paine Grande and Almirante Nieto.

DAY 13 to 15: The next three days will be spent on day hikes in and around the Paine Massif from our base camp. Possibilities include visits to Valle Frances and Valle de Ascencio, overnights to Grey Glacier or Lago Azul, or to Rio Serrano for excellent fishing.

DAY 16: Leave Paine and drive to the fishing and mining town of Puerto Natales.

DAY 17: Excursion on Seno Ultima Esperanza ("Last Hope Sound") to Balmaceda Glacier, viewing black-necked swans, cormorants, sea lions and perhaps even penguins.

DAY 18: Drive to the quaint port town of Punta Arenas.

DAY 19: Afternoon flight to Santiago, passing above the Patagonian icefields enroute.

DAY 20: Tour Santiago. Evening transfer to airport for late evening flight. Depart Santiago.

DAY 21: Arrive U.S. and connect with homeward-bound flights.

Cerro Torre (10,280'), "the unclimbable peak" until Americans Jim Bridwell and Steve Brewer reached its summit in 1979.

IT4EA1MT22

CHILE: THE ATACAMA DESERT MOUNTAINS

Archaeology, wildlife and trekking exploration

DATES: *Feb 2–Feb 23 (22 days)*
LEADER: *to be announced*
GRADE: *C-2*
LAND COST: *$1990 (8–12 members)*

Chile's Atacama Desert is one of the great natural wonders of the world. Soaring volcanoes, stark lava fields and huge, rolling track-less dunes dotted with tiny oases provide a wonderful contrast to its seemingly endless desert.

The Atacama extends about 600 miles from the restless Pacific up the high Andes and is famous for both its rich copper and nitrate deposits, and for the mysterious ruins uncovered here by archaeologists.

We begin in the port city of Arica, where we make an archaeological reconnaissance of the Lluta and Azapa valleys, with their geoglyphs, petroglyphs and Inca fortresses *(pucaras)*.

With three days in Lauca National Park, we trek for a day around Cotacotani and Chungara, two lakes at 15,000 feet, looking for vicunas and flamingos and enjoying views of the "twins," the snow-covered active volcanoes of Pomarapa (20,472') and Parinacota (20,767').

At Isulga National Park, set at about 13,000 feet on the Chilean *altiplano* (near the Bolivian border), we visit Aymara Indian villages and climb up Isulga Volcano to see its fumaroles, (volcanic steam vents).

Isulga Park is also the setting for our three-day foot journey across the wide, almost mystical expanses of the Atacama Desert. We'll camp each night and during the day, stop to explore Isulga's caves and petroglyphs.

We then circle south across the Pampa del Tamarugal, with its sparse desert vegetation, visiting various archaeological sites such as the Cerro Pintado petroglyphs and pre-Columbian sites at Chiu-Chiu and Caspana.

In the Cordillera De Los Andes on Chile's western border, we trek for three more days, climbing up Licancabur Volcano (19,409') to see its crater lake, and walking along the remnant of an Inca trail to the ruins of a remote Inca village.

Accommodations on the trip will be a combination of small hotels and our own tent camps.

ITINERARY:

DAY 1: Leave U.S. Fly to Arica, Chile, via Santiago. Transfer to hotel.

DAY 2: Tour of the port city of Arica, visiting the green, subtropical Lluta and Azapa valleys. Visit the typical *altiplano* village of Parinacota and the Sotoroma Inca ruins enroute.

DAY 3 to 5: Walks in Lauca National Park. Varied fauna inhabit these steppes including flamingos and vicunas. Camp in the park.

DAY 6: Travel across the *altiplano* by four-wheel-drive vehicle, crossing the Lauca River and Paquisa Lagoon. Different species of flamingos may be observed on the lagoon. Visit impressive Surire Salt Flats. Camp at Chilcaya.

DAY 7: Drive south to Isluga and camp in the national park.

DAY 8: Climb up Isluga Volcano to its fumaroles.

DAY 9: Travel to Colchane and the picturesque village of Isluga. Visit Cariquina to see strange rock formations.

DAY 10 to 12: Three-day desert trek from Quetaine to Aroma via Chiapa in Isluga Park. In the town of Chiapa, visit the remains of a small Inca *pucara.* Several of the gullies through which we walk have interesting petroglyphs. Nights spent in camp.

DAY 13: Drive to Mamina and visit unique Cerro Unitas anthropomorphous geoglyphs and the ghost towns of the "nitrate boom" days. Afternoon at hot springs at Mamina.

DAY 14: Morning at hot springs then drive to Pacific coast and tour port city of Iquique.

DAY 15: Travel southeast through the sparse vegetation of the Pampa del Tamarugal, stopping at Chuquicamata, the world's biggest open pit copper mine.

DAY 16: Travel to the towns of Chiu-Chiu, Lasana and Caspana, with archaeological sites dating back to pre-Colombian times. Continue to El Tatio, with its 40 geysers, 60 hot springs and 70 fumaroles.

DAY 17: Travel to San Pedro de Atacama. Afternoon horseback trip to pre-Colombian stone ruins.

DAY 18 to 20: Three-day trek: climb Licancabur Volcano and walk a section of an Inca Trail to Inca ruins.

DAY 21: Morning rest in San Pedro. Visit Pozo hot baths and Valle de la Luna (Moon Valley), with its exotic desert landscapes. Afternoon flight to Santiago.

DAY 22: Depart Santiago on homeward-bound flights.

IT3EA1MT20

THE ACONCAGUA EXPEDITION

Attempt highest peak in Western Hemisphere

DATES: *Jan 19–Feb 16 (29 days)*
LEADER: *Sergio Fitch-Watkins*
GRADE: *E-2*
LAND COST: *$1875 (9–10 members)*
$2100 (6–8)

At 22,834 feet, Aconcagua is the highest mountain in the Western Hemisphere and the highest outside Asia.

Aconcagua lies entirely within Argentina, just across the border from Chile. It rises some 4,000 feet above its neighboring peak and is easily visible from the Pacific on a clear day.

While not a technically difficult mountain to climb, weather and altitude make this peak a true mountaineering challenge requiring a range of skills.

Waterways of the Pantanal, Brazil/Terry Brian

We will attempt the Polish Route, first climbed in 1934, which involves some 1800 feet of technical ice climbing which, although low angle, can often present difficulties depending on weather and acclimatization of the party.

Members must be very fit and capable of carrying loads of up to 75 lbs. at high altitudes. All members will be expected to assist with expedition chores (load carrying, setting up tents, cooking, etc). All community climbing equipment will be provided.

The duration of the ascent can take as little as ten days, but usually requires two weeks or longer because of frequent storms. Aconcagua makes its own weather; caution and wise mountaineering judgement are required for a successful ascent.

ITINERARY:

DAY 1: Leave U.S. Arrive Buenos Aires, Argentina. Transfer to hotel.

DAY 2: Fly to Mendoza. Day free for organizing gear.

DAY 3: A day in Mendoza to finalize permits, have an expedition meeting and check gear.

DAY 4: Bus to Punta de Vaca (7,500′) and camp.

DAY 5 to 7: Approach hike to Aconcagua base camp at 13,500 feet, via Rio de Vacas and Rio Relincho.

DAY 8: At base camp.

DAY 9 to 24: Sixteen days will be devoted to the climb and descent to base camp. Establishing Camp I (15,500′) and Camp II (18,000′) will probably take six days (relaying loads, hacking out tent sites and acclimatizing). From Camp II to the summit and back should take about two days, with a high camp at 20,000 feet. Descent from Camp II to base camp takes one day, leaving a few spare days in case of storms and bad weather.

DAY 25 and 26: Hike out to roadhead.

DAY 27: Bus ride back to Mendoza. Afternoon free.

DAY 28: Free day in Mendoza.

DAY 29: Depart Mendoza and connect with homeward-bound flights.

IT5PA1SFMT14

BAHIA: A TASTE OF BRAZIL

Beach trekking, pre-Carnival celebration, wildlife of the Pantanal

DATES: *Jan 30–Feb 15 (17 days)*
LEADER: *Terry Brian*
GRADE: *B-2*
LAND COST: *$1550 (13–16 members)*
+ chtr. $330
$1690 (10–12)
+ chtr. $330

The highlight of this Brazilian journey is a five-day camping trek on the incomparable wilderness beaches of Bahia. We'll also enjoy "pre-Carnival" in Salvador, Bahia's colorful port city, and travel to the Pantanal of southwestern Brazil to tour by dugout canoe in wildlife-rich "everglades."

The journey starts with a visit to the famed waterfalls at Iguazu (which surpass both Niagara and Victoria Falls in size and grandeur).

We then make a short visit to "the Pantanal," a unique swampland in the state of Matto Grosso do Sul. The rainy season annually floods the Pantanal river system until the area becomes a shallow sea dotted with tiny "islands." There is excellent wildlife (particularly avifauna) which we observe as we explore for three days by dugout canoe. We camp at night on quiet spots by the water.

On the islands are concentrated the local fauna: capibaras, tapirs, marsh deer, jaguars, monkeys and caymen, as well as large concentrations of caracaras, vultures, buteos, kites, guans, curassows, parrots, macaws, herons, ibis, ducks, rails, kingfishers, toucans, storks, egrets and anhingas.

Heading for the beaches of Bahia, we first visit Salvador, Bahia's capital, which has a strong African influence in its dance and dress. Here we soak up the flavor of a classic tropical port town, strolling in the fish markets and sampling seafood delicacies sold by colorfully-costumed street vendors. Preparations for Carnival go on for weeks before the actual four-day festival. We'll see (and maybe participate in) spontaneous street dances, serenades, costume displays and dress rehearsals for parades. Carnival in Salvador is very different than in Rio (less commercial, more uninhibited and largely unexploited by tourism).

Flying to the coast of southern Bahia, our last excursion is a splendid five-day trek along remote and spectacular wilderness beaches.

We'll hike about 7 or 8 miles a day, sometimes along rocky coastal bluffs, sometimes along palm-fringed beaches. Camp supplies and food will be transported for us by small boat so we don't need to carry heavy packs. This is a very remote and idyllic part of Brazil's coast; there is no road access and the only inhabitants are in a few scattered fishing settlements.

A cook and camp staff will be with us on both the Bahia beach trek and at the Pantanal camps.

The trip ends in Rio, a spectacular city famed for its food, dances and attractions such as Corcovado, Copacabana and Ipanema.

Carnival Option (Feb. 16–Feb. 20): At the end of the trip, we can arrange an optional four-day stay in Rio to experience what may be the wildest four-day celebration in the world. Price quoted on request.

ITINERARY:

DAY 1: Leave Miami. Arrive Rio and fly to Iguazu Falls. Tour Brazilian side of the falls.

DAY 2: Tour Argentine side of the falls, then fly to Campo Grande, capital of the state of Matto Grosso do Sul. By bus to Hotel Cabana da Lontra, a "jungle" lodge.

DAY 3: Begin three-day river safari. Camp on the Rio Vermelho.

DAY 4: Continue along the Rio Vermelho, camping at Fazenda Redacao.

DAY 5: All-day return trip by river, arriving back at Hotel Cabana Da Lontra.

DAY 6: Drive to Corumba, a commercial center on the Paraguay River, and fly to Salvador, arriving late afternoon.

DAY 7: Time to explore Salvador.

DAY 8: Another morning in Salvador, then afternoon flight to Ilheus. Drive to Porto Seguro and camp.

DAY 9: Begin five-day beach trek, with boats carrying the camping gear.

DAY 10 to 13: Beach trekking.

DAY 14: Drive to Ilheus and fly to Rio, arriving late afternoon.

DAY 15: Half-day tour. Afternoon free to enjoy pre-Carnival in Rio.

DAY 16: Day free, then farewell dinner and late-night transfer to airport for homeward-bound flights.

DAY 17: Arrive Miami and transfer to domestic flights.

Camping on the wilderness coast of Bahia, southern Brazil.

Bahian street vendors of Salvador wear African-influenced dress.

Costa Rica has exceptional birdlife and unmatched flora that includes over 1,000 species of orchids alone. Its national park system is known throughout the world.

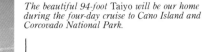

The beautiful 94-foot Taiyo will be our home during the four-day cruise to Cano Island and Corcovado National Park.

NATURAL HISTORY OF COSTA RICA

By yacht on Pacific Coast, by canoe on Atlantic inlets

DATES: #1 *Dec 18–Dec 29, 1984 (12 days)*
#2 *Jan 12–Jan 23 (12 days)*
#3 *Jan 23–Feb 3 (12 days)*
#4 *Feb 9–Feb 20 (12 days)*
#5 *Dec 21, 1984–Jan 1, 1986 (12 days)*
LEADER: #1: *Sara Steck*
#2, #3, #4, #5: *to be announced*
GRADE: *A-2*
LAND COST: *$1450 (9–12 members)*
$1690 (6–8)

We discover Costa Rica's natural history from two different vantage points: from a 94-foot two-masted Brigantine which sails us to the biological reserves of Cano Island and Corcovado National Park, and by dugout canoe in the tropical luxuriance of Tortuguero National Park.

Tortuguero National Park, a protected region of pristine Caribbean jungle, is known for its system of natural canals and lagoons which penetrate the green "walls" of the jungle. We'll be able to explore deeply into this region as we travel by motorized dugout, gliding over a maze of tranquil lagoons above which tower 180-foot-tall trees.

Wildlife possibilities on the water include manatees, crocodiles and fresh water turtles. On nature walks, we may see sloths, howler and spider monkeys. The avifauna includes 300 species (notably aquatic) including parrots, hawks, herons, toucans, pelicans, kingfishers and much more. Our accommodations will be in a well-appointed jungle lodge.

Tortuguero is also famous for the thousands of giant green turtles which come to nest on the beaches each year, and we will visit its turtle research station.

On the Pacific Coast, we travel to Puntarenas and board the *Taiyo*, a lovely sailing vessel with six double cabins, a spacious salon and scuba equipment on board. With

Gliding through the waterways of Tortuguero National Park.

our experienced crew, we sail to Cano Island, a beautiful spot which offers fine scuba and snorkeling in calm, clear waters. Sailing to nearby Corcovado National Park, one of Costa Rica's most famous attractions, we'll enjoy some light hiking or horseback rides on its various trails, forests and beaches.

ITINERARY:

DAY 1: Leave U.S. Arrive San Jose. Transfer to hotel.

DAY 2: Day tour to Poas or Irazu volcanoes.

DAY 3: Drive to Turrialba and visit Guayabo National Monument. Afternoon visit to the Tropical Agricultural Research Center and continue to the Caribbean coast at Limon.

DAY 4: Drive to Moin and transfer to Tortuga Lodge. Morning boat trip on canals of Tortuguero National Park. Optional afternoon wildlife walk. Evening visit to the green turtle research station.

DAY 5: All-day nature tour in motorized dugout.

DAY 6: Morning walk to the beach, afternoon hike up Cerro Tortuguero for views over the whole of Tortuguero National Park.

DAY 7: By charter flight to San Jose, drive to Puntarenas, and board the *Taiyo* in the evening for a four-day sail cruise. We'll spend the next four nights on the boat.

DAY 8: Arrive Cano Island in the morning. Snorkeling, scuba diving, exploring the island. Evening sail to Corcovado.

DAY 9 and 10: Arrive at Corcovado at breakfast time and spend two days enjoying this glorious beach park. Trail hikes or horseback rides on the beach are available.

DAY 11: Sail along the coast to Puntarenas. Overnight at hotel.

DAY 12: Depart Puntarenas and connect with homeward-bound flights.

Leo and Bill Le Bon horseback riding on the beaches of Corcovado/ Michael Kaye

VOLCANOES OF MEXICO

Learn basic mountaineering skills

DATES: #1 Dec 23, 1984–Jan 5, 1985
        (14 days)
        #2 Feb 23–Mar 8 (14 days)
        #3 Mar 10–Mar 23 (14 days)
        #4 Oct 20–Nov 2 (14 days)
        #5 Dec 22, 1985–Jan 4, 1986
LEADER: *Sergio Fitch-Watkins*
GRADE: *C-3/D-2*
LAND COST: *$890 (5–15 members)*

On this trip we'll make climbs of Orizaba (18,851′) and Popocatepetl (17,887′), the third and fifth highest mountains in North America, plus a third peak, Ixtaccihuatl (17,343′).

Many now-famous mountaineers started their careers on these snowy peaks, which provide a good introduction to climbing. We've been operating successful Mexican volcano climbs for 14 years.

The climbs require the use of ice axe and crampons and are not technically difficult. Instruction on the necessary techniques will be given by the leader. The real criteria for reaching these high altitude summits are desire and stamina.

Looking over the lip of the gigantic crater of Popo, one wonders how Cortez' men managed to get into it and return with the sulphur they needed for gun powder in their conquest of the Aztecs.

The approach to these giant volcanoes is through the Mexican countryside, where one still sees women weaving serapes of natural colored wool, farmers reaping crops with hand scythes and woodcutters hauling firewood to their villages on burros. Part of the charm of the trip lies in visits to small villages; there will be a one-day visit to the pretty colonial town of Puebla.

Richard Goldin and Peter Goodsell with the summit of Popo, as seen from the summit Ixta/ Mike Farrell

VOLCANOES OF MEXICO

ITINERARY:
    DAY 1: Leave U.S. Arrive Mexico City. Overnight at hotel.
    DAY 2: Free day in Mexico City (7,000′).
    DAY 3: Drive to base camp on Ixtaccihuatl at Alcalican Canyon at 11,000 feet.
    DAY 4 to 6: Climb and descend Ixta, and drive to Tlamacaz.
    DAY 7: Day free in Tlamacaz.
    DAY 8: Early morning start for the climb of Popocatepetl, via the Ventorrillo Route.
    DAY 9: Drive to Puebla.
    DAY 10: Drive to Piedra Grande Hut (13,776′) on the north side of Pico de Orizaba.
    DAY 11: Early morning start to climb and descend Orizaba via the Glacier de Jamapa.
    DAY 12: In Puebla.
    DAY 13: Drive to Mexico City.
    DAY 14: Depart Mexico City and connect on homeward-bound flights.

The Mexican volcanos are ideal for gaining high altitude experience and learning or practicing a range of basic mountaineering skills/ Sergio Fitch Watkins

Hanging out at the local cantina after the climb, Amecameca, Mexico/Sergio Fitch-Watkins

On the trail to Ixta/Mike Farrell

Climbers' hut on Popo/John Fischer

*The author
with freshly-caught dinner*

Camping in the wilds of Glacier Bay/Leo Le Bon

CANOEING & KAYAKING IN ALASKA

by Anne Wilder

Anne Wilder is a semi-retired reporter for the Miami Herald who still contributes a weekly column, travel articles and special features. She teaches journalism at a local community college, is a competitive Master swimmer and loves traveling to strange new places. In her own words, she is "living proof that you don't have to be under 35 to enjoy treks and adventures" (she is presently 70). Her first real trip in a wilderness setting was in 1976, when she took a Mountain Travel trip in the fjords of Greenland with Mike Banks. Since that time she has trekked in Kashmir, Mongolia and Peru.

You can drive to Alaska, fly there, or glide in on a cruise ship.

Some of the young strike out for themselves with backpacks and maps. Others prefer most of the comforts of home while touring this frontier state, still largely a wilderness.

But there is a middle approach for travelers whose view of new scenes is neither hitched to soft beds and hot showers nor to far-out roughing it.

Mountain Travel provides a middle way—a first-hand

Lakeside picnic, Admiralty Island/Anne Wilder

view of wilderness areas with the excitement and occasional discomfort of wilderness living, along with good guides, careful pre-planning and top-grade equipment.

That was how 14 of us explored two beautiful areas in southwest Alaska—tree-covered Admiralty Island with its carelessly flung jewels of blue-green lakes rimmed with yellow water lilies, and the icy majesty of Glacier Bay, with its steep cliffs, its rookeries, its short growth of bushes and flowers and its blue-green-white and sometimes dirty-looking glaciers.

We had a week in each area on an expedition that was challenging.

"Challenging" means that at intervals all of us muttered that Becoming One With Nature was a mistake.

Like the morning in Glacier Bay when we were kayaking across the cold waters, shivering in an icy wind blowing from a glacier (whose name was Marjorie), with muscles aching from our new experience of wielding the double-headed paddles.

At the low moment, a big white cruise ship rounded a bend, looking at first no bigger than a bathtub toy. As it approached, we could hear the ships's loudspeaker announcing the first lunch call.

"I could be there," said one of the campers. "I could be going down to lunch right now and be warm and dry."

But none of us would really have traded our little seats in the two-man kayaks for a box spring bed on a cruise ship.

The two-week trip started from Juneau, the capital of Alaska.

We were flown from Juneau to Mole Harbor, where we started a canoe trip through the lakes of Admiralty Island and later were flown to Glacier Bay for kayaking and camping.

The 14 persons who met in Juneau the first night for a preliminary briefing and equipment check eyed each other with some curiosity.

This was to be our family for the next 16 days. As it turned out, the family got along very well.

Our guides were Chuck Horner, a former chief ranger, assisted by Hayden Kaden, a young attorney from Texas who had deserted briefs and torts for kayaking and guiding, and Rob Bosworth, who had done an Alaskan environmental study as a college student and decided Alaska was his real home.

The group was a mixed bag of individuals with varying degrees of camping experience and an interest in trying something new. The roster included Leo Le Bon, head of Mountain Travel, and his children Bill and Suzanne.

Other trip members included a Nobel Prize winning professor of physics with his wife (a concert harpsichordist) and their two children, a professor of orthopedic surgery, a retired businessman turned computer science teacher, a biology teacher, a freelance writer for ski magazines, and myself, with a modest background in wilderness experience.

Tents and cooking equipment were provided. Our leaders insisted we have plenty of rain gear, and issued us rubber boots to replace our cherished hiking boots.

Once on the trail we found that the rubber boots were essential for splashing in and out of canoes and kayaks and slogging over muddy trails.

The first week in Admiralty Island centered around some of the beautiful lakes. We camped by the lakes and traveled by canoe.

Gliding over the smooth waters in the canoes, we spotted deer along the wooded margin, saw otter scrambling up the bank, caught a glimpse of a bear and got cricks in our necks looking up at birds, including several bald eagles.

At Admiralty, the challenge was portaging—the most demanding activity of the two weeks. A portage is made

Flat-water kayaking in two-person Kleppers/Leo Le Bon

when you have to carry your gear and canoes overland from one lake to another.

Though the portaging caused some grumbling, the setting was a compensation. Hemlock and spruce towered overhead and in the clearings the ferns grew shoulder-high. Gigantic skunk cabbage leaves were light green banners against the darker green of the moss and trees.

We also met a very beautiful and very nasty plant called devil's club. It has prickers on the stems, tops and bottoms of the leaves. We learned to hold our hands away when we saw the big flat leaves by the side of the trail.

Admiralty Island is one of the last refuges of the brown bear. Horner said bears usually leave people alone, but adolescent two-year-olds can be mean. And hungry. We were cautioned never to leave food around to attract them.

At one lakeside spot, Horner wrapped freshly caught salmon in skunk cabbage leaves and baked the fish in the fire. At the same campsite, Horner and Kaden collected wild greens for salad.

We had the wilderness to ourselves except for a doctor and his family in one of the few Forest Service cabins.

Then there was the salt chuck at Mitchell Bay Salt Lake. This is a narrow inlet where the tides from the ocean rush in with such force that it creates a waterfall and some real white water. After a period of calm, the whitewater's direction is reversed when the tide changes six hours later.

In this tidal area we spent a lot of time hanging over the side of the canoes and looking down into the water at sea anemones (some as big as cantelopes), sea urchins and a wide variety of starfish.

Our Admiralty Island trip ended at the Indian village of Angoon, where we stayed in a motel named Kootznahoo Lodge, which had good beds, hot water and a laundromat.

We were flown to Glacier Bay for the second half of the adventure. By this time, the shakedown phase of the trip was over. We put up tents automatically, knew how to find things in our packs and were convinced that the gasoline stoves would not blow up in our faces.

Glacier Bay was spectacular—and slightly forbidding—with steep barren cliffs, scrubby greenery sprinkled with a variety of bright flowers, ice from the glaciers floating in the water and views of some of the most spectacular (and probably the noisiest) glaciers in Alaska.

When big chunks of ice fall from the glaciers (called calving, and you tell me why), there is a roar and rumble; and the glaciers roar and rumble at random intervals day and night.

Our first assignment at Glacier Bay was learning to handle the two-man kayaks. Built with air sponsons (sort of an internal inflated pontoon), the kayaks were very stable. With some squeezing you could pack in two people and a lot of gear. You pulled the rubberized cover up around your waist, hoisted your two-headed paddle and felt the icy water running down your elbows.

Starting the canoe traverse across the small fresh-water lakes which dot the Admiralty wilderness/Leo Le Bon

Wet elbows are a sign of an amateur kayaker. After a few tries, we learned how to keep dry.

We also learned that Herr Klepper, who designed and built the kayaks, had good ideas about stability, but some strange ideas about human anatomy. Most of us came away from our first kayaking experience with aching rears. Later we learned to fold canvas bags under us to ease the strain.

Kayaks move smoothly, but the paddling develops some new muscles. If we had any reservations about kayaking on Glacier Bay, they were answered the first afternoon when we paddled—rather awkwardly—toward the nearest glacier.

Our crafts slid quietly among the ice floes and we saw harbor seals relaxing on the ice. Some were motionless, others were stretching and one was nearly turning himself inside out in an effort to scratch the middle of his back.

The sun touched the snow-covered peaks behind the glacier and a big chunk of ice fell into the bay.

The next day we broke camp in the rain and that was when we saw the first of several cruise ships.

We also saw humpback whales.

We heard the whale first—a loud snort. Then there was a geyser of spray, then the curve of a dark back, and finally the double fan tail vertical for a moment as the whale dove below the surface.

In the rookeries, we saw the young gulls trying to balance on the slippery rocks, flailing their wings. We saw an oyster catcher, black with an orange bill. Uneasy about spectators, he shuffled behind a rock. He may have felt secure—but his orange bill remained in plain sight.

Those who felt like it hiked the hills around the bay, took out the kayaks for bird-watching paddles or relaxed and listened to the glaciers calving.

If you had a non-travel day, you were free to spend the day relaxing if you didn't want to take to the trail.

You also learned to ignore the frequent rains which, though steady, were not stormy or driving. Our tents stayed dry, as did the sleeping bags. And the sunny days appeared twice as bright by contrast.

As the trip came to an end, we tallied the pluses and minuses, and came out far ahead. For the price of a few minor discomforts, we had gained an inside look at a country of beauty and fascination.

NORTH AMERICA
& HAWAII

Trip leader Chuck Horner doing what he does best. . .on the Tatshenshini River, Alaska/Fred Faye Hiltner

WASHINGTON • NEW HAMPSHIRE • ALASKA • HAWAII

Mountain Travel North America & Hawaii

Alaska, "the great land," is a huge wilderness encompassing four time zones, 33,000 miles of coastline and fourteen of the highest peaks in North America.

For 1985, there are fourteen Alaskan adventures to choose from, each with emphasis on a particular activity, perhaps rafting, backpacking, climbing or a combination of several outdoor pursuits.

In Southeast Alaska's water-bound wilderness, our journeys witness nature in action, watching tidewater glaciers shed giant icebergs into deep fjords.

In central Alaska, we field treks, expeditions and mountaineering seminars on Mt. McKinley, highest peak outside the Himalayas and Andes, and one of the most spectacular mountains in the world.

In the jagged Brooks Range, south of the Arctic Slope, we explore a primal wilderness where brown bears fish in swift arctic rivers and the glow of the northern lights illuminates the sky.

In the "Lower 48", we offer backpacking, llama trekking and climbing in Washington's North Cascades, a "range walk" in New Hampshire, and a hiking trip in Hawaii.

Our groups are very small (maximum of 12 on North America trips), our leaders are expert, and our itineraries are flexible enough to accommodate a wide variety of individual interests.

Looking down on the upper Noatak river valley, Alaska/Dave Ketscher

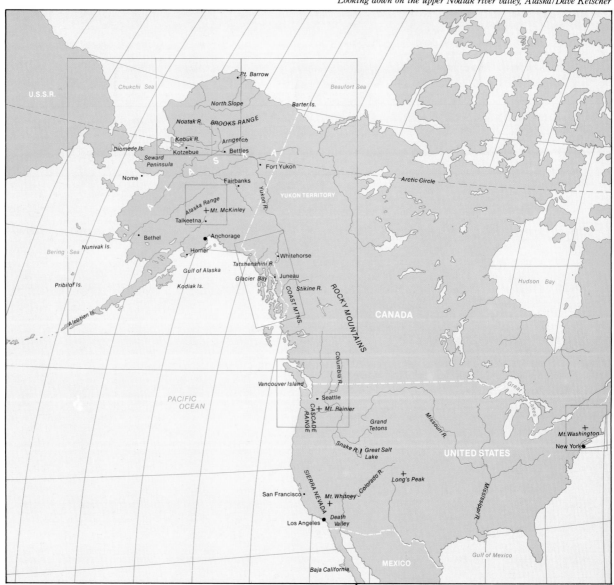

GARY BRILL, 35, is a professional guide with extensive climbing experience in the Pacific Northwest. He teaches rock, snow and ice climbing and has guided back-country ski tours and helicopter skiing.

GARY BOCARDE, 37, in his 16 years of climbing, has been involved in many difficult ascents, including the first ascent of the Shield on El Capitan, the first big wall route in Alaska (Moose's Tooth), first winter ascent of Mt. Hunter, and many other ascents throughout the Alaska Range. He has guided for ten years on Mt. McKinley, Mt. Foraker, Mt. Hunter, and Mt. Sanford and was a member of two mountaineering expeditions in China: 1980 Gongga Shan and 1981 Everest East Face.

JOHN & IDA BURROUGHS lead our White Mountains hiking trip in New Hampshire. They have spent considerable time exploring the mountains of New England as well as climbing in the American West, Alaska and Mexico. Jon is a former White Mountain hut-man and guide.

FRED FAYE HILTNER, 30, spends his winters as a ski patrolman and his summers as a river guide. He has taught rock and ice climbing, whitewater kayaking, canoeing and has worked as a wildlife biologist for the U.S. Forest Service.

CRAIG HOHENBERGER, 30, is a zoologist and research biologist with a special interest in arctic ecology. He has worked as a field ecologist on the North Slope, conducting a marine mammal census for the Alaska Fish & Game Department. Craig is an experienced kayaker and backpacker with extensive river travel experience throughout Alaska and the Yukon Territory.

CHUCK HORNER, 54, is Chief Ranger for the Southeast District of the Alaska Division of Parks and is an active canoeist, kayaker and cross-country skier.

HAYDEN KADEN, 40, is an outdoorsman and naturalist with 14 years' experience in kayaking and camping in southeast Alaska. A lawyer turned wilderness guide, he lives on a homestead at the mouth of Glacier Bay.

DAVE KETCHER, 34, is an Alaskan river runner, bush pilot, dog team guide and wilderness enthusiast who resides in the bush community of Bettles, Alaska.

MIKE & DEBBIE O'CONNOR are professional wilderness guides. A high school counselor in Angoon during the school year, Mike guides backpacking and kayak trips in the summer. Debbie teaches special education and also spends the summers guiding wilderness trips.

PETER OURUSOFF, 44, is an inveterate nature enthusiast and trekker. A former school teacher (science), counselor, park naturalist and landscape gardener, he has led adventure trips for 20 years and for the last five years with Mountain Travel in Mexico, Hawaii and Africa.

NIC PARKER, 35, is a lifetime Alaskan climber and explorer with over fifty first (and first winter) ascents in the ranges of Alaska. He has twenty years of alpine experience and has been a professional mountain guide for ten years. He has extensive mountain rescue training and is qualified as a medic-EMT. He lives in the village of Talkeetna, near the foothills of the Alaska Range.

ERIC SANFORD, 32, has been climbing, skiing and guiding for more than 15 years in the U.S., Canada, Alaska and Europe. He has many major climbs and first ascents to his credit and has worked with Colorado Mountain Rescue and the Yosemite Rescue Team.

RON STORRO-PATTERSON, 43, is a naturalist and marine biologist. He has led natural history trips for 20 years to numerous places including Africa, the Amazon, the Galapagos and Alaska. Since 1975, he has spent his summers observing the wildlife of Southeast Alaska. He helped found the Whale Center, an international non-profit organization dealing with the conservation of whales.

DOUG VEENHOF, 28, is a professional mountain guide and nordic ski instructor with extensive experience in the North Cascades in both summer and winter conditions.

Gary Bocarde   *Ronn Storro-Patterson*

Peter Ourusoff   *Eric Sanford*   *Mike and Debbie O'Connor*

Craig Hohenberger

Dave Ketscher

Fred Faye Hiltner

Chuck Horner

Please Note:

Nic Parker

Hayden Kaden

CLIMB THE VOLCANOES

Ascents of Rainier, Baker, Glacier Peak

DATES: *#1 Jun 30–Jul 13 (14 days)*
#2 Jul 28–Aug 10 (14 days)
LEADER: *Gary Brill*
GRADE: *D-3*
LAND COST: *$1050 (6–10 members)*

This is a mountaineering seminar with ascents of Washington's major glaciated volcanoes: Mt. Baker (10,750'), Glacier Peak (10,541') and Rainier (14,410').

Mt. Baker is a beautifully proportioned peak which soars a full 7,000 feet above a green skirt of forest in the North Cascades. The whitest of the Cascade volcanoes, it has one of the heaviest snowfalls in the state and has twelve active glaciers.

Ice-mantled Glacier Peak, in the heart of the Cascade Range, is an eroded volcanic cone which is prominently etched into the Cascade skyline.

Mt. Rainier, highest peak in Washington, rises 8,000 feet above surrounding ridges and lesser peaks, and has been called "an arctic palace floating on a sea of green trees." This massive volcano has a circumference of 20 miles and 26 named glaciers.

Members must have basic mountaineering skills, but the climbs are more physically demanding than technically difficult. Backpacking is required on the approach to the peaks. There will be one guide for every four members.

ITINERARY:

DAY 1: Meet group and leader in Seattle, drive to Mt. Baker National Forest and camp.

DAY 2 and 3: Hike to Kulshan Cabin on the slopes of Mt. Baker. Spend day on Coleman Glacier learning or brushing up on snow and ice climbing and crevasse rescue.

On the summit of Corteo, North Cascades.

DAY 4: Climb Mt. Baker via the Coleman Glacier route. Descend to Kulshan Cabin.

DAY 5: Hike out, drive to Darrington and camp nearby.

DAY 6: Drive to trailhead. Hike to Kennedy Hot Springs (3,300') and camp.

DAY 7: Hike to base of Sitkum Glacier (7,000') and practice ice climbing.

DAY 8: Climb Glacier Peak and descend to Kennedy Hot Springs.

DAY 9: Hike out, drive to Darrington for rest and relaxation.

DAY 10: Drive to south side of Mt. Rainier and camp.

DAY 11: Hike to Camp Hazard (11,300').

DAY 12: Climb Mt. Rainier via Kautz Glacier and return to Camp Hazard.

DAY 13: Descend to Paradise. Farewell dinner in Mt. Rainier National Park.

DAY 14: Drive to Seattle and connect with homeward-bound flights.

On Liberty Bell, North Cascades, Washington.

Simitar Glacier, Glacier Peak, Washington.

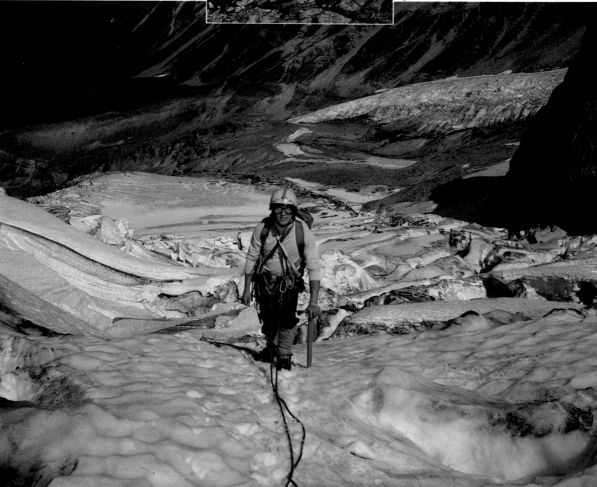

Summit, Liberty Bell, Washington.

THE PTARMIGAN TRAVERSE

Classic "American Alps" backpacking

DATES: *Aug 10–Aug 23 (14 days)*
LEADER: *Gary Brill*
GRADE: *D-3*
LAND COST: *$1050 (4–7 members)*

This is the classic North Cascades high mountain traverse, known for its superb scenery as well as challenging and varied climbing. First traveled in the 1940's, the route has drawn some of the nation's finest climbers to test themselves on many of the rugged peaks along the way. Participants should be prepared for changing climbing conditions. Cold, wet mountain weather may be encountered on the crossing of several major glaciers and high mountain passes. Time permitting, we will make ascents of several of the Cascades' finest peaks along the way. The trip begins with a three-day practice session to hone your mountaineering skills for the trip ahead, since once you begin, there's no turning back. If you're ready for a challenge and are up to the demands, these are the "American Alps" at their finest.

ITINERARY:

DAY 1: Meet group and leader in Seattle. Drive to Marblemount and pack up for practice course. Camp at trailhead.

DAY 2 to 4: Three days of shake-down training before the actual traverse. Practice climbing in Boston Basin and Eldorado Peak.

DAY 5: Rest day and pack up for Ptarmigan Traverse.

DAY 6: Hike over Cascade Pass (5,400') to Cache Col (7,000').

DAY 7 and 8: To Cool-Aid Lake. Climb Hurry-Up Peak (7,800'); to Yang-Yang Lakes via Spider-Formidable Col (7,400') and Middle Cascade Glacier.

DAY 9 and 10: Climb La Conte Mountain via La Conte Glacier; climb Sentinel or Old Guard Peak (8,200') and descend to White Rocks Lakes (6,200').

DAY 11 and 12: Traverse to Dana Glacier and climb Spire Point; climb Dome Peak (8,800') and return to Spire Camp.

DAY 13: Descend to Cub Lake and continue down Bachelor Creek and Downey Creek.

DAY 14: Hike out, drive to Seattle and connect with homeward-bound flights.

NORTH CASCADES SEMINAR & CLIMB

Pacific Northwest mountaineering

DATES: *Jul 7–Jul 20 (14 days)*
LEADER: *Eric Sanford*
GRADE: *B-3*
LAND COST: *$1050 (5–10 members)*

This two-week course is designed to teach all the basics for safe and efficient mountain travel. While little or no previous mountaineering experience is required, it is advised that members be in top physical shape and well broken-in to the rigors of extended back-country travel. Trip members will learn belaying, knots and rope work, rock, snow and ice climbing techniques, route selection and safety, crevasse rescue and glacier travel, mountain first aid, safety and rescue, use of ice axe, crampons and other climbing equipment, and rapelling and descending techniques. The seminar will take place in several locations in the Cascades depending on weather and climbing conditions. Several major Cascade peaks, including Mt. Baker (10,750') will be climbed during the course.

ITINERARY:

DAY 1: Meet group and leader in Seattle. Drive to Mazama and camp.

DAY 2 to 4: Hike into Wing Lake (5 miles) and camp. Climb Black Peak (8,970'). Instruction will include basic rock climbing, knots, rapelling and some basic snow climbing skills.

DAY 5: Hike out from Wing Lake, drive back to Mazama and camp nearby. Afternoon rock climbing practice and re-pack for the next trip.

DAY 6 to 8: Hike up to Blue Lake and our high camp in the Liberty Bell basin. Very close to our camp are a number of fine rock peaks and spires which provide excellent practice. These include Blue Peak and the Liberty Bell and Early Winter spires. Camp at the lake.

DAY 9: Drive to Mt. Baker and hike into Kulshan Cabin.

DAY 10 to 12: Establish a high camp on the Coleman Glacier and practice snow and ice climbing and crevasse rescue.

DAY 13: Climb Mt. Baker and return to high camp.

DAY 14: Hike out, drive to Seattle and connect with homeward-bound flights.

Mountain rescue practice: moving a rescue litter up a rock face

Practice climbing.

Members of the North Cascades Climbing Seminar receive instruction in basic and intermediate mountaineering skills. Many people attend these courses to prepare for a wider range of trips such as our climbs on McKinley and Ecuador's volcanoes.

North Cascades photos by trip leader Eric Sanford

Campsite on the Ptarmigan Traverse. West face of Mt. Shuksan (9,127') in background.

Llamas travel and forage like deer without destroying wilderness trails and meadows.

NORTH CASCADES LLAMA TREK

12-day Pacific Crest Trail hike

DATES: #1 *Jul 28–Aug 10 (14 days)*
       #2 *Aug 11–Aug 24 (14 days)*
LEADER: *Doug Veenhof*
GRADE: *B-2*
LAND COST: *$1200 (5–8 members)*

One of the most spectacular parts of the North Cascades is the northern border of the Pasayten Wilderness which stretches along the Canadian border in Washington.

We'll undertake a 12-day trek through this region, using llamas for pack animals. These delightful, furry beasts can carry a lot of weight (so we don't have to), and their antics and personalities will keep us entertained for hours.

We'll hike the entire Pasayten Wilderness from east to west, connecting sections of the Pacific Crest and Cascade Crest Trails, crossing high, hidden mountain passes and skirting alpine lakes. The total distance covered is just over 100 miles.

Llama and friend.

Trip members will share in camp chores. There are optional rest days or side trips along the way, great wildlife viewing and wildflowers galore.

ITINERARY:

DAY 1: Meet group and leader in Seattle, drive to Mazama and camp.

DAY 2: Drive to Thirtymile Campground, meet with llamas and begin hiking on easy terrain along the Chewack River for eight miles to a camp on Tungston Creek.

DAY 3: Hike eight miles on easy terrain to Remmel Lake.

DAY 4: Day hikes to Cathedral Lakes, Cathedral Peak and Amphitheatre Mountain. Fishing and easy climbing.

DAY 5 and 6: Hike a moderate ten miles to Ramon Lake; 11 miles to Dean Creek via Park Pass, Peeve Pass and around Sheep Mountain and Quartz Mountain.

DAY 7 and 8: Hike an easy 11 miles to Hidden Lakes; hike to camp on the Middle Fork of the Pasayten River via Tatoosh Buttes, 12 moderate and spectacular miles.

DAY 9 and 10: Gradually uphill along the West Fork of the Pasay-

ten River to Holman Pass, an easy 13 miles; along Cascade Crest Trail over Sky Pilot Pass, Deception Pass and enjoy magnificent views along the way to Devil's Pass. Eight moderate miles.

DAY 11: Day hike to Devil's Dome. Easy climbing, great wildlife viewing and many flowers.

DAY 12 and 13: Hike six miles to Devil's Park via Anacortes Crossing; downhill to the North Cascades Highway via Macmillian Park. Drive back to Mazama.

DAY 14: Drive to Seattle and connect with homeward-bound flights.

Llamas, members of the cameloid family, have been used as pack animals for thousands of years, most notably during the Inca Empire, when they transported goods from sea level to 16,000 feet in the Andes.

Llama trek photos by Eric Sanford

WHITE MOUNTAINS OF NEW HAMPSHIRE

60-mile New England trek

DATES: #1 Jul 12–Jul 21 (10 days)
    #2 Aug 30–Sep 8 (10 days)
LEADER: *Jon or Ida Burroughs*
GRADE: *B-3*
LAND COST: *$635 (10–15 members)*
    $750 (7–9)

This is one of New England's classic treks—a nine-day, 60-mile "range walk" from Franconia Notch to Pinkham Notch by way of Mt. Washington (6,288'), highest peak in the northeastern U.S.

Although these mountains are not high, they are extremely rugged and demand a high level of fitness. Despite the many steep "ups and downs" of this walk, it is a popular one for its scenic beauty. Trip #2 takes advantage of New England's glorious display of autumn colors.

The White Mountains have a system of well organized huts, maintained by the Appalachian Mountain Club. Bunks and blankets are provided, as are homestyle breakfasts and dinners. Each hut has a distinctive New England ambience —rustic, friendly, alpine and wholesome. The Hutmasters and their assistants are generally young men and women from eastern colleges who are energetic and more than willing to share their knowledge of these mountains.

ITINERARY:

DAY 1: Leave hometown. Arrive Boston. Meet with trip leader and transfer to bus for three-hour ride to Franconia, New Hampshire. Hike six miles to Lonesome Lake hut.

DAY 2: Descend the Lonesome Lake Trail, ascend Falling Waters Trail past three sets of waterfalls to Mt. Little Haystack (4,800'). Continue over Mts. Lincoln and Lafayette (5,249') to Greenleaf Hut (4,200'). 7 miles.

DAY 3: Ascend over the summits of Mt. Lafayette and Mt. Garfield (4,488') to Galehead Hut (3,800'), a strenuous 7.6 miles.

DAY 4: Steep ascent of Mt. South Twin (4,926') and descend to Zealand Falls Hut. 7 miles.

DAY 5: Either a demanding but spectacular 14.2-mile hike up to Mt. Webster (3,910'), with views into Crawford Notch, site of the Willey House (immortalized by Nathaniel Hawthorne) and over Mt. Jackson (4,052') to Mizpah Spring Hut, or take the moderate Avalon-Zealand Trail to Mizpah Spring Hut, a considerably easier 7.7 miles.

DAY 6: An easier but no less spectacular day over the Southern Presidential Range to Lake Of The Clouds Hut, located on the shoulder of Mt. Washington near three alpine lakes. 5 miles.

DAY 7: Along famed Crawford Path to the summit of Mt. Washington (6,288'), highest peak east of the Mississippi and north of the Carolinas, and crowded with a cog railway, auto road, museum observatory/weather station. From here, we traverse the beautiful Northern Presidential Range with optional side trips over the summits of Mt. Clay (5,532'), Mt. Jefferson (5,715') and Mt. Adams (5,798'). Descend to Madison Spring Hut (4,825'). Total hiking distance 7.7 miles.

DAY 8: Down the precipitous Madison Gulf Trail to the Glen House and a gentle ascent up to the beautiful Carter Notch Hut with its two sparkling lakes and numerous caves. Hiking distance 8 miles.

DAY 9: A rugged 6.8 miles over the summits of the Wildcat Ridge, with its beautiful views of the Northern Presidential Range and Mt. Washington. Down to Pinkham Notch Camp, summer headquarters of Appalachian Mountain Club activities.

DAY 10: Return by bus to Boston to connect with homeward-bound flights.

Glen House, one of the huts maintained by the Appalachian Mountain Club.

White Mountain photos by Jon Burroughs

GOVERNMENT PERMITS:

We work with outfitters or agents properly licensed for the government areas in which the trips operate. Appropriate federal and state governments may contact Mountain Travel for further information.

Brown bear fishing for sockeye salmon, Alaska/ Rollie Osternick

Moose, McKinley National Park, Alaska/ William Boehm

The wide Alsek River near the Gulf of Alaska is lined with vast meadows and glacial deltas/Fred Faye Hiltner

ALASKA WILDLIFE SAFARI

5-day high arctic camp, 4-day Denali cabin camp

DATES: *Jun 7–Jun 23 (17 days)*
LEADER: *Chuck Horner*
GRADE: *A-2*
LAND COST: *$2190 + $350 chtr. (10–12 members) $2350 + $375 chtr. (8–9)*

Note: Commercial flights between Fairbanks and Barter Island are not included in Land Cost.

This safari begins in "ultimate wilderness park" set in the northernmost reaches of the North American continent—the 8.9-million acre William O. Douglas Wildlife Range (formerly the Arctic National Wildlife Range).

Here, in the luxury of almost 24 hours of daylight, we spend five days experiencing the high arctic in summer, making optional day hikes into this rugged land where caribou, moose, and wolves roam. Our trips are times to take advantage of the caribou migration and best wildlife viewing season.

From Fairbanks, we take the train to the sub-arctic splendor of Denali (McKinley) National Park, home to 37 species of mammals and 132 species of birds. With five days in comfortable cabins at Camp Denali, we'll have an unregimented schedule during which we can hike, fish, photograph, or just relax and enjoy the beauty of the alpine tundra world.

At the end of the trip, we can arrange an optional visit to the very isolated Pribilof Islands in the Bering Sea, renowned as the breeding ground of the largest fur seal herd in the world and of literally millions of birds (more than 180 species, including kittiwakes, puffins, murres, and cormorants): two-day, three-night Pribilof Option is $675.

ITINERARY:

DAY 1: Leave hometown. Arrive Fairbanks. Transfer to hotel.

DAY 2: Fly to Barter Island in the Beaufort Sea.

DAY 3 to 7: By charter flight from Barter Island to a very remote part of the William O. Douglas National Wildlife Range. Here in America's largest wildlife refuge, a place of quiet beauty, the great caribou herds will migrate from near Barter Island southeastward toward the Yukon. We hope to see a part of the migration and there is also a chance to see bear, sheep, wolves and waterfowl. Nights are spent at a lake camp from which we will take daily hikes.

DAY 8: Return by charter flight to Barter Island.

DAY 9: Fly to Fairbanks.

DAY 10: Day free in Fairbanks, or to adjust itinerary if weather has delayed flights.

DAY 11 to 15: By train to Denali, then continue by bus about 90 miles to Denali National Park. At Camp Denali, we will have four days for wildlife viewing, panning for gold, and enjoying the beauty of the surroundings. The cabin camp is set in tundra and spruce woods with splendid views of Mt. McKinley (20,320′).

DAY 16: By bus and train to Anchorage.

DAY 17: Depart Anchorage on homeward-bound flights.

TATSHENSHINI/ ALSEK RAFTING

9-day journey from mountains to the sea

DATES: *Aug-3–Aug 14 (12 days)*
LEADER: *Fred Faye Hiltner*
GRADE: *A-3*
LAND COST: *$1390 incl. chtrs. (8–15 members)*

Known by seasoned river runners the world over, the Tatshenshini/ Alsek is one of the world's premier wilderness raft trips. From the lush green hills at the start to the glaciated mountains near the end, this journey reveals nature in its most pristine state. As we approach the coast, the horizon seems to shrink as the great St. Elias Mountains rise from the river's edge. Wildlife abounds, including grizzlies, bighorn, Dall sheep and bald eagles. But the single most impressive thing about this river trip is the immense blue-white glaciers we'll see on route.

Once the Tatshenshini joins the Alsek, glaciers flow right down to the river banks. The sights and sounds of the seven-mile-wide Alsek Glacier are an experience not to be missed. Huge icebergs will accompany our rafts downstream. Coming ever closer to the Gulf of Alaska, we'll be able to feel and smell the sea.

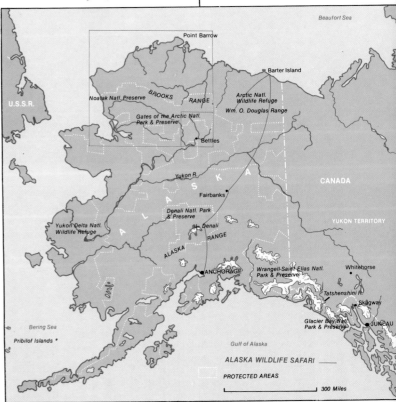

Floating on the Tatshenshini River, Alaska/ Bruce Klepinger

We return to civilization on a scenic bush flight over the Fairweather Range and the immense Brady Glacier before touching down in Gustavus, gateway to Glacier Bay National Park.

We travel five to a raft with an experienced oarsman. No previous rafting experience is necessary.

ITINERARY:

DAY 1: Leave hometown. Arrive Juneau. Continue by ferry or air taxi (cost not included) to Haines. Overnight in hotel.

DAY 2: Drive about 100 miles to the put-in point near Dalton Post, Canada. Set off down the river. On the upper Tatshenshini, we enjoy exhilarating rapids in the Tatshenshini Gorge. Emerge from the gorge into more placid waters.

DAY 3 and 4: The river slowly builds momentum as we wind our way towards the beautiful Alsek and Noisy Ranges. There are many good short hikes to take in this area.

DAY 5: The river gets increasingly broad as huge unnamed tributary creeks add their silted water to the Tatshenshini. This is prime country for moose, bear and wolf. Rounding one last fast bend in the river, we camp in the immense valley of the Tat's confluence with the Alsek.

DAY 6: A day of hiking and exploring the vast meadows, glacier deltas and ridges of the Alsek Valley. Several glacier-fed streams offer icy baths for those with fortitude.

DAY 7: A short but dramatic day on the Alsek brings us to the Walker Glacier, named by rafters because of the ease of walking onto his moraine-covered glacier. Hike onto the glacier and explore the base of the spectacular icefall from the upper glacier.

DAY 8: The Alsek quickly carries us through terrain where high peaks rise steeply from the river. This is ice age country and dozens of large and small glaciers fill every vista around our tiny rafts.

DAY 9: Enter the grandeur of Alsek Bay, a spectacular place. At the foot of the St. Elias Range (highest coastal mountains in the world), Mt. Fairweather looms 15,000 feet above us across the bay. We hear icebergs the size of ships calving off the face of Alsek Glacier, while smaller sculpted icebergs drift slowly by. Hike up to an overlook on Gateway Knob, then paddle the rafts quietly among the icy giants of Alsek Bay.

DAY 10: Leaving high country, we will begin to smell and feel the salt air of the ocean, as the Tatshenshini/Alsek system empties into Alaska's coast on the boundary of Glacier Bay National Park.

DAY 11: De-rig the boats at Dry Bay, then afternoon pickup by floatplane for a ride over Brady Icefield, along the Fairweather Range and over Glacier Bay to Gustavus. Continue by commercial flight to Juneau (cost not included). Overnight at hotel.

DAY 12: Connect with homeward-bound flights or Alaska State Ferry.

GLACIER BAY & CHILKOOT TRAIL

4-day kayak exploration, 4-day backpacking trip

DATES: #1 Jul 6–Jul 17 (12 days)
       #2 Aug 3–Aug 14 (12 days)
LEADER: *to be announced*
GRADE: *B-2*
LAND COST: *$1150 + chtrs. $300 (6–12 members)*

This trip combines a four-day kayaking/camping journey in the heart of Glacier Bay National Monument and a four-day backpack trip across the historic Chilkoot Trail of the 1898 Gold Rush.

In Glacier Bay, we'll travel from camp to camp in Klepper kayaks, paddling near the faces of the Riggs and McBride glaciers, witnessing the dramatic spectacle of huge chunks of ice "calving" off the glaciers into the serene blue waters of the bay.

In Gold Rush country, a four-day backpack trip takes us from Skagway to Lake Bennett over the Chilkoot Trail, "the meanest 32 miles in history," or so the gold stampeders called it, since they were required to carry a year's worth of supplies over it in the dead of winter! The trail has splendid mountain scenery and many remnants of the Gold Rush.

ITINERARY:

DAY 1: Leave hometown. Arrive Juneau. Transfer to hotel.

DAY 2: Visit Mendenhall Glacier then fly to Gustavus, near Glacier Bay National Park headquarters.

DAY 3: Board M.V. Thunder Bay for a cruise through the Muir Arm of Glacier Bay, disembarking at Riggs Glacier. Assemble the Klepper kayaks and paddle toward the face of Muir Glacier, with a good chance of observing seals and marine birds such as kittywakes, cormorants, puffins, gulls and eagles. Camp near Muir Glacier.

DAY 4: By kayak towards Riggs Glacier, passing sculpted icebergs and the active face of Muir Glacier, camping on the high limestone ledges south of Riggs Glacier. Beautiful view of upper Muir Inlet.

DAY 5: By kayak to McBride Glacier, then on across the Muir Arm to Wolf Point. Evening camp at Wolf Point.

DAY 6: Walk up to White Thunder Ridge, or hike along a remnant of the Muir Glacier. Late afternoon pickup by floatplane for a scenic flight through Endicott Gap, over the mountains and down to the little town of Skagway.

DAY 7: Travel by van to the abandoned mining site of Dyea. Explore the historical site and old avalanche graveyard. Then begin the Chilkoot Trail hike, walking along an abandoned logging road through mature spruce rainforest.

DAY 8 and 9: Continue hiking through deep forest, exploring old gold mining camps; enter alpine country and scramble over the steep Chilkoot Pass.

DAY 10: Once we have crossed the pass, we are in Canada. Hike along through high alpine country to the shores of Lake Lindeman.

DAY 11: Hike to Lake Bennett and the junction of the old cog railway. Return to Skagway by highway and continue by charter flight to Juneau. Overnight at hotel.

DAY 12: Depart Juneau and connect with homeward-bound flights.

About Raft, Kayak & Canoe Trips

Our adventures on the wilderness waterways of Alaska are conducted by professional guides, each of whom is an expert in making a wilderness experience a pleasant and safe one. Previous camping experience is recommended, but certainly not required. No previous experience with kayaks, canoes or rafts is needed. Trip members are expected to pitch in and help with camp chores such as packing and unpacking group gear from the boats, pitching tents, etc. Breakfast and dinner will be hot, hearty meals served in camp; lunch will be picnic-style. All boat gear (including life jackets) is provided, and the boats are stable, easy-to-handle and fun to use. Camp supplies are transported from place to place by raft, canoe or kayak (depending on the particular trip). Mountain Travel's Alaska leaders are all members of the Alaskan Association of Mountain and Wilderness Guides.

Day hike up to White Thunder Ridge from camp at Wolf Point, Glacier Bay, Alaska/ Pam Shandrick

One can learn basic kayaking skills in the pristine wilderness environment of Glacier Bay, Alaska

A short portage to Guerin Lake, Admiralty Island, Alaska.

Glacier Bay & Admiralty Island photos by Chuck Horner

Gone fishin'

Canoeing the lakes of Admiralty Island, Alaska.

GLACIER BAY & ADMIRALTY ISLAND

4-days of travel by kayak, 6-day canoe journey

DATES: *#1 Jul 20–Aug 2 (14 days)*
#2 Aug 10–Aug 23 (14 days)
LEADER: *Hayden Kaden*
GRADE: *B-2*
LAND COST: *$1390 + chtr. $330*
(8–12 members)
$1590 + chtr. $425
(6–7)

This two-week adventure takes place in the water wilderness of Southeast Alaska, a wonderful place to learn how to explore by kayak and canoe.

We start on the east shore of Admiralty Island National Monument, the "fortress of the bears," connecting five blue wilderness lakes by canoe with short portages. Enjoying great salmon fishing (and salmon feasts) along the way, we'll end up at the Indian village of Angoon, where hunting and fishing are still the main occupations.

From here we fly by floatplane to John Muir's beloved Glacier Bay, where snow-covered 15,000-foot mountains rise above ice-choked fjords. Glacier Bay's mountains are habitat for brown and black bear, coyotes, wolves and mountain goats; the waters are home to seal, sea lion, humpback and killer whales, salmon and trout. There is an abundance of waterfowl, including guillemots, puffins, murrelets, cormorants and kittiwakes.

From a very remote inlet, we'll have five days of easy kayaking in the turquoise waters amidst ice floes and tiny coves. There will be time for hiking on shore to explore several glaciers. Our two-man Klepper kayaks are simple and fun to use, allowing easy access to remote coves and inlets.

ITINERARY:

DAY 1: Leave hometown. Arrive Juneau. Transfer to hotel.

DAY 2: By charter flight from Juneau to Mole Harbor on the east side of Admiralty Island. Organize gear and hike 2.5 miles to Alexander Lake, one of the most beautiful lakes along the Admiralty Island Trail System.

DAY 3: To Beaver Lake, setting up camp on the outlet of Beaver Creek. Time for sightseeing on Hasselborg Lake or fishing for cutthroat trout.

DAY 4: Paddle across Hasselborg Lake, short portage into Guerin Lake and paddle to the creek flowing from Distin Lake. Camp near an old Civilian Conservation Corps shelter.

DAY 5: Paddle through a slough created by beaver dams in Davidson Lake. Portage between Davidson and Distin Lakes, then make a 3-mile backpack trip to Salt Lake, where we pick up another set of canoes.

DAY 6: Layover day at Salt Lake, a great campsite for wildlife viewing, fishing and laying about.

DAY 7: Paddle through Mitchell Bay and the island complex between Mitchell Bay and the village of Angoon. Good tide pools and, with luck, a chance to see eagles, martin, deer, porpoise, otter, humpback whales and an occasional bear. Arrive in Angoon, a native village where the old traditions still survive. Overnight at hotel.

DAY 8 to 12: By charter flight from Angoon directly into Reid Inlet, a remote region of Glacier Bay. From different campsites each night, we'll have five days to travel to inlets and nearby glaciers by kayak and on foot. The waters are home to seals, sea lions, porpoises, and whales and an abundance of fascinating birds. On shore, we may see eagles, brown and black bears, coyotes and mountain goats.

DAY 13: Pack up gear for pickup by charter flight to Gustavus. Continue by commercial flight to Juneau.

DAY 14: Leave Juneau and connect with homeward-bound flights.

NATURAL HISTORY CRUISES IN SOUTHEAST ALASKA

Beach combing and whale watching

DATES: *#1 Jun 30–Jul 9 (10 days)*
#2 Jul 9–Jul 18 (10 days)
#3 Jul 20–Aug 29 (10 days)
#4 Aug 1–Aug 10 (10 days)
LEADER: *Ronn Storro-Patterson*
GRADE: *A-1*
LAND COST: *$1490 (8–10 members)*
$1790 (6–7)

The waterways of Southeast Alaska are among the most fascinating and beautiful "ocean passages" on earth.

Biologically, this region is a virtual marine wilderness. Numerous islands support sea bird and marine mammal colonies; the waters team with fish, dolphins, porpoises and whales. The most intensive summer feeding areas for humpback whales in the entire eastern Pacific are located here. In addition to superb wildlife attractions, the Inland Passage has a unique blend of native American culture. Russian heritage and a frontier spirit.

The Delphinus, *our 50-foot natural history crusing ship.*

We will explore these reaches aboard the *Delphinus,* a custom-built 50-foot natural history cruising ship which accommodates ten passengers and a crew of three, including a naturalist guide.

"Breaching" humpback whale in Frederick Sound, Alaska/Ronn Storro-Patterson.

The small size of the boat allows us to travel into the most remote and scenic coves and inlets, a far different experience than that offered by larger boats. We will also be able to explore and observe in the small skiffs which the *Delphinus* carries, and go ashore for hikes, berry-picking, "botanizing," viewing and photographing animals, and beachcombing. Optionally, it may be possible to spend an evening or two ashore in your own tent.

The *Delphinus* has windows throughout the galley, salon and pilot house which allow uninterrupted visibility from inside. The spacious high decks, cockpit and flying bridge permit outstanding viewing and freedom to move about. She provides three double cabins and a four-bunk cabin, two bathrooms with shower facilities and a full galley which serves excellent meals.

Cruise #1 begins in Ketchikan and explores Misty Fjords National Monument, one of the newest and most spectacular national monuments, notable for deep fjords and 3,000-foot-high granite cliffs rising straight up from the waters' edge. Many have called it "a Yosemite to explore by boat." Shore trails make it convenient to explore on foot along the edges of this two-million-acre wilderness, home to brown bears, moose, mink, otter, bald eagles and waterfowl. We can also visit Wrangell at the mouth of the Stikine River or other more remote coves. We arrive in Petersburg via the Wrangell Narrows, one of the most amazing navigational features in southeast Alaska.

ITINERARY:

DAY 1: Fly to Ketchikan. Board boat.

DAY 2 to 8: On cruise.

DAY 9: Arrive Petersburg.

DAY 10: Depart Petersburg on homeward-bound flights.

Cruise #2 begins in Petersburg, a town aptly called "Little Norway," a hard-working fishing and lumber town little affected by tourism. From Petersburg, we travel to the LeConte Glacier to witness a thunderously calving tidewater glacier, then move to Frederick Sound for some of the most spectacular whale watching in the world. The sights and sounds of leaping humpback whales will probably cause us to linger here a few days. Afterwards, we visit Admiralty Island's Seymour Canal, with its extraordinary wildlife viewing and fishing. Continuing up Stephens Passage, we are treated to exceptionally fine views of a series of active glaciers:

the Dawes, Saywer, Sumdum and Taku. As time allows, we will explore numerous arms along the mainland side with their icebergs, snow-capped mountains and rivers of ice. The cruise ends with time to visit Juneau.

ITINERARY:

DAY 1: Fly to Petersburg. Board boat.

DAY 2 to 8: On cruise.

DAY 9: Arrive Juneau.

DAY 10: Depart Juneau on homeward-bound flights.

Cruise #3 begins and ends in Juneau, with time to visit the state museum and sample Juneau nightlife before heading up the Lynn Canal and Icy Strait to magnificent Glacier Bay, where we spend three days exploring and viewing many active glaciers. We will also see the important Indian settlement of Hoona, explore a portion of Frederick Bay on remote Chichagof Island, and make a visit to the fishing outpost of Elfin Cove near the head of Cross Sound. Much of our time will be spent exploring bays and coves, viewing wildlife, whale watching, visiting dense rainforests, fishing and relaxing.

ITINERARY:

DAY 1: Fly to Juneau.

DAY 2 to 8: On cruise.

DAY 9: Return to Juneau.

DAY 10: Depart Juneau on homeward-bound flights.

Cruise #4 begins in Juneau and emphasizes the wildlife found on Admiralty and adjoining islands, along with the culture and flavor of native American villages and Alaskan outposts. We first travel to Glacier Bay for an overnight visit, then stop in at Angoon, one of the most important native American settlements in Alaska, where at the conclusion of the Native American Settlement Act, the locals decided to pursue a traditional hunting and fishing lifestyle. Across Chatham Strait are the remote outposts of Tenakee and Baranoff Hot Springs. A further highlight of this cruise is Frederick Sound, with its old canneries and abandoned whaling stations, sea lion rookeries and, of course, its outstanding population of humpback whales. We end the cruise in Petersburg, with time to explore its colorful waterfront.

ITINERARY:

DAY 1: Fly to Juneau.

DAY 2 to 8: On cruise.

DAY 9: Arrive Petersburg.

DAY 10: Depart Petersburg on homeward-bound flights.

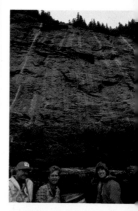

Traveling by boat is an ideal way to botanize, beachcomb and discover the beauty of Alaska with a naturalist guide.

Photos by trip leader Ronn Storro-Patterson

THE MCKINLEY TREK

8-day backpack trip onto McKinley's glaciers

DATES: *Aug 9–Aug 22 (14 days)*
LEADER: *Gary Bocarde*
GRADE: *B-3*
LAND COST: *$1290 (7–10 members)*
$1450 (5–6)

This is a fantastic trek which takes advantage of McKinley's full 17,000-foot rise above the Alaskan plains. It leads right up onto the glaciers of Mt. McKinley, North America's highest peak, known in the native language as Denali—"the great one."

Starting near Wonder Lake in Denali National Park, the eight-day trek begins at the mile-wide McKinley River and proceeds up Cache Creek to the alpine meadows of McGonagall Canyon. Crossing McGonagall Pass, we'll stop for a day of instruction on safe glacier travel and the use of ice axe and crampons.

We then ascend the Muldrow Glacier (from which the pioneer ascent was made in 1913) to a point near the lower icefall beneath McKinley's great northern flanks. From a central camp, we'll make day hikes near the Tralieka and Brooks glaciers and optional scrambles on several easy peaks before retracing our route over McGonagall Pass to Wonder Lake.

Camp at 8,000 feet on the Kahiltna Glacier, the area from which most McKinley climbs begin.

This will be a very spectacular trek involving simple glacier travel, vigorous hiking and a few difficult river crossings. No mountaineering experience is required.

ITINERARY:

DAY 1: Leave hometown. Arrive Anchorage. Transfer to hotel.

DAY 2: By Alaska Railroad to Denali National Park. Camp at Park Headquarters.

DAY 3: Scenic bus ride to Wonder Lake Camp nearby.

DAY 4: Begin trek. Cross the mile-wide McKinley River and hike the trail to Clearwater (Camp I) Creek. We'll carry all our own supplies in backpacks; however, our loads will be reduced somewhat by supplies that have been cached in advance.

DAY 5 and 6: Hike up to Cache Creek drainage, McGonagall Canyon and cross McGonagall Pass.

DAY 7: Ascend the Muldrow Glacier to the base of the Lower Icefall and Gunsight Pass.

DAY 8: Ascend Gunsight Mountain; spectacular views of the north side of McKinley.

DAY 9: Day trek up the Tralieka Glacier, with possible ascents of small peaks.

DAY 10 and 11: Walk out to Clearwater Creek.

DAY 12: Bus to Park Headquarters.

DAY 13: Train to Anchorage.

DAY 14: Leave Anchorage and connect with homeward-bound flights.

MCKINLEY CLIMBING SEMINAR

Learn mountaineering in the Alaska Range

DATES: *Jun 14–Jun 27 (14 days)*
LEADER: *Gary Bocarde & Nic Parker*
GRADE: *B-3/D-1*
LAND COST: *$1590 incl. chtr.*
(8–12 members)

This climbing seminar takes place in a spectacular mountain setting surrounded by the big peaks of the Alaska Range including McKinley (20,320'), Foraker (17,402') and Hunter (14,573').

We will fly to the southeast fork of the Kahiltna Glacier, the starting point for most McKinley ascents. From here, we ski or snowshoe to the base of Control Tower Peak (8,060'). From this base camp, we begin instruction in rope handling, glissading and snow climbing techniques.

After a few days of instruction, we make a night ascent of Control Tower Peak. The seminar continues with instruction in technical rock and ice climbing techniques, and the final few days are spent climbing Radar Peak (8,670') and Mt. Francis (10,450').

The seminar is suitable for strong backpackers (capable of heavy load carrying) who want to learn a full range of mountaineering techniques.

ITINERARY:

DAY 1: Leave hometown. Arrive Anchorage. Transfer to hotel.

DAY 2: Drive or take the train to Talkeetna. Continue by spectacular charter to the Kahiltna Glacier at the base of Mt. McKinley.

DAY 3: By ski or snowshoe for 1½ hours to the western base of Peak 8060 (Control Tower Peak). Establish a base camp, learning winter camping techniques.

DAY 4 and 5: Begin the seminar: basic knots, belaying, basic rope handling, self arrest, glissading, snow climbing techniques, rappelling, use of ice axe and crampons.

DAY 6: Continue seminar: glacier travel techniques, crevasse rescue, avalanche rescue procedures, discussion of mountain safety and first aid. Night climb of Control Tower Peak.

DAY 7 and 8: Technical ice climbing instruction and practice, using modern techniques and equipment.

Camp life, Kahiltna Glacier. The McKinley Climbing Seminar is suitable for strong backpackers (capable of heavy load carrying) who want to learn a full range of mountaineering techniques.

DAY 9 and 10: Basic rock climbing instruction: climbing techniques, use of pitons and chocks, setting up belay anchors, rappelling.

DAY 11: Move camp to north of the landing site, set up camp. Nighttime ascent of Mt. Francis.

DAY 12: Night ascent of Radar Peak.

DAY 13: Fly out to Talkeetna and return to Anchorage.

DAY 14: Depart Anchorage and connect with homeward-bound flights.

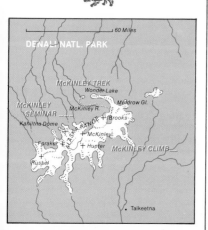

MT. MCKINLEY EXPEDITION

Climb North America's highest peak

DATES: *May 3–May 24 (22 days)*
LEADER: *Nic Parker*
GRADE: *E-2*
LAND COST: *$1950 incl. chtr. (8–10 members) $2100 incl. chtr. (5–7)*

Mt. McKinley (20,320′) is the highest point on the North American continent. It is a beautiful and impressive mountain by any standards, soaring a dazzling 17,000 feet above the plains—one of the greatest base-to-summit rises of any mountain on earth. It was first climbed in 1913; subsequent ascents were few until the 1950's.

The West Buttress route, first climbed in 1951, has become the standard approach to the summit. This will be our route of ascent, beginning at a base camp on the Kahiltna Glacier at 7,000 feet.

A climb of McKinley is physically demanding and requires a range of mountaineering skills. Technically, it is of moderate difficulty. Weather and altitude make it a true mountaineering challenge. The duration of the ascent can take as little as ten days, but can require 15 or more because of frequent and prolonged storms which hit the peak.

Members must be very fit, and capable of carrying loads of 75 lbs. or more at high altitudes and

assisting with expedition chores. All community equipment will be provided. The party will be flown in by charter from Talkeetna.

ITINERARY:

DAY 1: Leave hometown. Arrive Anchorage. Transfer to hotel.

DAY 2: Drive to Talkeetna. Prepare expedition gear for tomorrow's flight onto the Kahiltna Glacier.

DAY 3: By charter flight to the 7,000-foot level on the southeast fork of the Kahiltna Glacier. Establish base camp. Note: weather conditions may delay the departure of this mountain flight.

DAY 4 to 7: Carry loads from 7,000 feet to 10,000 feet at Kahiltna Pass. Conditioning and acclimatization during this period.

DAY 8 to 10: Move camp from 11,000 feet to 14,200 feet in a basin below the West Buttress, in accordance with weather conditions, acclimatization and strength of party.

DAY 11 to 14: Load carrying up fixed lines to 16,400 feet on the West Buttress. Establish high camp.

DAY 15 and 16: Move to high camp at 17,200 feet.

DAY 17 and 18: Summit attempts, depending on weather conditions.

DAY 19 and 20: Descend and return to Kahiltna Glacier pick-up point.

DAY 21 and 22: Charter flight from the Kahiltna Glacier to Talkeetna. Return to Anchorage by bus or train and connect with homeward-bound flights.

Note on itinerary: The daily schedule listed above is a guideline only and will vary in accordance with conditions on the mountain.

McKinley photos by trip leader Gary Bocarde

Students at the McKinley Climbing Seminar

An ascent of McKinley is one of the greatest mountaineering experiences outside of the Himalayas.

Muldrow Glacier, northern side of McKinley.

NOATAK RIVER BY CANOE

Float trip in the Brooks Range

DATES: *Jun 16–Jul 29 (14 days)*
LEADER: *to be announced*
GRADE: *A-2*
LAND COST: *$1575 incl. chtrs.*
(8–12 members)
$1690 (5–7)

Note: Commercial flights between Fairbanks and Bettles are not included in Land Cost.

Born in the melting snows of the Brooks Range and emptying 400 miles later into Kotzebue Sound, the Noatak is a majestic wilderness river, all of it above the Arctic Circle. It is now protected as a national park, called Noatak National Preserve.

This trip features a leisurely week-long float trip by canoe on the Noatak's headwaters where the peaks of the Brooks Range rise on both sides of the river. There will be time for day hikes on tributary creeks and fishing. Wildlife is abundant here: we'll see caribou, Dall sheep, grizzly bear and possibly bald eagles. No previous canoe experience is necessary.

ITINERARY:

DAY 1: Leave hometown. Arrive Fairbanks. Transfer to hotel.

DAY 2: Fly Bettles, continue by chartered float plane to the headwaters of the Noatak. The flight will be spectacular, with views of the distant Arrigetch Peaks and Mt. Igikpak, highest peak in the central and western Brooks Range. Land at the farthest upstream lake where the river is still navigable and camp on smooth tundra.

DAY 3: Today we'll hike most of the day, looking for Dall sheep and caribou.

DAY 4: Portage gear and canoes to the Noatak and begin leisurely float by canoe, stopping along the way to photograph and explore.

DAY 5: Hike up the gravel beaches along Kugruk Creek to visit secluded hot springs. Excellent fishing for grayling and arctic char.

DAY 6: By canoe to camp at Igning Creek confluence, a very scenic area with many grizzly bears. Excellent grayling and pike fishing.

DAY 7: Free day to explore Igning Creek, fish, hike or look over old gold mining claims.

DAY 8 to 11: On our final day canoeing on the Noatak, we will pass by a denning area for wolves, which are easily seen by the careful observer. Numerous ground squirrels live here, too, unwilling food for the growing wolf families. Our last two days will be spent canoeing and exploring Matcharak Lake. There is excellent fishing for lake trout. Often, the weather is warm enough for swimming.

DAY 12: Charter flight back to Bettles.

DAY 13: Commercial flight to Fairbanks.

DAY 14: Leave Fairbanks and connect with homeward-bound flights.

NOATAK KAYAKING

15 days on a high arctic river

DATES: *Jul 30–Aug 18 (20 days)*
LEADER: *Mike & Debbie O'Connor*
GRADE: *B-3*
LAND COST: *$1965 incl. chtrs.*
(8–12 members)
$2115 incl. chtrs.
(5–7)

Note: Commercial flights between Fairbanks and Bettles and from Kotzebue to Anchorage are not included in the Land Cost.

In a fascinating geological display, the Noatak River pours from the jagged Brooks Range, over broad tundra plains, between steep, carved canyon walls and finally through deep spruce forest and out into the Bering Sea. There is only one permanent human settlement on its entire 400-mile length. Otherwise its inhabitants are moose, bear, caribou, wolves, hawks and eagles.

Using two-man "Folboat" kayaks, we will journey for fifteen days on the Noatak from its headwaters all the way to the Eskimo village of Noatak near Kotzebue Sound. Along the way, we stop to hike, photograph and fish for delicious arctic char, grayling and salmon.

No previous kayak experience is necessary.

ITINERARY:

DAY 1: Leave hometown. Arrive Fairbanks. Transfer to hotel.

DAY 2: Fly to Bettles, continue by spectacular chartered float plane to the headwaters of the Noatak.

DAY 3: Hike to the top of the mountains to look for Dall sheep and caribou.

DAY 4: Portage to the Noatak River and float to the confluence of the Noatak and Kugruk Creeks.

DAY 5: Hike up Kugruk Creek and visit hot springs.

Not all of our time is spent in canoes.

Canoeing the pristine Noatak from its Brooks Range headwaters is a true wilderness experience.

Kayaking the Kobuk River from Walker Lake to the Eskimo village of Kobuk reveals a fine array of arctic wildlife.

DAY 6: Continue float to Lake Matcharak, passing a wolf denning area and prime grizzly bear country. Careful observers will probably see some wildlife.

DAY 7: Layover day for exploring Lake Matcharak, a transition area where the mountains give way to wide rolling tundra vistas.

DAY 8: Float from Lake Matcharak past Class II rapids below Douglas Creek. Caribou are commonly seen in the Aniuk Lowland area.

DAY 9: The Noatak waters pick up speed in the Aniuk lowland and Class II rapids make the day's travel exciting. This is a good opportunity to learn the art of "reading the water."

DAY 10: Float to Aniuk Creek and Cutler River, one of the larger tributaries of the Noatak. Here the river becomes at least 100 yards wide.

DAY 11: Float beyond Okak Bend, where there are several Eskimo archaeological sites. Sometimes whalebone sleds and old hunting camps are seen.

DAY 12: Now the flat, rolling terrain gives way to rugged hills. Small groves of cottonwood trees grow along the river—the first trees we've seen since Bettles.

DAY 13: Enter the "Grand Canyon of the Noatak," a beautiful broad valley with stratas of various types of vegetation on the hillsides which give it tremendous depth and color.

DAY 14 and 15: Float to Sisiak Creek and an area where the farthest extension of spruce forest in North America meets the river.

DAY 16: In the "grand canyon" section of the river, where colorful vertical-walled cliffs rise from either side of the river.

DAY 17 and 18: To the Kelly River, one of the finest spots in Alaska for arctic char, and continue to Noatak Village. Visit Eskimo settlement.

DAY 19: Fly by charter to Kotzebue. Overnight in hotel.

DAY 20: Fly by commercial flight to Anchorage and connect with homeward-bound flights.

KOBUK RIVER KAYAKING

7-day river journey in the arctic summer

DATES: *Aug 11–Aug 24 (14 days)*
LEADER: *Dave & Tamara Ketscher*
GRADE: *B-2*
LAND COST: *$1775 incl. chtr.*
(8–12 members)
$1890 (5–7)
Note: Commercial flight from Fairbanks to Bettles is not included in Land Cost.

This trip features a week-long journey down the swift Kobuk River by kayak, through a scenic region recently designated as Kobuk Valley National Park. Enroute, we stop often to enjoy the sunny, sandy beaches and, on the lower river, try our hand at fishing for migratory salmon and sheefish. We'll also visit some Eskimo fish camps and see remnants of abandoned gold mining operations. The beaches are a rock hound's paradise since the area is highly mineralized—jasper and jade are especially common.

The Kobuk is one of the richest rivers in all the arctic for fishing and it supports an amazing abundance of birdlife, including bald and golden eagles, osprey, kingfishers, ravens, arctic terns, and many varieties of gulls and predatory birds. Grizzly and black bears, moose, fox and wolves are also common.

No previous kayaking experience is necessary for this trip. We paddle stable, easy to use, two-man Folboat kayaks.

ITINERARY:

DAY 1: Leave hometown and arrive Fairbanks. Transfer to hotel.

DAY 2: Fly to Bettles, north of the Arctic Circle. Continue by chartered floatplane to beautiful 16-mile-long Walker Lake. Barbecue dinner at camp.

DAY 3: Free day for exploring around Walker Lake or fishing for lake trout, arctic char, arctic grayling and northern pike.

DAY 4: Begin kayak trip with a short paddle through some easy and fun rapids on an outlet river which joins with the Kobuk River about four miles from Walker Lake.

DAY 5: Continue float trip down river through rolling hills and prime arctic wildlife habitat. The river picks up speed as we pass through the upper Kobuk canyon, with its 200-foot rock bluffs.

DAY 6: Enter lower Kobuk Canyon, with its exciting but safe whitewater, the last rapids on the Kobuk.

DAY 7 to 12: Continue float trip on the now-placid Kobuk. Salmon will be spawning up small creeks and bears are commonly seen. At the Pah River confluence, we will spend half a day on the sandy beaches and try our luck at catching arctic sheefish, a tarpon-like fish distantly related to salmon and whitefish. There is an abandoned gold mining operation nearby and also some Eskimo archaeological sites in the area. We will have an extra day here to adjust the itinerary as desired, depending on water conditions. Arrive on Day 12 at the village of Kobuk.

DAY 13: Visit with Eskimos of Kobuk, watching them cutting and drying fish. Fly by scheduled charter to Kotzebue.

DAY 14: Fly to Anchorage and connect with homeward-bound flights. 🐎

Porcupine, just one of many species we might see along the Noatak.

Noatak and Kobuk photos by trip leader Dave Ketscher

The group and gear are flown from Bettles to Walker Lake by bush plane.

Arctic loon

Willow ptarmigan

Red phalarope

Bar-tailed gadwit

Wildlife photos by trip leader Craig Hohenberger

Northern phalarope

NATURAL HISTORY OF THE NORTH SLOPE & BROOKS RANGE

11-day kayak journey down the Colville River

DATES: *Jun 21–Jul 8 (18 days)*
LEADER: *Craig Hohenberger*
GRADE: *B-2*
LAND COST: *$2250 incl. chtrs.*
 (7–12 members)
 $2350 (4–6)

Note: Commercial flights from Fairbanks to Bettles and Prudhoe Bay to Fairbanks are not included in Land Cost.

A river trip in the arctic summer is a naturalist's dream. Traveling with our guide, a research biologist, we will see that the briefness of the arctic summer causes an accelerated pace of natural activity, as we witness the unfoldings of arctic flora and fauna in a condensed microcosm of time.

The north slope of the Brooks Range is special for several reasons: its mid-summer weather is among the best in Alaska, it is remote in the extremest sense, and it has an incredible abundance of wildlife, including one of the highest densities of grizzlies in Alaska.

This region also has the highest breeding densities of any place in the U.S. and allows a rare opportunity for the lay person to observe displaying and breeding shorebirds, a glimpse of natural selection and evolution at work. Here we'll find the endangered peregrine and gyrfalcon and even some rare Asiatic breeding birds (bluethroats and wheatears).

We begin at the Nigu River, a swiftly flowing tributary of the Etivluk and Colville rivers, and journey through three major geographical provinces as we follow the river northward on its course to the Beaufort Sea, gradually floating from the majestic cliffs of the central Brooks Range to our ultimate destination, the Colville River Delta.

Foraging Dall sheep, grizzly, caribou, moose and fox will be our constant companions. The timelessness and silence of the long arctic days will be punctuated with the ubiquitous cries of jaegers, falcons and loons and the piercing calls of the arctic fox. The nights will be illuminated by the midnight sun and our days will be filled with kayaking, hiking, fishing, photography, swimming and extensive exploration of the arctic environment. No previous kayak experience is necessary.

ITINERARY:

DAY 1: Leave hometown. Arrive Fairbanks.

DAY 2: Fly to Bettles and continue onward by air charter over the continental divide to the headwaters of the Nigu River. Introductory natural history hike amidst glaciated mountains and alpine tundra.

DAY 3: Day hike into the heart of the Brooks Range. Search glaciated cliffs for Dall sheep, hike over alpine tundra locating nesting shorebirds.

DAY 4: Begin kayak journey toward the Colville River Delta. Paddle through the swift upper sections of the Nigu, enjoying extraordinary views of displaying birds, foraging mammals and snow-clad peaks.

DAY 5: Continue float toward the confluence of the Colville River, stopping to photograph, fish and botanize.

DAY 6: Explore a nearby Eskimo archaeological site, hike and perhaps fish for lake trout and grayling.

DAY 7: Today we join the Etivluk River. Fishing for lake trout and grayling will be excellent throughout the trip.

DAY 8: As we travel north, the scenery of the Etivluk begins to change. The distinct Nigu River valley, bordered by mountains, gives way to a bluff-lined river flowing through rolling hills. Grizzly bears are often observed feeding in the willows or digging for ground squirrels here.

DAY 9: We reach the confluence of the Colville and Etivluk rivers. With the changing landscape, we get a new association of plants and animals.

DAY 10: Day hike into the rolling hills of the Kurupa River region, studying the evolutionary and social adaptations of the breeding avifauna.

DAY 11: While entering the low-lying sedimentary/limestone bluffs and hills of the lower Colville, we encounter the domain of the rare and endangered peregrine and gryfalcon. There will be ample time to stop and observe these graceful birds during their rarely-observed breeding cycle.

DAY 12: The river broadens and is braided between numerous islands and serpentine loops. Spectacular horizons are a conspicuous part of the scenery as we enter into the two-dimensional habitat of the arctic foothills and coastal plain.

DAY 13: Morning walk to study the carpets of blooming arctic wildflowers. We begin to see the first fledging shorebirds and perching birds. Many family groups of fox and caribou are visible.

DAY 14: Stop and explore the community of Umiat. Afterwards, continue to our northern destination of Ocean Point along the Beaufort Sea.

DAY 15 and 16: Eroded river bluffs, a plethora of ponds and lakes and luxuriant stands of grasses and sedges are characteristic of the lower arctic coastal plain. This region contains the richest breeding habitat in North America for swans, geese, ducks and loons. We will spend the last couple of days of our river journey alternating between paddling and studying the coastal flora and fauna.

DAY 17: Arrive at Ocean Point, Colville River Delta. Continue by charter flight to Prudhoe Bay. Connect with commercial flights to Fairbanks.

DAY 18: Depart Fairbanks on homeward-bound flights.

Caribou

Camping along the Alatna River.

THE ARRIGETCH WILDERNESS

6-day Brooks Range backpacking trip

DATES: #1 Jul 15–Jul 28 (14 days)
        #2 Jul 27–Aug 9 (14 days)
LEADER: *Dave Ketscher*
GRADE: *B-3*
LAND COST: *$1525 incl. chtr.*
        (8–12 members)
        $1680 incl. chtr.
        (5–7)
Note: Commercial flight from Fairbanks to Bettles is not included in Land Cost.

The impressive granite spires of the Arrigetch Peaks, now part of "Gates of the Arctic National Park," are perhaps the most spectacular part of the entire Brooks Range. The name Arrigetch in the native language means "fingers of the hand outstretched," and these peaks seem to reach up toward the sky, rising out of delicate alpine valleys.

To reach the Arrigetch wilderness, we fly to Bettles (above the Arctic Circle) and continue by floatplane to Circle Lake. From here, a two-day backpack trip takes us to our base camp in the heart of the Arrigetch Peaks, where we'll spend a few days hiking and photographing among the peaks. Dall sheep, black and grizzly bears are often found in the remote valleys. The hike into the Arrigetch is strenuous but the spectacular scenery makes it worth the effort.

We then hike out to the Alatna River for a float trip on a gentle arctic river which meanders through scenic bluffs and mountains. Moose, wolves, beaver and waterfowl are seen along the river. We will set aside ample time for hiking to nearby lakes to fish for lake trout and northern pike.

ITINERARY:

DAY 1: Leave hometown. Arrive Fairbanks. Transfer to hotel.

DAY 2: Fly to Bettles, north of the Arctic Circle. Continue by chartered floatplane to Circle Lake and camp nearby.

DAY 3: Today's hike, although only about 3 miles, is a difficult and strenuous one through bogs and terrain with tricky footing.

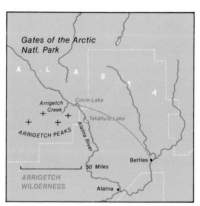

Camp on flat bluffs overlooking Arrigetch Creek in Gates of the Arctic National Park.

DAY 4: Six miles to our base camp in the Arrigetch Valley, a little easier than yesterday's hike, but with some bushwacking and fording icy streams.

DAY 5 and 6: From our base camp we will explore and hike up to the spires, past emerald glacial tarns. We carry only day packs on the walks during these two days, and return to base camp each night.

DAY 7: Break camp and retrace our route back to Arrigetch Creek.

DAY 8: Hike along Arrigetch Creek down to the Alatna River.

DAY 9: Begin float trip on the gentle Alatna River, a nice change of pace after our strenuous backpack trip. We'll drift slowly downriver, observing wildlife along the river.

DAY 10: Continue float trip and arrive at Takahula Lake. Portage the gear to the lake and camp on the lakeshore.

DAY 11: Free day at Takahula, a scenic lake nestled below majestic mountains. Time for fishing for lake trout and northern pike.

DAY 12: Afternoon pickup for charter flight back to Bettles. Barbecue on the Koyukuk River.

DAY 13: Fly to Fairbanks.

DAY 14: Depart Fairbanks on homeward-bound flights.

Floating the gentle Alatna River.

Arrigetch photos by trip leader Dave Ketscher

The 1983 Mountain Travel "Arrigetch Wilderness" group.

Haleakala Crater, Maui

Snow-covered Mauna Kea from the east. Large sugar cane plantations ring the mountain.

THE OTHER HAWAII

Camping, hiking, natural history

DATES: #1 *Apr 6–Apr 20 (15 days)*
　　　 #2 *Oct 5–Oct 19 (15 days)*
　　　 #3 *Dec 19, 1985–Jan 2, 1986)*
　　　 (15 days)
LEADER: #1: *Sara Steck*
　　　 #2 & #3: *Peter Ourusoff*
GRADE: *B-2*
LAND COST: *$990 (11–14 members)*
　　　 $1190 (6–10)

During our sojourn in the other Hawaii, we will hike, camp and explore the exotic natural beauty of the Hawaii of old, as it still exists on the outer islands.

With ten days on the "big island" of Hawaii, we will hike the Waipio Valley, swim and snorkel in the warm waters of Hapuna Beach, then make a summit hike on Mauna Kea (13,796'), highest peak in the Pacific.

Driving down the beautiful Kona Coast, we stop at Hawaii Volcanoes National Park to hike across the still-steaming Kilauea Caldera to explore Mauna Ulu, a very active volcano.

Our five-day sojourn on Maui includes a memorable sunrise from the summit of Haleakala (10,023'), followed by a two-day backpack trip across the moonscape of craters which form the volcano's floor. Our accommodations will be in beach camps and state park cabins, with our last night spent at an inn in the picturesque whaling port of Lahaina.

ITINERARY:

DAY 1: Leave hometown. Arrive Hilo, Hawaii. Transfer to hotel.

DAY 2: Early morning drive up Hamakua Coast for a walk in the Waipio Valley, a six-mile long valley bounded by 2,000-foot high walls. Swim under a beautiful waterfall and camp at Keokea.

Mountain Travel trip members Walker, Amanda and Pomo in the Waipo Valley.

DAY 3: A day's hike on the Pololu Trail, with its fantastic seascapes and profusion of native plants. Overnight at Hapuna Beach.

DAY 4: Morning swimming at the white sand beach of Hapuna, the best beach on the island of Hawaii. Afternoon drive to cabins at 6,000 feet in the saddle between Mauna Kea and Mauna Loa.

DAY 5: On our way before sunrise for a round trip day hike, we drive to the trailhead and begin hiking, reaching the summit of Mauna Kea (13,796′) by noon. From here, there are grand views of the "Big Island" below us and distant views (if it's clear) of Haleakala Volcano on the island of Maui.

DAY 6: Morning visit to the town of Kamuela, afternoon of body-surfing or snorkeling on Hapuna Beach. Sunset barbecue.

DAY 7: Drive along the Kona Coast, stopping at Kailua, the Place of Refuge, and Captain Cook's monument. Camp at a beach park.

DAY 8: At the southernmost point on the island, we'll walk along the coast and see canoe moorings which were part of an ancient Hawaiian civilization. Overnight at cabins.

DAY 9: Spend the day at Hawaii Volcanoes National Park, walking across the crater of Kilauea, with its active fumaroles.

DAY 10: Visit the bird park and hike to Mauna Ulu, a recently active volcano. Drive down to the rugged southern coast for a short walk and a freshwater swim in a natural pool.

DAY 11: Drive to Hilo and fly to Kahului on the island of Maui. Drive to the slopes of Haleakala Volcano and camp at Hosmer Grove, a beautiful hardwood forest at 8,000 feet.

DAY 12: Very early start for a drive to the summit of Haleakala (10,023′). Watch the magnificent sunrise from the summit, then don 30-35 lb. backpacks for a long day's hike down and across the huge seven-mile-long crater. Walk on Sliding Sands Trail in a landscape of colorful cinder cones and rare silversword plants. Overnight at cabins or in camp.

DAY 13: Hike the Halemauu Trail back through the crater to camp at Hosmer Grove.

DAY 14: Enjoy a last morning on the beach, then drive to Lahaina. Overnight at Pioneer Inn.

DAY 15: Transfer to airport to connect with homeward-bound flights.

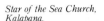

Star of the Sea Church, Kalapana.

City of Refuge Historical Park, Kona Coast.

Lunch break at Volcanoes National Park.

Hawaii photos by trip leader Sara Steck

Pololu Valley beach.

Trip Physicians

Mountain Travel seeks the services of a physician on trips to areas remote from medical care, such as the Himalayas and Andes. Physicians who undertake this job are given a reduction in Land Cost of up to 50%, depending on the trip (for specific information on discounts, write for our "List of Trips Requiring Physicians").

Applicants are considered on an individual basis: flexibility, a broad background, the ability to improvise and a sense of humor are important prerequisites. Our preference is for general surgeons, internists, well-qualified G.P.'s, full-time emergency physicians, orthopedists and other subspecialties that are not too far removed from care of the total body.

The job of the trip physician is to provide necessary minor medical care to our trip members and to be prepared for major problems, should they occur. Mountain Travel provides well-stocked field medical kits. Trip physicians assemble their own small medical trail kit to carry with them each day on the trail.

Prior to the trip, trip members complete our Medical Certificate, have it signed by their personal physician. We then send the Medical Certificates to the trip physician for his/her review and use.

Mountain Travel enjoys an enviable record of health and safety in the field and we want to keep it that way.

As our experience continues to grow, we find that we are able to pass on to our trip members more and more hints and suggestions concerning preparations for the trips they are about to take.

IMMUNIZATIONS

Only a few immunizations are LEGALLY REQUIRED for entry to certain countries, but it is very unwise to take only those shots needed to travel legally. Mountain Travel trips are by definition designed to get you away from the "usual tourist routes" and into what U.S. Public Health Service calls "rural or remote sections." While every effort is made to ensure proper sanitation, there is always the chance of disease exposure.

These suggestions should be used *only as a guideline.* Requirements are subject to change and travelers should check with their local Health Department, the Center for Disease Control and/or your personal physician.

YOU MUST START EARLY (at least two months before leaving) so that the shots can be sensibly spaced for maximum protection and minimum discomfort. All immunizations must be entered on your yellow "International Certificate of Vaccination" form which you should keep with your passport while traveling.

DIPTHERIA-TETANUS BOOSTER

Normally needed every 8 years, unless you are injured. BUT almost everyone on a walking trip will get a minor scrape or cut and we do often share trails with the local livestock. Get a booster!

ORAL POLIO

Regulations change periodically; check with your Health Department. If you have had the original 3 doses, a single oral booster is all that is needed. This is still a real disease in much of the world. Get a booster!

SMALLPOX

The disease no longer exists and vaccine is no longer available or required.

TYPHOID

This is desirable for anyone traveling and camping in rural areas—even in the U.S. It is essential for Mexico, South America, Asia, Africa and the Middle East. A booster is good for 3 years and gives about 60% protection. The Typhoid-Paratyphoid combination is no longer recommended since paratyphoid protection is minimal and the combination often causes reactions (i.e. fever, aches).

GAMMA GLOBULIN

An injection of 2 cc. (varies with weight) given as close to departure time as possible is for protection against hepatitis. The immunity is passive and does subside within a few months. Some trip members report their physicians are reluctant to give Gamma Globulin, but it is no longer controversial. The U.S. Public Health Service recommends it for travelers to "tropical areas," "developing countries," and those who "bypass the ordinary tourist routes." Get it.

TYPHUS

Its value is debatable and it is generally not recommended.

YELLOW FEVER

This is a legal requirement for travel to many countries that either have the disease or fear its introduction. The yellow fever zone covers central and the northern half of South America and a band across Africa. Yellow fever immunization is mandatory for travel in the areas above, and is strongly recommended for all travel in Africa or South America. A few Asian countries fear its introduction and MAY require it.

CHOLERA

Often required by local authorities and subject to change on short notice. All travelers to Africa, the Middle East and Asia should have a current cholera shot. This immunization is only valid for 6 months, but a booster is all that is ever needed once the primary series has been completed. Get it even though its value is questionable, since at least you'll get it with a clean needle in the U.S.

MALARIA

Malaria pills (Chloroquine Phosphate) are recommended for anyone traveling and camping in tropical areas. In some areas where malaria is prevalent and exposure cannot be avoided, some physicians recommend taking Primaquine during the six-week follow-up. In addition some areas require other medication for Chloroquine-resistant strains. Consult your physician in this matter.

FOOD AND DRINK

On Mountain Travel trips, food is prepared by experienced cooks using the highest possible degree of sanitation. The water we use for cooking and drinking is boiled and/or filtered. However, in hotels, restaurants and on your own, *take the following precautions seriously:*

Drinking tap water or brushing your teeth with it is dangerous. Use the bottled water which is available in most hotels, preferably after adding your own disinfectant. Ice cubes are generally made from the local water supply, which may be contaminated. Streams may look enticing, but germs are invisible.

Eat no food which is uncooked or which is bought from sidewalk vendors. Thoroughly cooked food which is still hot from a hotel kitchen is generally safe. Beware of salads! Custards, ice cream and creams in pastries and desserts are not safe in areas where refrigeration is primitive. Unboiled milk is suspect.

In order to stay well hydrated, which is essential to good health, you must keep up your fluid intake. Fill your water bottle with boiled water at night.

WATER PURIFICATION

For purifying questionable water sources, we recommend iodine tablets (available from camping stores) or iodine crystal solution (available by prescription from your physician. Iodine in crystal form should be used with care, as it is poisonous if ingested). Consult your physician and/or druggist.

Linda, Fran and Laurie display their trusty water bottles, Nepal/Barbara Kaplan

Dr. Richard Wohns performing emergency appendectomy on a Balti porter on the K2 trek, Baltoro Glacier, Pakistan. Mountain Travel endeavors to secure the services of a doctor on every trip where the need is obvious./ Dick McGowan

"Dinner is served" Nepal/Dick McGowan

PERSONAL FIRST AID SUPPLIES

The following suggestions are based on past trekking experience. Your own experience and preferences will, of course, influence your choice. Do not forget to bring medications used for individual conditions, since these are not generally available overseas. *This list is a guideline only, to be used as a basis for discussion with your physician.*

MILD PAIN, HEADACHE, FEVER

Aspirin, 5 gr. or Tylenol, if allergic to Asprin.

PAIN, COUGH, DIARRHEA

Aspirin w/Codine 1/2 gr. (Ascodeen-30), or Tylenol w/Codine, 1/2 gr.

ANTACID, UPSET STOMACH, ULCERS

Maalox, Gelusil M, or Mylanta antacid tabs. Donnatal tabs are good for stomach cramps, mild diarrhea, and are a mild sedative.

Sherpas preparing lunch below Pandim (21,952'), Sikkim trek/Ken Scott

DIARRHEA (symptomatic relief)

Codeine compounds listed above. Avoid Lomotil which has been reported to prolong illness with some types of dysentery. Some people find Peptobismal effective.

DIARRHEA (prevention)

Small daily doses of tetracycline, or its long-acting relative, doxycycline, have been shown to decrease the incidence of "traveler's diarrhea." This is certainly desirable when one has limited time and has invested a lot of money in a trip. This treatment is still somewhat controversial. Some people become sun sensitized by the drugs and can acquire a truly disabling sunburn. Also there is at least theoretical reason to fear that these drugs, while protecting against minor (albeit annoying) diarrheas, may be limiting the normal flora in the intestine and making one more susceptible to the more virulent organisms responsible for truly lifethreatening dysenteries. *Please discuss the pros and cons carefully with your own physician before taking these medications.*

COLDS, ALLERGIES (symptomatic relief)

Chlorpheniramine Maleate tabs., 4 mg. Actifed tabs (good for 4 hours) or Tuss-Ornade Spansule caps. (12-hour relief).

TOPICAL ANTIBIOTIC

Most antibiotic ointments contain one or more of the following in about the following proportions: Neomycin (3.5 mg.)/Bacitracin (400 units)/Polymyxin (5,000 units). Neosporin is typical.

SUN PROTECTION

The sun can be fierce! PABA preparations such as Pre Sun (applied often because of perspiration) are usually okay to about 10,000 feet. At higher altitudes, the only sun protection that works for many of us a total mechanical blocking agent—a hat, bandana around the back of the neck, etc. Don't forget reflected sun on areas such as under the chin and nose—especially when on snow. A-Fil Sun Sticks (Texas Pharmaceutical) are good for lips, and inside of nose.

SKIN

Mycolog ointment is very useful for itching, chafing and irritation in moist areas (especially after diarrhea).

MISCELLANEOUS

Band-Aids, Moleskin, foot powder, spare glasses, personal drugs, etc.

Breakfast at Huayabamba on the Inca Trail/ Sara Steck

Trip physicians often find that caring for the local people is a trip highlight. Those of us on the Mountain Travel staff who have come to know and care about the people of these remote areas feel an obligation to do what we can, and it seems only fair to share the benefits of some of the technology we are attempting to escape momentarily when we choose to spend our vacations in underdeveloped areas. Trip physicians often find that a little effort, concern and medicine can do wonders, particularly with infants and children, and the gratitude is overwhelming. Acting as a health educator is important, too, encouraging local people to take advantage of any nearby dispensaries and facilities which can deliver continuing care.

"Sick call" for the porters/Dick McGowan

For each trip, we make up a specific list of recommended clothing and equipment, based on our 16 years of experience. Items are selected from the complete list below, tailored to the conditions of each particular trip. Many trips involve the logistical support of small aircraft, boats, porters or pack animals, so your trek baggage should not weigh in excess of 30 lbs. (plus what you carry in your day pack), and must be packed in a sturdy duffle bag. On most trips, a suitcase of your "city clothes" can be stored in a hotel while you are on trek.

Taking proper clothing and equipment for your trek is an important ingredient to enjoying your adventure. Take time to look at what's on the market, don't underestimate the unpredictability of weather, and let your own experience guide you.

On the way to a refugio (climber's hut) on Mt. Ixtaccihuatl (17,343') in Mexico. On Climbing Seminars and Mountaineering Expeditions Mountain Travel supplies all high altitude technical equipment. Trip members need bring only personal gear. See equipment list on this page.

CASUAL CLOTHES FOR TRAVEL IN CITIES
SHIRT
- [ ] Wool, long-sleeved.
- [ ] Cotton, long-sleeved.
- [ ] Cotton, short-sleeved, or T-shirt.
- [ ] Windshirt.

An umbrella is for protection against the sun as well as the rain/ Lanny Johnson

SWEATER
- [ ] Heavy wool or pile/bunting jacket.
- [ ] Light wool or synthetic.

TROUSERS
- [ ] Full length trousers or knickers, wool or blend, or "pile/bunting" pants coupled with windpants & polypro underwear.
- [ ] Cotton hiking trousers (khakis, Levis).
- [ ] Windpants (Goretex) with side zipper, large enough to go over boots (and crampons) for wind, rain or snow.
- [ ] Hiking shorts.

UNDERWEAR
- [ ] Long—thermal, nylon or wool/ synthetic blend; polypropelene.
- [ ] Regular, everyday type.

HEADWEAR
- [ ] Silk or nylon facemask.
- [ ] Bandana.
- [ ] Balaclava, wool.
- [ ] Light hat with wide brim or visor for sun.
- [ ] Ski cap.
- [ ] "Sou'wester" hat for rain.

INSULATED CLOTHING
(The choice between down fill and synthetic fill is largely personal. Synthetic fill is preferred for wet climates.)
- [ ] Expedition parka, 16–20 oz. down or 20–30 oz. fiberfill, with hood. Must fit over bulky clothing.
- [ ] Medium-weight parka, 10–12 oz. or 16–20 oz. fiberfill.
- [ ] Down or fiberfill vest or sweater.
- [ ] Down or fiberfill overpants with zipper and/or snaps on the legs.
- [ ] Skiers' warmup pants or quilted underwear.

FOUL WEATHER GEAR
(With ANY rain garment, make sure the seams are sealed.)
- [ ] Gortex parka for rain and wind; or anorak, mountain parka, or cagoule. Large enough to fit over bulky sweater or insulated clothing.
- [ ] Poncho—lightweight but sturdy.
- [ ] Backpack rain cover.
- [ ] Waterproof (not just water repellent) rain suit including parka, pants and hat (e.g., traditional nautical foul weather gear such as Helley Hanson, Universal, Peter Storm, etc.).
- [ ] Rain pants (not necessary if you bring windpants).

HANDWEAR
- [ ] Silk or nylon glove liners.
- [ ] Heavy wool mittens (e.g., Dachstein).
- [ ] Light wool gloves or mittens.
- [ ] Cotton garden gloves for sun/ wind protection.
- [ ] Expedition mitts—down or fiberfill (must fit over wool gloves).
- [ ] Light down or fiberfill mitts or pile mitts.
- [ ] Overmitts—must be wind-and-water-proof and fit over wool mitts.

SOCKS
- [ ] Heavy duty socks, short or knee length (depends on length of trousers), at least 80% wool.
- [ ] Cotton athletic socks.
- [ ] Thin cotton or synthetic undersocks.

BOOTS AND SHOES
(Boots should be waterproofed, well broken in and worn with one lightweight & one heavyweight pair of socks.)
- [ ] Tennis or running shoes.
- [ ] Light hiking boots, with padded ankle and lug sole (size 9 weighs approx. 3 lbs. 8 oz.)
- [ ] Medium-weight hiking boots (size 9 weighs approx. 4 lbs. 10 oz.).
- [ ] Alpine, heavy mountaineering boots or model like Koflach "Viva" double boot. (size 9 weights approx. 5 lbs. 13 oz.)
- [ ] Korean vapor barrier boots with lug soles (also called K-boots or bunny boots—U.S. Army made). Include a patching kit.
- [ ] Booties—down or fiberfill.
- [ ] Rubber boots or shoe pacs. Sturdy, up-to-the-knee length, weight about 3 lbs. (e.g., L.L. Bean Maine Hunting Boots, Goodyear, Sorrel, etc.).

Practical mountain clothes ensure comfort in all weather conditions. Cho La Pass, Gokyo Valley, Nepal. Trip members are provided with a list of recommended equipment and clothing made up specifically for each trip/Gordon Wiltsie

GAITERS AND OVERBOOTS

- ☐ Overboots with rugged bottoms, insulated with foam or ensolite (for single alpine heavy mountaineering boots.)
- ☐ Full length gaiters up to the knee Or for use with double boots on grade D trips.
- ☐ Short gaiters for gravel and occasional snow.

SLEEPING BAG
(with waterproof stuff sack)

- ☐ Expedition weight (approx. 48 oz. down-fill or 72 oz. fiberfill).
- ☐ Medium weight (approx. 32 oz. down-fill or 48 oz. fiberfill).
- ☐ Lightweight (approx. 24 oz. down-fill or 36–48 oz. fiberfill.
- ☐ Sleeping bag sheet liner (recommended for trips in hot climates as occasional substitute for sleeping bag).

SLEEPING PADS
(select from below)

- ☐ Open cell foam, 3/4 length or full length, 2″ thick with waterproof cloth cover (not recommended for cold weather use).
- ☐ Closed-cell, like "Ensolite" 3/4 length, 3/8″ thick.
- ☐ Closed-cell, like "Ensolite" full length, 3/4″ thick (if on snow, Thermobar recommended.)
- ☐ Air mattress, top quality, 3/4 or full length (e.g., Therma-Rest, Air-Lift).
- ☐ Ground sheet.

CLIMBING EXPEDITIONS
(only for Grade D or Grade E)

- ☐ Ice axe (70–90 cm., as required by your height). Metal or fiberglass shaft recommended. Sling for wrist or body attachment of ice axe.
- ☐ Crampons (10 or 12-point HINGED, not rigid). With good straps (Neoprene) which have an extra 4″ so the ends can be easily grasped by a mittened hand. They must fit your boot perfectly (with overboots, if needed). Know how to use them!
- ☐ Carabiners.
- ☐ Locking carabiner.
- ☐ Descender—C.M.I. figure eight, or a total of 6 carabiners.
- ☐ Pully—Mountain Rescue type.
- ☐ Ascenders—Jumars, Gibbs, etc.
- ☐ Prusik loops—5 feet finished length, 12 feet in circumference of 5–6 mm Perlon joined with double fisherman's knot or grapevine knot.
- ☐ Slings—runners of 2.5 cm (1 inch) nylon tubular webbing, approx. 1.5 meters in circumference, ends to be joined with water knot.
- ☐ Swami belt (5 meters of 2.5 cm tubular webbing).
- ☐ Seat harness—adjustable, must permit dropping drawers without unroping.

- ☐ Chest harness (adjustable).
- ☐ Climbing helmet.
- ☐ Avalanche cord—20 meters with directional markers.
- ☐ Ice screw (one).

WINTER TRAVEL

- ☐ Snowshoes—wooden (e.g., Alaskan Trail) for soft snow; make sure lacings are well coated with plastic or resin to protect from abrasion.
- ☐ Snowshoes—aluminum (e.g., Sherpa, Black Forest, Early Winters); make sure lacings are well coated with plastic or resin to protect from abrasion.
- ☐ Ski poles.
- ☐ Cross country skis.
- ☐ Alpine skis.

PACKS AND BAGS

- ☐ Expedition framepack, with top quality aluminum frame, padded hip belt, roomy outside pockets (approximately 4500 cu in. capacity).
- ☐ Backpacking framepack, outside pockets (approx. 3800 cu. in. capacity).
- ☐ Large internal frame rucksack—approx. 4100 cu. in. capacity.
- ☐ Day pack with approximately 1500 cu. in. capacity to carry bulky jackets, camera gear, etc. One with waistbelt preferable.
- ☐ Small day pack, approx. 1000 cu. in. capacity.
- ☐ Duffle bag—largest available, made of strong material with full length zipper and wraparound straps. A padlock is also suggested.

EATING UTENSILS

- ☐ Cup, large, heavy duty plastic.
- ☐ Spoon, fork, bowl (plastic).
- ☐ Pocket knife with can opener and scissors.
- ☐ Leakproof plastic water bottle (1 or 1.5 qt. capacity).

ACCESSORIES

- ☐ First aid kit.
- ☐ Toilet kit—soap, toothbrush, toilet articles. Disposable towelettes (e.g., Wash n' Dries) are useful for hygiene.
- ☐ One roll of toilet paper per camping week.
- ☐ Insect repellent
- ☐ Repair kit—needle, thread, 1/8″ nylon cord, ripstop tape, etc.
- ☐ Regular sunglasses. Spare pair if you wear prescription lenses.
- ☐ Sunglasses or goggles for high altitude and snow travel with DARK (85% absorbency of visible light) lenses.

- ☐ Sun-blocking lotion—(e.g., Coppertone, Pre-Sun, Eclipse.)
- ☐ Glacier cream or zinc oxide to screen ultraviolet rays.
- ☐ Sun-blocking lip creme (e.g., A-Fil, Labiosan).
- ☐ Flashlight—with spare batteries and bulb.
- ☐ Head lamp—lightweight for night climbing or reading, plus spare batteries and bulb.
- ☐ Fire producer—2 butane lighters or 100 or more of "strike anywhere" type matches (pack carefully—they sometimes ignite by themselves!).
- ☐ Whistle (plastic coaches' type).
- ☐ Compass (good quality, light and simple).
- ☐ Maps (if desired).
- ☐ Waterproofing boot sealer (e.g., Sno Seal).
- ☐ Small lockable suitcase for city clothes (can be stored in hotel while on the trail).
- ☐ Stuff bags of assorted sizes and colors; good for keeping gear dry and in order.
- ☐ Plastic bags—various sizes, heavy duty, ziplock for film, books, small items.
- ☐ Accessory straps or cords to strap gear onto the outside of your pack.
- ☐ Baggage tags—one per bag (supplied by Mountain Travel).
- ☐ Towel.
- ☐ Swimsuit.
- ☐ Camera and film. Bring an ample supply of film as purchase abroad is difficult and expensive.
- ☐ Binoculars.
- ☐ Watch (waterproof).
- ☐ Reading material, writing material, playing cards.

PACKING TIPS

We recommend that you hand-carry on the plane (in your daypack or hand luggage) your boots, camera, important documents, medicines and other irreplaceable items. Make sure you attach a Mountain Travel baggage tag to all luggage. It is also a good idea to have identification inside your checked bags.

Duffle bags are loaded on a yak and ready for the trail, Khumbu, Nepal. On Mountain Travel treks animals or porters are used to carry personal equipment and supplies— freeing the trip member to enjoy the experience unencumbered.

"Of all the treks I have taken with Mountain Travel, the Zanskar trek has to be one of the most rewarding. Frits Staal—one of the best trek leaders I have ever been with; Siddiq Wahid an asset to any trek in Ladakh or Tibet; his ability to speak several dialects of Tibetan helped in several touchy situations."

L.B.

Zanskar: A Hidden Kingdom
1983 (Cultural Expeditions)

"The trip itinerary provided the diversity which allowed exposure to a good cross-section of Kenya in a relatively short time. The hard-working and pleasant camp staff also contributed to making the trip an enjoyable one. All in all, I'm a very satisfied customer and have already recommended Mountain Travel to several friends contemplating "adventure travel."

J.C.

Discover Kenya *1983*

"My husband and I thoroughly enjoyed the tour Tour du Mont Blanc. Rory was certainly familiar with the area and we felt that he was a fine leader. We felt the clothing list very helpful and never wished for an item we didn't bring. The support van was great! We look forward to joining another trek in the future.'

D.S.

Mont Blanc Circuit *1983*

Yes, I was wildly satisfied with the trip to Peru, as I always have been with Mountain Travel's trips—which is why I keep coming back."

F.R.

Inca Blanca Trek *1983*

"During May of this year, I took part in a very successful climb of Mt. McKinley which was organized by Mountain Travel and led by Nic Parker. I was very impressed with the organizational ability of Mountain Travel. Nic Parker's leadership and judgement were excellent during the entire climb."

H.T.

McKinley Expedition *1983*

WHY JOIN A MOUNTAIN TRAVEL TRIP?

We offer a truly *different* travel experience. Our groups are small—averaging 8 to 12 members, which helps to ensure mobility and comfort. We are pleased to report a repeat clientele of more than 35% (warning: Mountain Travel trips can be habit-forming!).

Veteran Trip Leader Bruce Kelpinger's expertise ranges from expedition logistics to mountain medicine to natural history. He's equally at home on the summit of a 21,000-foot peak in Nepal or in the jungles of Peru and has led more than 50 of our trips.

Leader Scot Macbeth has acquired the Sherpa nickname of "Seto Bhalu" (white bear) during many years of traveling in Nepal. His enthusiasm for the Himalayas is infectious and he enjoys great rapport both with the local people and his fellow trekkers. Here he gives the traditional "namaste" greeting of Nepal.

EXPERT LEADERSHIP

Our leaders are an important part of what makes Mountain Travel trips work so well. They come to us with a wide variety of backgrounds. Some are well-known authors or naturalists. Some are chosen for their knowledge of local language or culture, others for their outdoor skills. Above all, they are chosen for their ability to assure a safe, enjoyable and successful trip.

A QUALITY EXPERIENCE

Even though the major focus of our trips is outdoor travel, we don't skimp on the amenities. We hire experienced cooks and camp assistants to make outdoor living a pleasurable experience. We outfit every camping trip with the finest quality tents, roomy enough to comfortably accommodate two people and all their gear. On the vast majority of our trips, we hire porters and/or pack animals to carry all your personal gear, so you are free to walk, photograph and enjoy the scenery unencumbered by a heavy pack.

We will endeavor to secure the services of a doctor on every trip where the need is obvious (such as some South American and Himalayan treks). Medical attention and drugs will be administered free of charge to trip members by these trip doctors in the field.

In the cities, we stay in First Class hotels and sightsee by private car or small mini-bus with the best available guides.

WHO GOES ON THESE TRIPS?

Basically, our trips are made up of active, healthy people who love the outdoors. Most enjoy physical activities as an integral part of their lives (hiking, jogging, tennis, skiing) and they like the idea of being able to remain physically active while on vacation. They come from all walks of life and from all over the country. About 50% of our trip members are between the ages of 30 and 50. Anyone in good health who has a spirit of adventure is welcome on our trips. There is no upper age limit for participation.

Linda Goldsmith modeling the Mountain Travel T-Shirt, Nepal, 1984

Our mountain tents are roomy enough to accommodate two trekkers and all their gear. Rongbuk Valley, near Everest, Tibet
Leo Le Bon

GOOD FOOD

Yes, you can have "gourmet" dinners in a tent at 12,000 feet! Whether in Peru, Nepal, China, Africa or Alaska, our cooks are experienced professionals. We can't guarantee that the food will be exactly what you like, but our cooks often come up with delightful culinary treats. Some examples in the past have been home-made wonton soup at camp in China, a *pachamanca* (whole barbequed lamb) on the trail in Peru, cheese omelets served by a roaring stream in Nepal, just-caught salmon and crisp salads in the wilds of Glacier Bay, Alaska . Food on the trips is as varied as the trips themselves.

Expedition "kitchen" on the Kahiltna Glacier, Mt. McKinley, Alaska/Gary Bocarde

"Mediterranean" lunch of feta cheese, olives and pita bread aboard felucca while sailing on the Nile, Egypt/Ken Scott

A hearty brunch of eggs, cheese, spam and French fries is standard fare in Nepal/ Alla Schmitz

FULL-SERVICE TRAVEL AGENCY

Our task, as experts in "adventure travel," is to smooth your way through the maze of details involved in travel to the most remote regions of the world. We will procure your visas and permits, advise you on questions of clothing and equipment, book your airline tickets and make any independent travel reservations you desire in conjunction with your Mountain Travel trip. Our staff handles the needs of every trip member on an individual basis.

We welcome The American Express Card.

HOW TO SIGN UP

Look for the Trip Application Form in this book (if you don't find one, call us—toll-free outside California at 800-227-2384—and we'll send you a copy). Fill out the Application Form and send it in with your deposit of $200 per person. Well handle the rest.

TRAVEL AGENTS

If you have a favorite travel agency, take your Application Form to them and they'll be glad to book your Mountain Travel trip for you.

Leader John Thune with group in Urumchi, Sinkiang, China

Mountain Travel has been at the same address for over 10 years. Albany is adjacent to Berkeley, ten minutes north of Oakland off of Interstate 80 and twenty minutes from San Francisco via the Bay Bridge. Drop by if you're in the neighborhood.

About the Mountain Travel Logo:

The snow lioness depicted in our logo is an image taken from a Tibetan coin in use until 1959.

The white lioness, with her turquoise mane, was adopted by Mountain Travel as a symbol of the beauty of the high mountain environment of glaciers, peaks, sun and sky where we often travel.

The snow lion is a mythological symbol which dates from paleolithic times in Africa, and is usually associated with the sun—undying, renewing, energy-giving. The age of the lunar-bull was replaced by the age of the solar-lion in Egypt about 2600 B.C. The lion was the foremost animal symbol in the ancient Vedas of India. Hinduism adopted the lioness as the symbol for Vishnu and earlier portrayed the lioness as the goddess consort of Shiva.

The snow lioness came to Tibet from Iran via Turkestan, along with other bits and pieces of religious mythology, and was adopted as the symbol of that country.

In Tibet, the snow lioness is the animal symbol of the high mountains and glaciers, mythological site of the highest of the Seven Heavenly Thrones. These seven levels represent the domains of the first seven kings of Tibet. The mountain abode of the snow lion represents the highest, or seventh, mystical step to Buddhist heaven.

We would like to express our gratitude and thanks to our many trip members, those derring-do travelers who have participated in our adventures in the last 18 years. Without their interest and support, Mountain Travel would not exist.

It is the sharing of some small and unique adventure somewhere on our planet with these special people that has made it all worthwhile.

On Kala Patar (18,192'), a rock outcrop below Pumori (in background) high point of the Everest Trek/Brian Weirum

CREATED BY: **INPRINT** *International Promotions in Travel*
EDITOR: *Pam Shandrick*
DESIGN & PRODUCTION: *Ken Scott*
TYPOGRAPHY: *Linda Davis, Ann Flanagan Typography, Berkeley*
MAP PREPARATION: *Hugh Swift*
PRINTING: *Dai Nippon Printing, Japan*

Children from Liu Baxaing, a small Tibetan commune near Mt. Minya Ke in western Sichuan, China/Leo Le

ORDER FORM

To order a Regional Catalog, check the appropriate box and return this envelope with $2 for the first catalog, $1 for each additional catalog (or $5 for all six).

☐ ASIA & THE PACIFIC

Nepal • Mongolia • China • Tibet • Pakistan • India
Sri Lanka • Maldive Islands • New Zealand • Bali • Korea
Japan

☐ AFRICA & THE SAHARA

Kenya • Tanzania • Rwanda • South Africa • Botswana
Namibia • Zambia • Zimbabwe • Zaire • Egypt • Algeria

☐ EUROPE & THE U.S.S.R.

Greenland • Iceland • Norway • Ireland • United Kingdom
France • Switzerland • Italy • Germany • Austria • Corsica
Spain • Portugal • Greece • Bulgaria • Romania • Yugoslavia
Czechoslovakia • Turkey • U.S.S.R.

☐ SOUTH AMERICA & MEXICO

Peru • Ecuador • Bolivia • Chile • Argentina • Brazil
Costa Rica • Mexico

☐ NORTH AMERICA & HAWAII

Washington • New Hampshire • Alaska • Hawaii

☐ CULTURAL EXPEDITIONS

These tours empahsize the art, religion, culture and/or history of little-visited places within China, Tibet, Nepal, India, Egypt, Turkey, Israel, Italy, Peru and are escorted by a Mountain Travel trip manager plus an expert scholar/lecturer.

☐ THE MOUNTAIN TRAVEL BOOK OF TREKS, OUTINGS, & EXPEDITIONS

The 1985 "wish book": describes more than 130 outings in 40 countries; illustrated with hundreds of color photos and many maps; INCLUDES REGIONAL CATALOGS (see above) plus five essays by trip leaders and trip members, adventure travel equipment checklist, health tips for adventurous travelers. Makes a great gift! 180 pages. $12.95 postpaid.

Please send _____ copies. Check enclosed ☐

☐ MOUNTAIN TRAVEL POSTER

"The Potala at the end of the rainbow." 24 × 36 color photo by Galen Rowell. $5 (in a mailing tube) postpaid.

☐ MOUNTAIN TRAVEL T-SHIRT

Navy blue with orange design. $7.95 postpaid. Specify size (Men: S M L XL, Ladies: S M L XL). California residents add sales tax.

TO HELP YOU DECIDE

If you want a Mountain Travel staff member to call and help with any questions you might have about a particular trip, please list your *daytime* phone and indicate times when you are available.

Name: _____

Telephone: ( ) _____

I can be reached during (indicate hours): _____

I have questions about (indicate trip): _____

NAME _____

ADDRESS _____

CITY _____

STATE/ZIP _____

Please affix peel-off mailing label (if available)

MOUNTAIN TRAVEL
1398 SOLANO AVENUE
ALBANY, CALIFORNIA 94706-1892

PLACE
STAMP
HERE

TRIP
APPLICATION

Please print all information and mail with your deposit of $200 per person payable to Mountain Travel or your Travel Agent.

NAME OF TRIP:

DEPARTURE DATE:

APPLICANT'S NAME:

MAILING LABEL ACCOUNT NO.
(To facilitate our helping you)
ADDRESS:

CITY:

STATE/ZIP:

PHONE: (DAY) _____(EVENING)

AGE:_____SEX:_____HT:_____WT:_____

SMOKING PREFERENCE ☐ (NON)   ☐ (SMOKER)

OCCUPATION

PASSPORT NUMBER

ISSUE DATE OF PASSPORT

EXPIRATION DATE OF PASSPORT

PLACE OF ISSUE

CITIZENSHIP

DATE OF BIRTH

PLACE OF BIRTH

IN CASE OF EMERGENCY PLEASE NOTIFY:
(include address and phone number please)

STATE OF HEALTH:
(a medical questionnaire will be sent to applicants)

DESCRIBE YOUR BACKGROUND IN OUTDOOR ACTIVITIES
such as camping, hiking, skiing, mountaineering (indicate dates). Not necessary for "A" trips.

PREVIOUS MOUNTAIN TRAVEL TRIPS?
(indicate date and name of trip leader.)

HOW DID YOU FIRST LEARN OF MOUNTAIN TRAVEL?

For Travel Agent Bookings:

IATA *or* ATC #

AIR TRANSPORTATION:
Unless we hear to the contrary, we will assume that you wish Mountain Travel to prepare your airline tickets, including domestic space. It is usually to the passenger's benefit to have domestic and international ticketing done together due to fare concessions.

FROM:

AND RETURNING TO:

You may use a credit card to purchase your air tickets. Please fill in the information below if you wish to do so:

NAME OF CARD: _____ ACCOUNT NO. _____

EXP. DATE _____ SIGNATURE_____

HOTEL ACCOMMODATIONS:
☐ OK for sharing double room. Share with:
☐ I prefer a single room.
   Note: People who occupy single rooms, either by choice or by circumstance, must pay a single Supplement Fee (which will be quoted on request). Hotels only—single tents not always available.

AMERICAN EXPRESS
I wish to charge the LAND COST on
The American Express Card.
☐ Regular Payment Plan
☐ *Extended Payment Plan
   (circle number of months for extended payment)

   3   6   9   12   18   24

   *Non-U.S. Cardmembers: Extended Payment terms (if any) will be determined by your American Express Cardmember Agreement.

SIGNATURE_____

ACCOUNT NUMBER:_____

EXPIRATION DATE: _____

RELEASE AND ASSUMPTION OF RISK
   I am aware that during the mountain trip, expedition, ski tour, cruise, or other trip or vacation that I am participating in under the arrangements of Mountain Travel and its agents or associates, certain risks and dangers may occur, including but not limited to, the hazards of traveling mountainous terrain, accident or illness in remote places without medical facilities, the forces of nature and travel by air, train, automobile or other conveyance.
   In consideration of, and as part payment for, the right to participate in such mountain trips or other activities and the services and food arranged for me by Mountain Travel and its agents or associates, I have and do hereby assume all of the above risks and will hold them harmless from any and all liability, actions, causes of action, debts, claims and demands of every kind and nature whatsoever which I now have or which may arise of or in connection with my trip or participation in any other activities arranged for me by Mountain Travel and its agents or associates. The terms hereof shall serve as a release and assumption of risk for my heirs, executors and administrators and for all members of my family, including any minors accompanying me.
   I have read and agree to the conditions, especially noting the policy on cancellations and refunds, as stated under "Booking Information" in the Mountain Travel Catalog.

DATE: _____

SIGNATURE: _____

Parent or legal guardian must sign for person under 21.

TRIP GRADING

The whole notion of "trip grading" ould be considered in light of your n experience. Trips that may be enuous for some are quite easy for ers!

ur trips are rated by both a letter d a number. The letter B or C otes objective factors such as what tude is reached on the trip (B is der 15,000 feet, C is above 15,000 t) or if mountaineering experience is uired (Grade D and E). The number ng takes into account subjective tors such as trail conditions and gth of daily hikes.

EASY
MODERATE
STRENUOUS

RADE A:
hese "hiking optional" trips can be lertaken by anyone who is in good lth and enjoys a moderately active . None of our trips, however, is igned for the sedentary.

RADE B:
)n "B" trips, there is some form of uired physical activity, such as hik-. Hiking time might vary from three seven hours per day, depending on particular trip. A few "B" trips uire backpacking, in which case y are graded "B-3" (strenuous). wever, we design the majority of our s so that members don't have to ry heavy packs, (just a light day-k with personal items such as nera, jacket, and water bottle). vious camping experience is recom-nded but not required. Anyone who energetic, in good health and who oys the outdoors is qualified for a " trip. *Perhaps the most important lification is a positive mental attitude l a spirit of adventure.*

RADE C:
hese trips are different from "B" s in that some of the hiking takes ce at altitudes above 15,000 feet. e reason we separate them from "B" s is that hiking at high altitudes is enuous. However, we make things as nfortable as possible by hiring pack mals or porters to carry all the ds. We hire a staff of camp assist-s to do the cooking and camp chores.

RADE D:
his rating assumes that you are a ong, physically fit hiker who has ic mountaineering experience. You uld be familiar with the use of nbing equipment (ropes, ice axe, mpons) and have general mountain wledge (use of small stoves, route ding, etc.).

RADE E:
hese trips require at least 3 years of d experience in the skills appro-ate to the expedition. A detailed ume of your climbing experience is uired.

If you want a Mountain Travel taff member to call and help with any questions you might have about a particular trip, please fill in the appropriate information at the bottom of the order form envelope and return it to us.

GRADE A

GRADE B

GRADE C

GRADE D

GRADE E

RESERVATIONS

A $200 deposit, along with a completed Trip Application will reserve a place for you.

A second payment of $400 is due four months before departure.

Final payment of Land Cost and air fare is due two months before departure.

Prices are quoted in U.S. dollars. All payments must be made in U.S. dollars.

Reservations for most trips are accepted up to 21 days before departure. However, some trips fill up well in advance so early signup is advised.

If you have purchased a copy of our Book of Treks, Outings & Expeditions and later book a Mountain Travel trip, we will credit you for the cost of the book. Just attach your book receipt to the Trip Application.

SEE YOUR TRAVEL AGENT

Any travel agent can book a Mountain Travel trip for you. It costs no more to use a travel agent, and an expert agency can provide many special services for you free of charge.

MULTIPLE RESERVATIONS

If you have sent in a deposit on a trip for which the departure is in doubt and wish to be covered on a second-choice trip, you may reserve space on the second-choice trip by sending in an additional $200 deposit. If your first-choice trip does not go, all funds will be transferred to the second-choice trip. The process works in reverse if your first choice trip does go—all funds will automatically be transferred to that trip. Should you cancel from your first-choice trip, handling fees will be charged as per cancellation policy.

TRIP WAITLISTING

If you cancel your reservation while still waitlisted, the full deposit of $200 will be refunded. Upon notification of confirmation, you must advise us within 15 days if you do not wish to remain on the trip roster. If you cancel your reservation after this 15-day period. the usual cancellation policy will apply.

TRIP INFORMATION SUPPLEMENTS

The following material is sent out to participants.

IMMEDIATELY AFTER SIGN-UP:
Detailed itinerary, medical certificate, Health Matters bulletin.

FOUR MONTHS BEFORE DEPARTURE:
Equipment list, documentation, baggage and insurance information, air itinerary, medical immunization recommendations, invoice for 2nd deposit and final payment.

ONE MONTH BEFORE DEPARTURE:
Last minute information on the trip, including air tickets, baggage tags, trip roster, rendezvous instructions, insurance policy (optional), visaed passports (if required), and maps if available.

VISAS

Mountain Travel will process the necessary visas for your trip. If for some reason a visa is not granted to you, Mountain Travel is not responsible if you must therefore cancel your trip.

LAND COST

THE AMERICAN EXPRESS CARD
We accept The American Express Card for payment of Land Cost. You may charge on your usual basis or on an Extended Payment Plan of up to 24 months. (see Trip Application Form).

TIER PRICING:
While we make every effort to fill each trip to the point of maximum economy for everyone (and do all possible to avoid cancelling trips with low signup), we tier-price some of our tours in order to operate them with smaller numbers of passengers.

Tier pricing is based on the number of full revenue tour members. Not included are guests or staff of Mountain Travel, the trip doctor (if applicable), or members of the press or media who are occasionally invited to join our tours.

If a member cancellation reduces the group size to a higher tier within 29 days of departure, remaining members will not be charged the resulting higher Land Cost.

Rates quoted are per person, based on sharing a double room or tent.

SHARE BASIS FOR SINGLE TRAVELERS:
If you are traveling alone and wish to share accommodations, we will assign you a roommate, if one is available. If there is no one with whom you can share, you must pay a Single Supplement Fee which will be listed in the itinerary.

LAND COST INCLUDES IN THE CITIES:
Hotels with private bath where available, airport transfers for members using the group flights, baggage porterage and hotel porterage, all sightseeing arrangements as indicated in the itinerary, entrance fees, leadership, local guides, visas, permits. All meals included on China, Mongolia, and USSR trips.

IN THE FIELD:
All camp meals, porters or pack animals (if applicable), guides, cooks, ground transport, community camping and commissary equipment.

NOT INCLUDED:
Meals in the cities (except China, Mongolia, and USSR) to allow for individual choice of restaurants, cost of medical immunizations, insurance of any kind, excess baggage charges (if any), airport taxes (if any), alcoholic beverages, laundry charges and other items of a personal nature.

Medical costs (except for the ordinary services provided on trips), evacuation by helicopter or other conveyance or costs of hospitalization are not covered in the Land Cost.

If any trip has to be delayed because of bad weather, trail conditions, river levels, road conditions, flight delays, government intervention, sickness or other contingency for which Mountain Travel or its agents cannot make provision, the cost of delays is not included.

*FOR INFORMATION OR
RESERVATIONS
CALL TOLL-FREE
800 227-2384
(outside California only)
or 415 527-8100 (within the state)
or
SEE YOUR TRAVEL AGENT*

TRANSFER & CANCELLATION POLICY

At the time we receive written notice that you must cancel your trip, the following fees will apply:

More than 180 days
before departure $50
90 to 180 . . . .$100
60 to 89 . . . .$200
30 to 59 . . . . .20% Land Cost
14 to 29 . . . . .30% Land Cost
1 to 14 . . . . .75% Land Cost
No show . . . . .100% Land Cost

If you transfer from one trip to another between 180 and 60 days before departure (of the trip you are transferring from), the Transfer Fee is $100. If you transfer within 59 days of departure, you are subject to the usual Cancellation Fees outlined above (appropriate to the date you notify us that you want to transfer). We recommend that you purchase Trip Cancellation Insurance to protect yourself.

TRIP CANCELLATION INSURANCE

We encourage you to take out Trip Cancellation Insurance. This insurance protects all deposits and payments for both Air and Land Cost should you have to cancel your trip due to personal or family illness. Trip Cancellation Insurance costs $5 per $100 of Air and Land Cost. We will mail you the necessary forms on request. We recommend that you purchase it soon after signing up.

BAGGAGE AND ACCIDENT/LIFE INSURANCE (sample rates): $69 for 30-day $800 baggage insurance: $26 for 30-day $25,000 accident/life and illness insurance.

CANCELLED TRIPS

Mountain Travel reserves the right to cancel any trip due to inadequate sign-up which makes the trip economically unfeasible for us to operate. In such a case, a full refund of land cost is given, but Mountain Travel is not responsible for additional expenses incurred by members in preparing for the trip (i.e., non-refundable "Advance Purchase" air tickets, visa fees if applicable, equipment, medical expenses).

REFUNDS

No partial refunds will be given for unused hotel rooms, meals, sightseeing trips or trek arrangements for any reason whatsoever. Land Cost is quoted as a package and credits are not given for services not used.

PRIVATE TRIPS

In addition to the trips listed in each regional catalog Mountain Travel assists in setting up privately organized trips for small groups in East Africa, Nepal, Peru, Costa Rica, India, the Galapagos Islands, Alaska and other areas. Write for details.

AIR TRAVEL

Mountain Travel has a specialized agency staff and a fully automated computer system for handling ticketing and reservations worldwide. Our staff is experienced in scheduling air travel to the most remote and obscure destinations. In addition, we can book hotels and other services in most cities in the world.

You may purchase your air tickets with any major credit card. See the Trip Application Form. ALL AIR FARES QUOTED (in U.S. dollars) ARE SUBJECT TO CHANGE. They are valid as of April 1, 1984. Contact Mountain Travel for the most current information.

SAMPLE AIR FARES
ASIA
Round trip to
Nepal, India and Pakistan
Pakistan via PIA:
N.Y./Rawalpindi
(14/120-day exc.) $1288
S.F./Rawalpindi
(14/120-day exc.) $1567
India via British Airways or Pan Am:
N.Y./Delhi
(14/120-day exc.) $1326
S.F./Delhi
(14/120-day exc.) $1544
Nepal via Thai International:
S.F./Bangkok/Kathmandu
(120-day exc.) $1501
Nepal via Air India or Pan Am:
N.Y./Delhi/Kathmandu
(14/120-day exc.) $1590
Delhi/Kathmandu
(14/120-day exc.) $1876
Round Trip to Japan and China
S.F./Tokyo (Apex) $930
S.F./Beijing (Apex) $1375

AFRICA
Round Trip to Africa
via British Airways and KLM:
N.Y./Nairobi
(Apex) $1360
N.Y./Johannesburg
(Apex) $1303
N.Y./Johannesburg
(IT/SAA) $999
N.Y./Kilimanjaro (Tanzania)
(Apex) $1360
N.Y./Tamanrasset (Algeria)
(Apex) $850
N.Y./Cairo $786

EUROPE
Round Trip to England, Ireland, Switzerland, Paris, Athens, Oslo and Moscow via SAS, Aer Lingus, Air France, TWA and Aeroflot:
N.Y./London
(Apex, 7/60-days) $579
N.Y./Ireland
(Apex, 14/45-days) $559
N.Y./Athens
(Apex, 7/60-days) $849
N.Y./London/Oslo
(Apex, 14/45-days) $697
N.Y./Geneva
(14/60-day exc.) $800
S.F./Paris
(Super Apex) $1192
N.Y./Paris
(Apex) $749
N.Y./Moscow
(Apex) $950

SOUTH AMERICA
Round Trip to South America
via Eastern and Pan Am:
Miami/Cuzco
(YLE 150 exc.) 544
Miami/Cuzco/Puerto Maldonado
(YLE 150 exc.) $610
L.A./Cuzco
(YLE 150 exc.) $852
Miami/Quito/Guayaquil
(Apex) $512
L.A./Quito/Guayaquil
(Apex) $790
Miami/Punta Arenas (Patagonia) .$1428
Round Trip to Costa Rica and Mexico
via Pan Am, Lacsa and Mexicana:
S.F./Mexico City $415
Miami/Costa Rica $220

NORTH AMERICA
Round Trip to Alaska
via Alaska Airlines:
Seattle/Anchorage $396
Seattle/Juneau $290
Seattle/Fairbanks $475
Round Trip to Hawaii
via World Airways:
S.F./Honolulu $439

EQUIPMENT

Mountain Travel provides all group camping equipment such as tents and cooking gear. Trip members must supply their own sleeping bag.

A detailed list of recommended clothing and suggested personal equipment is made up specifically for each trip.

BAGGAGE

Most major carriers have "piece" baggage restrictions. Under these rules, Economy Class passengers are permitted free baggage allowance for two bags, total dimensions not exceeding 106 inches. Carry-on baggage (one or more underseat bags not exceeding 45 inches) is also permitted free. More detailed information will be sent to trip members.

MEDICAL & HEALTH

It is vital that persons with medical problems make them known to us well before departure. The trip leader has the right to disqualify anyone at any time during the trip if he feels the trip member is physically incapable and/or if a trip member's continued participation will jeopardize the safety of the group. Refunds are not given under such circumstances.

Mountain Travel will endeavor to secure the services of a doctor on every trip where the need is obvious (such as some South American and Himalayan treks). Medical attention and drugs will be administered free of charge to trip members by these trip doctors in the field.

Hospital facilities for serious problems are often unavailable and evacuation can be prolonged, difficult and expensive. Mountain Travel assumes no liability regarding provision of medical care. Trip members will receive our "Health Matters" bulletin, and a medical certificate which must be filled out by both the trip member and his/her doctor (not necessary for "A" trips) and returned to us.

Once you have been confirmed on a trip, there will be no refunds if your doctor does not approve your medical certificate.

TRIP PHYSICIANS

We offer a discount of up to 50% of the Land Cost on trips requiring the services of a trip physician. We prefer that trip physicians be general or orthopedic surgeons, internist, emergency physicians or general practitioners. Write for the list of trips requiring a physician.

BOOKS, MAPS, ETC.

Write for our complete book and map list. We sell more than 80 books and 25 maps pertaining to the trips we offer.

MOUNTAIN TRAVEL T-SHIRT
Made of the best quality heavyweight cotton with the circular M.T. Logo (taken from a Tibetan coin) silkscreened on the front. Short sleeved, color-fast, and washable, it makes a great gift. Color: Navy blue with orange & light blue design. Send check or money order for $7.95 postpaid (California residents add applicable sales tax). Specify quantity and size (Men: S,M,L,XL; Ladies: S,M,L,XL). See back of Trip Application to order.

MOUNTAIN TRAVEL POSTER
A 24" x 36" color poster of a rainbow above the Potala, former palace of the Dalai Lama, in Lhasa, Tibet. Photograph by Galen Rowell. $5 postpaid (rolled in a mailing tube). See back of Trip Application to order.

RESPONSIBILITIES OF TRIP MEMBERS

Trip members have certain responsibilities to Mountain Travel and to other trip members: trip members are responsible for comprehending the conditions implied in the Mountain Travel trip grading system and selecting a trip (perhaps in consultation with Mountain Travel) which is appropriate to their interests and abilities; for preparing for the trip by studying the itinerary and supplemental trip information sent by Mountain Travel; for bringing appropriate clothing and equipment as advised by Mountain Travel; for following normal standards of personal hygiene in order to lessen risk of travelers' diseases, as advised by the trip leader and trip doctor (if a trip doctor accompanies the trip); for following normal social behavior patterns with fellow trip members; for acting in an appropriate and respectful manner in accordance with the customs of countries visited; for completing the trip itinerary as scheduled (or as adjusted in the field as necessary).

RESPONSIBILITY OF MOUNTAIN TRAVEL

PLEASE READ CAREFULLY

Mountain Travel, Inc., (its Owners Outfitters, Agents, and Employees) give notice that they act only as the agent for the owners, contractors, and suppliers providing means of transportation and/or all other related travel services and assume no responsibility howsoever caused for injury, loss or damage to person or property in connection with any service resulting directly or indirectly from: acts of God detention, annoyance, delays and expenses arising from quarantine, strike, thefts, pilferage, force majeure, failure of any means of conveyance to arrive or depart as scheduled, civil disturbances, government restrictions or regulations, discrepancies or change in transit or hotel services over which it has no control. Reasonable changes in the itinerary may be made where deemed advisable for the comfort and well being of the passengers. On advancement of deposit to Mountain Travel, Inc., the depositor therefore agrees to be bound by the above recited terms and conditions.

AIRLINE CLAUSE:
The airlines are not to be held responsible for any act, omission or event during the time passengers are not on board their planes or conveyance. The passage contract in use by the airlines concerned, when issued, shall constitute the sole contract between the airlines and such purchasers of these tours and/or passenger. Such conveyance, etc. is subject to the laws of the countries involved.

REFERENCES
BANK OF AMERICA
Albany Branch, 1615 Solano Avenue
Albany, Ca. 94706

ALBANY CHAMBER OF COMMERCE
1108 Solano Ave. Albany, Ca. 94706

*Validity of this catalog is
from Jan. 1, 1985–Dec. 31, 1985*